THE TEMPEST
IN CONTEXT

T0346495

ANTHEM PERSPECTIVES IN LITERATURE

Titles in the **Anthem Perspectives in Literature** series
are designed to contextualize classic works of literature for readers
today within their original social and cultural environments. The books
present historical, biographical, political, artistic, moral, religious and
philosophical material from the period that enable readers to understand
a text's meaning as it would have struck the original audience. These
approachable but informative books aims to uncover the period and the
people for whom texts were written; their values and views, their anxieties
and demons, what made them laugh and cry, their loves and hates.
The series is targeted at high-achieving A-level, International
Baccalaureate and Advanced Placement pupils, first-year
undergraduates and an intellectually curious audience.

THE TEMPEST IN CONTEXT

SIN, REPENTANCE AND FORGIVENESS

Keith Linley

ANTHEM PRESS

Anthem Press
An imprint of Wimbledon Publishing Company
www.anthempress.com

This edition first published in UK and USA 2015
by ANTHEM PRESS
75–76 Blackfriars Road, London SE1 8HA, UK
or PO Box 9779, London SW19 7ZG, UK
and
244 Madison Ave #116, New York, NY 10016, USA

British Library Cataloguing-in-Publication Data
A catalogue record for this book is available from the British Library.

Library of Congress Cataloging-in-Publication Data
Linley, Keith.
The Tempest in context : sin, repentance and forgiveness / Keith Linley.
pages cm. – (Anthem Perspectives in Literature)
Includes bibliographical references and index.
ISBN 978-1-78308-375-6 (papercover : alk. paper)
1. Shakespeare, William, 1564–1616. Tempest. 2. Literature and
society–England–History–17th century. I. Title.
PR2833.L56 2015
822.3'3–dc23
2014049137

ISBN-13: 978 1 78308 375 6 (Pbk)
ISBN-10: 1 78308 375 1 (Pbk)

Cover image © Andrew_Howe/iStockphoto.com

This title is also available as an ebook.

CONTENTS

INTRODUCTION

About This Book

This book concentrates on the contexts from which *The Tempest* emerges, those characteristics of life in early Jacobean England which are reflected in the values and views Shakespeare brings to the text and affect how a contemporary might have responded to it. These are the primary central contexts, comprising the writer, the text, the audience and all the views, values and beliefs held by these three. The actions taken and words spoken by the characters do not all represent Shakespeare's own views, but they will have evoked ethical judgements from the audience in line with the general religious and political values of the time. There would have been a range of differing responses though the fundamentals of right and wrong would have been broadly agreed. These primary contexts, this complicity of writer, audience and text and their shared mediation of the play, are the prime concern of this book.

Where relevant, the book also focuses on a range of secondary contexts. A play does not come into being without having a background and does not exist *in vacuo*. It will have its own unique features, but also characteristics inherited from its author as well as sources derived from and traits resembling the writing of its time. Other secondary contexts – the actors, their companies, the acting space, the social mix of general audiences – do not figure in this study except as occasional incidentals. The first recorded performance was at the king's palace at Whitehall on 1 November 1611. The book discusses that space and that unique audience; this is a play about three fictional courts and would have evoked reflection about the fourth real one.

There are tertiary contexts too. There is the afterlife of the text (its printed form, how subsequent ages interpreted it on stage and changed it) – what is called its performance history. And there is the critical backstory, showing how critics of subsequent times bring their agendas and the values and prejudices of their period to analysis of the text. These are referenced incidentally where they seem useful and relevant, but are not a major concern. The 'Further Reading' list provides broad guidance on the critical and performance history and any scholarly edition of *The Tempest* will cover these areas in greater detail.

This book is for students preparing assignments and exams for Shakespeare modules. The marking criteria at any level explicitly or implicitly require students to show a consistently well-developed and consistently detailed understanding of the significance and influence of contexts in which literary texts are written and understood. This means responding to the play in the ways Shakespeare's court audience would have done in 1611. You will not be writing a history essay, but along with considering the play as a literary vehicle communicating in dramatic form, you will need to know something of how Shakespeare's audience might have reacted. A text is always situated in some way within its historical setting. The correlatives in this case would have been the classics (for the educated), the Bible, Christian ethics and the society of the day, the latter meaning they would see the play in the light of what had happened in recent history and what was currently happening in the court, in the city, in the streets, on the roads and in the villages. No one could watch Prospero's behaviour and manner and not think of King James, nor hear Antonio's comments on the moral cowardice and corruptibility of the Milanese court and not think of England's court.

The following material will enable you to acquire a surer grasp of this cultural context – the socio-political conditions out of which the play emerged, the literary profile prevailing when it was written, and the religious-moral dimensions embedded in it. Because *The Tempest* was written in an age of faith, when the Bible's teachings and sermons heard in church formed part of everyone's mindset, it is vital to recreate those factors, for the actions of the characters would have been assessed by Christian criteria. You may not agree with the values of the time or the views propounded in the play, but you do need to understand how belief mediated the possible responses of the audience that watched the piece.

Key to this book's approach is the idea that *The Tempest* is full of sins, transgressions, boundary crossing and rule breaking – in the personal world and in the public and political arenas. Prospero's backstory (Act I Scene ii) provides information about where the sinning began, with a ruler neglecting his role and his brother usurping power. Accumulating sins invite judgements, until the final scene when the play turns round on itself, reverses the revenge Prospero seems intent upon taking and embarks upon the more positive Christian line of reconciliation and forgiveness. Alerted to the subversive behaviour of the characters the audience would expect the unrepentant to be punished and those repenting to find forgiveness and new understanding. In the event a positive mood prevails and the play ends with apparent hope for a better future. Though biblical values may underpin much of the action, there is much more going on scene by scene than a series of echoes of what the Bible says about virtue and vice. Interwoven are political concerns about rule (of the self, of a state – or an island), parenting, education, colonialism and considerations relevant to attraction and love.

What Is the Primary Context?

Any document – literary or non-literary – comes from the environment which produced it, the biographical, social, political, historical and cultural circumstances which form it (the author's and the viewers'), and the values operating within it and affecting the experience of it, including what the author may have been trying to say and how the audience may have interpreted it. These features are embedded in it, overtly and covertly. This is its primary context.

A text in isolation is simply an accumulation of words carrying growing, developing meanings as the writing/performance progresses. It is two dimensional – a lexical, grammatical construct and the sum of its literal contents. It has meaning, we can understand what it is about, how the characters interact, but context provides a third dimension, it adds value, making meaning comprehensible within the cultural profiles of the time. Primary context is the sum of all the influences the writer brings to the text and all the influences the viewer/reader deploys in experiencing it. It is an amalgam of writer, text and audience. This book concentrates on the archaeology of the play, recovering how it would have been understood in 1611, recovering the special flavour and prevailing attitudes of the time, and displaying the factors that shaped its meaning for that time and that audience. Knowing the cultural context enriches our experience of the text, unearthing the significations of society embedded in the text that, added together, make it what Shakespeare intended it to be – or as close as we can be reasonably sure for, of course, it is impossible to definitively say what the author may have meant at any one point or whether the words of a character represent the author's opinions. This cluster of attitudes will not be the same as those an audience today will bring to a performance. Our views about the text stem from our attitudes, our prejudices and our priorities, but we always have to understand the context in which something from the past was said or done if we are to understand what the text was meant to mean. Recovering the mindset, nuances and values Shakespeare worked into *The Tempest* and how his audience would have interpreted them means recreating the Elizabethan-Jacobean period. To achieve that a range of aspects is considered, but two key contextual areas dominate the approach of this book: the religious-moral and the socio-political. The play has a number of explicit verbal echoes of or allusions to the Bible, but the audience would have interpreted the multiple transgressions it presents in terms of the scriptural upbringing most of them would have had. Set among courtiers, focusing on the breakdown of a governing family and the past entanglements of an ex-duke, a current duke and a king, the play considers issues related to kingship, rule, family and education, subjects constantly debated in pre–Civil War England.

Cultural historians aim to recover 'the commonplaces' and 'the unargued presuppositions', and 'the imperative need, in any comparative discussions of epochs, [is] first to decide what the norm of the epoch is'.[1] Once the typical and orthodox values are established, it is then essential to register significant divergences from them. Because sin, subversion, transgression and reversals abound in the play, Part I, 'The Inherited Past', looks broadly at the 'world view' of the time, the normative inherited past which shaped how the Jacobeans thought about God, the world, sin, death, the Devil, the social structure, family and gender relationships. Connections are made between the play and the wider literary world. Most importantly, the book considers the religious beliefs informing the likely judgements made of the actions in the play and suggests a number of socio-political allusions that gave the drama a topical dimension. *The Tempest* has recently suffered from the tendency of directors and critics to interpret texts according to their own agendas and the preoccupations of their time. Consequently, rather than explicating the play in the ways the Whitehall audience would have understood, it has been interpreted as avoiding engagement with feminist discourses while reflecting European post-colonial guilt. These are incidentally addressed but are not the main concern of the book. Part II, 'The Jacobean Present', discusses the contemporary contexts – education, politics, magic, colonialism, literature, authority and morality – that enhance and clarify some of the issues addressed in the play.

The book refers throughout to the religious beliefs that informed the audience's likely judgements of the action and suggests a number of socio-political allusions that gave the drama a topical dimension. Crucial to the religious context are the moral matrices against which conduct in the play would have been measured: the Ten Commandments, the Seven Deadly Sins and the Seven Cardinal Virtues, and secondarily the Corporal and Spiritual Works of Mercy. You need to absorb them thoroughly as they recur constantly (Chapters 3 and 4). These ethical contexts decode the hidden nuances and inflexions of meaning which would have coloured a contemporary audience's responses to the story of Prospero, his daughter, their island and their visitors. There will have been many different responses, but in the area of religious and moral values there will have been many shared reactions.

A gulf always exists between what people are supposed to do or believe and what they actually do or believe. The idealized fantasies of conduct and rule are countered in *The Tempest* by the harsh realities of necessity. Machiavelli's version of the 'mirror for princes' claimed:

> I have thought it proper to represent things as they are in real truth, rather than as they are imagined. [...] The gulf between how one should live and how one does live is so wide that a man who neglects what is actually done for what should be done learns the way to self-destruction rather than self-preservation.[2]

Ignorance, indifference, rebelliousness, purposeful wickedness and laziness account for these discrepancies. Sebastian and Antonio's deviations from expected normative behaviour are motivated by deliberate ambition and innate evil. They know they are doing wrong, but do not care. Their goal is power and any means that gives them dominance is acceptable. Their tendency towards lying, mocking and secret plotting is highlighted by how they are often presented standing apart from the other characters, cynically commenting and intriguing in asides. In the words of the Lord's Prayer, their trespasses are forgiven, but only because Prospero is omniscient (all-knowing), can pre-empt their plans and reaches a state where he is readier to forgive than punish.

Further Reading

Introductions to editions of The Tempest

Frank Kermode, *The Tempest*, Arden edition (London: Routledge, 1989).
David Lindley, *The Tempest*, New Cambridge Shakespeare (Cambridge: Cambridge University Press, 2002).
Stephen Orgel, *The Tempest*, Oxford World's Classics (Oxford: Oxford University Press, 2008).
V. M. Vaughan and A. T. Vaughan, *The Tempest*, Arden edition (London: Bloomsbury, 2011).

Other critical reading

Francis Barker and Peter Hulme, 'Nymphs and Reapers Heavily Vanish: The Discursive Con-Texts of *the Tempest*', in *Alternative Shakespeares*, ed. John Drakakis (London: Routledge, 1985).

G. Wilson Knight, 'The Shakespearean Superman', in *The Crown of Life* (London: Methuen, 1958).

Jan Kott, 'Prospero's Staff', in *Shakespeare Our Contemporary* (London: Methuen, 1967).

Simon Palfrey, *Late Shakespeare: A New World of Words* (Oxford: Clarendon Press, 1997).

D. J. Palmer (ed.), *The Tempest: A Casebook* (Basingstoke: Macmillan, 1968).

Ann Thompson, 'Miranda, Where's Your Sister?', in *Feminist Criticism: Theory and Practice*, ed. Susan Sellers (London: Harvester Wheatsheaf, 1991).

A. T. Vaughan and V. M. Vaughan, *Critical Essays on Shakespeare's 'The Tempest'* (London: Prentice Hall International, 1998).

R. S. White (ed.), *The Tempest: William Shakespeare*, New Casebooks (Basingstoke: Macmillan, 1999).

Journal articles

Curt Breight, '"Treason Doth Never Prosper": *The Tempest* and the Discourse of Treason', *Shakespeare Quarterly* 41 (1998).

Barbara Fuchs, 'Conquering Islands: Contextualizing *The Tempest*', *Shakespeare Quarterly* 48 (1997).

John Gillies, 'Shakespeare's Virginian Masque', *English Literary History* 53 (1986).

Trevor R. Griffiths, '"This Island's Mine": Caliban and Colonialism', *Yearbook of English Studies* 13 (1983).

Rob Nixon, 'Caribbean and African Appropriations of *The Tempest*', *Critical Inquiry* 13 (1987).

Stephen Orgel, 'Prospero's Wife', *Representations*, 8 October 1984.

Meredith Anne Skura, 'Discourse and the Individual: The Case of Colonialism in *The Tempest*', *Shakespeare Quarterly* 40 (1989).

B. J. Sokol and M. Sokol, 'The Tempest and Legal Justification of Plantation in Virginia', *Shakespeare Yearbook*, vol. 7 (1996).

Robert Wiltenburg, '*The Aeneid* in *The Tempest*', *Shakespeare Survey* 39 (1987).

Note: All quotations from the text are from the Kermode, Arden edition.

Prologue

THE SETTING

Hallowmas nyght was presented at Whitehall before the kings Maiestie a play called the Tempest.[1]

Thus the Revels Accounts for 1611 announce the first known public performance of this strange play. The dais in front of the stage is empty. The king has not yet arrived. Slowly the court assembles, with the usual shuffling, chattering, giggling and greeting of friends as the galleries fill. Some of the young gallants are rowdy. The wines were various and they have sampled copiously. Some lean over eagerly awaiting the queen's gentlewomen, others scan for pretty, new faces. The Palace of Whitehall's banqueting hall is ablaze with candles. Silk dresses shimmer, jewels glitter. There is excitement and expectation. Gathered to watch a new play by Master Shakespeare, no one knows what to expect – blood and intrigue, bawdy comedy maybe.[2]

As far as we know no one had seen it before and there is no literary source on which it was based to provide a central storyline that people might already have known. The only feature they could reasonably have anticipated was that there would be a storm, but that was a common enough stage effect. Shakespeare alone had recently presented the audience with several storms. In *King Lear* (1606) a storm outside indicates the king's approaching madness and there is the horrible scene on the heath with thunder and lightning as the sad old man rages against Fate and his daughters. *Macbeth* (1606) opens with thunder and lightning as the three witches meet, and thunder accompanies them at each subsequent entry. A tempest shipwrecks the eponymous hero of *Pericles* (1608–09). It is only described by the chorus figure, Gower, but the mention of thunder might have been accompanied by sound effects. In *The Winter's Tale* (1610–1611) a storm and a shipwreck bring Antigonus to the fictional coast of Bohemia. That storm too is over, though background sounds might have been used. Marlowe's *Faustus* (1598) utilizes thunder to herald the appearance of Lucifer and thunder and lightning mark the hero being dragged off to Hell at the climax. Thunder was 'produced' by rolling cannonballs along a wooden trough or playing drum rolls. Lightning could be achieved by waving candelabra aloft backstage or setting off squibs to give a crack of sound and flashes of light.[3]

The play begins not only with a storm but a storm at sea. It is a dramatic, explosive, shocking opening, immediately creating edginess and tension. Storms and shipwrecks were stock features in literature, either to start the plot by bringing the hero to a new land or to disperse characters to other locations in order to develop new strands in the story. *The Aeneid* begins with a long description of Neptune's rage and the storm he creates, casting Aeneas upon the shores of Carthage. Poseidon's anger also shipwrecks *The Odyssey*'s hero.[4] Renaissance verse romances used this convenient device to move characters from one place to another. Significant and archetypal for an age steeped in the Bible was the faith-testing shipwreck of St Paul (Acts 27).[5] This helps combine Christian allegory with classical models to make sea storms and wrecks into potent emblems. But reading such drama is not like seeing it acted out before you. Practicalities of stage effects aside, storms have symbolic value, representing approaching disorder and crisis, the anger of the gods, signifying a transgression already committed and being punished or heralding imminent emotional or physical conflict. Shakespeare's Hallowmas tempest heralds a crisis and confrontations that will right wrongs committed long ago, yet the title is misleading. Once the opening scene is over there are some unsettled, angry emotions but little tempestuous action to follow, though there are special effects galore. What the excited audience would not have known is that the setting is an isle full of noises, spirits, tricks and spectacle.

The Tempest is much like a masque (indeed has a short masque in Act IV) with its relatively straightforward storyline, allegory and magic. Masques were non-realistic dramas incorporating characters representing abstract concepts (concord, virtue, love, etc.) and/or classical deities acting out didactic (i.e., morally instructive) narratives. They increasingly featured in court entertainment and encouraged the development of ever more ingenious stage sets and gadgetry to produce spectacular effects. Aspects of masque staging seeped into the way traditional drama was presented. Unsurprisingly such developments influenced Shakespeare. Ben Jonson, an associate of the King's Men and friend and fellow playwright of Shakespeare, led the way in writing masques. He and Inigo Jones, court architect and stage engineer, developed many innovative stagecraft features like those pioneered by Leonardo da Vinci at the Sforza court in Milan. For the notorious *Masque of Blacknesse* (1605) Jones designed a forty-foot-square, four-foot-high mobile stage.

Once installed it remained *in situ* and was probably used for *The Tempest*. The understage space housed lift machinery to make ghosts and spirits appear to rise from Hell or the grave through a trapdoor, a standard feature of the public theatre stage. In the 'Heavens' (the roof over part of the open-air stage) was a machine for lowering a god or goddess onto the stage so that they could pass judgement on tangled human affairs.[6] In the Act IV masque 'Juno descends' (IV. i.), presumably using this *deus ex machina* device. Such machinery could be adapted to simulate flight for Ariel. Jonson's masque opened with a stormy sea effect created by painted cloths stretched across the stage, held at each end offstage and manipulated to make them billow like waves. In Jonson's *Masque of Blacknesse* the masquers 'were placed in a great concave shell [...] curiously made to move on those waters and rise with the billow'.[7] This wave effect was used in many later productions and may well have been part of the visual simulation in the opening scene of *The Tempest*.

The play is unusual in the amount of spectacle and music it contains. Music is used in many of Shakespeare's plays, as are a number of effects, but the amount of both in this piece is significantly greater. They are integral to a story about enchantment and magical control. The directions are unexpectedly detailed, from the relatively simple 'Enter Mariners wet' (I. i.) to 'Thunder and lightning. Enter Ariel, like a Harpy; claps his wings upon the table; and, with a quaint device, the banquet vanishes' (III. iii.). Other unusual effects abound: spirits, enchantment, disembodied music, 'strange shapes', a disappearing banquet, tricks and jokes played, and a tempest that turns out to be specially manufactured by magic. The tempest artificially simulated by the stage crew is also artificially raised by Prospero. Illusions within illusions are a feature of the play. Reported storms were used by Shakespeare often, bringing characters to strange shores where their virtues would be tested, but as stagecraft invented more elaborate machinery, he tended to bring the storms into the ongoing action.

So, a tempest seemed promised. What else would happen was a mystery, and therefore would create an air of excited expectation. As the court gathered, chattering, manoeuvring for places, waving to friends, watchful of their skirts, a little tipsy from too indulgent a dinner, they must have wondered what Master Shakespeare would serve up that night. It could be anything from high tragedy with plots and murders to a romp with farcical clowns and sighing lovers dancing the tangled maze of a 'sex war' comedy. He seemed to have become very romantic recently, with tales of loss, love and reunion, but always with that acid edge of cynicism and satire.

What the audience would see in this unknown play was a simple enough revenge storyline, but not the sort of Revenge Play they were used to. There is plotting and deviousness, the potential for brutal action, but in the event not a drop of blood is shed. The play will lack sustained drama and exciting incident. The characterization is broad but not penetrating. All dangers are contained and blunted, the love interest suffers no upsets or obstacles and the female lead, though delightful, lacks the wit and irrepressibility of Beatrice or Rosalind. The story is slight. A fleet returning from a royal wedding between the king of Tunis and Claribel, daughter of the king of Naples, is beset by a ferocious tempest. The ship carrying the king, his son, his brother, the Duke of Milan and other courtiers is separated from the rest and is apparently about to sink. Act I Scene i closes with cries of 'We split, we split!' and Gonzalo, last on stage, exits delivering himself into the hands of the gods and wishing not to drown: 'The wills above be done, but I would fain die a dry death.' The passengers are to be imagined leaping into the sea. In fact, the vessel runs aground safe and sound, with the sailors put into a deep sleep. The royal, courtly and common passengers are washed up separately on different parts of an island, each group thinking the others dead.

Act I Scene ii fills in the backstory, revealing that no one is drowned and the storm was artificially created by a master magician, Prospero, the previous Duke of Milan. This scene begins with a retrospective of the sort commonly found in the classical epics and in Renaissance romances. This device, informing us who the characters are and their background, is called *protasis* and is much used in narrative. Here it is much longer than usual (504 lines), but the scene is broken into four sequences. Prospero first tells his own story of duty neglected, usurpation, banishment and arrival on the island. Ousted by his brother, assisted by the King of Naples, he and his infant daughter were cast away at sea. 'Providence divine' (with some human assistance) brought them safely to the island. This tale is recounted to his eager daughter. After seeing the magician with Miranda, we see him dealing with his spirit servant, his savage slave and his son-in-law-to-be (the Prince of Naples). These are four parent–child relationships of very different sorts, for Prospero is a sort of father to Ariel, Caliban and Ferdinand as well as Miranda. The magician knew his traitorous brother and the king were aboard the ship and has drawn them to the island to take revenge and reclaim his rightful dukedom. The survivors display their various character flaws or strengths, are magically manipulated, made to wander the island, played with and tricked until in the final scene the magician calls them all into a magic circle, reveals himself as the banished duke, admits he created the tempest and proceeds to judge and sentence. Wrongdoers are exposed but by the time he is able to take revenge he has reached a state where he is readier to forgive his two offenders and create the potential for a positive future by arranging a marriage between Miranda and the prince. It is a revenge story with a reconciliation twist and some comedy. The contrived ending is another typical Shakespeare trick, something the audience was used in his most recent works and with the masques that had become popular. For some it might be heart-warming to see the apparent victory of hope over reality. A number of failed high-profile marriages had recently increased the hothouse temperature at court and negotiations for royal marriages were in the air too. Others might smile wryly at the silly optimism of it.

Frank Kermode described *The Tempest* as 'one of the most economically constructed of all Shakespeare's plays'.[8] The bare bones of the narrative make it sound like a folk- or fairy-tale romance; in many respects it resembles nothing so much as pantomime.[9] It is a multi-genre multi-thematic hybrid incorporating many current issues and discourses. Tragedy it is not, though it has conflictual elements that could have had disturbing implications (including three possible murders). Neither is it outright comedy, though incorporating a range of amusing situations. It is vibrantly a play of its time with cultural contexts of the early 1600s resonating through it, though it is curiously short of action or tension to create suspense and grip the audience. The driving impulse of revenge is eventually diverted with a final scene dénouement that is downbeat, for all its laudability as a truly Christian act. Other subsidiary plot features are also diverted or held up. Indeterminacy seems integral to the work, as if Shakespeare is saying, 'Nothing works out as expected, nothing ever quite finishes conclusively. Life is a series of inconclusive scenes.' Even Miranda and Ferdinand's union is planned rather than achieved. The play's charms are of another sort.

Critical responses have varied widely, seeing it as an allegorical moral pilgrimage of revenge turned to forgiveness and reconciliation, a series of parent–child relationships reflecting the contemporary education debate, an interrogation of the limitations of patriarchy, the nature of rule and authority, the morality of imperialism and the nature of art and illusion. These themes – all present, all active – are recapitulations of concerns recurrent throughout Shakespeare's work. A play does not have one meaning or one theme any more than it offers cut and dried answers. It can be all of these things and offer only partial solutions. Though it revisits many of the writer's subjects, it is also an innovative piece in terms of its content and style. Its thematic and ethical complexities are reflected in the sometimes difficult syntax. The degree to which magic and its effects operate is greater than even *A Midsummer Night's Dream*. *The Tempest* is like nothing else Shakespeare wrote; yet it is like everything he wrote. Many previous plays have elements found clustered in *Tempest*: the enchantment and mischief rife in *A Midsummer Night's Dream*, the sibling rivalries in *As You Like It, Much Ado About Nothing* and *King Lear*, the study of flawed kingship that runs through all the history plays and the Great Tragedies. One overriding theme is the struggle to control the passions.

Rule of the self (or failure to do so) is a common denominator in Shakespeare and in other contemporary dramatists, for it lies at the heart of the Christian view of how life was to be lived if damnation was to be avoided. For all his status as master magician and stage manager, even Prospero, the God-like puppeteer, is flawed as a ruler of others and himself and is unable to make his brother repent.

The first scene, an exciting way to start a play, concerns a real, dramatic event. Londoners and those at court, inhabiting a sea-trading port, would hear constantly about voyages, shipwrecks, dangers, escapes, monsters and marvels. The century preceding *The Tempest* was vibrant with accounts of seafaring adventures as pirates, traders and settlers began crossing the Atlantic to pillage and colonize the 'New World'. Indian Ocean crossings too were made. The East India Company (officially registered in 1600) made its first two exploratory forays in 1601 and 1604.[10] The American adventure began in 1584 with Sir Walter Raleigh and the failed Roanoke colony.[11] The Virginian colony was established in 1607 at Jamestown. From the East and the West stories were rife with exotic creatures and tribes with strange, sometimes barbaric customs. Exaggerated accounts grew in the telling, passing from person to person, tavern to tavern. In the absence of instant communication and film footage, news of savages morphed into the grisly or fantastic. The storms and hazards of the Atlantic crossing were real enough and in 1610 London buzzed; 'the new fleet for Virginia' had encountered horrific storms off the Bermudas and been dispersed. Most vessels made the American coast, but one, though surviving, had been driven aground on one of the islands. The crew underwent mutinies and hardships before fitting out a couple of boats to sail on to Jamestown.[12]

The illusory stage storm might well be acted in a stylized way, without ropes and rigging or masts and sails. Despite the possibility of fake waves there would probably be little attempt to replicate a ship's deck. The words would create the tempest (assisted by sound effects) and actions would represent men on a heaving deck buffeted by imaginary wind. Jacobean playgoers, accustomed to long sermons, were used to listening to the words and were not overly distracted by and did not need all the realistic effects we today cannot do without. That said, the court audience was used to and demanded more inventive machinery in the staging of the many masques performed for them.[13] The language of the play is dominated by imagery recreating and describing sounds and there is a deal of music – played by an offstage consort.

The Banqueting House built for James within the grounds of the Palace of Whitehall was the setting for the large number of masques that, encouraged by Queen Anne (James's wife) and Henry, Prince of Wales, became the fashion at court. Shakespeare may well have used some of the scenery and machinery commonly used in the masques. After the storm scene, the play moves suddenly into a world of enchantment and fantasy, though subtextually touches on a number of very real topical debates. For all the apparent simplicity of the outline narrative this is an intricate piece and the hymeneal masque (incorporated to bless the planned Ferdinand–Miranda union, though it sits oddly in some respects) contributes integrally to the seriousness of the overall concerns. The Act IV masque apart, of all Shakespeare's works, *The Tempest*'s amalgam of action, formal speechifying, magic and spectacle, and its range of lexical registers, music and dance, is closest to the style and handling of the masque genre. This aristocratic art form, mixing classical deities and allegory, 'gave a higher meaning to the realities of politics and power'. Its fictions 'created heroic roles for the leaders of society'.[14] Masque demanded exotic and lavish costumes (many designed by Jones) made from expensive cloths. In a play full of illusions, the idea of 'the leaders of society' taking away the Christian message of how their duty to lead should be shaped is the greatest, ironic trick of all. No documents tell how the audience reacted to the play. Curiosity before it began might have given way to pleasure as the revenge and love stories unfold in an atmosphere of constantly surprising magic and mayhem. The audience would have noted the lessons of the play related to rule, authority, parenting and imperial ambitions. Whether they would have acted on them is doubtful. They were largely an idle, feckless lot, more intent on pleasure than duty. Their lack of concern for their responsibilities and the political problems of the age would lead inexorably to civil war (1642–49).

The play perplexed critics from early on. Davenant and Dryden's collaboration (1667), for which they rewrote the script and brought in new characters, suggests dissatisfaction with the original. Shadwell turned it into an opera (1674). No one quite knew how inhuman or subhuman to make Caliban. Nineteenth-century productions went overboard for elaborate staging, feeling perhaps the original text was too light and needed bulking out with theatrical sensation. No one could agree either what sort of creature the play was and how to define it. It is a generically modified clone of different types, mixing knockabout comedy, a love story, political skulduggery, trickery, serious comment on courts and loyalty, singing, dancing, a masque, a ghostly banquet, unearthly music and characters frozen immobile, sent to sleep or played with as Prospero, the enchanter, mocks and manipulates them like God as a manic puppeteer. If it resembles nothing so much as a pantomime, it is an edgy pantomime with dark corners.

Strange that a piece so full of spirits, magic, illusion, deceptions, manipulation of appearances and non-natural happenings should be acted on 1 November. Hallowmas (also known as All Saints' Day, All Hallows' Day, the Solemnity of All Saints, or the Feast of All Saints),[15] commemorated all the saints. The Church of England no longer permitted celebration of Halloween because of its pagan connections with rites of the dead and the release of evil spirits, but Halloween and Hallowmas were once important festal days, traditionally part of a three-day celebration starting at sunset on October 31 (Halloween – the 'eve' before All Hallows'), running through All Saints' Day (1 November) and continuing into All Souls' Day (2 November). The trio of days metamorphosed in Christian Europe into a memorial of the holy ones of the faith, celebrating first the banishment of evil spirits, then memorializing those who died for their faith and were canonized, and then into a remembrance day for all souls. In Tudor times the king wore purple and the court black in mourning for the departed. Bells were rung at intervals throughout the three days and community meals were taken as a form of wake (with feasting, drinking and dancing). The underlying concept was too papistically superstitious for the reformed English church. The break with Catholicism did away with much of the ceremonial, but kept Hallowmas in memory of the saints. But, as Ronald Hutton points out, the Anglican Church retained Hallowmas 'as a celebration of saints as outstanding godly human beings, and not as semi-divine intercessors'.[16] Halloween and All Souls' were discontinued by the Church of England, though it took a long while for communities to fully conform. Prosecutions for illegal bell ringing and junketing were still being made into the 1580s. Halloween was banned for its pagan connections – the release of spirits, witches' covens and devil worship. Both All Saints' and All Souls' were especially connected in the common mind with the expectation of 'spiritual appearances' and the English Church had doctrinal difficulties with spirits, spectres and ghouls in general.[17]

Halloween seems more appropriate for a play concerned with the witch Sycorax's extraordinary black magical strength and Prospero's own powers. As the night when all the evil spirits are let loose, it fits with the mood and action of Prospero's pervasive trickery, Antonio and Sebastian's evil, Caliban's malice and Trinculo and Stephano's foolish ambitions. Yet, the benevolent and hopeful outcome, a peaceful end after a stormy beginning, is a conclusion fitting a day dedicated to the virtues exhibited by the huge array of saints that had built up the positive side of Christian belief. And Prospero is a white magician, harnessing the elemental powers of the world, creating illusions, but doing no evil. Though the Reformation banned the idolatrous reverence given to statues of saints and chapels and prayers dedicated to them, the habit was still powerful in the minds of the faithful. What the saints represented in terms of the virtues – faith in adversity, readiness to sacrifice for Christ, chastity and abstinence when surrounded by temptation – was still valued by the Church of England and the day continued to be celebrated. A thoughtful member of the Banqueting House audience might have felt that a play ending by relinquishing magic and the mish-mash of references to the classical gods, turning to forgiveness and anticipating a hopeful marriage, was well fitted to such a day. After all, the saints fought to banish evil, and the sometimes harsh though never evil Prospero finally turns aside his vengefulness, pardons those who trespassed against him and promotes a marriage which it is hoped will bring redemption to the next generation. Someone clearly thought it fitting enough to be performed at court during the 1613 celebrations of the king's daughter's marriage to the Elector Palatine along with 14 other dramatic pieces presented during the usual Christmas season's plethora of entertainments.[18] It is a hopeful piece in which, like *The Winter's Tale*, man's potential for destructive emotions and the critical contemporary matters relating to authority, rule and the court are eventually vanquished in favour of redemption, healing, reconciliation and new beginnings. In both these late plays, the characters are delivered from evil, and despite satirical barbs against courts and courtiers, the unrelieved cynicism of the Problem Plays and Great Tragedies (1600–1606) is less prevalent and the mood is lighter.

Part I

THE INHERITED PAST

Chapter 1

THE HISTORICAL CONTEXT: AN OVERVIEW

In 1603 Elizabeth I died and James VI of Scotland became James I of England. The play was written between 1610 and 1611, so falls into the Jacobean period (after *Jacobus*, Latin for James). In the wider European literary and political contexts, the period is the waning of the High Renaissance. Historians today call it Early Modern because many features of it are recognizably modern while being early in the evolution that shaped our world.

The new king, ruling until 1625, was of the Scottish family the Stuarts. They were a dynastic disaster; none was an effective ruler, and rule and authority are key themes in *The Tempest*. James was a learned but flawed monarch. Prospero announces his own failings when he claims, 'My library/Was dukedom large enough' (I. ii. 109–10). James too shirked the routines of work involved in government, but was a worse ruler than Prospero for he disliked contact with his people, drank heavily, was extravagant, impulsive, tactless, hectoring and bullying, and constantly in debt. He was a hard line right-winger in religion who backed the repression of Catholics and Puritans and was in perpetual conflict with Parliament. Sir Anthony Weldon dubbed him 'the wisest fool in Christendom'.[1] The epithet captures the discrepancy between his writings on political theory and his practice as a lazy man only intermittently engaged with his role. London celebrated with bonfires when he succeeded peacefully. His apparent engagement with his regal duties generated hope, reflected in the mass of appalling, sycophantic, eulogistic verse published.[2] During the royal procession through the city on 15 March 1603 two St Paul's choristers sang of London as Troynovant (New Troy),[3] no longer a city but a bridal chamber, suggesting a mystical union and new hope.[4]

This sense of promise soon evaporated as his failings and inconsistencies emerged. *The Tempest* is underpinned by concerns about authority and rule (or misrule) of self and others. Misrule of self is a theme running through all Shakespeare's plays. Parental rule over a child, the difficulties of ruling a recalcitrant 'subject' and the extent and limitations of authority over others are themes running through the play from its opening scene to its last. The major characters, even Miranda, are guilty of misrule of themselves; each transgresses in some way.

The previous monarch, Elizabeth I, a Tudor, was much loved and respected and had been a strong ruler, indeed strong enough to suppress the addressing of many problems which by James's time had become irresolvable. The Tudors (Henry VII, Henry VIII, Edward VI, Mary I and Elizabeth I) ruled 1485–1603. Though dysfunctional and brutally absolutist, they successfully brought stability after the turmoil of the Wars of the Roses (though there were various short-lived rebellions against them). Questions of succession, the nature of rulers, the use and limits of monarchical power, the influence of the court and the qualities of courtiers were matters that concerned people throughout the period and are among the contexts of *The Tempest*. Religion was a major area of conflict,[5] with Dissenters and Catholics fighting for freedom from tight central control by the new Established Church. The effects on society and individual morality of the wealth that the new capitalism and the expansion of trade were creating also worried Jacobean writers. The new individualism, another context of the play, emerges in the self-centred ruthlessness of Sebastian and the established amorality of Antonio.

Henry VIII's great achievement (and cause of trouble) was breaking with the Catholic Church of Rome and setting up an independent English church. It was to remain essentially Catholic until the reforms of his son Edward aligned it with the Protestant movements on the Continent. This period of seismic change was called the English Reformation. There was some limited alliance with the Protestant Reformation led by Martin Luther, but in many ways the English went their own way. Monasteries and convents were dissolved and the infrastructure of Catholicism banished. Altars were stripped of ornaments (leaving only the cross), churches emptied of statues and relics and many murals whitewashed over. New church services and prayers were inaugurated in English rather than Latin. New English translations of the Bible began to appear and there was a Book of Common Prayer to be used in all parish churches. Holy shrines and saints' days were done away with as idols and superstitions. The vicar was to be the only intermediary between a person and God. After a brief fiery and bloody return to Catholicism under Mary I (1553–58), Elizabeth I succeeded and bedding-in of the new church continued. The new freedom of a reformed English religion, stripped back to its simple original faith, encouraged the rise of more extreme reformist Protestant sects (not always to the liking of the infant Established Church).

These groups, called Non-Conformists, Independents or Dissenters, included the Puritans, Calvinists[6] and Presbyterians – all Protestant, but with doctrinal differences. Some eccentric sects grew up too, such as the Anabaptists, Brownists and the Family of Love. Religion and the tensions between different sects is a persistently present consideration at this time, but despite all the official changes, the essential beliefs in sin, virtue, salvation, the centrality of Christ and the ubiquity of the Devil (the idea that he was everywhere, looking to tempt man) were the same as they always had been, as were the beliefs that punishment and possible perdition followed sin and that the world was in decline and would shortly come to an end. Sin and virtue are persistently referenced throughout *The Tempest*.

Another persistent feature is the political discourse on kingship. Elizabeth I (adoringly nicknamed 'Gloriana' after her identification with a character in Spenser's *The Faerie Queene*) ruled from 1558–1603, a time long enough to establish her as an icon, particularly as she headed up strong opposition (and victory) against the Spanish. But while external threats were repulsed, the Elizabethan-Jacobean period was one of unstoppable internal changes.[7] These gradually altered the profile and mood of society. Religion, commerce, growing industrialization, increase of manufacture, social relationships, kingship and rule were all in flux. One feature of the period was the unceasing rise in prices, particularly of food, bringing about a decline in the living standards of the poor, for wages did not rise. The rich and the rising middle class could cope with inflation, but the state of the poor deteriorated. Enclosure of arable land (very labour intensive) and its conversion to sheep farming (requiring less labour), raised unemployment among the 'lower orders' or 'baser sort', who constituted the largest proportion (80–85 per cent) of the four to five million population. Rising numbers of poor put greater burdens on Poor Relief in small, struggling rural communities and added to the elite's fear of some monumental uprising of the disenchanted. Most of the population worked on the land, though increasing numbers were moving to the few existing cities. Later ages looked back on the Elizabethan era as a 'Golden Age' and talked of 'Merry England' – it was not, except for a small section of rich, privileged aristocrats. Also enjoying greater luxury and comfort were canny merchants making fortunes from trading in exotic goods from the 'New Worlds' of Asia and the Americas and those manufacturers making luxury goods for the aristocracy and the increasingly wealthy, acquisitive 'middling sort'. The emotional detachment of the governing classes from awareness of the state of the poor was a resonant feature of contemporary England and there is some sense in *The Tempest* of social tensions – between the mariners and their privileged passengers, in Trinculo and Stephano's views and other characters' attitudes towards them. On Sunday 13 March 1603, the Puritan divine Richard Stock delivered a Lent sermon at the Pulpit Cross in St Paul's churchyard, commenting: 'I have lived here some few years, and every year I have heard an exceeding outcry of the poor that they are much oppressed of the rich of this city. […] All or most charges are raised […] wherein the burden is more heavy upon a mechanical or handicraft poor man than upon an alderman.'[8]

The Jacobean period was quickly perceived as declining from the high points of Elizabeth's time, with worsening of the continuing problems she had been unable or unwilling to rectify during her reign. Economic difficulties, poverty, social conflict, religious dissent and political tensions relating to the role and nature of monarchy and the role and authority of Parliament all remained unresolved. Charismatic, strong rulers (like Elizabeth and Prospero) carry their followers with them, generating loyalty though often through an element of fear. Emerging problems are ignored or masked because the ruler prevents them being discussed and councillors are afraid to raise them. Elizabeth, for example, passed several laws that made it treason to even discuss who might succeed her. It is a tenable argument that the younger Prospero did not deserve to rule since he had detached himself from the day-to-day running of the Milanese state. Antonio's means of usurping power were unacceptable, devious and Machiavellian, and legitimacy of succession was a recurrent concern throughout the period. Antonio gradually suborned the court and government to his side and then launched a coup. A polity needs an active ruler, engaged with the key problems and petty matters of the state. States needs rulers who engage physically and sympathetically with the people, not reclusive scholars who shut themselves up in their libraries improving their mind. Contemporaries would have condemned any man who claimed there were 'volumes/I prize above my dukedom' (I. ii. 167–8). Dereliction of duty deserves the loss of privilege and power. Monarchical commitment and an unwillingness to seek advice were often queried in James's time. In his first speech to Parliament James claimed he was as a husband wedded to England as his bride. It was to be a union in which the husband would bully, boss, insult and generally repress his 'helpmeet'. James's flaws consisted in regular absence from court (most often for hunting), delegation of power, inconsistency and a dictatorial manner. He issued a royal proclamation prohibiting the English from discussing 'causes of state'.[9] In making decisions of state James relied too much on favourites as advisers, gave them too much power and tended to lecture and bully Parliament rather than consider its input. This high-handed approach encouraged his son to make similar mistakes and would contribute to the unavoidable move towards civil war.

Strong, purposeful central rule dwindled under James into rule by whim and capricious diktat. His court became more decadent and detached from the rest of the population than in his predecessor's time. Commerce and manufacture expanded rapidly, triggering a rise in the middle class that provided and serviced the new trades and crafts. Attitudes to religion and church authority began developing into resistance, and science began slowly to displace old superstitions and belief in magic. Like all times of transition, the Jacobean period and the seventeenth century in general were exciting times for some but unsettling for most, profitable for a few but a struggle for the majority. As always, the rich found ways to become richer, and the poor became poorer. Gradually the poor found men to speak up for them in the corridors of power, in the villages of England and in the overcrowded streets of the cities. *The Tempest* appears at first sight a light-hearted mix of romance and playful humour appealing to the idle, pleasure-loving court, but it is also a typical Jacobean play – dark at times, cynical, satirical, violent (threatened rather than actual) and psychologically disturbing, hinting deep character flaws and suspect motives. It is also much concerned with sin, punishment, repentance, redemption and reconciliation.

The first known audience was the court. Its entertainments – particularly the many masques – its fashions, lifestyle and attitudes, indicate a ritualization and artificiality that were fast detaching it from life outside. The new reign and new century were still much overshadowed by the past. Just as Prospero's past relationship with his brother resonates in the present, so past events resonated in Whitehall Palace on 1 November 1611, while a cluster of new problems were developing outside, in London, in the nation.

Chapter 2

THE ELIZABETHAN WORLD ORDER: FROM DIVINITY TO DUST

Cosmology

How the cosmos was thought to be structured was formalized in the second century AD by Ptolemy (Claudius Ptolemaeus), a Graeco-Egyptian astronomer, geographer and mathematician living in Alexandria. His model of the universe was geocentric (centred around Earth) and conceived as a set of revolving transparent crystal spheres, one inside the other, each containing a planet. Moving out from Earth in the middle, encased in its sphere, next came the Moon's sphere, then Mercury, Venus, the Sun, Mars, Jupiter and Saturn, like the rings of an onion.[1] Each planet in its sphere circled Earth at different orbital angles and different speeds. After Saturn came the firmament or fixed stars (divided into 12 zodiac sectors). Outside this were 'the waters above the firmament' (Genesis 1:7) and the tenth sphere, the *Primum Mobile* (First Mover), which drove the spheres. Finally came the all-surrounding Empyrean, the domain that was all God's and all God (i.e., Heaven). Here he was accompanied by the angels, the saints and the blessed. The set of concentric balls was imagined by some to hang from the lip of Heaven by a gold chain. In Tudor times his *Cosmographia* was still recommended by Sir Thomas Elyot for boys to learn about the spheres.[2]

The Ptolemaic system

In the ages of faith medieval and Renaissance man thought of Creation as an all-enveloping Godliness that incorporated Heaven, the human universe and Hell.

Men could see the stars and sometimes some of the planets, but not beyond, their vision being blocked by the 'waters'. The Empyrean (Heaven),

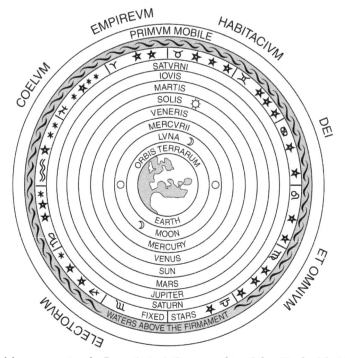

Adapted from engraving for Peter Apian's *Cosmographicus Liber* (*Book of the Universe*, Antwerp 1524). Enclosing the spheres is the 'COELUM EMPIREUM HABITACIUM DEI ET OMNIUM ELECTORUM' (The Empyrean sky, home of God and all the elect – i.e., those judged worthy of Heaven)

the destination for the virtuous saved, was thus made invisible. But people wanted to know what Heaven was like, they needed a visualizable image. It was easier to imagine the blessed 'living' in a celestial city rather than existing vaguely and spiritually in the heavenly ether, so the idea grew of a fortified city with towers and gates made of different substances. At the Gate of Pearl, St Peter was supposed to receive each approaching soul and consult his 'Book of Life', recording all the good and evil a person had done, to see if the soul was worthy of entry. Medieval paintings show the *Civitatis Dei* (City of God) resembling the walled cities of Italy, France or Germany. Painters often simply depicted the city they knew.[3]

By Shakespeare's time the Ptolemaic system was beginning to be undermined by the revolutionary ideas of Copernicus, Galileo, Kepler and others, who put the sun at the heart of the universe. The idea entered the public domain with Copernicus's study *De Revolutionibus Orbium Coelestium* (*On the Revolutions of the Celestial Spheres*, 1542), but was only slowly accepted by scientists and took even longer to filter down to ordinary people.

The church blocked dissemination of iconoclastic research that might disturb the orthodox theology of the universe. Heresy and atheism were useful charges to block scientific advances. In 1603 Sir Christopher Heydon, displaying his knowledge of the new advances, declared, 'Whether (as Copernicus saith) the sun be the centre of the world, the astrologer careth not.'[4] This references the triple belief system in which most people lived: 1. Christian doctrine existing uneasily alongside, 2. the new astronomy and sciences, and 3. old semi-magical beliefs in the authenticity of astrology. Heliocentrism, opposed by the scepticism of other astronomers (including John Dee), was bloodily repressed by dogmatic, authoritarian churches. The Catholic Church's Inquisition enforced conformity persuasively with thumbscrews, the rack and many other grisly tortures. The English church had its own courts to question and punish deviations from customary practice and belief; diocesan visitations enabled bishops to keep vicars and congregations in line and serious infractions could be brought before the Star Chamber.[5] Prison and the rack were used to encourage orthodoxy in England too.

The principle underlying the inner organization of Creation was order, an intricate and beautiful arrangement ordained by the Creator. Cosmology (how the audience thought their universe was structured), theology (how they saw God and religion) and sociology (how their place in the order of things was organized) were ruled by strict hierarchy (everything having its place according to its importance in God's order) and organic harmony (everything being part of a whole and having a function to perform). Hierarchy and harmony were still the natural laws by which the early seventeenth century believed the world functioned. The disorders and disharmonies upsetting the roles and expectations in *The Tempest* stem from Prospero's initial fault in neglecting his duties as a ruler. His comment 'My library/Was dukedom large enough' (I. ii. 109–10) strongly indicates faulty leadership. Also transgressive are Antonio's usurpation, Prospero's appropriation of rule on the island, Caliban's attempted violation of Miranda, Antonio and Sebastian's plan to assassinate Alonso and Gonzalo, Stephano's planned coup and Ferdinand's enforced slave labour. The initial trope of the tempest and Prospero's other claimed environmental disruptions act as metaphors emblematic of a world turned upside down. His magic too is perilously close to trespassing into the domain of God. A series of other reversals are presented before the play reaches a degree of harmony. Disturbances of normal order were unsettling to an audience living under a strict etiquette of precedence and whose social power relied on their being seen and accepted as the pinnacle of society.

Most people knew where they were placed in the universal order, the Great Chain of Being.[6] God ruled all, was omnipotent (all-powerful) and omniscient (all-knowing). Man was inferior to God, Christ, the Holy Ghost, all the angels, apostles, saints, the Virgin Mary and all the blessed, but superior to all animals, birds, fish, plants and minerals. God ruled Heaven, kings (and princes, dukes, counts, etc.) ruled on Earth and fathers ruled families, like God at home. The great hierarchical chain stretched from God through all the lesser hierarchies of existence to the very bottom in descending order of importance – from divinity to dust – all interconnected as contributory parts of God's creation. The chain links were each a separate group of beings, creatures or objects, each connected to the one before and the one after, semi-separate, dependent but partly independent, separate yet part of something greater. Each link had its internal hierarchy. The human link contained three different ranks: the 'better sort' (kings, nobles, gentry), the 'middling sort' (merchants, shopkeepers, farmers) and the 'baser sort' or 'lower orders' (artisans, peasants, beggars). The word 'class' was not used then, but these ranks, degrees and estates are equivalent to our upper, the middle and lower classes.

Other beliefs concerning the structure of our world were being transformed. Magellan's circumnavigation of the world without falling off the edge (1522), showed the Flat Earth theory was inaccurate. Drake's 1580 voyage brought this home more directly to British people when the queen permitted an exhibition to publicize his discoveries. A map displayed at Whitehall Palace made the spherical world graphically clear. But how many people saw it? Shakespeare knew of the new development in thinking about the world's shape, as evidenced by Puck's referring to putting 'a girdle round about the earth' (A Midsummer Night's Dream, 1595–96) and Lear's demand the gods 'strike flat the thick rotundity of the earth' (King Lear, 1606). He clearly knew much too about the recent travel writing describing the discovery and conquest of the Americas. To most people, unenlightened by new discoveries, heliocentricity and Earth's roundness were unimportant and largely still unknown. In an age when the nearest town was often as alien as the moon, the 'New Worlds' were a bestiary of fantasy and nightmare, places inhabited by strange animals and unnatural beings, like the cannibal anthropophagi and 'men whose heads/Do grow beneath their shoulders' (Othello I. iii. 144–5).[7] Looking at the sky from your fields at dawn then at dusk, it seemed the sun moved round the Earth. As long it shone bright to ripen corn and fruit and assist in telling the time and the season, most people were indifferent. The village was the centre of their universe. Caliban's astronomical knowledge extends only so far as distinguishing the 'bigger light' (the Sun) from 'the lesser' (the Moon). The ordinary farmer would know the stars and some of the planets but thought of them as belonging to the mystical world of superstition, astrology, weather lore and magic rather than to the measurable world of science and astronomy.

The Great Chain of Being

The set of hierarchical links making the world order placed man at the top of earthly creation, followed by animals, birds, fish, plants and minerals, and each stratum of existence was internally organized in order of importance. Man was the pinnacle of God's animal creation, though not entirely perfect. Flawed by Original Sin, with animal weaknesses and negative passions, he was nevertheless part angel, endowed with soul, reason, language, intelligence and sensitivity. A human being acting morally was an imitation of Christ. Choosing the left-hand way, the path of sin, he resembled the Devil. The conflict between these two aspects made man an angel with horns, but the tensions between virtue and passion, the perpetual *psychomachia*[8] of life, sparked the interest of literature.

As a construct of human imagining, the Great Chain of Being helped people from the early medieval period to the Renaissance picture how the universe was put together socially and how it worked physically. It was a general belief still held by the majority of people in Shakespeare's time, though its physical structure was increasingly challenged by new astronomical research and by socio-economic changes. Most people still thought the universe geocentric. The Renaissance is regarded as a time of change, new learning and new knowledge. Men were discovering new lands and new ways of thinking about God and society, but this only slowly affected everyday life. The iconoclastic, rationalist, free-thinking Renaissance Man, daringly breaking through barriers and questioning old orthodoxies, was an oddity often in conflict with the authorities and general orthodox beliefs, and confined to small minority groups of progressive artists/scientists/intellectuals.[9] Seventeenth-century Everyman was conservative and backward-looking in his beliefs and daily lifestyle. If literate, he would have few books apart from a Bible.[10] He still went to the wise woman for semi-magical medical help, believed in divination, went to an astrologer to predict a suitable day for travelling or a suitable mate, and still believed the Chain of Being was constructed by God.

The chain, arranged hierarchically, reflecting descending importance, usefulness and perfection, was sometimes imagined instead as a ladder of nature (*scala naturae*). In the physical world each man had his place on the social ladder, might rise or descend, but was largely expected to stay where he was born. Christian thinkers found the ladder image agreeable as a spiritual metaphor, suggesting rising towards the divine (or descending towards perdition), as each person was supposed to do by a life of virtue that would cleanse away their earthly faults, purifying them as they metaphorically rose rung by rung to a holiness that prepared their soul for Heaven. Walter Hilton's *The Ladder of Perfection* (written between 1386 and 1396) reflects in its title the image of the step-by-step rise from sin to virtue, presented as a spiritual journey towards the peace given by Christ and the peace which was Christ. He is the perfection achieved in climbing the ladder, reached by denying the primacy of the 'anti-Trinity' of mind, reason and will, and trusting faith alone.[11] In the busy, corrupt world of London in1611, the same belief persisted among the godly sort. These were not just fervent Puritan zealots, but those ordinary folk who believed their Christian duty was to live the good life. The good life meant not the carnal life of fleshly pleasures, but the hard-working, devoted life of the family man or woman, whose days were struggled through with the example of Christ as their perpetual model. It is important not to underplay the general piety of most people at this time. They listened regularly to preachers of different sorts and attended church regularly. The literate bought, borrowed, read or had read to them more and more of the religious pamphlets pouring off the presses. Production of printed pamphlets accelerated from a trickle in 1600 to a flood by the Civil War.[12] Though they lived physically 'by the rule of the flesh', as St Augustine put it, they were dominated by 'the rule of the spirit'.[13] While many lived dedicated Christian lives, most lived at various intermediate stages ranging from occasionally lapsing piety to a more sinful existence, less concerned with virtue than bodily pleasures, and shading down towards outright irreligion and criminality. This vast spectrum was much represented in the City Comedies of the 1600s and in the Revenge Tragedies (1580s–1630s). Shakespeare's Problem Plays (*Troilus and Cressida*, 1601–02; *All's Well That Ends Well*, 1602–04; *Measure for Measure*, 1604) and the late Romances (*Pericles*, 1608–09; *Cymbeline*, 1609–10; *The Winter's Tale*, 1610–11; *The Tempest*, 1611) all address the ethical complexities and ambiguities focused in the tensions between flesh and spirit. *The Tempest*, without being very specifically topical and satirical, does nevertheless question conduct in areas that were of contemporary interest. The audience's responses will have largely been made within the Christian, Bible-based context.

Chain or ladder equally suggest unbroken interconnection between the Creator and dust and all the intervening phases of existence. Originating in the pre-Christian philosophy of Plato and Aristotle, this idea of hierarchies reflects a Western obsession with taxonomy (classification). Medieval Christian theology assimilated the heavenly hierarchy to fit above the feudal system of human society and the descending levels of the rest of creation. Below earthly life (physically and morally) came the hierarchy of Hell traditionally thought to be in the bowels of the Earth. Dante (1321) placed it below Gehenna, the rubbish dump outside Jerusalem.[14] The orderliness of God's creation was so imbedded in people's minds that disassembling it was like an attack on the foundations of life and faith. Order was part of everything and the maintenance of order was a form of worship, an acceptance of God as author of that order. Within each dominion – Heaven, Earth and Hell – there was a series of graduated structures.[15] In Christian thought the domains of Heaven and Hell, equivalents of the classical world's Olympus (home of the ancient gods) and Hades (the underworld, the place of the dead), had their inhabitants ranked according to priority and power like the various types of earthly creation. All three realms had rulers and below them were ranks of diminishing power and diminishing virtue. This was 'a society obsessed with hierarchy'.[16]

Heavenly Hierarchy - God > Christ > the Holy Ghost > Seraphim > Cherubim > Thrones > Dominations > Principalities > Powers > Virtues > Archangels > Angels > the Virgin Mary > the disciples > the saints > the blessed (saved, elect, good souls admitted to Heaven after a virtuous life).[17]

Saints were still intermittently prayed to as intercessors for specific concerns in Protestant England. Though the Church disapproved, having banished such idolatry, it takes generations to change a mindset that has for centuries been integral to thought and belief.

Hierarchy of Earth: Man > animals > birds > fish > plants > rocks/minerals

Hierarchy of Hell: Devil/Lucifer/Satan > first hierarchy (Hell's 'nobility'): named devils like Beelzebub, Mephistophelis, Mammon, Belial, etc. > second hierarchy: demons > goblins > imps > incubi/succubi[18] > familiars

Familiars are spirits controlled by a witch/wizard and acting as an assistant. Often they are in animal form. A black cat is commonly thought to be the standard witch's demon familiar, but records include frogs, dogs and toads. They could take human shape too. Seventeenth-century witch confessions regularly describe a good-looking, blond-haired young man, but with giveaway cloven hoofs. A familiar attached to a necromancer/witch was thought to be a malevolent servant/assistant imp/demon, a limb of Satan, sometimes even Satan himself. If it was benevolent and assisted a white wizard/cunning woman it was sometimes called a fairy. The latter could have mischievous tendencies, as Ariel does at times. They were capable of appearing as three-dimensional forms or remaining invisible. Ariel is essentially benevolent, imprisoned by Sycorax for having a moral sense 'too delicate/To act her earthy and abhorr'd commands' (I. ii. 272–3). Presumably these were simply horrible acts of black magic. Ariel is a spirit of air and fire (qualities associated with the divine) rather than of earth and water (heavy qualities suited to darker arts). The cast list describes him as an 'airy spirit'.

He flies swiftly over distances (as far as the 'Bermoothes'), is able to flame amazement, 'burn in many places' (I. ii. 199) and leave the ship 'all afire with me' (I. ii. 212), but also acts as an all-purpose spirit/servant sometimes associated with water and earth too. Prospero talks of him being sent

> [...] to tread the ooze
> Of the salt deep,
> To run upon the sharp wind of the north,
> To do me business in the veins o' th'earth
> When it is bak'd with frost. (I. ii. 252–6)

His confederates are benign spirits, though they take on frightening aspects when wrongdoers need to be chastened. They are all controlled/commanded by the white magician, the theurgist, who has learned to harness the powers of nature.[19] Ariel is more a creature of light and air, Caliban of dark and earth. These binaries reflect the four elements and echo the old morality plays, but reflect also the paired allegories common to the masque.

Human society was arranged in three main ranks, degrees or orders: the 'better sort', the 'middling sort' and the 'lower orders' ('commoners' or 'baser sort'). It was thought those of highest rank were there by the grace of God and were therefore automatically thought more virtuous. They certainly thought themselves superior. Among the classical texts they studied at university was Aristotle's *Nichomachean Ethics*. In his conclusions, they would have found a view to endorse their sense of superiority:

> While [arguments] seem to have power to encourage and stimulate the generous-minded among our youth, and to make a character who is gently born, and a true lover of what is noble, ready to be possessed by virtue, they are not able to encourage the *many* to nobility and goodness. For these do not by nature obey the sense of shame, but only fear, and do not abstain from bad acts because of their baseness but through fear of punishment.[20]

This ignores the fact that many elite men did wrong because they knew they could escape penalty by buying off the law, by family influence or by the psychological power they had over the subordinate majority. The lower orders were thought to be naturally sinful, the middle ranks dour money-grubbers. The three-tier medieval feudal system (those who fight, those who pray, those who work) was refined in the Renaissance. The clergy ranks were diminished by the Dissolution of the Monasteries and the remaining personnel assimilated into the upper ranks. 'Those who work' were split into the 'middling sort' and 'commoners'. The former included the important expanding new masses of bourgeois entrepreneurs (bankers, projectors [speculators], merchants, wealthy clothiers, industrial manufacturers, etc.) that had hardly existed before, but which were driving the astonishing explosion of culture and commerce that was the Renaissance. As money and investment spread through the arteries of European trading, so the bourgeoisie expanded. This rising class was to be a vital feature in Elizabethan-Jacobean social change, hugely increasing the numbers of the 'middling sort', creating confusion about whether powerful 'merchant princes' and 'captains of industry' belonged within the middling rank or among the better sort.[21] Many became investors in ships sent to establish American plantations or search for the Northwest Passage. In *Tempest* the top tier includes Prospero, Miranda, Ferdinand, Alonso, Sebastian, Antonio and the courtiers. The middle rank is represented by the shipmaster alone, and the baser sort by Trinculo, Stephano, the boatswain and the mariners.

In general terms, the old, simple world of the Middle Ages, unified in religion by Catholicism and unified socially by the feudal system, was morphing into dynamic new forms. Rising wealth created new types of employment. Developing industries created new roles and services. The broad social stratifications were still the same, but within them the three levels were diversifying into complex new forms while social/political/commercial interactions were changing in destabilizing, disturbing ways with which many could not easily cope. Some of these social tensions are suggested in the play (between the boatswain and the titled passengers and in 'King' Stephano's transgressive pretensions), but it largely focuses on the splits between the courtly characters – between the old values of virtue and loyalty in Gonzalo and the new, self-obsessed ruthlessness of Antonio and Sebastian. The rest of the court, docile sycophants with moveable morals, reflects James's court audience. The state of official corruption was highlighted in the oration delivered to James on his arrival in the city. It demanded, 'No more shall bribes blind the eyes of the wise, nor gold be reputed the common measure of a man's worth.' The burden of monopolies, generating taxes that went into the pockets of the monopoly owner, was described as 'most odious and unjust' and sucking the marrow out of the life of the people.[22] The legal profession too is indicted: 'Unconscionable lawyers and greedy officers shall no longer spin out the poor man's cause in length to his undoing and the delay of justice.' The speaker, Richard Stock, demanded benefices no longer be sold, the nobility be encouraged to shoulder their responsibilities to the poor, and placemen rebuked for their 'abuse [of] the authority of his Majesty to their private gain and greatness'.[23] Ironically, the spur to these pointed demands was the recent republication of James's own book on kingship.[24]

Seven copies were published in Edinburgh for private circulation in 1598, but James had thousands reprinted in London on his accession. Some in the audience must have read it. *The Tempest*'s anti-court satire is minimal but exists and is important – in Antonio's suborning the Milanese court with offices given, suits granted and promotions awarded, in his comment that if Alonso and Gonzalo are killed the entourage will say nothing, do nothing and meekly accept whatever they are told:

> They'll take suggestion as a cat laps milk;
> They'll tell the clock to any business that
> We say befits the hour. (II. i. 283–5)

How far from Castiglione's requirement that 'the aim of the courtier is to make his prince virtuous'.[25] The open flatterer and the morally timorous courtier become important figures in satire and polemic as the age engaged with questions of power and morality in the royal court. To Elyot the silent onlooker was as bad as the flatterer.[26] Both block truth being told to power. Many watching the play might feel a little awkward at hearing Antonio's remark, for it indicts those who betray allegiance and moral principles by doing nothing, neither standing up against wrongdoing nor condemning it, in order to live a quiet life and keep their status. Dante condemns to the anteroom of Hell the morally bland, those of weak character who do nothing disgraceful nor anything worthy of praise;[27] likewise those angels who did not actively support God in the struggle against the rebellion led by Lucifer. Satire is there in the silence of Alonso's attendants, non-entities described in the cast list as 'and others' or '&c.'.

Human Hierarchy: The Social Pyramid of Power

Each man inhabited different hierarchies relating to 1. society in general, 2. work and 3. family. It is usual nowadays to see human hierarchies as layered pyramids. This simple sociological model classifies according to priority, power and function. First you had a place in the social pyramid (better, middling or lower). Every rank had its inner hierarchy, its duties and its role to play. The precedence of a duke over an earl or a merchant over a shopkeeper was a matter of importance. It showed your standing, how you were thought of by society and re-enforced your self-image. At work you were in another pyramid where position depended on age, experience, seniority, qualification and success. Within the family pyramid an unmarried man was subordinate to his father and other male elders. Once married, he was still subordinate within his extended patrilineal family but ruled his own nuclear family – wife, children

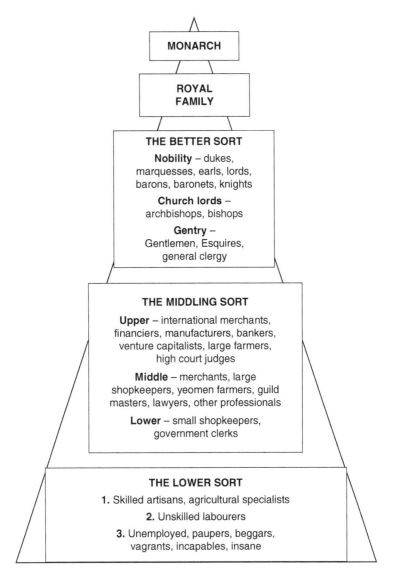

and servants. For each of these social structures obedience to those above was paramount, resistance to change was the default attitude and threats to order were seen as blasphemy, defying God's arrangement. Deference was meant to flow upwards and authority (with respect) to be shown to those below you. Those with most to lose were most in favour of things staying the same and so in history and literature noblemen and kings promote order and hierarchy as God-ordained and not to be overthrown; maintaining the status quo guaranteed the perpetuation of their power and privilege. The Bible authorizes this privileged view: e.g., 'Remember them that have the rule over you' (Hebrews 13:7) and the Commandment 'Honour thy father and thy mother'.

Antonio's usurpation gives a blasphemous edge to the origin of the plot. This is re-enforced as he encourages Sebastian to repeat the crime. Further potential subversion lies in Caliban's attempted suborning of Stephano and Trinculo into assassinating Prospero. Betrayal (of family, country or liege lord) and murder were not only damnable sins but carried resonant overtones given recent history. Ferdinand usurps his father's title before he is dead and will usurp Prospero's role in Miranda's life, but the one is a mistake to be corrected, the other the process of nature.

Topping the pyramid the ruler reflected God's dominance. The idea of Divine Right is founded on the belief that kings are chosen by God as his representatives on Earth. This endows monarchs with immense psychological (or superstitious) influence. As God's vice-regent a king could no more be questioned, tried, imprisoned or executed than you might think of questioning or dethroning God. James, like Prospero at times, could become aggressively angry when opposed. He began increasingly to think of himself as a god in a manner disturbingly close to megalomaniac mental instability. The king's will was sufficient for anything to be done unquestioningly by willing courtiers. It was the magic password for absolute power, though increasingly James found his will thwarted, often because there was no money to execute it, but increasingly because Parliament opposed him. Here we encounter the uneasy tension between the divine aura attributed to kings and the daily experience of their human failings.[28] Prospero behaves sometimes as an unquestionable bullying autocrat – specifically in his reactions to Ariel's and Caliban's complaints. How fallible this divine representative is, but then he has already been seriously betrayed and is perhaps over-wary. In ruling his little 'state' he has overcompensated for earlier laxness by becoming excessively controlling. As the play progresses this extreme relaxes somewhat. Given the ritualistic, emotional reverence accorded to monarchs, customary obedience to hierarchical superiors and the range of arbitrary punishments James had shown himself willing to mete out to those who crossed him, the audience would probably endorse Prospero's sometimes harsh patriarchalism. To answer the question whether Prospero is a bad parent we have only to look at Miranda.

The better sort

Below the king came the royal family, the nobility and gentry. Prospero and Alonso, the King of Tunis, represent the top rank, for though he is only a duke Prospero was the governor of a sizeable state spreading far beyond the city of Milan itself. Royal family members are represented by Sebastian, Antonio, Miranda (whom her father calls a 'princess'), Ferdinand and Claribel. Gonzalo ('an honest old Councellor'), Adrian, Francisco ('lords') and undefined 'others' are of the nobility and represent the court (most of which is in the other vessels of the fleet). The middling sort is represented by the shipmaster. He is a licensed professional, the captain, responsible for the crew's well-being and safety, responsible for the cargo and passengers. He is perhaps also the owner. In this period shipmasters often were owners or co-owners of their ships, therefore shifting into entrepreneurship, contracts and speculative carrying of goods. Within the little world of the boat he tops the work hierarchy. Like a king his orders carry weight. Below him is the boatswain (a commoner but at the top of the lower ranks as a skilled and experienced sailor) and at the bottom (also commoners) are the ordinary mariners. In addition Trinculo and Stephano are of the 'baser sort'. Both are servants of the king: Trinculo is a professional entertainer, a jester, Stephano is a slightly elevated household servant in charge of the *bouteillerie* (i.e., the wine cellar) from which comes his title as butler. It is appropriate that he floats to safety on a wine cask and carries a homemade bark bottle as a symbol of his role and a parody sceptre.

The descending ranks of the nobility – dukes, marquesses, etc. – were highly stratified, jealously preserving distinctions of precedence. This upper section included archbishops and bishops, men of immense power and wealth. Part of the upper sort, but untitled, was the gentry – men eligible to be called esquire and gentleman. They were ranked – upper, middle and lower – according to size of fortune, size of landholding, civic profile and ancientness of family title. The 'better sort', the 'quality', was the governing elite. What did they actually do? Some were ministers, privy councillors, government officers, MPs, army or navy officers (when there was a war) and local magistrates.[29] Those with estates might 'manage' them (though probably through a steward). They were essentially idle, a leisured class pursuing their own pleasures (hunting, gambling, drinking, whoring and lounging about at court), a do-nothing aristocracy doing nothing. Yet they had clear social duties as outlined in the Corporal and Spiritual Works of Mercy (see Chapter 4). Increasingly there were men who never had an estate (or had lost it through debt) but who called themselves gentlemen on the grounds of having (or having had) some sort of independent means, university education, officer rank, skill with weapons, no need (or intention) to work for a living, gentry parents and a coat of arms. The City Comedies of Dekker, Middleton, Heywood and Jonson are filled with impoverished gentlemen, living on the edge of high society, scrounging meals, hustling for an heiress or favour at court.

The distinguishing material feature of the nobility and gentry was land ownership. Estates meant tenants (farmers and land workers) paying rents. Rent rolls provided the basic unearned family income.[30] Many titled men held sinecure government posts (requiring little actual work), enabling them to sell other places to family members, friends and political contacts who formed an obligated clientage. This nepotism (giving jobs to relatives), once a sin, now accepted, added to the growing grievances about the court and government corruption.[31] Wealth could be materially improved if the monarch gave or sold you a monopoly, giving you control of the taxes and other charges on a commodity or service, like imports of wine, tobacco, sugar or starch.[32] This provided further opportunities for selling posts within the infrastructure. The upper sort thought themselves superior in virtue, born with innate leadership abilities and with better moral qualities than other ranks. Probitas (physical and moral courage) was believed to pass through the male bloodline (a reason for ensuring the legitimacy of your heir), giving each generation innately the qualities of prowess, honour and magnanimity. Noble in rank, supposedly noble, courageous and generous in nature, they thought themselves deserving of respect from all below them. They were the contemporary evolution of the medieval warrior class, now demilitarized and without apparent function. Many were fine and decent people, living on their estate and doing their social-moral duties. Many others were simply weak personalities, extravagant, in debt, idle, sexually decadent, syphilitics, drunks, fools, inveterate gamblers and incompetent estate managers, indifferent to their role as social exemplars and leaders. James did nothing to encourage reform.

The discrepancies between the expected conduct of the ranks and how people actually behaved were regular targets for satire. Knowing how to behave and actually conducting themselves decorously, respectfully and modestly were two different matters. The drunken butler is a stock character. He fails to do his duty: wardship of the cellar has become too great a temptation. Caliban too fails to accept his hierarchical role of grateful submission. They are typical of how the lower sort were expected to behave. But Sebastian and Antonio also lack the deference and supportive co-operation expected of their roles. Driven by ambition which has wakened 'an evil nature' (I. i. 93), they are further blackened by their cynical mocking of any belief in virtue. Evil themselves, they sneer at good. They are those in society who belittle, obstruct and subvert any attempt to organize to make things better. Like Caliban they are indefatigably evil, denigrating others with cynical asides, yet never doing anything positive. Reserving a modicum of doubt about people's motives is sensible, but it should not be excessive. Their attitude to the boatswain and Gonzalo displays them as 'new men', belittling old values and social distinctions. True gentlemen would respect the boatswain's superior knowledge of maritime matters and show respect to Gonzalo's experience and wisdom while politely enduring his portentous manner, but to them their own will, their own ends, dominate. They constantly seek new distractions to amuse them and pass the time. Gonzalo defines them precisely: 'You are gentlemen of brave mettle; you would lift the moon out of her sphere, if she would continue in it five weeks without changing' (II. i. 177–9). Running after the latest fashion or innovation was becoming a feature of court life, fed by leisure and the expanding availability of luxury goods as commerce and capitalism took hold in England. It was encouraged too by the increasingly closed nature of the court as a separate world in a protected bubble.

Contemporary plays are full of men claiming gentlemanly status but behaving badly. Drunken, roistering, lecherous misconduct highlights serious discrepancies between the expected behaviour of aristo-gentry men and their actual comportment.[33] Inconsistently, bad behaviour often co-existed with oversensitive alertness to offences to their honour. 'Upon my honour' was so common an oath it became a cliché, and was often spoken when a man was behaving dishonourably. Reacting to the slightest perceived insult to their conceived status and the respect they believed it deserved, the response was usually angry and violent. To assert their honour they often were drawn into dishonour by inflammable temper and a readiness to commit violence. In an age when gentlemen habitually wore swords the ready resort to arms was all too easy, especially when alcohol played its part in the constant outbreaks of street and tavern brawls. This gives a very topical context to the swaggering braggadocio of the Montagu/Capulet bravo boys of *Romeo and Juliet*. The use of the word honour by any character is a trigger to activate judgement of their conduct, to see if it fits with true honour or merely with the arrogant, snobbish aggressiveness it often resembled. Jacobeans were obsessed with genealogy and proving the ancientness of their origins. Many family trees, however, were fabricated, claiming descent from Norman knights, Saxon thegns, the pre-Roman Trojan roots claimed for the British nobility by pseudo historians like Geoffrey of Monmouth, even from Old Testament kings. Suitable payment to the College of Heralds bought you an 'authenticated' coat of arms and genealogy. The court audience knew full well that young men of titled or gentry background often behaved like rowdy boors, and that some of them were currently watching the play – or probably ogling the waiting gentlewomen.[34] In the 1600 City Comedy *Eastward Ho!* Francis Quicksilver claims gentlemanly status because his mother was a gentlewoman and his father a senior Justice of the Peace. He feels it is beneath him being apprenticed to a goldsmith, and spends his time drinking, whoring and scamming money out of other gallants.[35] To him idleness, drunkenness, violence and carelessness over money, are gentlemanly markers:

> Do nothing [...]. Be idle [...]. Wipe thy bum with testons [sixpences], and make ducks and drakes with shillings. [...] As I am a gentleman born, I'll be drunk, grow valiant, and beat thee.[36]

Golding, the industrious apprentice, scorns Quicksilver as 'a drunken whore-hunting rake-hell' (I. i. 125). Sexual licence was common in the elite. A 'rake-hell' was a trouble maker and alludes to the gang mentality and hooliganism of the many unsupervised, upper-class young men floating around London.

Despite the intense stratification of society, dividing lines between groups were becoming blurred by individual cases of social mobility, the proliferation of new knights, growing bourgeois wealth and the increasing complexity of society. People became obsessively fussy about precedence, about being treated according to their rank and preserving fine differences that made them feel superior. Ambition is a subset of pride or vanity, so overambition is seen as pushy, selfish and sinful. A little ambition was proper use of your God-given talents. However, to avoid becoming overproud of advancement, you should humbly thank God for the good fortune of your rise, downplaying the extent and effect of your own efforts.

Political theorists and moral polemicists formulated programmes emphasizing the upper ranks' duty to serve the state and the people. Elyot's *The Boke Named the Governour* (1531) proposed careful education combining a reverence for virtue and a readiness to assume social responsibilities. This meant residing on your estate, leading the community, helping the poor and establishing schools and alms houses, as enshrined in the Corporal and Spiritual Works of Mercy. These justified living comfortably off income derived from the labours of tenant farmers and tenant labourers. Rank and privilege were counterbalanced by a requirement to put something back into the community, but one of the features of the growing new individualism was that civic spirit and charitable work were increasingly discarded by elite young men. This was assisted by the growing tendency of the governing class to gravitate to London and become detached from their locality. A responsible role for the ruling classes, built upon a virtue-based humanist education, was promulgated by many writers throughout the decades leading to the Civil War, but the actual behaviour of many gentlemen conformed more to Viscount Conway's definition: 'We eat and drink and rise up to play and this is to live like a gentleman; for what is a gentleman but his pleasure?'[37] Antonio's assessment of the docility of the court is correct and implies moral indifference. The pursuit of personal pleasures dulled the ability or willingness to make moral distinctions if they threatened enjoyment or social status among one's peers.

The middling sort

The next layer down is the newly enlarged bourgeoisie or 'middling sort'. In the Middle Ages, the feudal system included them with 'those who work' (anyone earning a living – 90 per cent in medieval times). This group then comprised everyone from day labourers to the wealthiest merchant. The country arrangement was village centred with the lord of the manor (living in or near the village) governing and guarding his 'flock' of farmers and labourers like a shepherd guards and guides his sheep. The workers lived in or near the village, where the priest represented 'those who pray'. The professional 'middling sort' (lawyers, doctors, produce factors, clothiers, etc.) hardly existed in country areas, and were numerically an insignificant demographic nationally. By the Renaissance the pattern had changed. With the growth of commerce and the growth of towns, the 'service' industries expanded and with them the numbers of the bourgeoisie. Although 80 per cent of the population was still rural – farmers and labourers – 15 per cent were now largely town-dwelling middle class. The remaining 5 per cent was the aristo-gentry which had absorbed the clergy, whose numbers were drastically cut by the Dissolution of the Monasteries. The upper ranks thought the middling sort were greedy, obsessed with making money, virtuous enough, but lacking taste, elegance and culture. They were mocked as 'cits' (citizens, city dwellers – i.e., not landowners), derided as social climbers whose wives and daughters were snobbish, fashion mad, empty-headed, and easy prey for lascivious, gold-digging courtiers. Some were like that, but many were educated, cultivated people, looking after their families (especially their children) better than many of the nobility. Most were hard working, eager to put a comfortable buffer between themselves and poverty, but modest in lifestyle and personal behaviour. They showed civic spirit, were pious and drove conservative church reform.

The big social change in Elizabethan-Jacobean England was the rise of the middling sort. Division into upper, middle and lower classifications distinguishes between, say, a very rich international merchant, the farmer of a largish thriving farm and a small shopkeeper. The upper echelons were merchant bankers, financiers, large-scale traders, major clothiers, wealthy manufacturers, leading lawyers and judges, and large-scale farmers – men of wealth and local (and increasingly national) power. The middle group would be comfortably wealthy merchants and masters of guild trades, living in cathedral cities and market towns. The lower 'middling sort' were small shopkeepers, small farmers who owned a little land and growing numbers of low-paid metropolitan-based government clerks. What differentiated between the upper, middle and lower 'middling sort' was money. More money meant access to mayorships, masterships of guilds and alderman or councillor status. Money brought the capacity to invest in speculative capitalist enterprises and loan cash, thus becoming a sort of local banker or simply a moneylender. Usury (lending money at interest), a sin in medieval times, was acceptable by the seventeenth century, a natural development of the growing cash richness of the expanding commercial world. As the economy grew and fortunes were made and wasted, satire against moneylenders, money-amassing citizens and the debt-fuelled lifestyles of parasite gentlemen became regular features in contemporary plays.

The middle ranks looked up to the aristo-gentry and showed public respect. Privately they thought themselves morally better than the upper sort. Pious, hard working, earning their living, living moderately, paying their debts, establishing schools and hospitals, doing civic duties, and giving their children disciplined home lives, education and love, they saw the gentry and nobility as vain, idle, showy wastrels, parading in silks they did not pay for, gambling, drinking, acting promiscuously and demanding deference not always deserved. Yet, many merchants longed to rise and put on the outer show of gentlemanly status – a fine country house, a coach and horses, fashionable clothes and social power. 'The old English gentry were powerfully reinforced [...] by an influx from the professional and mercantile classes. Lawyers, government officials, and successful merchants bought land not only to better their social standing but also to increase their incomes.'[38]

As England became a more active trading nation the middle class expanded and became wealthier and more upwardly mobile. Those at the very top could be awarded or buy titles. They tended also, with this status rise, to move into the country, selling their business, cutting themselves off from the taint of trade or distancing themselves from it by hiring a manager. Legislation restricting bourgeois land ownership was increasingly ignored, circumvented or simply not applied. The bourgeoisie was unstoppable, buying estates, thinking themselves equal to the nobility; some even became nobility. Money power enabled such men to push out the cash-strapped yeoman farmer. Agricultural depression led to many of these freemen, who owned their own farm, selling up to opportunist incoming merchants-turned-landowners looking to add to their holdings. Small, independent farmers were also under pressure from some gentry augmenting their estate.[39] Another expanding bourgeois group was top civil servants administering the proliferating departments of government. The three most prestigious power posts were those of Lord Treasurer, Lord Chancellor and the King's Secretary.

These were political as well as royal household appointments. Below them was another internal pyramid of court power – the bureaucrats – reaching down to the lowliest 'base pen clerks'.[40] The most junior dreamed of catching the eye of a superior or a titled courtier and being promoted. Once in a higher place your future was made. Place was gained by patrimony, patronage or purchase. A poor clerk without family connections or money to help him advance had to find a patron. It was difficult to penetrate 'the grand efflorescence of nepotism' if you could not buy promotion or inherit a post from your father.[41] The court was awash with idle young men seeking opportunities for advancement. In *Eastward Ho!* the idle apprentice, Quicksilver, cast off by his irate master, declares, 'I'll to the Court, another manner of place for maintenance […] than the silly City!' (II. ii. 54–5). If your courtier patron had some measure of power you were made. In the plots, counterplots and intrigues of the Jacobean court there are innumerable examples of servants ready to bear false witness, cheat and slander to get on. Prospero, already victim to placeholders turning blind eyes in order to retain power, observes from on high the devious ploys afoot and thwarts them. King James never bothered to lead or control in this way.

The lower orders

The mass of the population formed the broad base of the pyramid. Skilled artisans were at the top along with farm workers with a specialism (shepherds, horse men, cattle men, etc.). Apprentices, learning a trade or craft, would count themselves as being in the middle of the lower orders, but with diligence and industry aspired to move into guild membership and shop ownership, thus becoming bourgeois. Below was the mass of unskilled labourers (hired by the day), with the unemployed, paupers, beggars, vagrants, the insane and the incapable at the very bottom. Farm labourers were severely squeezed at this time. Food prices rose steeply throughout both Elizabeth's and James's reigns. Common land, where game could be caught, firewood gathered and vegetables cultivated, was being enclosed by greedy landowners, thus diminishing the augmenting of food and comfort. This sector of society too was growing alarmingly, not because of a high birth rate but because the changing economy caused 'casualties' that fell out of working society into unemployment. The growing unemployed poor put pressure on local Poor Relief resources and represented a dangerous underclass with the potential for social unrest and riot. A 1597 law aimed at reducing poverty by banishing vagbonds to Newfoundland and the East and West Indies, but remiss or reluctant justices of the peace meant the law failed to reduce or repress the problem.[42]

The lower orders were thought by those above to be lazy, delinquent, ignorant, feckless and vicious (in the physically brutal and morally unsound senses). There was much truth in that, particularly among the growing numbers of urban poor. But there were hard-working men and women living godly lives and bringing up families despite hardships. Those living in the countryside were particularly susceptible to rent rises, fluctuations in labour needs, prices of produce and winter feed for livestock, and changes in land usage brought about by local enclosure. A series of disastrous harvests in the 1590s exacerbated matters, bringing famine to many doors. Piety, thrift and frugality could not feed hungry children. Nor could hard work and decent living protect you from market shifts caused by the greed of others in higher ranks. The self-satisfied court audience and the negligent king knew well that outside the comfort of Whitehall beggars thronged the streets; there were about twelve thousand in London in 1600 and economic conditions would have added to that by 1611. Some were indolent fraudsters preferring begging or thieving to work, but many were genuine victims of hard times. They were all the responsibility of those with wealth and rank and privilege. They were all morally and metaphorically (some literally) sons and daughters of the nobility. It was the job of the king and court to look after them; most did not. Shakespeare had already roundly criticized the detachment of the rich from the poor in the opening to *Coriolanus* (1607–09) where the privileged senator Menenius and the arrogant Martius clash with starving citizens of Rome:

> 1 *Citizen*: We are accounted poor citizens, the patricians good. What authority surfeits on would relieve us. If they would yield us but the superfluity while it were wholesome, we might guess they relieved us humanely. But they think we are too dear. The leanness that afflicts us, the object of our misery, is as an inventory to particularize their abundance. (I. i. 13–19)[43]

If the governing orders had responsibility to aid the poor, the poor had a duty of grateful, controlled conduct; the three base men of sin (Caliban, Stephano and Trinculo) fail to live up to that. The ignorance, timorous superstitions and drunkenness of Trinculo and Stephano marks them as base. Their language register too is a social marker. As usual in Shakespeare, commoners speak in prose. The duo are brought together to form a homicidal plot against Prospero as a subsidiary to Prospero's main plot. They are presented as comic and clownish, though there is an element of instinctive human care shown to Caliban until they realize his exploitability. Social difference and tensions between the ranks is not a major theme, but it relates to the duty of kingship, the Christian duty of charity, the concept that brothers (in Christ) and neighbours should take care of one another. At the end Prospero has become more embracingly understanding and declares to Alonso:

> Two of these fellows you
> Must know and own; this thing of darkness I
> Acknowledge mine. (V. i. 274)

'Own' means 'ownership' (some aristo-gentry thought of their servants as property) but also 'responsibility'. Prospero claims his 'property' and acknowledges responsibility for the 'darkness' in Caliban, like a father accepting that a son's misconduct is a reflection of a darkness (evil) he has inherited (or learned) from his parent and is something the father must deal with. Ariel and Caliban are Prospero's good and bad angels, separate parts of his psyche. One represents the power of mind, of imagination and spirit. The other is all the dark in man – his raging appetites, sinfulness, anarchy and viciousness.

The Theory of the Humours

There was a hierarchy of the inner man too. The head, like a monarch, ruled (theoretically) as a symbol of the primacy of reason. The major organs, like the nobility and gentry, came next as key to the functioning of the body. The limbs, like the commoners, were the mere labourers. This imprecise image was less important than the connection of the body to the outer world, the macrocosm. Correspondences between the inner and outer world were multiple. Organs were responsive to weather, foodstuffs and the zodiac. The alignment of stars, planets and the ascendant zodiac sign at the precise hour of your birth fixed your fate and personality, enabling predictions to be made concerning your future fortune. From classical times until the end of the eighteenth century people believed that the body contained four fluids (humours) influencing personality, attitude and behaviour. While your astrological sign provided your broad personality characteristic, the proportions of the four humours determined more precisely your temperament. Whatever these proportions were at birth defined your unique healthy normal state and your psychological type. The humours were: phlegm, yellow bile (choler), blood and black bile. Four temperaments were associated with the humours. The phlegmatic person was normally easy-going and stoical, remaining calm in crises and seeking rational solutions. The choleric man was inclined to temper, was bossy, aggressive, ambitious and liked to take charge. Prospero shows some symptoms of this 'complexion'. At times he is quite snappy, particularly with Ariel. The sanguine man (in whom blood predominated) tended to be positive, active, impulsive, pleasure-seeking, self-confident, sociable, open, friendly and warm-hearted. Those in whom black bile was dominant tended to be considerate of others but melancholic, negative, overly introverted and inclined towards pessimism about the imperfections of the world. The many permutations and proportions of these four cardinal types explained the huge variety of character types and the range of emotional phases to which an individual might be subject.[44] Illness was caused by an increase or decrease in one fluid and led to (and explained) mood changes. The medical practices of bloodletting and purges were thought to rebalance the humours, getting rid of an excess of one fluid, while certain foods or drinks redressed deficiencies. Some natural philosophers (scientists and rationalists) were beginning to question this theory, believing parental attitudes, early life experiences and education formed personality. Some physicians were beginning to ascribe other causes to illnesses, though today's knowledge of chemical imbalances causing maladies and mental aberrations shows the humours theory was not entirely wrong. Belief in these characteristics led to 'humour' stereotypes in literature that were sources of comedy (grumpy fathers, shrewish wives, romantic lovers, bloodthirsty soldiers, gold-mad misers, sex-mad widows, scheming villains, etc.). The character flaws of tragic heroes and villains fall easily into these broad categories as well.[45] There were those who rejected astrological origins of personality and claimed they created their own destiny. In *King Lear* the Machiavellian individualist Edmund rejects the idea of the stars forming personality. Conceived 'under the dragon's tail' and born 'under Ursa Major', he would be expected to be 'rough and lecherous' (I. ii.), but his belief in himself as maker of his own destiny ('I should have that I am had the maidenliest star in the firmament twinkled at my bastardizing') was a minority view. The questions of why Caliban is evil and why Prospero and Antonio are so different are raised later.

The Rest of Creation

Below humankind come the other animals – mammals, birds, fishes, insects, etc – able to move, reproduce, experience appetites (e.g., hunger, thirst, heat, cold, sexual urges), with limited sensory responses, limited problem-solving intelligence, lacking capacity for a spiritual life, without ability to reason or make moral decisions and unaware of God. Animals were thought not to have souls, logic or language.

Animals were also ranged hierarchically though less precisely than humankind and often according to conflicting ideas about their nature. Some were highly regarded, while others were denigrated for what were thought to be their distasteful characteristics. The lion topped the animal world because of its imagined links to courage, nobility and kingship (reflected in the use of lions as royal heraldic emblems). Tigers were noted for ferocity. A mother tiger's protectiveness of her young is admired but tigers could also display an unreliable, savage aspect – a quality ascribed to ruthless humans. Foxes were lowly ranked for their cunning, wolves and hyenas because of their savage, predatory, scavenging nature. Apes and goats were thought particularly lustful. Reptiles were low in the hierarchy, snakes particularly being associated with evil, temptation and Original Sin in the Bible. Frogs, toads and bats had associations with witchcraft. Lowest of all were rats, mice and other vermin. Domesticated animals were ranked by usefulness. Dogs (guards and hunters), listed with the working creatures, could be highly prized and Elizabethan-Jacobean gentlemen endlessly compared the qualities of their hunting dogs. Canine loyalty was highly regarded, but there were negatives – a fawning, flattering nature, greediness and readiness to follow anyone who fed them.[46] 'Whoreson dog' and 'cur' are common abusive epithets in plays.

Birds were highly thought of because of flight's association with air, thought to be a divine element along with fire. Birds of prey, used for the chase, were ranked according to their suitability to be linked with different social levels – an eagle for an emperor, gerfalcon for a king, peregrines for the nobility, goshawks for yeomen (small-scale landowning farmers), sparrowhawks for priests and kestrels for knaves (servants). After the birds of prey (including the owl, synonymous with wisdom) came the carrion eaters (vultures, crows, kites, etc.). As scavengers they were ranked lowly, like hyenas in the mammal hierarchy. Kites (many combed the rubbish tips in London) are always represented negatively, linked with the parasitical behaviour of those feeders and sycophants hanging around the households of men of power.[47] The parasite (the yes-man toady, like Mosca in Jonson's classic play *Volpone* [1606] and Oswald in *King Lear*) was a familiar figure of scornful fun on stage, originating in Roman comedy and satirical poetry. A parasite was anyone attaching himself to a rich, powerful man in order to curry favour, be rewarded for running errands (including pimping), and to flatter his master's self-esteem. At the very least he hoped to be invited to dinner, at most retained as a household member and personal assistant-cum-fixer. Mosca, the paragon of parasites, is so called after the Latin for fly since flies are the lowest carrion eaters. Volpone is named after the Latin for fox, since he is both devious and cunning. Jonson names his fortune hunters after the allegorized animal figures of the medieval-Renaissance didactic fable – Voltore (a vulture-like advocate), Corbaccio (a raven-like miser) and Corvino (a crow-like merchant). Below the scavengers came the worm- and insect-eating birds and then the seed eaters.

Abusive name calling occurs plentifully in Jacobean drama and involves animal/avian epithets that use negative characteristics associated with these creatures. A few animal epithets are positive, but likening human behaviour to animals is mostly negative, a reminder that the animal side of man was sinful – lustful, brutal, devious, greedy and slothful. The worst type of reference involves monsters – unnatural, mythical, animal hybrids. The word applied to humans connotes anyone behaving outside the acceptable parameters of civilized conduct and signifies an extreme shift from what is regarded as decent, normal human form and behaviour to brutal and uncivilized in manners and deformed in appearance. Caliban, described in the cast list as 'a salvage [savage] and deformed slave' is regularly called 'monster'. He represents the primitive savagery in man and the ungovernable sex drive of the brute. It is a savagery Prospero's love and care could not nurture into goodness. There is savagery inherent in Antonio and Sebastian for all their cultured, educated backgrounds, suggesting civilization is a thin veneer. But Caliban also represents the wild men Europeans were meeting as they explored the Americas, what Lear calls 'unaccommodated man'. Early contacts describe the natives as 'gentle' and 'simple', but this lexis soon changes. 'Barbaric', 'primitive' and 'uncivilized' soon intrude, often meaning simply that tribesmen had different customs and were non-Christian, though it also applied accurately to flaying and eating enemies, unregulated sex and human sacrifice. Meetings with 'uncivilized' tribes threw into sharp relief questions about just how truly civilized Western society was with its institutionalized torture, witch burnings, rampant urban sex trade, epidemic STDs and court plots and murders. Its selfish, ruthlessly individualistic conduct, disregarding the ancient traditions of respect for the vulnerable, is another collision of old and new philosophies that casts doubts on European cultures.

Shakespeare, while displaying the evil of Antonio and Sebastian, also portrays Caliban as far from innocent or virtuous. He is not a 'noble savage'. Europe too had its wild men, regular characters in pageants and folk plays in the Renaissance period, linked to pagan rites and the woods that once covered England, and therefore inevitably to the Green Man who continued to be venerated through medieval times, despite church opposition. In Book VI Canto iv of *The Faerie Queene*, Spenser introduces a 'Salvage Man', a wild man of the woods (a *wodwo*). Bremo in *Mucedorus*, a 1598 romance drama, is nominated 'a wild man' in the cast list. He too lives in the woods, is brutal and captures the heroine with the intention of forcing her to be his bride. Revived at court in 1610, acted by the King's Men, the play may have inspired Shakespeare to create a similar character.[48] The 2011 Arden editors suggest 'Caliban may be a "salvage man", but […] he proves to be more rational and sympathetic than the two Neapolitan conspirators or the drunken servants who represent European culture's corrupt underside.'[49] This view is coloured by the editors' sympathy with the body of criticism that has inflated the slavery/colonialism allusions in the play into Shakespeare having written a discourse on imperialistic land appropriation in Virginia. Caliban's savagery is understandable, given his background, but he is no more rational or sympathetic than the Europeans. The Westerners are worse only in that they have had advantages that Sycorax's son has not.

The final groupings of animals were the fish, reptiles, amphibians, insects and sessiles (unmoving shellfish). Fish were ranked low, as water was thought to be a dull heavy element like earth. Reptiles, amphibians and insects were thought of as even lower, fleas and lice being seen as verminous like rats. Bees and ants were positively regarded for their industry and apparent social organization which suggested something approaching intelligence. This period valued any form of corporate, civic or community co-operation as a mark of moral engagement with civilized behaviour.[50]

Lower still, the plant world had only the ability to grow and reproduce. But it too had its hierarchy. Trees were at the top with the oak as the prime form – useful, because of its hardness, for ships and houses – associated with stability, rootedness, imperturbable fortitude and Englishness. A king was seen as a great oak, sheltering his people as the tree did birds and insects.[51] Shrubs and bushes came next, along with flowers. The rose was thought to be the most beautiful, associated with love and with the Virgin Mary (the rose without a thorn). The lily signified purity, chastity and death. There was panoply of floral/herbal significations: pansies for thought, rosemary for remembrance and so on, plus the useful plants – edible and medicinal. Ferns, weeds, moss and fungus were such basic forms they furnish pejorative metaphors for useless, troublesome, threatening humans. The rising bourgeoisie was sometimes described as 'so many early mushrooms, whose best growth sprang from a dunghill'.[52]

At the bottom of creation were rocks and minerals. Even they were ranked by their values as gemstones, precious metals or their usefulness for building or yielding minerals. Many were thought to have magical/medical power. Pearls were much prized in the Renaissance (by Queen Elizabeth particularly) and long associated with purity. Among the metals gold was king, succeeded by silver, iron (and steel), bronze, copper and lead. Gold had particular power over the Renaissance imagination; it was the regal metal, used for crowns and sceptres, superior to silver and lowly lead. Gold also had its negative side as a symbol of man's greed, the means to suborn, seduce and corrupt. Its corrupting power is most forcibly, comically and sadly expressed in *Volpone*, where, blasphemously, gold has become Volpone's god. Flamineo in Webster's *The White Devil* (1612) succinctly describes this idolatrous blasphemy:

> O gold, what a god art thou! And O man, what a devil art thou to be tempted by that cursed mineral [...]. There's nothing so holy but money will corrupt and putrify it. (III. iii. 21–8)

For Romeo gold is 'saint-seducing' (I. i.) and King Lear's reference to gold's power to corrupt justice, making it a buyable commodity, is particularly pointed considering the persistent contemporary pleas to reform and purify public life and James's ignoring of complaints about venial judges.

> Plate sin with gold,
> And the strong lance of justice hurtless breaks;
> Arm it in rags, a pigmy's straw does pierce it. (*King Lear*, IV. vi.)

Gold became a Renaissance obsession. People longed for it, got it, then wanted more. Foolish speculators gave huge amounts of money and metal objects to alchemists experimenting to turn base metals into gold. Some seriously believed this possible; others used its potential for lucrative scams. This avaricious dream became the subject of Jonson's powerful satire on human greed, *The Alchemist* (1610). Exploration of America was triggered by the belief that huge amounts of gold could be found there to rival the spoils brought home by the annual Spanish treasure fleet. Balboa wrote to King Ferdinand that in Darien (in Columbia) there were rivers of gold.[53] The Roanoke settlers lost interest in building the plantation once they realized there was no gold or silver available.[54] Sir Walter Raleigh exaggerated about a South American city of limitless gold – El Dorado.[55] Gold thread woven into cloth, gold jewellery, gold plates and gold drinking goblets all showed off your pride in your wealth. Pride, vanity and display were all sins.

Among rocks marble was most prized, followed by granite, sandstone and limestone. Even lowly chalk and clay had their practical and commercial uses, though clay was connected metaphorically with man's mortality. Last of all are the particle forms – sand, gravel, soil and dust. Sand and gravel represented the precariousness of man's attempts to build a solid life. Earth was thought a dull, heavy element, appropriately typifying man's last state: 'earth to earth, ashes to ashes, dust to dust'.[56]

Order

Not only were humans ranked in an order reflecting how they were valued, but the preservation of that order was seen as a guarantee of social harmony. Orderliness reflected, therefore affirmed, God's ordering of the universe. Order and hierarchy are present in tension in the opening scene of *The Tempest* and then extended in Prospero's revelation of the hierarchy-threatening coup that supplanted him and the underhand (but all too common) means by which Antonio subverted the court. The audience would have felt uneasy at this; they may have bribed, flattered and blackmailed their way into that holy of holies. Their position at court and in the world at large relied absolutely on preserving order, the status quo. They had recently undergone the nervousness naturally accompanying a handover of power. The new king calmed anxieties by announcing all posts held under Elizabeth I would continue in the hands of the current placeholder, but then (not the last time would he go back on his word) replaced with Scots all the gentlemen of his Bedchamber (responsible for organizing his bed linen, night clothes, day clothes and washing and toilet needs). These salaried posts gave the holders valuable access to the king. The increasingly elaborate ritualization of all aspects of the king's life meant nobles and titled men doing menial tasks. Some enjoyed the honour, some found it degrading but necessary to maintain their influence. Sir Philip Gawdy describes the king's dinner served not by ordinary household servants but by titled courtiers:

> [The king] was serued wth great State. My Lo: of Southa [Southampton]: was caruer [carving the meat], my L. of Effingham Sewer, and my Lo: of Shrewsberry cup bearer, my poore selfe carried vp ij [2] dishes to his Maties [Majesty's] table.[57]

Courtiers struggled indecorously for these places, flattering, bribing and defaming rivals. James unsettled the order of things by rearranging the tenancy of these posts. The tense uneasiness and ever-watchfulness of the court was something the audience well understood, as was Prospero's description of Antonio's conniving machinations:

> Being once perfected how to grant suits,
> How to deny them, who t' advance, and who
> To trash for over-topping,[58] new created
> The creatures that were mine, I say, or chang'd 'em,
> Or else new form'd 'em; having both the key
> Of officers and office, set all hearts i' the state
> To what tune pleas'd his ear. (I. ii.79–85)

In this precarious world, power and place struggles were everyday happenings. Loss of post meant shame, dishonour, loss of influence with the king, and loss of valuable patronage saleable to those wanting your help accessing the monarch. The disassembling of Prospero's power would have had uneasy political relevance for the audience, the feeling of a takeover of power, a new force, adding to the general mood of uneasiness in a society as a whole that sensed the world was in decline. The Privy Council was expanded and among the new members were five Scots, two of whom were additionally given top legal and financial posts. New monarchs usually brought in favourites, but James gave unprecedented power to men regarded as foreigners. This Scottish usurpation generated grievances to add to others accumulating around the wholesale Scots incursion into London and Whitehall. Crucial in any court was who controlled access to the ruler. The Venetian ambassador, Giovanni Scaramelli, recounted how English courtiers complained:

> No Englishman, whatever his rank, can enter the Presence Chamber without being summoned, whereas the Scottish Lords have free entrée of the Privy Chamber, and more especially at the toilette; at which time they discuss proposals which, after dinner are submitted to the Council, in so high and mighty a fashion that no one has the courage to oppose them.[59]

Gawdy complained that the king put Scots 'in all offices' and 'put out many English, meaning to make us all under the name of ancient Britons'.[60] James's blatant favouritism had the effect of uniting rival English courtiers and politicians. Scaramelli observed: 'The English, who were at first divided amongst themselves, begin now to make common cause against the Scots.'[61] This weakness of the king worsened when favourites began to emerge; the Carr and the Villier factions in particular gained huge influence and huge amounts of money. While there might be sympathy for Prospero's situation and understanding of his vengefulness, there is danger in his barely suppressed anger. It distorts his manner and character as wrath is liable to do. His threats to Ariel and Caliban appear petty, using power to cow those he should control by kindness. Montaigne's comment, 'No passion disturbs the soundness of our judgement as anger does',[62] echoes a theme schoolboys knew from studying Seneca's *De Ira* (*On Anger*). James was well established as an intemperate, irascible monarch liable to burst into rants and swearing if opposed. Hasty, ill-considered action and rash judgements are unwise. When the actor is a father the consequences can devastate lives; when he is a king the consequences are national. In his essay 'Of Anger', Bacon quotes Seneca: 'Anger is like ruin, which breaks itself upon that it falls.'[63] Prospero's occasional outbursts of sharpness are minimal, are counterbalanced with many little endearments and do not affect Miranda's love. Ephesians 426 warns, 'Be angry, but sin not' and Luke 21:19 exhorts us to 'In your patience possess ye your souls.' Wrath is one of the Seven Deadly Sins, but largely Prospero controls himself and patiently sets about restoring order in a Christian manner. There is disorder in the ferocity of the opening storm. Some dangers develop that might threaten life and order, but this is not a tragedy. Keeping order, preserving the distinctions of rank, was essential; they are eventually restored.

Orderliness is given its most famous and detailed definition in *Troilus and Cressida* (1602). Ulysses upbraids the bickering Greek leaders for neglecting the 'specialty of rule'. If the clarity of 'degree' is blurred the unworthy will appear no different from the meritorious. James himself blurred degree when, relieved at the welcome of his people as he progressed south, he made hundreds of unworthy knights.[64] The specialty of rule is founded on the traditional belief that 'some things are so divided right from birth, some to rule, some to be ruled'.[65] Ulysses points out that the whole universe follows an ordained rule:

> The heavens themselves, the planets, and this centre,
> Observe degree, priority, and place,
> Insisture, course, proportion, season, form,
> Office, and custom, in all line of order. (I. iii. 85–8)

If orderliness is disturbed:

> What plagues and what portents, what mutiny,
> What raging of the sea, shaking of the earth,
> Commotion in the winds. (I. iii. 96–8)

Disorder affects human society when rank is disrespected:

> O, when degree is shaked,
> Which is the ladder of all high designs,
> The enterprise is sick! How could communities,
> Degrees in schools, and brotherhoods in cities,
> Peaceful commerce from dividable shores,
> The primogenitive and due of birth,
> Prerogative of age, crowns, sceptres, laurels,
> But by degree, stand in authentic place? (I. iii. 101–8)

Order is the cement bonding human society and Ulysses warns of the consequences of its disassembling:

> Take but degree away, untune that string,
> And hark what discord follows! each thing meets
> In mere oppugnancy: the bounded waters
> Should lift their bosoms higher than the shores,
> And make a sop of all this solid globe;
> Strength should be lord of imbecility,
> And the rude son should strike the father dead. (I. iii. 109–15)

Shakespeare was always concerned with order – nationally, socially, personally and spiritually. Rebellion, usurpation and collapse are political themes found in all his history plays (including the Roman ones). Disorder, excess and misrule figure too in his tragedies and comedies. Like many writers in the early 1600s, he was preoccupied by political and social questions relating to how society should be run. Loss of 'degree' meant force would dominate society, justice would be lost, and illegitimate power, will and appetite ('an universal wolf') would rule. James warned his son, 'Beware yee wrest not the World to your owne appetite, as over many doe, making it like A Bell to sound as yee please to interpret.'[66] Ulysses uses images of natural order turned upside down, unnatural human behaviour and the dominance of sin. The irony is that history shows repeatedly that what is natural for man is that the strongest oppress the weak, the brutal take control and the ruthless rule. The need and desire to co-operate creates society and unites community, but such bonding is often weak when faced by strong men backed by pitiless, armed henchmen ready to shed blood to gain power. Shakespeare's history plays and tragedies show time after time how devious men gain power and how decency and virtue are slow to react. Prospero's story proves the saying 'It is necessary only for good men to do nothing for evil to triumph.' The duke in his library was, in political terms, doing nothing: he permitted evil to enter his court by being too absent from it. In a Christian context, evil was thought ever present, the Devil constantly trying to tempt people into sin. Constant vigilance was crucial.

The seventeenth century was much concerned with political theory. Playwrights, especially Shakespeare, picked up on sixteenth-century interest in how society was best to be administered. Elyot's *The Boke Named the Governour* (1531) and the various editions of *The Mirrour for Magistrates* (between 1559 and 1603) were influential. James contributed two theoretical conduct books on kingship: *The True Law of Free Monarchies* (1598) and *Basilikon Doron* (1598). Sadly, though typically, there was a discrepancy between his ideas and his actions. So too the theory of order, the desire for peace and harmony, were belied by the actualities of life. Order seemed continually under attack and the fear of disorder added to Jacobean angst. Rising crime figures in the 1600s contributed to the general gloomy sense of decline and decay. On 15 March 1604 James made a formal procession through the city to Westminster. At one of the seven highly ornamented gates set up for him to pass through, a Latin oration was delivered (among many sycophantic speeches). It spoke of 'this sixt age of the world […] in the declyning age of our Kingdome'.[67] These factors feed into those dramas which reflected the feeling of increased dishonesty, licentiousness, greed and brutality. The City Comedies are peopled by petty criminals, shysters, cozeners, cony catchers, usurers, legacy chasers, greedy merchants and braggart, penniless, heiress-hunting gentlemen. London itself emerges as the subject and often the setting of critical dramas in the 1590s. Though foreign cities (especially Italian) are often the setting (especially for Revenge Tragedies), they are only a mask; the virulent satire, the abuses and 'ragged follies' are transparently English and associated with London and the court. The increase in the crowded metropolitan population (200,000 in 1600, 575,000 in 1700)[68] provided a huge variety of human types and writers revelled in portraying the seedier characters, enjoying their vitality while deprecating their immorality and trickiness. *The Tempest* is less topically specific than *Measure for Measure* or *King Lear* and much less so than Jonson's comedies, but its overall mood still reflects those neurotic fears of collapse. Antonio and Sebastian's plotting is curiously underplayed. They are almost inept villains of a pantomime. At the moment when they appear about to stab Alonso and Gonzalo, the action is diverted by Sebastian's 'O, but one word' (II. i. 291) and then Ariel wakes the intended victims. The message is that with monarchical vigilance (Prospero overviews all that happens) and with luck (or magic), evil can be monitored and thwarted. In *The Tempest* the subversions that destroy happiness and peace in other dramas are successfully neutralized. The plot is driven by intended acts of transgression, intended subversion of accepted norms, planned tricks, cruelty, lies, lust, ambition and other sins, but they are turned aside.

Geographically the nation was arranged to reflect the authoritarian orderly social structure. Divided into a network of counties, each with a Sheriff or Lord Lieutenant, hierarchy imposed order on what might otherwise be, and sometimes was, a restless population. Below the Sheriff, a patchwork of estates owned by rich, titled, powerful men imposed local authority. Estates varied in size, but within reach (sometimes within the actual perimeter) of even the smallest would be villages, parishes and individual dwellings rented by families dependent on the landowner's good will. Grand nobles often owned huge estates in different parts of the country, each providing income from rents and farm produce. Increasingly, though land gave status its value was diminishing, but the power of rank was never far away and localities could always feel the pressure of aristo-gentry, magistracy and priestly presence. Something like 90 per cent of the land was owned by 5 per cent of the population. Even if the magnate was absent his representatives imposed his wishes.

The depression in land values encouraged landowners to become entrepreneur-employers, exploiting mineral deposits on their domains and other natural advantages like water, timber, rush for thatching and clay for bricks. Men of lesser title and less money, with smaller estates, would still have dependent, rent-paying tenants and a home farm to provision the family. With high produce prices and little profit to be made from agriculture by any except the great farmers, landowners raised rents, reducing the profit margins of husbandmen holding leases from them and forcing many labourers into homeless unemployment. The gentry might only own a house, maybe a fortified manor, and their land might be no more than a small acreage surrounding the house, but as part of the ruling class – magistrates and justices of the peace – they further imposed the values of their privileged elite. Hierarchy even penetrated parish churches, where the better sort had boxed-in family pews near the pulpit, the middling sort sat on benches and the poor stood at the back. The gentry monopolized parish councils through the so-called 'select vestry' that barred lower ranks from attending. Local politics was controlled by landed families and Parliament was 88 per cent upper orders and 12 per cent merchants and civic authorities. The top 5 per cent had the whole country under their nominal control. The few large cities – London, Bristol, Norwich and York – also had their networks of power, with aldermen, beadles, mayors and the wealthy liveried companies. Richard Stock's 1603 Lent sermon in St Paul's churchyard, directly addressed the Mayor of London, the aldermen, nobility and privy councillors:

> You are magistrates for the good of them that are under you, not to oppress them for your own ease. I would speak to him who is chief of the city for this year. What is past cannot be remedied, but for the future, as far as lies in your power, prevent these things.[69]

'The wealthier sort feared sudden uproars and tumults, and the needy and loose persons desired them.'[70] The older generation of the gentry largely resided in the country, while titled men spent much of their time at court and Parliament. Increasingly gentry heirs and younger sons drifted to the capital, forming a large, shifting population of troublesome young men, hanging about the court seeking posts or heiresses. Some were enrolled at the Inns of Court, though their attendance was sporadic. All saw London as a pleasure ground, removed from immediate parental disapproval. Drinking, whoring, gambling, fighting, theatre-going and chasing rich merchants' daughters, they were generally a nuisance.

Many titled families were founded by men who, coming to power under Henry VIII, bought, or were given by the king, church lands that came onto the market at the Reformation. These once-new families were now the old upper-rank families. A few titled dynasties could trace their ancestry to the Conquest. Most were of relatively recent authority, some paying the College of Heralds to manufacture fake genealogies that gave them more respectable and ancient descent.[71] This network of power and privilege was intended to keep the king's peace. It largely did so, despite outbursts of local unrest, but at the expense of the physical and political repression of the 'baser sort'. Generations of psychological pressure established a fear of the upper ranks, a belief that, like the king, they were part of God's order and opposing them was a grave blasphemy, pitting your puny, sinful self against the divinely ordained state of creation. The civil power was not the only repressive network controlling England. Hand in hand with government, often synonymous with it, the church attempted to guide conformity and forcibly dissuade dissent. In 1549 Thomas Cranmer, Archbishop of Canterbury, re-enforced this in upbraiding rebels: 'Though the magistrates be evil and very tyrants against the commonwealth and enemies to Christ's religion, yet the subjects must obey in all worldly things.'[72] This encouragement to submit even to injustice was repeated in *The Second Tome of Homilies* (1571) in the sermon 'Against Disobedience and Wylful Rebellion'. Tyranny was a divine punishment against a sinful people who should not 'shake off that curse at their owne hand'.[73] Identifying hierarchical deference with submission to God was part of seeing the social order as ordained by God. By making it an aspect of church doctrine the Anglican hierarchy aimed to curb rebellion, maintain power and enforce doctrinal uniformity. Social and religious submission to the established power structure, however unjust its actions, would work for the mass of fearful superstitious people. But opposition was slowly rising.

Each English diocese had a bishop responsible for ensuring priests and congregations followed the Anglican form of worship. These dioceses totalled between nine and a half and ten thousand parishes, each (theoretically) with a priest and an average of 300 parishioners (450 in the less controllable, expanding cities). Pluralism (holding more than one living) was a growing practice whereby already rich vicars could augment their wealth or a poorly paid vicar could augment his stipend. Either way it was a corrupt practice.[74] Non-resident parsons employed curate substitutes, so there was religious presence to oversee the social and spiritual state of congregations. The priest, representing the church's might, was a figure to be respected, part of the ruling establishment. Part of his aura of power was his education. the ability to read and write gave priests special, magical status (though not all were highly literate). Additionally, as supposed mediators between this world and the next, they had immense psychological influence. Education enabled them to advise on moral and practical matters and their spiritual role made them privileged mentors in matters related to living the virtuous life. Not everyone in a village would necessarily defer to the priest. Some saw him as an arrogant snob, allied to the gentry, parading his learning, an outsider speaking an incomprehensible, elite language.[75] Closet Catholics and Dissenters paid only lip service. Puritan dissidents were increasing in numbers and were increasingly vocally critical of the church. More worrying for the church's elite was the spread of vicars of Puritan sympathy. In the 1590s large numbers of progressive, radical-thinking young ordinands graduated from Cambridge, adding yet another destabilizing factor to an age already undergoing disturbing changes. Precepts learned from the teachings of Cambridge don William Perkins inclined them to be less obsequious to gentry parishioners, more mindful of the hardships of the poor and keen to simplify vestments, rituals and sermons. Some gentry families, sympathetic to reform, protected Puritan-minded vicars from church persecution. This was particularly evident in the 'Pilgrim Quadrilateral' and the Boston area of Lincolnshire in the years 1600–1610.[76]

Another burgeoning force undermining the establishment was the irreverent, radically minded university-trained playwrights. Vitriolic in criticizing purse-proud citizens, their ostentatious wives, the explosion of greed, the obsession with luxury, vanity and lust, the idle and incompetent aristocracy, and particularly those many ungentlemanly profligate gentlemen buzzing like flies around the court, they also deplored the state of the lower orders. Many plays, set firmly in the contemporary city, are morality based, harking back to medieval values. Shakespeare tended to skirt round overt attacks on the establishment by setting his plays in other countries or in other periods. *The Tempest*'s probable Mediterranean island setting should not fool us into thinking the play is not about current issues.[77] The original audience would not be gulled either. The economic and political system of England was firmly organized for the benefit of those who already had much. The Prospero who acknowledges Caliban's darkness as his own will perhaps be more receptive to the needs of a broader range of his subjects when he returns to Milan and perhaps more cognizant of the necessary limitations to the scope and style of autocracy.

King James expressed the principle that concern for 'the well-fare and peace of his people' identifies a king 'as their naturall father and kindly maister'. In 'subjecting his owne private affections and appetites to the weale and standing of his subjects' he shows himself better than the tyrannical king who 'thinketh his people ordained for him, a pray to his passions and inordinate appetites.'[78] Unfortunately, James soon revealed himself as stand-offish to the 'baser sort' and obstinately pursued his own appetites. *The Tempest* is a gentle reminder of the necessity of socio-political engagement.

Detachment from people encourages desensitization, which leads to brutal attitudes to them. Experiencing major setbacks teaches Prospero his duty to use his power properly, to engage with it fully and to use it for the good of all the community. Acknowledging Caliban's 'darkness' hints at reconnection with the savage part of his 'family' and the savage in himself. The court should feel awkward hearing this, for it reminds the rich man of his duty to help the poor, and to show God gratitude for being wealthy by not wasting his excess fortune on pointless extravagances but to put it to the good of the whole polity. The Bible is clear about this: 'For unto whomsoever much is given, of him shall be much required' (Luke 12:48). Gonzalo's fantasy ideal state emblematizes unworkable daydreams. His commonwealth would have no drive, no impelling principle of co-operation. It is a paradigm of courtly literature's Golden Age fantasies of pastoral idleness. The middling and lower orders had obvious work to do to live; those with wealth and rank did not need to work. However, the standard view was that 'none are less exempted from a calling than great men'.[79] The Bible story of Dives and Lazarus (Luke 16:19), a popular text for sermons, told how the rich Dives refused to pass the crumbs off his table to the poor Lazarus. Dives dies, goes to Hell and in his sufferings sees Lazarus among the elect. The rich and powerful had a duty to be fathers to their neighbours, shepherds to the flock around them. Brathwait put it starkly: 'The higher place the heavier the charge.'[80] Many privileged lords and ladies sent unwanted food to the poor, endowed alms houses and schools and did other acts of charity. Many did nothing. Each new generation inheriting wealth needed reminding that charity

> [...] should flow
> From every generous and noble spirit,
> To orphans and to widows.[81]

The concept of *caritas* (love expressed through charitable acts), integral to medieval church teaching, was derived from canon law's delineation of the basic duty of the rich to assist the needy. It was taken up in Protestant thinking too. Compassion was a necessary virtue in a Christian and essential for those who had never experienced adversity or affliction. Miranda's very first speech expresses the pity a sensitive soul feels for the sufferings of others. Her father acknowledges 'the very virtue of compassion' in her (I. ii. 27). The Jacobean governing classes had detached themselves from the rest of society, living their own self-interested, selfish, narcissistic lives at court or isolated in their mansions on their estates. What a prick to the consciences of the pampered young women in the audience Miranda would be. Corrupt, ineffective, arrogant kingship was another feature of the time and the period is full of admonitions to kings and nobility. In 1609 the Earl of Northumberland wrote:

> There are certain works fit for every vocation; some for kings; some for noblemen; some for gentlemen; some for artificers; some for clowns [country people]; and some for beggars. [...] If everyone play his part

well, that is allotted him, the commonwealth will be happy; if not then it will be deformed.[82]

God's judgement against Adam and Eve at the Fall condemned men to live by the sweat of their brow. Adam had a second chance. Saved from destruction by the mercy of God, he left Eden and sought salvation elsewhere. Prospero is given a chance at redemption in a second paradise. The Bible (e.g. Ezekiel, Proverbs, Ecclesiastes, Thessalonians and Timothy) strongly criticizes idleness and recommends employment. That included kings and courtiers.[83] The Whitehall audience knew they had a job to do, a duty to perform, but it was an injunction increasingly ignored. King James did read state papers and attend councils, but only when it suited him; he might just as readily disappear suddenly on a hunting trip. His effectiveness diminished, bribery and favouritism became the norm and his court became increasingly idle and debauched in its pursuit of pleasure, increasingly corrupt and self-seeking in its administration of the realm. *The Tempest* is about both flawed kingship and flawed fatherhood. Female input in Prospero's parenting has been negligible, but despite some minor flaws, he has nurtured his 'princess' well.

Chapter 3

SIN, DEATH AND THE PRINCE OF DARKNESS

Stand thou in rightwiseness and in dread, and make ready
thy soul to temptation, for temptation is a man's life on the earth.[1]

An inescapable factor in every aspect of Jacobean life was the ever-present possibility of sin. Jacobeans were neurotically alert to the temptations surrounding them. People's sinfulness was the greatest threat to order. Conflicting Christian sects shared basic beliefs when it came to right and wrong: man was perpetually open to sin and temptation was all around him, the Devil was to be defied, and Christ was man's redeemer and the way to salvation. The religions may have differed homicidally about doctrine, but the moral bases of life were agreed.

The Ten Commandments were the foundational start point for Christians:

The Ten Commandments (abridged from Exodus 20:19)

1. Thou shalt have no other gods before me.
2. Thou shalt not make unto thee any graven image.
3. Thou shalt not take the name of the Lord thy God in vain.
4. Remember the Sabbath day, to keep it holy.
5. Honour thy father and thy mother.
6. Thou shalt not kill.
7. Thou shalt not commit adultery.
8. Thou shalt not steal.
9. Thou shalt not bear false witness.
10. Thou shalt not covet […] any thing that is thy neighbour's.

They were paired inextricably with the Seven Deadly Sins to mark the way to avoid damnation and win salvation through godly living (the Seven Cardinal Virtues are discussed in Chapter 4):

The Seven Deadly Sins

1. **Pride** (arrogance, vanity, vainglory, *hubris*)
2. **Wrath** (anger, violence)
3. **Lust** (lechery, wantonness, lasciviousness)
4. **Envy** (covetousness)
5. **Greed** (avarice)
6. **Gluttony** (including drunkenness)
7. **Sloth** (laziness, despair)

Sin and Satan were as much a part of religious consciousness as the desire to emulate Jesus and live virtuously. Evil was real, sin was real. The church's cultural monopoly meant even those indifferent to religion would acknowledge faith was the common, underlying feature of life at all levels. The passing year was marked by religious events and each day was punctuated by aspects of faith. The parish church bell indicated the times of services, pious families gathered for morning and evening prayers, and individuals might visit the church during the day too. Schoolboys had communal classroom prayers with their teacher. A master craftsman, his journeymen and apprentices might start the working day with prayers. The formal ceremonies of their guild involved prayers, readings and sermon-like addresses. Children were taught the Bible, learned texts, creeds, catechisms and prayers and would kneel by their bedside to ask for protection during the dangerous hours of darkness. The Lord's Prayer was central to ordinary belief, asking for daily bread, the forgiveness of trespasses and protection from temptation. Those of weak faith attended Sunday service rather than be fined in a church court.[2] Those not particularly pious in their everyday life had scriptural grounding as children and like everyone else would know how they were expected to behave as Christians, would be aware of biblical allusions, echoes and ethics in what their neighbours said and did. They would observe too how stage plays displayed, reinforced and debated the basic Christian values of society. The church was omnipresent. When you were born, married, committed adultery, defamed a neighbour, were rowdy, sharp-tongued or shrewish, or traded on Sunday, the church was there approving or wagging its finger. You lived in public, your sins were easily made public and your punishment would be public. Your misdemeanours would be spied out by constables, beadles, the watch, servants or neighbours and dealt with in the local church court.

Anglicans were rarely left to solve a problem alone. Individual conscience was too weak to deal with matters of sin and morality without help. In times of national or personal stress many people turned to the consolations offered by being part of a communally held belief. When imminent disaster threatened communities coalesced and turned to the vicar; the church was a mental, spiritual and physical refuge.

All Shakespeare plays allude to or echo well-known biblical texts. *Measure for Measure* does so abundantly and, despite its basis in magic, *The Tempest* has an unspoken, indirect, implicit biblical context evoking Christian values, reactions and assessments. Christian values shadow the actions of the play. The second agent, after the author, in the mediation of a text was the reader or viewer, who provided a religious assessment. The text may lack direct allusions to Christian dogma, but Shakespeare knew his audience would make the connections. Every scene provokes a Christianity-focused judgement of what is said and done. The key plot movement, from Prospero as a despised, rejected, Christ-like figure desiring revenge but ultimately showing forgiveness, parallels the essential impulse of the New Testament. On the cross Christ requested, 'Father, forgive them, for they know not what they do' (Luke 23:34). Whatever the level of engagement with faith, Christian upbringing triggered a vigorous conscious or subconscious religious reaction to everything seen. Debauched libertines or audience members who had lost their faith still had vestigial memories of the values learned as children. The Bible was the standard of all conduct, the New Testament especially. Responses might vary according to education, upbringing, experience of and attitude to the world, class or political and/ or religious allegiance, but there would be broad agreement, since all the viewers – from the king on his dais to gallants in the galleries – shared this common Bible-based background. The ways in which time after time the characters offend the Commandments or commit sins would be glaringly obvious to the audience. It is an absolutely fundamental aspect of the play, informing every other motif in it.

Life was a journey, a pilgrim's progress towards holiness and union with God or a sinner's path to damnation. Prospero, having resolved his problem, intends to finish his journey with a return to his power base, but not apparently for long. He announces:

> I'll bring you to your ship, and so to Naples,
> Where I have hope to see the nuptial
> Of these our dear-belov'd solemnized;
> And thence retire me to my Milan, where
> Every third thought shall be my grave. (V. i. 307–11)

He seems to foresee his imminent death once he has set up the next generation, as if he sees himself merely as part of nature's cycle of rearing young, arranging for mating to perpetuate the family, while he quietly retires. From birth people were to pursue virtue, shun sin, imitate Christ, keep the soul pure and progress towards death, ready to pass through to the life everlasting. Life here was a transient state preparatory to the afterlife. In John Ford's late Revenge Tragedy *'Tis Pity She's a Whore* (c. 1629–31), when sexual sins and violent plots begin to gather and drive the drama, the character Richardetto states the basic situation of Christian existence: 'No life is blessèd but the way to heaven' (IV. ii. 21); he then encourages his niece to flee a vile world by entering a convent: 'Who dies a virgin lives a saint on earth' (IV. ii. 28). The virtuous life gained Christ's favour and a state of grace. No advantage in the fleshly, physical world was of any value if you lacked grace. The hitherto unregenerate Caliban ultimately declares the need to 'be wise hereafter/And seek for grace (V. i. 294–5). It may be a sudden comic end-of-show conversion, a ploy to evade punishment, or genuine penitence. Ford presents even good looks in a religious context:

> Beauty that clothes the outside of the face
> Is cursèd if it be not clothed with grace. (V. i. 12–13)

Prospero has earned grace. Miranda had it already by nature, along with virtue, chastity and compassion. Even her obvious passion for Ferdinand is controlled. Uncontrolled appetite was something the church feared and punished. Lust was the most common everyday sin, but any of the Seven Deadly (or Mortal) Sins could damn you eternally if unrepented. Miranda's virginity was saved from Caliban (the man of wild nature) and will be given as a sacrament to her husband (the man of better nature). Premarital sex was common; not endorsed by the church but grudgingly tolerated, it was beginning to be prosecuted more actively in the period in which *The Tempest* was being staged.[3] Shakespeare relied on his audience seeing the danger of youthful sexuality and the guiding restraint Christian morality offered. He relied too on their seeing how the court did not fit the moral framework of the time. A court audience, possibly more attentive than the social mix at the public theatres, perhaps on their best behaviour in the king's presence, had enough biblical knowledge (even if their faith was weak) to put the actions and words before them into a moral context that reflected poorly on them. Caliban is physically mature, but underdeveloped morally, unaffected by nurture and without grace. His witch mother and devil father represent evil magic, the antithesis of Prospero's benevolent 'Art'. Caliban is the once-reclaimed garden reverted to 'briers and darnell'. Evil and appetite have overcome cultivation.

The pervasive religious atmosphere made identifying sin instinctive. Sin was the Devil's portal, giving access to your soul to damn you. The Devil was a very real entity to people, not a metaphor of evil, but an actual horned, cloven-hoofed, fork-tailed, sulphurous and fearsome presence. Progressive thinkers tried to internalize the Devil as the evil in man, but most people believed he was a real creature. His earthly work, assisted by legions of demons, imps, goblins, incubi and succubi, was devoted to corrupting man and thwarting God's will. The Book of Revelation describes 'the great dragon' who 'was cast out, that old serpent, called the Devil and Satan, which deceiveth the whole world' (22:9). In John's Gospel he is called 'the prince of this world' (22:31) and in Corinthians 'god of this world' (4:4), suggesting that the fleshly world of greed, brutality, cheating and lust (ever-present in the plays of the 1600s) is the Devil's domain. Paul's Epistle to the Ephesians (2:2–3) goes further, placing the Devil firmly in this world, embodied in the waywardness and violence of men. Seeing the Devil manifesting himself through human evil suggests how the audience might see Caliban, Antonio and Sebastian. Ariel calls Alonso, his brother and the Duke of Milan 'three men of sin' (III. iii. 53). Their faults are betrayal, intended homicide and fratricide, disloyalty, subversion of hierarchy and covetousness. For all its romance form, with many sins contemplated not committed, it is a play showing how the Devil is loosed when Christian values and cultivated, civilized, sensitive and sympathetic behaviours are ignored. The unrepentant Antonio, like a pantomime villain, seems to be an emanation of the Devil in human form, and is worse than Caliban because privilege and the benefits of living in a cultured, civilized environment should have made him better. Caliban, born of evil parents, orphaned, already formed when Prospero tried to nurture him, has little choice but to be evil. Antonio, with all the advantages (we assume) of a cultivated background, has a choice. He knows the difference between right and wrong, has free will and chooses sin. Dante defined nobility in terms of virtuous conduct, not rank.[4] Castiglione highlights this too when, during a discussion on what makes the best sort of courtier, he has Pallavicino remark that while some 'of the most noble blood, have been wicked in the extreme' there were 'many of humble birth, who, through their virtues, have won glory for their descendants'.[5] Conduct is the determinant of true nobility. Nobility of spirit, expressed in courteous, gentlemanly, noble behaviour, counts for more than all the cultural accomplishments a lady or gentleman may have. Antonio's education to virtue discarded, his propensity for evil dominates. His actions are ignoble, he should theoretically be excluded from rule, but it is the nature of the world that ruthless men hold on to power while weak men let them.

Viewers would see *The Tempest* as not simply a tale of a cruelly banished man retrieving his status, but a *psychomachia*, an allegorical drama in which various emanations of evil are displayed in contrast to virtue, are shown understanding and forgiveness and are offered a second chance, an opportunity to redeem themselves through repentance, atonement, forgiveness, reconciliation and salvation. Only one (Alonso) accepts. Once cast ashore in separate groupings, the characters continue to experience tempestuous happenings and unsettled emotions, uncertainties and fears. Alonso is particularly cast down throughout the play, believing his beloved son dead. The punishment, for his crime in abetting the usurpation of Prospero's place, is to be kept in this belief until the revelation at the end. He atones through suffering and is rewarded for repentance by finding his son alive.

The fates of the others escape the scope of the play. Caliban may be left on the island. Sebastian is currently safe unless Prospero reveals his plotting. Of the remorseless Antonio we have no inkling. Prison? Execution? Fraternal reconciliation? The latter might work but might just as well lead to uneasy tensions in the Milanese court and further trouble (another forgiven brother, Don John in *Much Ado About Nothing*, sins again). He could be abandoned on the island. Miranda and Caliban are Prospero's good and bad angels, Gonzalo and Antonio are Sebastian's. Though not written in the style of the earlier Morality Plays, the subject and ethics are the same.

Vicars loved loosing their imaginations sermonizing about the workings of the Evil One and the torments of Hell awaiting unrepentant sinners. Creative writers too enjoyed the opportunities for fantasy descriptions offered by ideas of Hell, Sin, Death and the Devil. The awareness that sin is ever present, that life is a persistent battle between good and evil, that the lure of vice has to be constantly rejected, was reinforced by the witch trials that were common at the time. Witchcraft was another subject upon which King James delivered his opinions and his *Demonologie* (1597) captures the contemporary mood of fear and suspicion, an alternative world of dark deeds and Devil worship. Many painted representations of demons and the Devil gave visual concreteness to people's fears. Hell and the sufferings of the damned were popular subjects. Hieronymus Bosch (1450–1516) graphically depicts the horrors of perdition in *The Last Judgement*. Many medieval churches had depictions of Christ in Majesty, but in the late medieval period (in response perhaps to the holocaust of the Black Death) artists took to painting scenes of the Last Judgement. Many (but not all) were scratched out or whitewashed over during the Reformation. It was an age when hanged bodies were routinely publicly displayed strung up in chains, 'heretics' were burnt at the stake and Gunpowder Plotters had their entrails cut out and burned in front of them. The rack, thumbscrew and strappado were regularly used to extract information. Noses were slit and ears cropped for criticizing royalty or church, thieves were branded, and blasphemers had their tongue pulled out or a hole bored in it. Birching, blinding and being broken on the wheel were simply part of institutionalized cruelty. The gruesome acts portrayed in plays reflect a violent culture. Sin against the state, sin against God – the painful punishments were similar. These brutal punishments reflect the age and how people imagined the damned were tortured in Hell.

The threat of damnation and eternal torture if you were an extreme sinner, was a useful moral control device to frighten naughty children and a moral corrective for adults, but there were those who did not care about hellfire and damnation, and those who did not believe in Hell. Marlowe's Faustus declares that 'hell's a fable' (Scene v. 128). Despite Mephistophelis asserting 'this is hell, nor am I out of it' and 'where we are is hell', Faustus arrogantly laughs off the possibility:

FAUSTUS:	Think'st thou that Faustus is so fond to imagine
	That, after this life, there is any pain?
	Tush, these are trifles and mere old wives' tales.
MEPHISTOPHELIS:	But, Faustus, I am an instance to prove the contrary,
	For I am damn'd, and am now in hell.
	[...]
FAUSTUS:	How! now in hell!
	Nay, an this be hell, I'll willingly be damn'd here.
	(Scene v. 134–44)

People were beginning to question Hell's existence, claiming this life was our Hell. In 'Tis Pity, the reckless Giovanni, a scholar like Faustus, thinks reasoned argument can demolish the idea of Hell, and confidently announces to his confessor:

The hell you oft have prompted is nought else
But slavish and fond superstitious fear,
And I could prove it too. (V. iii. 19–21)

The friar replies, 'Thy blindness slays thee.' Giovanni's trust in rational arguments led him to believe sex with his sister was permissible – a moral blindness. His actions lead to spiritual death and physical slaughter. Most of the audience, if they thought about it, probably believed in both Heaven and Hell as places of reward and punishment in the afterlife. Most, except extreme libertines, believed sin was everywhere and virtue needed to be cultivated. This would not have prevented them committing sins or encouraged living a particularly good life. Like most people they would probably experience guilt and fear, resolve to improve, then lapse into their normal 'not very bad but not very good' everyday lives. An affecting play might well prick their consciences – temporarily at least.

In *King Lear* the mad king makes a brief mention of Hell in a comment on female lust that shifts from describing how from the waist down 'is all the fiend's' domain to recognizably describing the Christian idea of the Devil's kingdom:

> There's hell, there's darkness,
> There is the sulphurous pit – burning, scalding,
> Stench, consumption […]. (IV. vi.)

In *'Tis Pity* the friar, trying to frighten Annabella into repentance for fornication and incest, describes Hell:

> There is a place […] in a black and hollow vault,
> Where day is never seen. There shines no sun,
> But flaming horror of consuming fires,
> A lightless sulphur, choked with smoky fogs
> Of an infected darkness. In this place
> Dwell many thousand thousand sundry sorts
> Of never-dying deaths: there damned souls
> Roar without pity […]. (III. vi. 8–16).

He continues to describe the specific punishments meted out for specific sins:

> There are gluttons fed
> With toads and adders; there is burning oil
> Poured down the drunkard's throat, the usurer
> Is forced to sup whole draughts of molten gold;
> There is the murderer forever stabbed,
> Yet can he never die; there lies the wanton
> On racks of burning steel, whiles in his soul
> He feels the torment of his raging lust. (III. vi. 16–23)

Like a vengeful God Prospero threatens Caliban and Ariel with racking pains and Ariel with a return to imprisonment.

Sin and Death

The Prince of Darkness[6] was inexorably linked with temptation, reminders of what awaited after death and the very fact of death itself. In medieval and Renaissance art reminders of death are ubiquitous. Skulls, skeletons and the Grim Reaper appear regularly in church paintings and in the funerary furniture surrounding the congregation. Sin and Death are linked as a hellish duo in opposition to Christ and the Holy Spirit. The everyday world was a minefield for the morally unwary, full of devils waiting for any hint of ungodly, impure thought. Momentary lapses – a nasty comment, bitchy gossip, a bad-tempered, snappish reply, blasphemous expletives, temptations to gluttony, theft or the prickings of lust – were opportunities for 'the Enemy of Mankind'. I Peter 5:8 warned: 'Be sober, be vigilant; because your adversary the devil, as a roaring lion, walketh about, seeking whom he may devour.' Wary Christians prayed regularly for protection. Prayers at bedtime were especially important, calling on guardian angels as night security. A habit grew of eventide self-examination of your day, casting up your account of good and bad acts, making resolutions to improve, repenting and praying for salvation. It was end-of-the-day quiet time for assessing how well you had passed the day and resolving to be better if need be. James recommended to Prince Henry:

> Remember ever once in the foure and twentie houres, either in the night, or when yee are at greatest quiet, to call yourself to account of all your last dayes actions, either wherein yee have committed things ye should not, or omitted the things yee should doe, either in your Christian or Kingly duty.[7]

A marginal note references I Corinthians 11:31: 'For if ye judge your selfe, ye shall not be judged.' Temptation to sin was everywhere and everyone knew 'the wages of sin is death' (Romans 6:23). You had to fight constantly to win the gift of eternal life through Jesus Christ. What made it more difficult was that you were born a sinner, with the susceptibility to sin already in you. This 'Original Sin' was the curse Adam and Eve's fall brought to mankind. Their disobedience meant that all successive generations were weakened by being open to temptation – a weakness played upon by omnipresent devils and much utilized by playwrights. This idea provoked a rich language of condemnation among moralists – pamphleteers or preachers – and a delight in describing the pains of Hell.

In the turbulent times when *The Tempest* was written there was no shortage of targets named as the source of sin. Sin bred like disease in the growing capital. Disease itself was God's punishment for sin; not just the usual bodily sins of lust, gluttony and sloth, but pride in rank, the vanity of fashion and the greed of money making too. Society seemed falling apart; crime, alcoholism and illegitimacy were all rising,[8] and heresy and religious dissent were rife. Anglicans blamed Puritans, Puritans blamed Anglicans, everyone blamed the

Catholics, the Pope (the Antichrist), the French, the Spanish, the court or the king.

Life was a battle to preserve your virtue and live like Christ, cleansing sin by prayer. Prayer would involve repentance and begging forgiveness ('Forgive us our trespasses …'). An accumulation of unrepented sins, particularly grave ones, could damn you when you died, though repentance (even at the last minute) could save you. The terrified Faustus, about to be dragged down to Hell as payment of his side of the bargain with Satan, cries out:

> See, see where Christ's blood streams in the firmament!
> One drop would save my soul, half a drop. Ah, my Christ!
> Ah, rend not my heart for naming of my Christ!
> Yet will I call on him. (Scene xix. 146–9)

Death was never far away in those days of plague and illnesses easily brought on by a poor diet, unhealthy living conditions and ignorance of basic hygiene. Infections were a leveller making no distinction between rich or poor, though the better-off might be protected by superior food.[9] The world was an insecure place, made more uncertain by persistent Puritan claims that epidemic diseases were punishment for tolerating Catholicism or changing church ritual, performing plays, not keeping the Sabbath holy, the sinfulness of the court or the sinfulness of everyone in general.[10] There was no escape. Poverty, illness and sudden disaster were constant anxieties people lived with. As Montaigne put it: 'We do not know where death awaits us: so let us wait for it everywhere.'[11] Starting and ending the day with family prayers was part of that protection/salvation process, behaving piously during the day was another. James I advised his son, 'Pray […] God would give you grace so to live, as yee may everie houre of your life be readie for death.'[12] This life, though the gift of a bountiful God, was short and merely a preparation for the life eternal, spent in the torments of Hell or among the blessings of Heaven.

Increasingly in the seventeenth century small coteries of scientists and intellectuals, 'still climbing after knowledge infinite',[13] questioned the authority and authenticity of the concepts of sin, damnation and salvation.[14] Part of a growing rationalist movement, they encouraged cynicism, secularism and individualism. The idea that the individual was responsible for his own soul and for his personal relationship with God was refreshing and liberating, facilitating independence from a church increasingly mired in corruption and entangled in the establishment power structure.[15] But individualism, emerging contemporaneously with the capitalist practices of a profit-driven, go-getting selfish commercial world, threatened old ideas of humble self-effacement and dedication to the community's good. This individualism discounted others, prioritized your needs, disconnected you from moral restraints and promoted a world where personal will and private appetite were the measure of actions, where villainy thrived and where Antonio and Sebastian get their own way if not opposed strenuously. Traditional morality demanded the bad be punished in fiction. In real life villains often got away with skulduggery and dishonesty. Machiavelli was demonized because his works 'openly and unfeignedly […] describe what men do, and not what they ought to do'.[16] Machiavelli demonstrates how discrepancy between moral expectation and actual behaviour shows that rule breakers succeed. Man's unique features – the virtues of charity, mercy, sympathy, intellectual ability and reason, and the emotional faculties of imagination, love and sympathy – raised him above animals and closer to godlike status. But the pinnacle of God's earthly creation, part-divine, part-animal hybrid, was too easily tempted by fleshly failings. Mankind was God's second attempt after some of his first angelic creations rebelled with Satan. Because humans had animal traits life was a constant battle between the animal promptings of appetite and passion and the angelic demands of reason and virtue. The exploration of that struggle between our baser and our better nature is the domain of literature. The Ten Commandments, the Seven Deadly Sins and the Seven Cardinal Virtues specifically address this need to fight the impulses towards lust, violence, theft, gluttony and sloth. The presence of these appetites gives *The Tempest* its religious-ethical context. These conduct guidelines are implicit in all Elizabethan-Jacobean drama. Characters can be measured against them.

The list of sins, revised by Pope Gregory I in AD 590, was tabulated hierarchically by Dante in his influential poem *The Divine Comedy* (1321). Originating in Catholicism, these Mortal, Capital or Cardinal sins were still relevant to the sin-conscious Anglican Protestants and dissenting sectarians of Shakespeare's time. They are cardinal because they were thought grave enough to require God to renew His grace to the sinner and for the sinner to show repentance before forgiveness could be shown. They are mortal or capital because they were serious enough to warrant death ('For the wages of sin is death'). God was thought able to strike down great sinners by sudden death or to use human agents. The spirit Ariel claims he and his fellow spirits are 'ministers of Fate' (III. iii. 61). He works at the command of Prospero, who is an agent of Divine Providence bringing retribution to 'men of sin'. The Book of Proverbs lists as sins looking proud of yourself, lying, shedding innocent blood, having a heart ready to devise wickedness, a readiness to do mischief and stirring trouble. St Paul offers a longer list, any of which will lose you the kingdom of God: adultery, fornication, uncleanness, lasciviousness, idolatry, witchcraft, hatred, variance, emulation, wrath, strife, sedition, heresy, envy, murder, drunkenness, revelling 'and such like' (Galatians 5:19–21).

Fornication was sex between couples not married to each other. The principle was that sex should not take place at all unless permitted by the holy vows of matrimony. James's court was a hotbed of promiscuity which he did nothing to curb or punish. There are many other negative behaviours and vices regarded as sinful, though less serious. These are called venial sins. Committing them would not lead to you losing the grace of God, thus you could still be cleansed and saved, with effort on your part.

The idea of Hell as below the Earth, imagined as a fiery pit like a funnel, is formalized by Dante in *Inferno* (Hell), the first part of *The Divine Comedy*.[17] Each sin was tabulated and allocated its sector. The lower Dante goes in his visit to the nine circles of Hell, the worse the sins committed by the damned he meets. In 'Upper Hell' are those who committed sins of incontinence, failings effected by those constant enemies of mankind, the appetites. These mainly personal failings are, in descending order: the lustful, gluttonous, hoarders and spendthrifts, wrathful and suicides. In 'Nether Hell' – getting closer to Satan at the bottom of the pit – are sinners who committed planned transgressions – fraud or acts of malice. In descending order they are: panders and seducers (pimps and fornicators), flatterers, simoniacs (those who sold church offices), sorcerers,[18] barrators (those abusing the legal system to profit by groundless cases or false claims), hypocrites, thieves, those encouraging fraud, sowers of discord, falsifiers and traitors (to kindred, country, guests, their lord, etc.). These broad definitions comprise a number of sins against the community and against probity in public office. Some of them are present in *The Tempest* and the audience would easily identify them.

Pride was the first sin, committed by the Devil in thinking so well of himself he rebelled against God to replace him. As Lucifer ('the bright one'), he was God's favourite angel, but becoming ambitious, thinking that although God favoured him above the other angels he deserved even better and higher status, he rebelled, was defeated and was cast out of Heaven. He and his co-conspirators fell through Chaos into Hell, a fiery pit full of sulphur and smoke, specially created by God. Vanity is a form of pride. At a venial level it is conceit about your physical looks, clothes or status. Antonio's sin is initially the same as Lucifer's: overly high self-esteem, an overblown perception of his own worth that leads him to overthrow his rightful lord. The arrogance of thinking yourself better than others is a small vanity until it becomes active disregard and bad treatment of others, behaving as if you were above the common courtesies. Antonio betrays lord and family, but significantly shows no remorse. Alonso, almost equally guilty, does at least repent. Antonio further sins by flattering and bribing himself into a position from which to launch his rebellion. The audience sees him attempt to spread the same sin, and political machinations and recruiting support were strategies the court would readily recognize. Vanity related to appearance and fashion is minimally raised in Stephano's attraction to the trumpery clothes Ariel displays before Prospero's cell to distract the would-be attackers. Any reference to clothing as a moral distraction would be relevant to a peacock court audience whose wasteful extravagance on clothes was infamous. Antonio has the right to expect some role in government but wants all the power. In wrenching it away from his brother he subverts traditional primogeniture (the inheritance of land, estates, fortune and title by the eldest son).

Pride is the besetting sin of those with power, privilege, rank and wealth (like the audience). The Bible required people of rank to disregard their advantages and be humbly ready to serve those whom it was their duty to help. A king is most likely to be proud, but overweening self-regard was rife among courtiers too. And, comically, among butlers it seems. The slightly more elevated status of stewards among the household servants might well lead them to dream of greatness, like Oswald in *King Lear* and, most famously, Malvolio in *Twelfth Night*. Stephano's fantasies of rule too betoken an inflated sense of self and capacity. It is inappropriate for a butler to contemplate rule, and his pretension is suitably mocked and exposed.

Wrath ranged from any tiny moment of anger that flares and soon dies away, through escalating losses of temper to the irrational rage that becomes violence against another. This is relevant to those men in the audience ready to fall out and fight. Men (not just gentlemen) wore swords, carried concealed daggers and were prepared to use them. With too much wine tempers frayed easily – over cards, dice, women or a word taken the wrong way. The Day of Judgement was known as the *Dies Irae* (Day of Wrath, a term used in the Anglican Communion). It was the day when God's ultimate wrath would be shown. Irascibility (a tendency to lose one's temper) is a sin liable to occur in any rank of society, but particularly among hot-headed young men. Those of rank and wealth were most susceptible to it, believing themselves superior to others and ready to defend any perceived slur against their honour.

There is much anger in *The Tempest*. The boatswain shows it briefly towards the interfering courtiers. Sebastian and Antonio show a snobbish kind of anger towards the boatswain, whom they call a 'bawling, blasphemous, incharitable dog!' and 'whoreson insolent noisemaker!' (I. i. 40–41, 43–4). Caliban shows it persistently in his morose resentment of Prospero. Stephano becomes angry with Trinculo when he is tricked by Ariel (III. ii.). Prospero sparks into anger many times – with Miranda, with Caliban and with Ariel – usually in response to some questioning of his power or motives. His passing anger is soon assuaged, gradually diminishes and disappears as he gains full control of the situation and decides to relinquish his revenge. The tempest with which the drama begins blows out into calm as Prospero's anger subsides. William Perkins lamented 'the abuse of the tongue among all sorts and degrees of men everywhere'[19] but the inventive invective so common in Shakespeare is muted in The Tempest. This reflects how Prospero's anger, hoarded over 12 years, filters away into forgiveness.

Lust was a universal sin, felt by both sexes, all ranks and most ages. The 'disease of lust' was to St Augustine persistently intrusive and the most destructive of the appetites.[20] Necessary for the continuation of the species, the human sex drive was difficult to control and greatly concerned all churches. The sin of fornication was defined as any prohibited sex, meaning outside marriage – sex between two unmarried adults was forbidden. Sex with someone other than your husband or wife was both fornication and adultery. The intention to conceive a child was the only justification for intercourse within marriage. Sex for pleasure alone was lust and fornication. Lust comprised all unclean thoughts and unclean acts, including what were regarded as unnatural ones like bestiality, incest and homosexuality (condemned in Romans 1:26). Masturbation, rape and sexual thoughts were all lust. A perceived growing libidinousness in society, with an increase in unwanted pregnancies in all ranks, worried preachers and playwrights alike. 'In political libels, lampoons, satires, and other forms of writing and action, upper-class immorality is almost inevitably the object of sharp disapproval, reflecting the growing grip of Protestant attitudes to sin, social order, and divine vengeance.'[21]

The church's attitudes to sexuality centre on two problem areas: women as the source of sin (particularly the belief that women were more lascivious by nature than men)[22] and the central principle that appetites (passions) made men more like animals than angels and needed to be controlled or suppressed. The Christian ascetic tradition required avoiding all excess – simple food, simple clothes and a focus on the spiritual rather than the carnal. Every Deadly Sin was a form of appetite developed to excess. In 'Tis Pity calm reason is recommended to a jealous, vengeful husband: 'Sir you must be ruled by your reason and not by your fury: that were unhuman and beastly' (IV. iii. 83–5). Different sorts of unruly appetites (mostly for power, money or sex) were a recurrent theme in drama. Very slowly, marriage was established as a means of controlling and channelling lust. While theoretically chastity was preferable if full spiritual perfection was to be achieved, it was gradually conceded that marriage was the second best course if you could not effectively control your sexual impulses.[23] Marrying was preferable to promiscuity, but even within wedlock lust had to be restrained. Lust was a major topic for admonition in sermons and religious writing. Men and women even sat separately in church.

The Puritans, though in favour of marriage, had considerable difficulty with the whole area of sexuality.

Criticism of rampant lust is recurrent in plays of the 1600s. *Measure, Hamlet, Othello* and *Troilus and Cressida* express concern about the lasciviousness of both sexes. Sexuality also has a part to play in *The Tempest*, in the lust of Caliban (which he laughs off unrepentantly), in Prospero's protective father strictures to Ferdinand, in Stephano's song about prostitutes and in the excitement of Miranda meeting Ferdinand. These had a topical context considering the moral reformation drive of both church and legal authorities against brothels, whores and prenuptial sex even between betrothed couples. Orgel's assertion that Ferdinand is a 'violently libidinized adolescent' is entirely wrong.[24] Prospero pretends to believe Ferdinand is a sexual threat. It is part of his testing the prince, who is in actuality respectfully controlled. There is no evidence of any attempt to take advantage of Miranda. Each is excited by the other, but is suitably correct in conduct.

Envy or covetousness is jealous desire for what others have, a form of mental theft and discontent with the lot God gave you. Antonio's envy became actual theft, Stephano's did not develop as envisaged. Envy was not perhaps the reason for Prospero's taking of the island from Caliban so much as an imperious sense that he was destined to rule there and was senior to and more suitable than Caliban. Taking control does not appear to happen until Caliban's attempted rape showed him to be a danger. In the final scene, revealing himself to the gathered characters, he says:

> I am Prospero, and that very Duke
> Which was thrust forth of Milan, who most strangely
> Upon this shore, where you were wrecked, was landed
> To be the lord on't. (V. i. 159–62)

This suggests he believed it was Providence's plan he should become ruler. Similarly, the Europeans took control of the lands they discovered in the Americas with a sense of cultural superiority and a spiritual mission to bring light to the heathens. The expectation of boundless riches drew them there, especially the lure of untold amounts of gold. Theft of land and resources was at the heart of Portuguese, Spanish, French, Dutch and British colonialism. The missionary duty to spread the word of God was a *post facto* justification.

The grievances of the two younger brothers in the story not only indicts them as ambitious and envious, it implies a failure on the part of Prospero and Alonso to effectively satisfy natural ambition and greed by delegating responsibilities to them within government while keeping firm a hand on the reins of power.

It raises the age-old controversy of whether primogeniture was the best means of dealing with family property inheritance. Montaigne and Bacon address this difficult matter. Most English landowners believed in primogeniture because it was traditional, kept the estate intact and maintained the male bloodline. This theme is as old as families themselves, as old as Cain and Abel. Shakespeare uses the sibling rivalry motif many times; usually it demonstrates how younger sons envy the eldest's inheritance, so it is firmly focused on material longing. It also reflects concern with justice being done and expresses the jealousy of older sons towards the second's arrival, threatening his monopoly of love and attention. It raises the question of what should be done when the official heir is a wastrel, a spendthrift, irresponsible, evil, mentally incapable or unsuitable in some other way. The history plays address this in relation to inept kingship and the question of succession. Sibling rivalry is doubly present in *As You Like It* with Orlando and his brother, and the exiled Duke and his brother. In *Hamlet* it focuses on Hamlet Senior and Claudius. In *Much Ado About Nothing* there are Don Pedro and his bastard brother Don John. These all involve deceit, cheating, attempts to oust the hated rival, an actual murder of one brother by another (*Hamlet*), and a war between siblings (*Much Ado*). In *Richard III* the Duke of Gloucester is deeply envious of his handsome, golden, successful brother, Edward IV. In *The Taming of the Shrew* an older sister is jealous of the younger because she is seen as father's pet. In *King Lear* the long-held grievances of childhood surface in the jealousies of the king's three daughters and the conflict between a legitimate and illegitimate brother. It is deeply disturbing to see how little love can exist within a family, or how testing times can open cracks rather than strengthen bonds. In different ways, and to different degrees of seriousness, Shakespeare reworks envy as an unsettling, potentially destructive aspect of family relationships. The early Morality/Chronicle Play *Gorboduc* (1571) goes back to a period of British prehistory, focusing on the rivalry of two brothers who are given half the kingdom by their father, Gorboduc, who is resigning from power. The plot pivots on sibling rivalry and succession. The Mary Tudor/Elizabeth relationship had had its uneasy jealousies. The Mary Queen of Scots/Elizabeth cousin rivalry bedevilled English politics until the former was executed for yet another plot against the queen. Also pertinent is the support for Arbella Stuart as a more authentic claimant to the throne than James I. Plots, envious siblings and succession rivalries were all part of the ambient politics of the period.

Greed and **gluttony** are sins of physical excess. Avarice (greed), excessive desire for material goods or wealth, is the miser's sin – hoarding for its own sake. It is the sin of the money maker – the financier/speculator/entrepreneur – accumulating more than he needs. It is the sin of conquistador explorers like Sir Walter Raleigh and the Virginia Company. From a religious standpoint it is the sin of the man who does not 'shake the superflux' to the needy, a theme much discussed in the increasingly hard times of the 1590s and 1600s.[25] Gluttony is a bodily excess, largely applied to overindulgence in food and drink. It was believed that 'enough is as good as a feast'; if you had eaten and drunk in moderation, sufficient for the body's needs, anything more was unnecessary indulgence. The leftovers could be given to the old and the poor. It is the Dives and Lazarus story again, a story reminding the rich and comfortably-off to do their duty to the community. It was part of the harmony of society, payment for deference, putting back into the community.

Excess was a moral pivotal point; any form of excess was a sin. The early church was built upon moderation, asceticism, fast days, a lack of material possessions – the simple life. It failed to live up to that ideal, becoming a monolithic edifice of accumulated wealth, land, power, corruption and self-indulgence. Its decadence and worldliness triggered various reformist heresies violently suppressed in the name of preserving the faith, but actually defending Catholicism's monopoly hold over the people of Europe. The theoretical basis was moderation and simplicity. The Apollonian religion of ancient Greece had a tradition of controlled moderation. 'Nothing in excess' was inscribed on Apollo's temple in Delphi and the concept persisted. A late fourteenth-century proverb says, 'There is measure in all things.' St Augustine wisely remarked, 'To some, total abstinence is easier than perfect moderation.'[26] The Puritans revitalized the traditions of asceticism, leading to them being seen as killjoys, but excess was a moral danger marker. In tragedy (classical and Elizabethan-Jacobean), once a character behaves with excess in one aspect of their life disaster is unavoidable. Excess is fundamental to comedy too: Sir Toby's persistent drunkenness, Malvolio's social aspirations and Orsino's obsession with Olivia (just to take examples from *Twelfth Night*). Any form of obsessive/excessive behaviour is open to mockery. Gonzalo's tendency to pompous philosophizing, Prospero's need for control and his lectures on lust, Antonio's persistent evil, Stephano's love of his bottle and Caliban's unremitting moroseness are all excessive and sources of humour. The trigger of the story is Prospero's excessive love of his books. There is some mild absurdity too in the rather pointless excessive magical feats Prospero requires of Ariel – fetching dew from the Bermudas, treading the ocean's ooze and delving in the veins of the Earth. There is further absurdity in the theatrical spectacle by which the characters are played with, teased and confused. Shakespeare is both using and mocking the over-elaborate devices of court masques, which became increasingly sensational to please jaded palates that needed more and more ingenious stimulation. The over-effusive love of Ferdinand is another area of comedy excess, but then the exaggerations of love were always amusing to Shakespeare.

Virtuous, rational living was thought to be its own reward. Moderation, abstinence, chastity, renouncement and avoidance were all ways to concentrate your devotion to God and virtue, but not much practised at court. The principle of moderation was integral to Christian belief from its beginnings. The simple life of John the Baptist, Jesus, the hermits of the Thebaid Desert and many saints prioritized spiritual cleansing over the demands of the body. Regular fasting and frugal living were practices that continued in Protestant England among the godly. Periods of contemplation and prayer were encouraged, as was the rejection of luxury. Excessive, ostentatious display of your spirituality were sinful too. The aim was to put the corrupting influence of this world into perspective; diminishing its power over you gave you time to focus on the next world, but balance had to be kept. It was acceptable to work hard, enjoy your family, be an active, useful member of your community *and* take pleasure moderately in the good things of this world. Shakespeare is always subtextually smuggling in warnings for the audience. The court – an ostentatious, drunken, promiscuous, gambling-obsessed, garrulous, debt-ridden lot, mostly living away from home, thus neglecting their families and their local social duty – needed more instruction than most. Given the sometimes noisy, inattentive, food-munching, giggling, gossiping nature of audiences, we can only hope that the court spectators were more receptive to the lessons taught.

Sloth, another sort of excess – an overdeveloped laziness – was not just disinclination to work, but a psychological/spiritual state of not bothering. Your duty to God was to work hard at your trade and at being virtuous. Many didactic stories and plays illustrate the spiritual and material rewards of industry. A popular motif compared two apprentices – one hard working, who gets on well in his trade and gains his master's daughter, the other idle, who falls into bad habits and ends up in prison for debt. This is demonstrated in *Eastward Ho!* (1605). Industry meant more than working at your livelihood, it meant being a committed, active Christian, helping the community and actively working at guarding and improving your own spiritual state. The Latin word for sloth, *acedia* (or *accidia*), also applies to spiritual slothfulness or despair, the state in which you lose belief that God cares for and watches over you. It was a state akin to melancholy or depression.

Prospero's neglect of his duties, his selfish preference for his own inclinations, is a form of sloth. A sin he comes to regret and is eager to absolve, it is a sort of intellectual pride that leads him to see the daily routine of government as beneath him. The parade of sins would be easily spotted and a Jacobean audience would be of the mindset to interpret the drama before them in the light of these moral waymarkers.

Chapter 4

THE SEVEN CARDINAL VIRTUES

If the Seven Deadly Sins were the warning signs for avoiding damnation, the Seven Cardinal Virtues were signposts to salvation. The Seven Deadly Sins all had obvious opposites (pride/humility, wrath/calm forbearance, lust/abstinence or moderation, covetousness/generosity, greed/charity, gluttony/moderation, sloth/active engagement), but there was also an official list of virtues, some of which appeared as opposites to the sins, some of which related to broader matters of faith.

The Seven Cardinal Virtues

1. **Temperance** (abstinence, moderation)
2. **Prudence** (providence, foresight, circumspection, consideration, wise conduct)
3. **Justice** (justice, equity, fair judgement)
4. **Fortitude** (strength under pressure)
5. **Faith** (piety, duty to and belief in God)
6. **Hope** (hope of salvation)
7. **Charity** (love of, benevolence to, others)

A godly life won a heavenly crown. If life was a journey, each person a pilgrim on the highway, then conduct determined destination. Virtue's path was hard – steep, thorny, stony, winding and tiring. The way for the carnal man of weak character, Mr Worldly Wiseman, was easy – a 'primrose path', as Macbeth puts it – but it led to an 'everlasting bonfire' and 'sulphurous pit'. Because *The Tempest* is not designed as a tragedy, the potential for sins to take hold and destroy is persistently turned aside or thwarted. Sins hold our attention because they are intriguingly horrible. Virtue is evident in *The Tempest* in Prospero, Miranda, Ferdinand and Gonzalo, but it is engagement with sin which creates the *psychomachia* of the play. Sins raise questions that create suspense: Will Caliban's plot succeed? Will Antonio's? Will the sinful men be punished? If so, how? The two fathers are guilty of sin; Prospero has been punished and seeks redemption, but what will the outcome be for Alonso? The simple nature of the storyline leads us to suspect that all will artificially work out for the best.

The centrality of virtue to living the good life was not only recognized in Christian thought. Classical writings extolled virtue, particularly Plato's Socratic dialogue *Protagoras*, Aristotle's *Ethics*, Cicero's *De Officiis* (*On Duty* or *Obligation*), and Seneca's *De Ira* (*On Anger*) and *De Clementia* (*On Mercy*). Each listed those qualities required to live the good (i.e., virtuous and wise) life. Plato names wisdom, courage, justice, kindness, circumspection and holiness as essential components of excellence. Aristotle identifies courage, temperance, liberality, magnanimity, proper ambition, patience, truthfulness, friendliness, modesty and righteous indignation. Cicero was studied at school as a model of the Latin style, elegant but direct. In an age when one's first public duty was to others and not to selfish individual desires, *De Officiis* became the key *exemplum* of good citizenship. Studied at university as an essential guide to moral behaviour and public conduct for young men who might become active in national arenas, it advised how to discern false flattery from wise counsel, something of which Alonso is unaware (perhaps because he is driven to distraction by grief for his supposedly drowned son).

These classical qualities evolved into the four virtues of Christian thinking (temperance, prudence, justice and fortitude), then extended to seven with Paul's first letter to the Corinthians (13:13): 'And now abideth faith, hope, charity, these three: but the greatest of these is charity'. In his Epistle to the Galatians (5:22–3) Paul also says, 'The fruit of the Spirit is love, joy, peace, longsuffering, gentleness, goodness, faith, meekness, temperance.' Such characteristics are part of the moral excellence that constitutes a person's virtue. The Christian fathers St Ambrose, St Augustine and St Thomas Aquinas (*Summa Theologica*, II. i. 61), reacting to and refining St Paul, detailed what became the seven key characteristics of the pious Christian and incorporated them into the main body of church teaching. By the Renaissance (with its love of classical writings) they had become an amalgamation of classical and Christian virtues and proliferated into a huge mentoring literature aimed at any sort of leader or governor. For King James, temperance was not only an opposite to gluttony but meant moderation in all things, particularly in the exercise of justice, power and controlling anger – not something he actually followed himself, being an intemperate drinker, given to immoderate anger when thwarted and often inconsistent, unjustly arbitrary and capriciously absolutist in exercising his power. To Sir Thomas

Elyot, self-control and emotional balance were crucial qualities in someone with the immense potential for punishment available to a king. Within the fiction of *The Tempest*, Prospero's powers give him the potential to wreak a terrible revenge on both men who wronged him. His patience and restraint are therefore admirable.

Along with prudence or circumspection, moderation was fundamental to kingly rule. In defining the ideal courtier, Castiglione has Count Ludovico Canossa specifically pick out 'prudence, goodness, fortitude and temperance of soul' as essential to a man of 'honour and integrity'.[1] Not jumping to conclusions but carefully considering options and outcomes is a vital skill for any civic leader whose actions and judgements have widespread consequences. James would presumably approve of a play about the consequences of negligent kingship. If he saw his own failings in the past and present weaknesses of Prospero he may have felt awkward – all the more embarrassing since he had proclaimed in detail the virtues a prince needed in 'A King's Duty in His Office', the central second book of *Basilikon Doron* (thousands were in circulation). Watching any recent Shakespeare play he ought to have squirmed in his royal seat, recognizing the virtues transgressed on stage as his own failings and those of his court. Patience, perseverance, courage (the bravery to do the right thing and to face evil), fairness (justice for all who deserve it), tolerance, honesty, respect for others, kindness, generosity and forgiveness are very much in evidence in *The Tempest* (their opposites too: pride, intemperance, greed, sexual licence, envy, indulgence, irreverence, dishonour, projected murder, violence and deceit). Against Prospero's flaws we have to consider his claim that Antonio feared to kill him, 'so dear the love my people bore me' (I. ii. 141), and Ferdinand's comment that he is 'this famous Duke of Milan/Of whom so often I have heard renown' (V. i. 124). If true, both claims indicate something special in Prospero: the magic of majesty or an aura of virtue – perhaps both.

The black cynicism in many plays from 1600 onwards reflects a sense of spiritual and moral decline. For an age believing everyone was a sinner to a greater or lesser degree, the corruption of man was a given. Pessimism about individual probity (personal goodness, honesty and openness) extended into the wider workings of society and government. Individuals from all ranks were thought to be morally corrupt in different ways, but the supposed leaders of society – the titled governing elite, the expected exemplars of good practice – were persistently shown to be selfish, indifferent and morally bankrupt. Every age sees itself as corrupt in some way; satirists thrive on cynicism. Due to the religious aspect of Elizabethan-Jacobean ethics, the Deadly Sins inevitably parade through the drama of the period. Theatre demands tension and the conflict between sin and virtue provides that tension.

Three other moral schemas had become part of the thinking about how men should behave towards each other. All officially disappeared at the Reformation, but were still in people's heads and hearts, becoming absorbed into Protestant thinking, particularly in relation to social responsibilities:

The Seven Corporal Works of Mercy

1. To tend the sick
2. To feed the hungry
3. To give drink to the thirsty
4. To clothe the naked
5. To harbour the stranger
6. To minister to prisoners
7. To bury the dead

The Seven Spiritual Works of Mercy

1. To convert the sinner
2. To instruct the ignorant
3. To counsel those in doubt
4. To comfort those in sorrow
5. To bear wrongs patiently
6. To forgive injuries
7. To pray for the living and the dead

The Seven Gifts of the Holy Ghost

1. Counsel
2. Fear of the Lord
3. Fortitude
4. Piety
5. Understanding
6. Wisdom
7. Knowledge

These are the positives by which the characters would be judged by the contemporary audience. For all his failings, Prospero strives to behave according to the expectations of Christian rulers. (These positive aspects are discussed in relation to the play in Chapter 15.)

Chapter 5

KINGSHIP

Savage and relentless anger is unbecoming in a king. (Seneca, 'On Mercy', 193)

Now what shall I say about the courtiers? For the most part they are the most obsequious, servile, stupid and worthless creatures, and yet they're bent on appearing foremost in everything. (Erasmus, *Praise of Folly*, 176)

The aim of the courtier is to make his prince virtuous. (Castiglione, *The Book of the Courtier*, 320)

They do abuse the king that flatter him:
For flattery is the bellows blows up sin. (*Pericles*, I. ii. 39–40)

Prospero, as one-time Duke of Milan and now 'ruler' of a tiny island, master of the castaways and controller of their fortunes, is a prince figure. He must be measured by the various criteria applied to rulers. He misgoverned a sizeable and powerful state by failing to keep proper control of it, yet there is an aura of loftiness and dignity about him. In describing the devious means by which his brother infiltrated and subverted the state to his own rule, he uses a common metaphor for the suborning of legitimate power: Antonio was 'the ivy which had hid my princely trunk' (I. ii. 86). The regal, sheltering, nurturing tree (trees were common symbols of royal power in Renaissance iconography) had its life force sucked out by the parasitic ivy, the Machiavellian schemer. He refers to himself as 'princely' – the Renaissance term for all state leaders. Whatever their actual title, they were all generically defined as princes, governors or magistrates. This aligns him with any other ruler, whether the King of Spain commanding a vast empire, the elector of the tiniest German palatinate or the count of an Italian city-state. During the Renaissance, Milan had been of considerable power and influence, its domain spreading across a large part of Northern Italy (the city comprised 100,000 inhabitants, the

surrounding state another 800,000).[1] After the Sforza family's loss of power
the state became an adjunct of Spain, often vulnerable to French attack,
and altogether a place of tangled, precarious politics. It lost several dukes
in the constantly changing power balances of the time and eventually was
swallowed up by the Spanish rulers of Naples and Sicily. Prospero's conduct
there is certainly open to criticism, as he acknowledges, but so too is his
manner of controlling the island, its small size an apt reflection of what he
deserves after his negligence in Milan. These matters locate the play within
the contemporary discourses on legitimacy and rule and the experience
of constantly swinging power in European states. Prospero will, however,
gradually earn the right to return to power.

The education and conduct of princes much concerned moralists and
political theorists throughout the Renaissance. James I's two books on
monarchy written before he came to the English throne were followed by
two more that deal with regal power – *An Apologie* [explanation] *for the Oath
of Allegiance* (1608) and *A Premonition to All Most Mightie Monarchs* (1609).
James's persistent failure to marry personal behaviour and monarchical role
in conformity with his own well-publicized principles resonates throughout
the play. The matter of government (of people, of self) is common to all
Shakespeare's work. Though Prospero ultimately emerges as benevolent and
forgiving, his earlier rule of Milan and his current treatment of Miranda
and his pseudo-children are questionable in many aspects. Prospero was an
absentee ruler. Though physically present in Milan he was disengaged from
government, nominating Antonio as his deputy while he pursued his private
studies.[2] His dereliction of duty triggers a series of events leading to his arrival
on the island. His manner of control as 'ruler' of the island and some aspects
of his parenting relate to contemporary discourses and to some extent reflect
badly on him. Ferdinand (failing to understand that Prospero is testing him
with role play) complains he is 'crabbed,/And he's compos'd of harshness' (III.
i. 8–9). There is some truth in this criticism; his 'kingship' and fatherhood
are both flawed. Ambiguously, while absolutism can be harsh and must be
applied carefully, firm and strict rule appears necessary, as subjects (both the
privileged and the mob) are naturally inclined to anarchy, destruction and
vandalism. The disorderly behaviour of Antonio and Sebastian on the one
hand and Caliban, Trinculo and Stephano on the other proves the need for
Prospero to be more autocratic. The problem, as always, is getting the balance
right between authoritarianism and liberalism.

Kingship is inevitably an explicit theme in the history plays. Audiences
seemed insatiable for dramas revisiting the English past, displaying the
fortunes of heroes and villains, plotters arrested and executed, monarchs
succeeding or failing. The stories of Henry V, King John, Richard II and

Richard III were popular subjects that Shakespeare would later rework in his own way. The fall of kings was endlessly fascinating, and the history genre remained popular at the Swan and Rose theatres even into the 1600s,[3] when other writers at other venues, doubtful and discontented about the running of public affairs and the direction in which society seemed to be going, turned to topical satire to voice their anxieties. Reading or watching the many Chronicle Plays infesting the stage leads inevitably to the conclusion that although kings are theoretically honoured as God's vice-regents on Earth, in practice history shows them as persistently opposed, plotted against, harried from battle to battle, disrespected, often violently removed from the throne and violently disposed of. 'The contrast between the monarch as symbol of the independent English commonwealth, and the actual occupants of the throne, was too marked.'[4] In *The Tempest* we see the fall and rise of a prince who admits his failure as a public figure. His problem is a grave one for a man born to inherit power; by nature he is more drawn to the retired, private life of a scholar than to the public duties required of a ruler. Had Prospero shown in Milan the decisiveness, engagement and taste for control that he shows on the island, he would not have been banished. His addiction 'to closeness and the bettering of [his] mind' (I. ii. 90) encouraged his neglect of 'worldly ends':

> The government I cast upon my brother
> And to my state grew stranger, being transported
> And rapt in secret studies. (I. ii. 76–7)

He has made a prime mistake in governance: putting his own selfish ends before his duty. He describes himself as 'for the liberal Arts/Without a parallel' (I. ii. 72–3), much as James boasted of his intellectual prowess. Being 'rapt in secret studies' (I. ii. 77) euphemistically avoids admitting that like Faustus he was drawn into more arcane learning, pursuing mystic knowledge and seeking magic powers. King James had warned that such absorption in study was dangerous:

> Mounting from degree to degree, upon the slipperie and uncertaine scale of curiositie; they are at last enticed, that where lawfull artes or sciences failes to satisfie their restless minds, even to seeke to that black and unlawful science of *Magic*.[5]

Prospero makes no diabolic pact, using his art for protection and to help him resume rule. On the island he has continued to learn about harnessing nature, has practised with Ariel and within the play's timeframe is ready to make his attempt at restoration, presumably with the intention of doing better the second time. Good kings can be undermined by evil men; weak kings, however virtuous, can be misled by devious lords. Prospero has undermined himself and played into the hands of an opportunist brother. Bad kings have nasty ends, being shown as unworthy of their role, either on personal or political grounds. Alonso is redeemed by repenting his part in the plot to topple another ruler, chastened by the presumed loss of his heir. The process of the narrative then is to follow the final stages of a ruler's preparation to resume power. Strategically Prospero is ready. Tactically he has several more moves to make. Morally he is not quite ready, but the last remnants of negative qualities are sloughed off during the action as he loses his anger, becomes more positive and forgiving and achieves a readiness, humble but full of presence. Prospero now has an aura he perhaps lacked when governing (or not governing) Milan. Charismatic rulers generated powerful displays of patriotic loyalty and provoked a similar response in audiences when their stories were dramatized, but by the end of Elizabeth I's life a general cynicism about real-life leaders (nobles and monarchs) seemed to have pervaded public opinion. A strong leader's decline provokes consideration of failings that would otherwise have been diplomatically ignored while the ruler's strength was feared. Elizabeth's death precipitated open discussion of many long-repressed anxieties.

The Chronicle Plays crowding the early public stage reflected not just an interest in rethinking the nation's past, but sublimated contemporary anxieties about stability, masked and made palatable by dead personae and long-gone events. The inexorable approach of the end of the century released many superstitious fears of the Apocalypse and gloomy anticipation of the new era. These fears transferred into negative representations of magistrate figures. Jonson's *Sejanus* and the numerous Revenge Tragedies do not portray leaders as divine or their courts and advisers as anything other than basely human, grasping and unscrupulous. Roman history and recent Italian city-state politics afforded a useful means of dealing with current English concerns under the mask of foreign settings.

The question of government is not confined to the history plays, it is present too in the four Great Tragedies, focusing on the qualities that may enable proper or improper governorship of self or *polis*.[6] Be that *polis* a household, a city or a nation, the control of emotions, appetites and vices (and the consequences of not doing so) is always at the heart of Shakespearean drama. The restraint of appetite and emotion is central to Christian ethics and the problems passion and vice create are inevitably central to drama. The late plays are similarly focused though more interested in the personal politics of small courts and individual relationships. With restrictions on what aspects of contemporary life could be presented and portrayal of the monarch prohibited, indirection was the only means. *The Tempest*, while not a history play, is a study of faulty governorship, faulty parenthood and an exposure of personal and political ambitions. Its satire on authority and power, the corruption of courtiers and the ruling infrastructure in general would have interested a king who had contributed to the literature relating to the education of a prince, even if he was himself a secondary, unacknowledged target.

The story of the play, with Prospero so distinctly at its centre, present in so many scenes and directing the action even when not personally there, would inevitably have provoked questions about the rule of the man in whose court the play was being presented. Nothing is treasonable, but there are lots of little prompts that call King James to mind. His personal manner in conducting the court was certainly open to criticism, as was his variable administration of the government. Prospero's outcome was fortunate, James's too – in that he died before matters could develop into a civil war. Prospero might have been assassinated in the palace coup (several plots were planned against James), but was huddled away to exile; Antonio stopped short of fratricide. If Prospero's claim about his popularity is correct, then Antonio wisely chose not turn public feeling against him any more than it might have been inclined to be. There were precedents of brother murdering brother for power, but Antonio was wisely cautious. Even so, banishment had its dangers. Afloat in 'a rotten carcass of a butt' (I. ii. 146) Prospero might have capsized, but came ashore safely. Perhaps Antonio secretly hoped for a disaster at sea and a convenient disappearance. Twelve years later, providentially saved, a different man has emerged from the one who was cast ashore on the island, not perfect as a man, father or ruler, but much improved and certainly more engaged with 'policy decisions' and prepared now to rule. James's flaws only got worse.

Preparation for Rule

Did some fault in Prospero's education disincline him to govern? Tudor conceptions of preparation for rule were dominated by Sir Thomas Elyot's *The Boke Named the Governour* (1531). But there are other influences. Elyot's book echoes much of the thinking and conclusions arrived at in Castiglione, but then they shared a long tradition of works acting as *speculum principis* (a mirror for princes), defining the personality and conduct required to make a good ruler.[7] Castiglione moves from defining what makes the ideal courtier and court lady to a fourth and final book that situates the courtier as counsellor to a prince. Elyot focuses more upon the qualities of the governor, asserts the need of 'one souerayne gouernour [...] in a publike weale', but acknowledges the need for advisors and a nationwide group of 'inferior governours called magistratis'.[8] These fulfil the proper function of the courtier, not just as a finely dressed, cultured ornament, but as a voice of wisdom. Here was a role for Antonio, a focus for his energies and ambitions, but he becomes the corrupt deputy lured by power.

The basis for rule at any level is the proper upbringing of 'the chylde of a gentilman which is to have auctorite in the publike weale'. Elyot discusses lengthily the curriculum for this education because 'gentyllmen in this present time be not equall in doctrine to th'ancient noble men', due to 'the pride, avarice, and negligence of parentes', snobbery and a lack of teachers. Elyot complains that gentlemen believe 'it is a notable reproche to be well lerned'. The better sort of families paid high wages for skilled cooks or falconers, but not for a tutor to educate their child and inculcate virtue. A number of points are raised here relevant to Prospero's situation. He splits the rule, giving the day-to-day exercise of power to Antonio, while presumably keeping the name and prestige of duke and, probably, the prerogative of executive decision making. A precarious move, though he must have thought his much-loved brother trustworthy. King Lear had attempted to 'divest' himself of rule while keeping 'the name and addition of a king'. That tragedy had been performed before the court in 1606 and the outcome would still be vibrantly remembered by the current audience. Prospero is clearly 'well lerned' but not worldly enough to realize his private inclination should not have overshadowed his destiny. God made him a ruler, so he has a duty to rule. Pragmatic common sense should have warned him to be watchful of his deputy, brother or not.

The qualities needed by any man who was to govern at any level were prudence, industry, circumspection and modesty. Prospero lacked all these except modesty. Monarchs required comeliness in language and gesture, dignity in deportment and behaviour, a demeanour of honour and sobriety, affability, mercifulness, placability, humanity, benevolence and liberality, well-selected friends, sharp discernment of the 'diversity of flatterers', a sense of justice, personal fortitude and 'the faire vertu pacience'. Some of these qualities Prospero has from the beginning, others he lacks but seems to develop. His great flaw was a reluctance to engage in the drudgery of administration. Inclination to scholastic study was an unaffordable personal indulgence if it took him away from governing; in a man with responsibilities it is sloth. Much like King James, he has allowed a harmless enough passion to become excessive and therefore dangerous and sinful. A virtue, exercised excessively until it becomes a matter of pride, also becomes a vice. Prospero seems not to have gathered a court of carefully selected friends who would alert him to the growing danger of Antonio's insidious cuckoo behaviour. Elyot sees obstinacy as 'a familiare vice' among men with power and recommends a set of virtues for controlling passion: abstinence, continence, temperance, moderation, sobriety, sapience (wisdom) and understanding. These requirements, echoing the Seven Virtues and the Works of Mercy, are very demanding. Prospero had them, but did not apply them to the sphere of his God-given duty. Privilege, power and the money that comes with them bring responsibilities and responsibilities mean sacrifice. Yet, he has what Elyot calls 'the exposition of maiestie': he generates loyalty and love – witness the allegiance of Ariel, Miranda and 'the love my people bore me' (I. ii. 141). If Prospero's judgement is to be believed this suggests it was the court that betrayed him. That collection of greedy, power-hungry parasites allowed themselves to be bribed by Antonio, who:

> Being once perfected how to grant suits,
> How to deny them, who t'advance, and who
> To trash for over-topping, new created
> The creatures that were mine. (I. ii. 79–82)

The ability to inspire subjects with loyalty is crucial to kingship. It was one Elizabeth had pre-eminently and James did not. The ability to distinguish the users and predators from the genuine supporters was also vital. Elizabeth, for all her faults, was adored and allowed her subjects to approach her. James, though he enjoyed their enthusiastic welcome of him to the throne, had little sympathy for his new people, was sarcastic about them, and kept them at bay whenever possible. As long as he kept giving – titles, posts, presents, etc. – James's courtiers were loyal (to their own interests). The Milanese yes-men simply accepted a new duke. To complain would be to lose all chance of advancement. Antonio suggests the Neapolitan court would react similarly if Sebastian killed Alonso. Though Prospero had the people's love he did not promote it to the point where they were ready to rise to support him in the coup. Perhaps there was no time to rouse his followers, as it does look as if the usurpation was executed swiftly and secretly. Similarly he did not recruit strong support among the nobility. Machiavelli advised that 'one becomes a prince […] with the favour of the people or of the nobles'.[9] Prospero also failed to take account of Machiavelli's analysis of the principle motivation of courts: 'The nobles have more foresight and are more astute, they always act in time to safeguard their interests, and they take sides with the one whom they expect to win.'[10]

It is the governor's role to keep just harmony between the 'comunaltie' ('the base and vulgare') and those with honour and dignities (titles and responsibilities). Maintaining order is vital. The 'discrepance of degrees' (differences of ranks) is part of 'the incomprehensible maiestie of God'. 'Take away ordre […] what shulde then remayne? […] Chaos […] perpeyuall conflicte

[...] vniuersall dissolution.' This has an ideological affinity with Ulysses's degree speech in *Troilus and Cressida*. Elyot asserts that the hierarchies of Heaven are reflected on Earth – the elements have their 'spheris' and men do not all have the same gifts from God. Potters cannot administer justice, ploughmen and carters 'shall make but an feble answere to an ambassadour'. With Antonio and Prospero we have perhaps the two unacceptable faces of rule as defined by James in *Basilikon Doron*: 'extreame tyrannie' and 'extreame slacknesse of punishment' (64–5). A man evil enough to grab power will be evil in the administration of it. Central to the situation as viewed by most orthodox Englishmen is that Antonio subverted normative hierarchy – God's order. This disorder is metaphorically reflected in the tempest with which the drama begins and the multiple transgressions displayed during the progress of the narrative.

Key to the infant education of men destined to authority is that their formative early years be lived in a milieu of virtue, that the language and behaviour of mothers, nurses and maids be irreproachable. At the age of 7 boys should be removed from 'the company of women' and tutored by 'an auncient & worshipfull man' with grave demeanour, gentle manners and impeccable morality. Then began a course in the classics that would develop rhetorical skills, improve their Latin and perfect the fluency and accuracy of their English. Elyot does not preclude physical exercise in his regimen, recommending hunting, hawking, dancing, wrestling, running, swimming and weapons training – in moderation. This is standard Renaissance elite male education.[11] Elyot deplores the tendency of noble families to halt their children's education at 14 and 'sufre them to live in idelnes'.[12] He believes education to be a lifelong process and essential for the production of governors if they were to resemble Plato's philosopher-king. But Prospero has taken lifetime learning to an extreme. We do not know what sort of education he had, presumably the liberal arts (I. ii. 73).[13] Did Antonio receive the same?[14] There is no doubting Prospero's personal virtue, but his upbringing has encouraged a taste for mysterious studies and not for the everyday intricacies of governing. His brother, by contrast, has learned the truly Machiavellian method of using men's self-interests for the furthering of his own, and 'having the key of officer and office' has 'set all hearts i' th' state/To what tune pleas'd his ear' (I. ii. 83–5). King James deprecated the tyrannical distortion of the state to suit the monarch, but tried to do exactly that himself. Antonio, like Prospero, displays similarly unsuitable characteristics, albeit different ones: 'Good wombs have borne bad sons' (I. ii. 16). Prospero appears to have been 'trayned in the way of vertue' as Elyot recommended, had avoided the usual high-end lures of gluttony, avarice, lechery, swearing and gambling, but has developed the vice of excessive academic seclusion, 'dedicated/To closeness and the bettering of my mind', thus 'neglecting worldly ends' (I. ii. 89–90). Antonio has developed the sort of sibling envy typical of primogeniture and so common in Shakespeare's plays.

Elyot exhorts young men to 'lerne wisdom & fal nat [do not fall into sin]' and abide by Christian precepts of behaviour, for 'from god only procedeth all honour' and God 'shal examine your dedes & serch your thoughts'. Since no one man can know all that is happening in a realm, a king needs reliable deputies to act as his eyes, ears, hands and legs. The body image was often invoked. The nation was 'the body politic', the head was the monarch, the major organs the nobility, and the hands, legs and muscles were the labouring part of society. All had a job to do and if one part did not work properly the whole became less effective. Prospero has allowed his 'body' to be usurped by Antonio, but the play shows him to be reborn. Less than worthy as governor of Milan, now determined to force restoration, he is an authoritarian but basically loving father, and raises many questions about authority and rule. Orgel asserts that he is 'not the ideal ruler required by the harmonious vision that is so often summoned up in the play'.[15] By the final act he approaches that ideal.

The courtiers around Alonso reflect the court of James. Gonzalo is wise but garrulous and portentous. Adrian appears to be a dull pedant, Francisco a non-entity. Such subsidiary governors (courtiers, councillors/counsellors, etc.) should be men 'superiour in condition or haviour [and] vertue'. Elyot demands they have 'their owne reuenues certeine, wherby they have competent substance to lyve without taking rewardes: it is likely that they wyll not be so desirous of lucre'. This defence against bribery had disappeared by James's time. Jobbery, corruption and greed were standard at court as they appear to be in Milan. Two generations of luxurious living and extravagance left many high-end families financially embarrassed. An unseemly scrabble for lucrative posts, lobbying for monopolies and a readiness to accept bribes was one way to help recoup family fortunes. Another was a profitable marriage. In the sixteenth century, marriage for mainly monetary reasons stood at 20 per cent among titled families, rising to 34 per cent by 1660.[16] It would be unfair to judge either Prospero, Antonio or Alonso's courts by the limited evidence of the play, but the instinctive feeling is that they could not have been places of intellect and culture. Prospero was too inward-looking, too focused on developing his own knowledge, Antonio too concerned with the ready serviceability of his followers, Alonso too determined to have his own way – ignoring Gonzalo and Sebastian's advice against the Tunis–Naples marriage. Where we see Prospero's character most clearly is in his handling of his 'subject' family – Miranda, Ariel, Caliban and Ferdinand. He treats each differently, according to their relationship to his power, but the common feature is his dictatorial manner. He talks down to them all, adopts a high-handed tone, and threatens punishment at any sign of disobedience. He has, like God, ultimate control over them: Miranda is simply made to fall into a sleep when he wishes, Ariel is warned to obey or face reimprisonment in an oak, Caliban and Ferdinand are faced with cramps and bruising pinches if they do not work and behave. Though there is underlying affection for his daughter, his familiar spirit and his future son-in-law, it is rough love like his rough magic – stern, harsh, unbending, but not malign.

A King's View of His Office

Prospero's misrule, deposition and rebirth are contextualized by the real king's contribution to conduct literature on the role and nature of kingship. *Basilikon Doron* was structured as an advice book to his son, Henry, Prince of Wales. It is divided into three books: 'Of a King's Christian Duty towards God', 'Of a King's Duty in His Office', and 'Of a King's Behaviour in Indifferent Things' ('indifferent' meaning matters relating to leisure time). The first section, about a king's duty to follow the tenets of Christianity, strongly establishes the idea of a king as God's representative. This becomes a running motif throughout. Many ideas parallel Elyot and there are verbal echoes of the earlier work. Marginal notes indicate how much the book owes to Plato's *Republic* and Cicero's seminal *De Officiis*, the common source for books on the perpetual need to remind the governing ranks what their function in society was.

The key interests of *Basilikon Doron* in relation to *The Tempest* are threefold: 1. establishing the criteria for measuring Prospero against the idealized monarch presented, 2. as an ironic reflection of the discrepancy between James's theory and practice, 3. as a topical-satirical mirror reflecting how the Jacobean court failed to live up to its monarch's precepts. The play's lightness and relative brevity mean that these criteria are less prominent than in plays like *King Lear* and *Measure for Measure*, but the characters' conduct and the portrait of humanity emerging reflect some of the critical remarks made by James.

The book begins with an abstract of the 'Argument' in sonnet form:

> GOD giues not Kings the stile of Gods in vaine,
> For on his throne his sceptre doe they swey:
> And as their subjects ought them to obey,
> So Kings should feare and serue their God againe.
> If then ye would enjoy a happy raigne,
> Obserue the statutes of your heauenly King,

And from his Law, make all your Lawes to spring:
Since his Lieutenant here ye should remaine,
Reward the iust, be steadfast, true, and plaine,
Represse the proud, maintaining aye the right,
Walk always so, as euer in his sight,
Who guards the godly, plaguing the prophane:
And so ye shall in Princely vertue shine,
Resembling right your mightie King Diuine.

Overlapping the belief that kingship was divinely sanctioned with the image of God's 'lieutenant here', the king almost becomes divine. Few Jacobeans questioned that rule should be monarchical or doubted that the continuing English system should have a one-person government, but increasingly they questioned kingship's divinity, the relationship between ruler and ruled and what should be the limits to princely authority. It is often assumed Divine Right was universally accepted; it was and was not. The unthinking masses accepted that the king – a distant figure of power and awe to them – was like a god on Earth. Largely they were voiceless, but others spoke for traditional beliefs. Robert Filmer formalized these in *Patriarcha*. Written in the 1620s (published posthumously in1680), it summarizes the accumulated ideology of Divine Right. Filmer believes the model monarchical state is founded on the idea of familial patriarchy and asserts Adamic dominion established by God (in Genesis) as the origin of patriarchy and kingship. As fathers rule the domestic *polis*, so kings rule the state. Elizabeth's death foregrounded discussions increasingly focused on the complex concept of Divine Right and how kings should govern. The justificatory line of argument was that God made Adam lord of all creation, with dominion over his wife, family, and the fruits of the Earth. The male therefore had divine sanction for his rule and kings had similar incontrovertible, unopposable rule. Disagreement was a sin against God, against nature. Thus bulwarked against opposition, monarchy and patriarchy became firmly embedded in society and their power developed. Kings had absolute power over life and property, could have people executed or pardoned, declare war, make peace, levy taxes, regulate trade, charter markets, issue licenses for manufacture, legitimize bastards or send people to the Tower. Their will was law and the law bent to their will. Regal proclamations were made with the mantra 'Le roi le veult' (The king wills it). Laws were only passed if the king similarly authenticated them. He nominated government officers, bishops, judges and peers. His power was absolute, his favour vital. James declared of kings that 'even by God himself they are called gods'.[17] One might ask how he knew this. Prospero's sometimes snappy autocracy in personal relations (even when speaking without his magic mantle) and his power as a magician are theatrical versions of the aura and potency of a king who claims godlike supremacy.

The first book of *Basilikon Doron* opens with an orthodox declaration that immediately places Prospero in the wrong:

> He cannot bee thought worthie to rule and commaund others, that cannot rule [...] his owne proper affections and unreasonable appetites, so can he not be thought worthie to governe a Christian People [that] feareth not and loveth not the Divine Majestie. Neither can [...] his Government succeed well with him [...] as coming from a filthie spring, if his person be unsanctified. (1)

James stresses the need for kingly piety and a life lived according to the demands of Christianity (as an example to his court and people): virtue, self-control, respect for and obedience to scripture, conscience and faith ('the Golden Chaine that linketh the Faithfull Soule to Christ' [9]). The series of guiding precepts are as follows: 'Wrest not the World to your owne appetite' (4), 'The summe of the Law is the Tenne Commandements' (6), 'Wisely [...] discerne [...] betwixt the expres Commaundment and Will of God in his Word and the invention and ordinance of Man' (15), and 'Kythe [show] more by your deedes then by your wordes the love of Vertue and hatred of Vice' (16). Prospero should have acted as a role model for his people through his personal virtue, but, forever buried among his books, he was not visible enough to be effective in that respect. Public profile built through public appearance was an important aspect of Elizabeth's image, but James (and Prospero) failed to project theirs.[18]

The second book, 'A King's Duty in His Office', links the lesson of being a good Christian to the prince's second calling: being a good king. This office is discharged through 'justice and equitie [fairness]', achieved by 'establishing and executing good lawes' and 'by your behaviour in your own person, and with your servants, to teach your people by your example: for people are naturally inclined to counterfaite (like Apes) their Princes manners' (17–18). Miranda talking to Caliban is as authoritarian as her father, adopting a superior tone copying his abusive epithets ('abhorred slave', 'savage', 'brutish', 'thy vile race' [I. ii. 353, 357, 359, 360]). Both have an attitude of 'I command, you obey' common to the 'better sort'.

To James a true king is 'ordained for his people', while a tyrant 'thinketh his people ordained for him, a pray to his passions and inordinate appetites' (18). A good king 'employeth all his studie and paines, to procure and maintaine [...] the well-fare and peace of his people [...] as their naturall father and kindly maister [...], subjecting his owne private affections and appetites to the weale and standing of his subjects' (18–19). Prospero is a father and sometimes kindly to his 'family' on the island, but in Milan he was a prey to his passions, failing to look after the 'weale and standing' of his subjects. He was not a tyrant (and Renaissance Italian history provided plenty of examples) but was simply disengaged from his role.

James warns that new laws are always needed to deal with 'new rising corruptions' (20) and that 'a Parliament is the honourablest and highest judgement [...] as being the Kings heade Courte' (21). He repeatedly called Parliament when he needed money but regularly left the country in the charge of his Privy Council while he gallivanted off hunting for days on end. Of Parliament he once told an ambassador, 'I am surprised that my ancestors should ever have permitted such an institution to come into existence.'[19] James did not deal with the old or new corruptions that surrounded him, did not settle the country 'by the severitie of justice' (22), but left in place the endemic institutional corruption. He did not 'embrace the quarrel of the poore and distressed' (26). Neither did he live up to the precept that you should 'governe your subjects, by knowing what vices they are naturally most inclined to, as a good Physician' (27).

It is easy to see why such demanding duties as James outlined did not appeal to Prospero's bookish preferences. In a sense Antonio was God's punitive-curative instrument physicking Prospero's 'ailment'. The Prospero we see is more circumspect, more alert to the deviousness of people. Both fictional and real ruler bear responsibility for their failure to deal with the social necessities of their states. It is probable James simply found the English situation too complex and too deeply ingrained, gave up trying to reform either court or country in line with *Basilikon* and, hypnotized by the immense disposable income the English crown gave him, stopped bothering to try to be a good king and just enjoyed the ritual, the status and the luxury. James regarded England 'like a man that hath been wandering in the wilderness for forty years and hath at last come within sight of the Land of Promise'.[20] The failure to see that privilege, power and luxury come with responsibilities would lead James's son into civil war. Prospero claims that he was saved from murder by the love his people bore him. As the account of his past is mediated through him alone we cannot definitively judge. He admits to a degree of culpability for the consequences of leaving government to Antonio, but also implies that his brother betrayed not only the legitimate ruler but also the state in exchanging its freedom from fealty to Naples in return for military assistance in taking over the city. Dante condemned to Nether Hell those who betrayed kindred and state.

James never got to grips with any of the underlying social problems, seeming to let the nobility act as they pleased, despite his admonitions in

Basilikon about repressing pride and supporting the poor. The Scottish and English nobility were similar; 'although second in ranke, yet over-farre first in greatnes and power, either to do good or evill', with a 'fectlesse arrogant conceit of their greatnes and power', tending 'to thrall, by oppression, the meaner sort, [they] maintaine their servants and dependers in any wrong' and run to the law 'for any displeasure' (33). James advises taming arrogant nobles; a governor must 'teache' them 'to keepe [the] lawes as precisely as the meanest' (34). Echoing Elyot he advises, 'Acquaint your selfe […] with all the honest men of your Barrones and Gentlemen' (34) for 'vertue followeth oftest noble blood' (35) and such men 'must be your armes and executers of your lawes' (35). This expresses the common belief that the nobility are born innately virtuous. True for Miranda, Gonzalo and Ferdinand, but clearly not for Sebastian or Antonio. This view, promulgated by the nobility, ignores both Original Sin (the common belief that all men are born with a sinful tendency) and the daily evidence of aristo-gentry misconduct.

James's recommendation to 'bee well acquainted with the nature and humours of all your subjects' and 'once in the yeare […] visit the principall parts of the country' (40) was not something he did and clearly Prospero had no 'meet and greet the people' policy or popular revolt would have opposed his removal. After reading Polydore Vergil's *Anglica Historia*[21] James agrees that a king's actions determined his country's fate. The image of a 'filthie spring' polluting the stream (a ruler's corruption corrupting the country) occurs frequently in contemporary drama.[22] Prospero, though not personally corrupt, has corrupted good government by being disengaged, allowing temptation to lure both his brother and his court. The gap between precept and practice is made wider and more ironic in James's discussion of a prince and his court as exemplars:

> It is not enough to a good King, by the sceptre of good lawes well excute to governe, and by force of armes to protect his people; if he joyne not therewith his virtuous life in his owne person, and in the person of his Court and companie: by good example alluring his subjects to the love of vertue, and hatred of vice. […] All people are naturally inclined to followe their Princes example […] let your owne life be a law-book and a mirrour to your people. (45)

This was to be achieved 'in the governement of your Court and followers' and

> in having your minde decked and enriched so with all virtuous qualities, that there-with ye may worthilie rule your people. For it is not enough that yr [sic] have and retaine […] within your selfe never

so many good qualities and virtues, except ye imploy them, and set them on worke, for the weale of them that are committed to your charge. (45)

Prospero has 'decked and enriched' his mind but not ruled worthily. Care was crucial when appointing public officers who had responsibility for 'the weale of your people' (50). They should be men 'of knowne wisdome, honestie, and good conference [...], free of all factions and partialities: but specially free of that filthy vice of Flattery, the pest of all Princes' (51). We see little of Alonso's court in action and learn less of Antonio's or Prospero's. The Neapolitans seem loyal enough to be concerned for the king but self-effacing (perhaps cowed). Antonio suggests they would quietly accept Sebastian's takeover (II. i. 283–5). The Milanese courtiers were readily bought off by Antonio. James recommends: 'Commaund a hartly and brotherly love among them that serve you. [...] Maintaine peace in your Court, banish envie, cherish modestie, banish deboshed insolence, foster humility, and represse pride' (53–4). Brotherly love, modesty, banished insolence, repressed pride – the opposite of what we see in *The Tempest*.

As regards personal kingly virtues, James echoes many of Elyot's recommendations. Prospero may be measured against these qualities. A prince should follow the four cardinal virtues with 'temperance, Queene of all the rest' (62). The synonym for temperance used by both Elyot and James is 'moderation'. A king needs the quality of 'wise moderation [...] first commanding your selfe [...] in all your affections and passions, [...] even in your most virtuous actions, [so you] make ever moderation to bee the chief ruler' (63). If civility, education and cultured behaviour are to be part of social–civic interaction, moderation is vital in assisting the repression of those aspects of man's nature that are disruptive to the moral profile of a state. Prospero was temperate and kindly in his early interaction with Caliban, but nature was too strong, the beast inveterate and Prospero's intervention too late. Gratitude and affection were not strong enough to dowse the sexual instinct or to mollify resentment at having what Caliban regards as his right to the island appropriated. After temperance comes justice: 'the greatest vertue, that properly belongeth to a Kings office' (63). 'Use Justice [...] with such moderation as it turne not in Tyrannie' (63).[23] Prospero's behaviour looks like tyranny – peremptory, overly strict and inflexible. There is some degree of this with Miranda and Ariel, but much with Caliban for he is the greater threat. In this Prospero resembles Elizabeth I. Shakespeare had recently explored 'what difference is betwixt extreame tyrannie [...] and extreame slacknesse of punishment' (64–5) – the former in *King Lear*, the latter through Duke Vincentio in *Measure for Measure*. Prospero, initially soft in his approach, is now overcompensating; his apprenticeship in governance is incomplete. He has yet to learn that mercy and forgiveness may achieve much, though it is to be doubted if Caliban would ever, could ever, respond to what he would regard as weakness. The audience, learning of his attempt to rape Miranda and his brash lack of repentance, might agree that Prospero's harshness with his slave is justified.

> O ho, O ho! would 't had been done!
> Thou didst prevent me. I had peopled else
> This isle with Calibans. (I. ii. 351–3)

Orthodox paternalist belief favoured firm authoritarianism. James specifies 'Clemencie, Magnanimitie, Liberalitie, Constancie, Humilitie, and all other Princely vertues' (64) as essential. Clemency (mercy) should not, however, be shown without signs of repentance. Another recommendation (ignored by James himself) is the encouragement to 'haunt your Sessions [court hearings], and spie carefullie their proceedings' (67). He advocates 'reading of authenticke histories and Chronicles […], applying the by-past things to the present estate' (69), yet he learned nothing from history, seeming swamped by the complexity of English society's problems and the immoveable corruption of a court and government he could never fully control.

The Tempest was perhaps chosen for performance at Whitehall as an entertaining, light-hearted romance. In the event it is an embarrassing exposure of his and the court's failure to live up to his principles by representing venal courtiers. The second book of *Basilikon Doron* finishes with a series of pertinent precepts: 'Embrace true Magnanimitie […], thinking your offender not worthie your wrath, empyring over your owne passion, and triumphing in the commanding your selfe to forgive' (71). James implores the reader to 'foster true Humility […] banishing pride' (71) (relevant to Antonio and Sebastian), and warns, 'Beginne not, like the young Lords and Lairds, your first warres upon your Mother […]. O invert not the order of nature, by judging your superiours' (72). *The Tempest* begins with nature's order in turmoil – reflecting the deviance of Sycorax, Prospero's flaw and Antonio's sin. Nature is perverted/inverted, the world turned upside down, with the jester and butler envisaging themselves in power and the governors governed as they wander distracted, controlled by forces they cannot see. Most crucially, James concludes with an admonition to 'exercise true Wisedome; in discerning wisely betwixt true and false reports' (74), reminiscent of Montaigne's essay 'On the Vanity of Words'. Prospero's court was subverted by misuse of words and his inability to read the signs. He was the victim of the flattering ploys of rhetoric as Antonio won over the court. Montaigne deplored the art of fine speaking, 'deceiving not our eyes but our judgement, bastardizing and corrupting things in their very essence' so that feelings are 'inflated with rich and magnificent words'.[24] James's final dictum resonates with the ironies of his failings and Prospero's:

> Consider that God is the author of all vertue, having imprinted in men's mindes by the very light of nature, the love of all morall virtues. [...] Preasse then to shine as farre before your people, in all vertue and honestie; as in greatnesse of ranke [...] as by their hearing of your lawes, both their eyes and their eares, may leade [...] them to the love of vertue, and hatred of vice. (75)

Prospero signally failed to lead, teach or guide his people.

Prospero and King James

Prospero is not a fictionalized representation of James I. Some may see Prospero's marriage-themed masque and other masque-like features as decidedly linking the play to the court and therefore turning Prospero into a representation of James. One was too detached, the other all too interfering. However, an exploration of the consequences of neglecting absolute power's responsibilities, contrasted with autocracy maladministered by erratic whims and fancies, nevertheless throws up subtle similarities for the audience to identify. Prospero's failings are never specifically or definitively allied to James's. Prospero's ruling passion is for learning, James's was for hunting (though he wrote books and prided himself on his intellectual superiority). Overt identification of fictional ruler with the real ruler watching the play would not be allowed. All plays were licensed by the Revels Office and registered at the Stationers' Office only once the government officials were sure the work contained nothing treasonable or heretical. The definition of treason was elastically expanded to mean any criticism of the monarch. Direct representation of or critical reference to a reigning monarch was prohibited and would be removed from the script. The author could face imprisonment, and James had already shown a readiness to do that.[25] A marginal note in *Basilikon Doron* ('Witnesse the experience of the late house of Gowrie' [47]) alludes to the 1600 plot by the Earl of Gowrie to kidnap James.[26] In 1604 the King's Men rehearsed a new play, *The Tragedy of the Gowrie*, for the court Christmas celebrations. Politically sensitive, it necessitated an actor playing the king, and represented an incident from his life. The play was suppressed.[27] Shakespeare, however, knew how to cloak his concerns by indirection, smuggling in themes and presenting them in such a way as to not appear overtly critical of particular persons. As one of the leading King's Men he could ill afford to upset his employer. Gowrie had planned to kill the king, whereas Antonio saw how politically unwise that would be. Other political plays about misrule of the state, but less sensitive because they were not blatantly personal, were *Measure for Measure* (performed at court on 26 December 1604) and *King Lear* (performed at court on 26 December 1606). Satire of flawed leadership and the corrupt ruling classes is evident in all the last plays: *Measure* is set in Vienna, *Lear* in pagan times, *Macbeth* in the relatively recent past (but showing the restoration of a legitimate line from which James was descended), *Antony and Cleopatra* in the Roman era, *Timon of Athens* in Athens, *Coriolanus* in Rome, *Cymbeline* in pre-Christian Britain, *The Winter's Tale* in Sicily and Bohemia, and *The Tempest* on a Mediterranean island. Whatever the locational indirection or shift in historical period, the themes were resonantly contemporary.

At the same time, Prospero *is* James, but so obliquely as to be impossible for government censors to pin down definitively. Any ruler onstage automatically invited mental comparison by the audience. The critique of styles of rule aims at provoking thought and a possible adjustment of values. It effects this indirectly. Italian background, Mediterranean island, a master magician – nothing treasonable there. But there is enough reference to rulers and courts to make his audience think about current court behaviour. Shakespeare's defence could be: 'If you think I am talking about today or anyone particular you have seen parallels I didn't intend.'

James looked a very promising replacement as ruler of England: experienced as king of Scotland, something of a philosopher-king, author of books on witchcraft and smoking in addition to two kingship studies. *The True Law of Free Monarchies* (1598) gives a clear statement of his belief in Divine Right absolutism, but its subtitle 'Or the Reciprocal and Mutual Duty Betwixt a Free King and His Natural Subjects' suggests belief too in rule involving a contract between king and people. There is an unresolved contradiction here. A contractual relationship suggests that the two sides agree to organize government through discussion and compromise, and that one (the king) acts as the public voice for his subjects. James's actual style of rule, once in power, betrayed him as a wilful absolutist. *The True Law* (1598) demonstrated (illogically and by closed arguments) that kings derived power from God, that their authority was 'the true pattern of divinity' and, like God's, kingly authority was part of the laws of nature and the customs of the realm. Some already supported the contract idea, tying people and ruler together in a liaison of mutual responsibilities and authority. James's practice took less notice of the customs of his realm than of his own will and needs. Quoting the Book of Samuel he repeated the idea that all subjects' property was the king's to use as he chose. This was not well received by the Commons, whom he lectured on the subject, for they were all men of property. The great obstacle was the traditional claim that as God's deputy no one could judge him but God. Putting him above the law, blocking any suggestion that he could ever be judged by his people, diametrically opposed his one-time tutor George Buchanan. Buchanan's *De Jure Regni apud Scotos Dialogus* (*Dialogue on the Rule of Kings in Scotland*, 1579) made an important contribution to the contractarian debate, proposing that royal power originates from the agreement of the people, that kings hold power only as long as they conform to the terms by which power was given them by the people, and that a people may resist, depose and punish a king who breaks his contract by becoming tyrannical.[28] More and more voices questioned the manner of kingship as exercised by Elizabeth and James.[29] James's belief in his divine mission was well established by his accession and endorsed by the fawning verses, flattering speeches and obsequious courtiers that oozed around his arrival in London and his coronation. During his 1604 procession through the city he received an address at the Fenchurch Street gate in which a character, Theosophia (Divine Wisdom), announced 'Per me reges regnant' (By me do all kings govern).[30] It would not be long before people would doubt James's will was identical to God's. Prospero behaves like God throughout the play, manipulating like Providence, gathering and disposing. But this is a necessary fiction, a role he needs to play, to achieve his restoration and execute his plan of healing the past and securing the future. The man of the final act is different from the waspish master-father of Act I. His softer, gentler manner suggests he will be an affectionate father figure to his people once reinstated.

On ascending the throne James promised he would act 'like a good physician'. He immediately set up the Hampton Court Conference to deal with the 'millenary petition' he had been given coming south, a plea from Puritan-minded ministers for more tolerance of church reform. The conference looked promising, but it was a blind. James listened without ever intending to make any concessions. The philosopher-king persona was a mask only. The real James wanted his way and was fairly uninterested in debate, preferring to hector and lecture. He disappointed Catholics hoping for toleration, making clear he intended, like Elizabeth, not to permit two forms of faith in his kingdom. He also promised to consider the supplication made by poor petitioners against Cecil's and other landowners' increasing enclosure of common lands, fobbed them all off with promises to consider their cases, then did nothing once installed in Whitehall.

The master magician, while not a fictionalization of the king, shares some similarities with him. Inevitably comparison with the incumbent monarch will be made. This is particularly so with a personality like James.

Inviting identification with Prospero are his bullying manner, determination to have his own way on matters ranging from the highly political or religious to the most trivially personal and his conviction that he was always right because 1. he was more learned than anyone else, and 2. because he was a god on Earth. The inclination to academic reclusiveness is seen as a flaw in a ruler if it interferes with the demands of government. James was prone to fixations that distracted him from his administrative duties. His academic commitment to polemic writing did not particularly divert his energies, but he did have an intellectual snobbery that revelled in displaying his knowledge. This particularly related to his tendency to lecture on doctrinal matters and give mandatory directions to his overly compliant bishops. James also pressurized his leading judges, especially when they upheld appeals against the High Commission of the Church. The need to always be right suggests a sense of insecurity possibly resulting from his disjointed family life in his formative years.

Chapter 6

PATRIARCHY, FAMILY AUTHORITY AND GENDER RELATIONSHIPS[1]

Yet will not I forget what I should be
And what I am, a husband: in that name
Is hid divinity. (*'Tis Pity She's a Whore*, IV. iii. 135–7)

In drama, as in life, falling in love, courtship, marriage, married life and family life are all features of the complex of relationships at the heart of existence. Gender relationships are the common factor and gender relationships are influenced by the sometimes tense interactions between the sexes. The extent of patriarchy within the characters' families and the degree to which patriarchy will influence newly forged families are an integral part of the theatrical ambience. In drama, gender conflict – the 'sex war' – is more theatrically exciting if it is heightened by disagreements, mistakes, paternal pressure and filial opposition. Sex, money, true love and hidden motives are all part of the mix. Real-life gender relationships are similarly full of ambiguities, inconsistencies, prejudices, agendas, hidden motives and lies – from both sides. Amid the tenderness is jealousy, suspicion and a constant struggle for one or the other to establish their will. Each can be as devious as the other; each has internalized stereotypical views of the other. Fiction reflects this tangle, offers positives and negatives and delights in presenting stereotypes – lovelorn couples, intransigent fathers, lascivious widows, heiress-hunting rakes and title-seeking gold diggers. The Jacobean context is full of ingrained misogyny and female distrust of men, with predation and cunning by both sexes. Mixed in are some more enlightened views and, despite the suspicions and tensions, there is also love. Men and women seem locked in a love–hate struggle, what Beatrice (*Much Ado About Nothing*) calls a 'merry war'. A person of the opposite sex can bring the greatest joy or the deepest misery, passing through all the positives and negatives in between. Amid the ebb and flow of feelings within relationships, two features remain constant in the Jacobean context: theoretically men ruled and in practice women often subverted male domination. Custom, doctrine and law made husbands/fathers heads of families. God ruled creation, kings ruled nations and fathers ruled the home. God punished sin, kings punished earthly crime, and men could beat their wife, children and servants. Custom recommended moderation in corporal punishment, advocating its avoidance if possible, but its support in law meant it could happen. Beating causing bodily harm was not allowed. No doubt there were abusive and violent men who caused serious injury, but they were protected by an all-male legal system. Men had few civil rights. Women had even less. A wife/daughter was in a sense the property of the husband/ father. A husband/father was an authoritarian figure whose word was law and the law supported men. St Paul authorized male dominance in the New Testament, *the* primary conduct book: 'Wives, submit yourselves unto your own husbands, as unto the Lord. For the husband is the head of the wife, even as Christ is the head of the church.'[2] Theoretically, husbands were dominant, wives supposedly subordinate in all things – in legal status, physical strength, intelligence and virtue.

Patriarchy originates in Genesis. God makes man first, gives Adam dominion over all animals, then makes Eve out of Adam's rib and gives him rule over her. She is designated 'an help meet' (Genesis 2:18) – a companion and assistant, a partner but not an equal. Adam, tempted by Eve to eat the apple, is upbraided by God for listening to his wife and acting according to her encouragement rather than God's command against eating the forbidden fruit. This emblematizes the central complexity; man is too easily tempted by woman, women have verbal and physical means of persuading; nagging, tears, alluring, promising or prohibiting sexual favours. The story of the Fall, written by men, endorsing male superiority and rule, reflects the hierarchy of the chain of creation, establishes the female as moral danger, reflects how society was organized, and was re-enforced over centuries by a misogynistic Catholic Church deeply suspicious of women. Such views were ingrained in male thinking. To the fallen Eve God says: 'I will greatly multiply thy sorrow [...]. In sorrow thou shalt bring forth children: and thy desire shall be to thy husband, and he shall rule over thee.'[3] Thus the pains of childbirth are annexed as punishment for woman's sinfulness and misogyny given divine authority. The seventeenth century saw female inferiority as pre-dating the Fall. Made after Adam, Eve was always secondary, so were all women. The poet-satirist George Wither summed this up: 'The woman for the man was made/And not the man for her.'[4]

James I, advising his son about marriage, quoted Genesis 2:23 (where Adam claims Eve is 'bone of my bone, and flesh of my flesh'), commenting that the institution is 'the greatest earthly felicite or miserie, that can come to a man, according as it pleaseth God to blesse or cursse the same'.[5] His advice is largely orthodox. He tells Henry to 'marrie one [...] of your own Religion; her ranke and other qualities being agreeable to your estate'.[6] (In *The Tempest*, Ferdinand is instinctively drawn to Miranda's beauty and grace of mind without knowing she is of his rank.) James is aware of the partnership aspect of marriage but it is patriarchally slanted:

> Treate her as your owne flesh, commaund her as her Lord, cherish her as your helper, rule her as your pupil, and please her in all things reasonable [...] Ye are the head, as she is your body: [...] your office to commaund, [...] hers to obey; but yet with such a sweete harmonie, as shee should be as readie to obey, as yee to commaunde [...] suffer her never to medle with the politick government of the common-weale, but hold her at the Oeconomick rule of the house; [...] yet all to be subject to your direction: keepe carefullie good and chaste companie about her; for women are the frailest sexe.[7]

Publicly, it was a man's world. Regardless of theory, whatever the biblical and legal support, the reality varied greatly. In defining gender roles and attitudes it is always important to remember, whatever the stereotypes, in practice matters could be different. Men could be liberal and sympathetic and most women subverted patriarchy in many ways and in a variety of arenas. When their lives are restricted some people give way and accept it, others evade limitations by whatever means they can.

The long-established medieval position on women persisted, but there had been changes. Orthodoxy saw women as the origin of sin, the source of temptation, taking its authority from the Bible. Paul, particularly influential in matters of gender, told wives to submit to their husbands and keep silent in church (Colossians 3:18). In I Timothy (2:8–12) he wrote: 'I will therefore that the men pray [...]. Let the women learn in silence with all subjection. I permit not a woman to teach, neither to usurp authority over the man, but to be in silence.' The Bible's good women, the Virgin Mary and the huge array of female saints, were outweighed by evil women in scripture, in history and in the diatribes of the church fathers.[8] Biased selection of biased texts built up formidable prejudice against the sex. Tertullian (AD c. 160–c. 225) saw women as 'the devil's gateway'.[9] St John Chrysostom (AD c. 347–407) exclaimed: 'How often do we, from beholding a woman, suffer a thousand evils; [...] entertaining an inordinate desire, and experiencing anguish for many days [...]. The beauty of woman is the greatest snare.'[10] Clement of Alexandria (AD c. 150–c. 215), went further: 'Every woman should be ashamed that she is a woman' for they are 'the confusion of men, an insatiable animal […], an eternal ruin'.[11] Male mistrust of female sexuality, chiefly originating from male clerics, underlies much of the patriarchal system. It was a factor in the intermittent waves of witch trials and executions. The *Malleus Maleficarum* (*The Hammer of Witches*, 1496) declared, 'All witchcraft comes from carnal lust, which in women is insatiable.'[12] Women are commonly accused of sex with the Devil in accounts of witches' covens and other black mass rituals.

A woman was expected to be a housekeeper and largely to keep to the house. In rural areas women helped in the fields (particularly at harvest time), but many of their tasks were home based: cooking, feeding poultry, tending vegetable gardens, cleaning and making clothes. A shopkeeper's wife or daughter might help behind the counter, but saleable products (cooked foods, clothes, crafted items, etc.) were made by men (apprentices, journeymen and masters) and shop assistants were mostly men. Women were barred from the professions, public life and higher education. The standard view was that women were intellectually feeble, unreliable, irrational, shrewish, gossips unable to keep a secret, particularly susceptible to pride, vanity and lust, bad tempered, endlessly demanding, never satisfied and if given rein would monopolize any public/social meeting. They had to be protected from male sexual predation and from their own lustful inclinations. A common image in medieval comic writing was that while the man worked and the servants kept the house, the wife gossiped with friends, entertained her lover or gallivanted around wasting money shopping. This view persisted. It was generally believed women were overemotional and easily overheated sexually. Belief in the insatiability of the female sex drive reflected male insecurity and a man's uncertainty whether the child he was bringing up was indeed his own – fears related to questions of inheritance and keeping the family bloodline pure. It explains the obsession with the chastity of daughters and wives. A tainted daughter shamed the family, had little value in the marriage market and remained a drain on family finances. A wife who was 'loose i'the hilts'[13] degraded the husband's public reputation and honour, wounded his personal esteem, cast doubt on his children's legitimacy, and made him the butt of jokes about cuckolds and horns. Proverbs 12:4 declared: 'A virtuous woman is a crown to her husband: but she that maketh ashamed is as rottenness in his bones.'

Patriarchy's dominance explains why so many men had such low opinions of women, treating them unsympathetically and as sex objects. Such views are voiced frequently among the rakish male characters crowding Elizabethan-Jacobean comedies, though Hamlet and Iago are misogynistic too. This loose-living, loose-tongued, bawdy, joking brotherhood stretches from Lucio (*Measure for Measure*, 1604) through Willmore (Aphra Behn's *The Rover*, 1677) to innumerable libertines in later drama and novels. A counterbalancing philosophy offers the *gentils domna* (gentle lady) of Courtly

Love, the beautiful but virtuous woman whose example civilizes brutish men. Her self-effacing quietness is courtesy and confidence, not the silence of submission. Miranda has something of this quality as opposed to some of the negative women alluded to in *The Tempest*. With her father she is lively but deferentially obedient. With Ferdinand she is a new spirit – open, intelligent, alert, talkative and playful, with the liveliness of a young girl falling in love for the first time. While Ferdinand displays some features of the adoring lover of Courtly Love (smitten at first sight, undergoing tests of hardship for his lady, idolizing her, etc.), Miranda reciprocates his feelings and expresses them much more forwardly than the distant ladies of medieval lyric and romance.[14]

The 1571 *Second Book of Homilies* (XVIII, 'Of the State of Matrimony') declared woman 'a weak creature, prone to all weak affections and dispositions of the mind'. This indicates the Anglican Church was essentially little different from Rome. Greater respect for women, though still wary, emerged among the Puritans, who demanded abstinence from both men and women, but Puritanism, though spreading, was still a minority sect. Theatre commonly reverted to stock types of female for their comic or dramatic value. The garrulous nurse in *Romeo and Juliet*, the witty but overwhelming Beatrice in *Much Ado About Nothing*, and the scheming unscrupulousness of Lady Macbeth all follow stereotypical lines. Another stock character from drama, the widow – either rampantly free or easily victimized – reflects the standard view of predatory female sexuality and echoes anxieties about overhasty second marriage for women. Dynastic and financial concerns are involved. Family fortunes could quickly be lost to a predatory second husband and the children of the first union disposed of or simply sent to a faraway estate and neglected. The widow, whether truly loving, merely lascivious or as latent virago (as in *The Taming of the Shrew*) was not just a comic figure. *Hamlet* and *The Duchess of Malfi* present tragic examples of the difficulties second marriage could bring. In practice second marriages were common among both sexes and all classes. Moralists admitted that humankind was inordinately lustful, but since most were male they tended to be more tolerant of male libidinousness and more critical of female failings. Neither the wildfire spread of syphilis nor the widespread ecclesiastical condemnation of intercourse outside marriage as a Deadly Sin for both sexes curbed the natural lustfulness of either. With the blatant hypocrisy, chauvinism and prejudice that each sex brings to stereotyping the other, there was, on the male side, a double standard in accepting young men fornicating indiscriminately and regarding possession of a mistress as a sign of manhood, while demanding chaste behaviour among their own female family members. This hypocrisy is summed up in the contemporary adage 'Untill everyone hath two or three bastards a peece, they esteeme him no man.'[15]

Shakespeare's early 'sex war' comedy *The Taming of the Shrew* (1593–94) presents the orthodox male view of husband–wife relationships.[16] Petruchio, eager to marry in order to refill his coffers (as many of both sexes did), tells the assembled wedding guests:

> I will be master of what is mine own.
> She is my goods, my chattels: she is my house,
> My household stuff, my field, my barn,
> My horse, my ox, my ass, my anything. (III. ii. 229–32)

At the end of the play Kate, supposedly defines the theoretically submissive role of the wife:

> Thy husband is thy lord, thy life, thy keeper,
> Thy head, thy sovereign – one that cares for thee,
> And for thy maintenance commits his body
> To painful labour both by sea and land,
> To watch the night in storms, the day in cold,
> Whilst thou li'st warm at home, secure and safe. (V. ii. 146–51)

She sees wifely 'love, fair looks, and true obedience' as a duty like that 'the subject owes the prince' and criticizes rebellious wives seeking 'rule, supremacy, and sway'. Is this sincere or has she, like women before and since, discovered she can get all she wants by appearing submissive while secretly gaining control of the household and of husband? This is the comic discrepancy inherent in the gender relationship. Man plays the master and to all intents and purposes is so publicly, while the woman pulls his strings behind the scenes.

Manipulation, deviousness, sheer bloody-mindedness and simple evil (their weapons of mass subversion in the sex war) were attributed to women in the social comedies of the 1600s. While female tenderness and sensitivity are acknowledged, misogyny is accurate in its definitions too. In Middleton's *A Mad World My Masters* a country gentleman, surreally named Penitent Brothel, admits the superior acumen of the courtesan Frank (Frances) Gullman and associates it with inventive, devious female resourcefulness:

> The wit of man wanes and decreases soon,
> But women's wit is ever at full moon. (III. ii. 159–60)

He later comments:

> When plots are e'en past hope and hang their head,
> Set with a woman's hand, they thrive and spread. (III. ii. 246–7)

The aptly named Gullman ('man fooler'),[17] lures into marriage Follywit, the heir of Sir Bounteous Plenty. Shakespeare's comic heroines (e.g., Beatrice, Rosalind, Viola and Portia) are similarly clever, inventive, independent and resourceful women. Their virtue prevents them intending or doing evil, but they are irrepressibly wilful. Lady Macbeth and Goneril and Regan in *King Lear* are prime examples of devious Shakespearian women with ruthless and destructive ambition.

In the real world theory and practice diverge and diversify into a variety of relationships. Every marriage was unique – some conform to the orthodox model, in some the woman ruled unopposed, in most a compromise was negotiated or appropriated. There were happy marriages, arranged or not. In the upper and middle ranks many men and women married for fiscal or dynastic reasons. This did not always make for easy relationships, but neither did it preclude love, companionship and happiness. A slow shift evolved marriage into a partnership of physical and spiritual companions. Lord Montagu advised his son, 'In your marriage looke after goodness rather than goodes.'[18] Traditionally men sought love and sexual relief outside marriage. This was the negative aspect of arranged marriages where there was no initial attraction and none developed afterwards. The Earl of Northumberland advised his son: 'As you must love, love a mistress for her flesh and a wife for her virtues.'[19] Some women took lovers (though less openly), others sublimated their emotional needs through running estates and raising children, while their husbands attended court or parliament, joined the army or spent their time in usual male activities – hunting, gambling, drinking, theatregoing, whoring, etc. Many marriages were based on separate lives, but many thrived on the love and respect that formed the new companionate marriage. Puritan pamphlet/sermon input to the marriage debate promoted the development of the helpmeet/companion element.[20]

A play marking the emergence of the strong, independent woman is Fletcher's *The Woman's Prize, or The Tamer Tamed* (1610). Appropriating Shakespeare's Petruchio, the shrew tamer, Fletcher has him tamed (or humanized) by his second wife, Maria, who outwits the standard chauvinistic male. No longer 'gentle' or 'tame', her 'new soul' is:

Made of a north wind, nothing but tempest,
And like a tempest shall it make all ruins
Till I have run my will out. (I. ii. 77–9)

Her sister advises her to abandon her plans and accept her expected sexual destiny. Maria is implacable:

To bed? No, Livia, there be comets yet hang
Prodigious over that yet. There is a fellow [Petruchio]

Must yet before I know that heat – ne'er start wench –
Be made a man, for yet he is a monster;
Here must his head be [...]. (I. ii. 101–5)

No stage direction indicates where she points – to herself (as his head), her breast (where his head must rest lovingly), or under her foot? Her transgressiveness expresses something of the rebalancing of the gender roles of the time. Her cousin Bianca contextualizes Maria's stand:

All the several wrongs
Done by imperious husbands to their wives
These thousand years and upwards strengthen thee!
Thou hast a brave cause. (I. ii. 122–5)

This hints at an aggressive, vengeful impulse, a man-hating deviousness emerging. Maria's apparent goal is equality in marriage, declaring:

[...] That childish woman
That lives a prisoner to her husband's pleasure
Has lost her making and becomes a beast
Created for his use, not fellowship. (I. ii. 137–40)

This play contributes to the lively late sixteenth-/early seventeenth-century debate about just what women were like and what their place in society should be. Opinion was mounting against arranged marriages forced for dynastic and material reasons (characteristic of royal and aristocratic unions) where there was no attraction or love. Arranged royal marriages were traditionally a façade only, sometimes fruitful, sometimes not, often becoming a union of separateness masked by ritual and splendour. Thomas Becon, in his *Golden Boke of Christen Matrimonie* (1542), describes couples trapped unhappily in arranged/forced marriages cursing 'their parents even unto the pit of hell for coupling them together'. Unhappy elite couples could more easily afford to live separate lives. Among the middling sort this was less possible. In these two ranks forced/arranged marriages occurred more frequently, but the men customarily spent much more time with other men in business or leisure. Evidence for marriage practices and experience of married life among the common sort is scanty, but both in drama and in documentary sources it is also clear that there were many loving and happy unions at all levels.[21]

Prospero has planned for his daughter and Alonso's son to bring peace between Naples and Milan and arranges their meeting. This could effect the subsuming of Milan into the kingdom of Naples after Prospero's and Alonso's deaths, but it secures his daughter's future. He does not, however, arrange their falling in love; this happens naturally with no indication in the dialogue or stage directions that any magic is used other than natural chemistry. Though he at will makes Miranda sleep and freezes Ferdinand in self-defence, their attraction is mutual and free. Before Prospero is fully convinced the young man is a worthy mate, Miranda (who has seen no other males than Caliban and her father) has already become enamoured of his looks. Prospero foresaw it, watches it with the satisfaction of a plan coming together, but the process is driven by their own instincts. Love at first sight is a recurrent romance/comedy device. Antipholus of Syracuse falls for Luciana (*The Comedy of Errors*), Romeo for Juliet, Rosalind for Orlando (*As You Like It*), Viola for Orsino and Olivia for Viola (*Twelfth Night*), and Florizel for Perdita (*The Winter's Tale*). Gender politics have no overt part in *The Tempest* though individual audience members may have approved or deprecated Prospero's or Miranda's conduct. Miranda (an inexperienced, 14-year-old only child) is subject to stern, orthodox patriarchy, but diverted by paternal love, romance and an arranged marriage which she wholeheartedly supports.[22]

Women were beginning to record their private lives in journals and letters, and their increased vocal presence in society and at court, combined with their increased presence in print, ratcheted up the gender discourse. In public drama, however, gender issues were mostly addressed through male dramatists. The growth in the practice of printing play texts for commercial sale helped broaden the audience for this perennial concern. But in privately circulated manuscripts and in occasional printed texts, women were emerging as authors and raising gender issues from female perspectives.[23] One such view is *The Memorandum of Martha Moulsworth, Widow* (1632), which offers a touching verse account of her life and three happy marriages. A loving father brought her up 'in godlie pietie' and 'in modest chearfullnes & sad sobrietie'. Unusually, for her sex and rank (rural gentry), she was taught Latin, but lamented, 'Two universities we have of men/O that we had but one of women then!' (lines 33–4).[24] Martha married at 21 (quite late), was widowed after five years, mourned a year, then remarried. Widowed again ten years later, she married a third time after nearly four years. Of this last relationship she writes:

> The third I tooke a lovely man, & kind
> such comlines in age we seldom find
> [...]
> was never man so Buxome to his wife
> with him I led an easie darlings life
> I had my will in house, in purse in Store
> what would a women old or yong have more? (Lines 57–68)

She declares she loved all her partners, was very happy with them and enjoyed domestic responsibility: 'I had my will in house, in purse in Store' (lines 67–8). She completes her autobiography with a neat and witty couplet in keeping with her sense of satisfaction in marriage:

> the Virgins life is gold, as Clarks us tell
> the Widowes silvar, I love silvar well. (Lines 109–10)

There is insufficient evidence to form a distinct pattern or profile showing how widespread such education for girls was or how common such happiness was in marriage.[25] Martha is a positive example of a provincial woman – her education makes her an exception. Reading, writing and enjoyment of literature was largely confined to small groups of gentlewomen housed with an aristocratic mistress whom they served. She is not unique, but the bulk of women (and men) had little learning. How much love they found within arranged unions is impossible to tell. Miranda, schooled by her father, who has a natural scholarly bent, is acute and articulate. She therefore has education and seems naturally courtly. Her self-selected marriage partner seems a similar type so they look, potentially, set for happiness.

Work, running the estate or living a life of pleasure was a man's life. A woman's focused on the family, along with overseeing the household economy (though she was responsible to her husband for expenditure in both areas). Traditionally women were thought more naturally inclined to be loving and nurturing, while many fathers were distant, even when at home. King James warned his son that when he had 'succession' (children) he should 'bee carefull for their virtuous education: love them as yee ought', but 'contayning them ever in a reverent love and feare of you'. As regards inheritance:

> Make your eldest sonne *Isaac*, leaving him all your kingdoms; and provide the rest with private possessions. Otherwaies by dividing your kingdoms, ye shall leave the seede of division and discorde among your posteritie: as befell to this Ile, by the division and assignment thereof, to the three sonnes of *Brutus*, *Locrine*, *Albanact*, and *Camber*.[26]

Some mothers too were distant (especially court ladies), so that noble offspring were often reared by nurses and maids. Fathers tended to be strict, concerned to discipline children to conform to society's expectations of their gender role and attitudes. Formality and ritual deference were more common among the elite. In their parents' presence children stood in silence, speaking only when spoken to. In very strict aristocratic families they knelt. Even a citizen's children asked father's permission and blessing before beginning any undertaking – a journey, going to university, leaving home to marry, leaving the table, going to bed, etc. Addressing father or mother could be very formal – using their title or calling them 'Sir' and 'Madam'. In Act I Scene ii, Miranda calls Prospero 'sir' six times, 'good sir' once, 'father' twice, 'my father' three times speaking of him to Ferdinand and 'my dearest father' in her opening speech. Even later when criticizing his treatment of Ferdinand she maintains the same formality mixed with affection. Similar formality could apply between husband and wife. That said, in many families there was affectionate informality. Prospero is noticeably tender, calling Miranda 'my dear one', 'my girl', 'dear', 'cherubin', 'dear heart', 'wench' and 'foolish wench'.

Miranda's submissiveness is suitable to a young girl untried in the ways of the world and dependent upon her father. Such humility, valued in men too, was not merely a device for keeping women quietly deferential. Cultured people prized highly knowing when to give your opinion and how to give it least offensively and most courteously. Humility was valued as a form of personal modesty. It was equally prized in men and was not merely a chauvinistic desire to keep women submissive. Talkative, gossipy adults were unacceptable whatever their sex. There are blabbermouth males in the works of Shakespeare and other dramatists, but at least since the rise of medieval misogyny there was a belief that, given their head, many women would talk ceaselessly. The terms gossip, flibbertigibbet, scold and shrew range through the types of more ready female verbalizing. If women stereotype men as talking too little, men stereotype women as talking too much. The implication is that female vocalization is silly, pointless, idle gossip. As the saying had it, 'Every ass loves to hear himself bray.' Or herself. Gratiano (*The Merchant of Venice*) and Lady Would-Be (*Volpone*) are a male and female example of the comic figure of the incessant chatterer who makes little sense. Benedick, fairly vocal himself, expresses frustration at Beatrice being 'possessed with a fury' (*Much Ado About Nothing*, I. i. 160), 'huddling jest upon jest' (II. i. 214), nominating her 'my Lady Tongue' (II. i. 240). At no point does Miranda display the aggressive verbal independence of some of Shakespeare's female characters. Yet she is not a broken-spirited creature and persists in her expressions of attraction to Ferdinand, although aware she is disobeying her father's teaching. Dusinberre asserts, 'A woman suffers continually from the impotence which is exceptional in a man.'[27] Shakespeare's impotent women are far outnumbered by his resourceful, independent ones, reflecting perhaps his perception that despite patriarchy, despite the public limitations of their horizons, women did achieve a deal more of their own way than might be assumed if theory and orthodoxy alone are considered.

Legal and biblical authority made man the head of the woman and the family. His wife's money and property became his, his claim to custody of the children took precedence and theoretically he had the final say in all things. In practice many different arrangements were negotiated by individual couples. Some women were independent, bossy termagants.[28] Some efficiently ran households with the power of decision over menus, furnishings, hiring and firing servants, the education of the younger children. Some were docile shadows. There was an immense range of different male familial profiles too, from the ultra-chauvinist father, through the liberal, kindly, affectionate, caring father, to the weak or indifferent non-entity.

There was considerable debate about how fathers should behave to their children and how best children should be brought up. Montaigne and Bacon have much to say on the subject (see Chapter 13, 'Sources'). Largely, fathers were stern, distant and formal, partly because high infant/teenage mortality discouraged too close and affectionate a relationship developing, partly because strict fathers were thought better teachers of respect and discipline than mothers, who were thought too lax.[29] Fathers reflected the loving sternness of God. Children were thought to be like wild creatures needing taming and training if they were to be self-disciplined in later life and cope with the customs and practices of a highly stratified, ritual conscious, traditionalist society. The traditional suspicions men had of female irrationality, unreliability and emotional instability transferred into their attitude towards a mother's relationships with her children. In elite families boys were removed from female control at age 7, breeched and put under a tutor until ready to be sent away to complete their education.

Affective family relations did exist as did companionate marriages. Not all was male chauvinism or female submission, not all marriages were perpetual conflict. Many widows were thought competent to inherit estates and businesses and managed them effectively. There were many more of these than one might think since men tended to marry later than women and die earlier. It was not unusual or unexpected for a woman to remarry. In business a widow commonly married one of the journeymen or a senior apprentice. A journeyman was a skilled worker who had completed his seven-year apprenticeship. Not yet master of his craft, he was sufficiently skilled and experienced for it to be a practical union keeping the business going and money coming in. Among elite families marriage and family relationships were often thought of not as loving support networks developing within a sheltered environment, but as units of child production that would enable the family title, status, money and property to be kept together and handed on. It is a chilling fact that one-third of marriages did not last longer than 15 years, many women dying in childbirth or old husbands predeceasing. Remarriage was common, often swiftly following the funeral. These dynastic concerns seem inhumanly disagreeable to modern minds, but in an age when death was a constantly imminent possibility such severe considerations were crucial at every level of society where property (however minor) was held. At stake might be the tenure of thousands of acres, a family's home, a place at court, a commercial enterprise or simply the hedging tools of a farm labourer and the lease on his cottage. Apart from biblical authority for patriarchy there were practical reasons for it. Among the aristo-gentry, remembering the violent precariousness of the Wars of the Roses, men bred large families hoping at least one male would survive. This required a wife who was fertile and would be based at home in order to rear the offspring. Stone puts it thus:

> Among the landed classes in pre-Reformation England [the] objectives of family planning were the continuity of the male line, the preservation intact of the inherited property, and the acquisition of further property or useful political alliances.[30]

Such objectives persisted in the seventeenth century.

Feminist historians and literary critics have drawn attention to the marginalized role and restricted potential of women throughout the ages.[31] This useful counterbalance to the male-dominated view of history and sociology has simultaneously overemphasized the negative aspects of male domination and underemphasized the forms of covert petticoat power. The behind-the-scenes and in-the-bedroom influence of women at court is an acknowledged but underexplored factor. Because women had no official political role, it has been assumed they had no power, yet literature shows their incitement of and complicity in tragic and comic plots and history is increasingly revealing the influence they wielded in political, social and personal arenas. The most material sign of male dominance was his appropriation of his wife's property and money to do with as he wished, though sometimes family wealth could be held combined and administered jointly. Where the husband was a cash-strapped, debt-ridden thriftless wastrel (whether eldest son or a younger) this led to the dowry being swallowed up, laying grounds for resentment and tension. Liberal and less chauvinist men often left their wife's money and property in her hands.[32] Less publicized was the jointure arranged by parents and lawyers. This was an agreed annuity payable to the wife from the husband's fortune if he predeceased her, and could represent a considerable sum if paid over a long period. Women heir hunters would unashamedly access a husband's wealth, title and status. Debts accrued by a wife were legally payable by the husband and extravagant female spending, a traditional feature of satire, is frequently referenced in Jacobean drama and particularly targeted at women of the better sort and citizens' wives. Materially and emotionally every arranged union had two potential victims.

Men too could be trapped unhappily in forced marriages. The patriarch keeping family property intact through primogeniture may himself have been forced into marriage with a wealthy but old, ugly or ill-tempered woman. Until younger offspring had been found appropriate partners they were an expense to keep in a style suitable to their status. Sons, always problematic, tended to drift into similarly cash-short homosocial groups at university or in London, unsupervised, uncivilized and antisocial. They were increasingly pushed into high-status professions – the church, law, government service, the army, etc. – but often dropped out. Many young high-status women remained unmarried but without a vocation, without the chance to work other than at relatively trivial domestic and social accomplishments (sewing, embroidery, music, etc.). Those who married had to be provided dowries.

While parental wishes, influenced by financial, hierarchical or political interests, were dominant in choosing a partner, increasingly the child's consent was sought. This approach was particularly evident in the wealthy upper middle ranks. If a child did not like and was not attracted to a possible partner that could end negotiations. In *'Tis Pity She's a Whore* a fellow citizen seeks Florio's daughter as wife for his booby fop of a nephew. Florio tells him:

> My care is how to match her to her liking:
> I would not have her marry wealth, but love;
> And if she like your nephew, let him have her. (I. iii. 10–12)

Ironically, this liberal approach is voiced while Annabella is in bed with her chosen lover – her brother.[33] Drama presents a mass of different conflicts over courtship and marriage because it offers excitement and more plot possibilities than demure agreement or immediate attraction. Largely, however, in real life, it seemed that parents commonly chose a suitor or bride when they saw there was already attraction. In the case of a candidate picked by the parents but unknown to the prospective bride/groom, proposed by the suitor/ bride's family or self-presented by a free bachelor, again the son/daughter's response was taken into account. But if a candidate was strongly preferred by the parents on material grounds and rejected by the son or daughter, then patriarchal weight (threats of disinheritance and other punishments) would be applied. Marriage without parental consent was illegal, putting the archetypal romantic lovers, Romeo and Juliet, outside the law. King Lear, in his anger, disposes of Cordelia to the lowest bidder without her say. Prospero, a more caring father, approves of the mutual attraction between his daughter and future son-in-law.

Though the odds might appear against it, there is evidence of loving marriages and happy families 'long before the eighteenth century'.[34] Studies show that 'patriarchal authority applied in theory to this period, but could be modified in practice, by illustrating the range of experiences of married couples in which much depended upon factors such as the personality and relative status of the husband and wife'.[35] More importantly, counterbalancing the idea of women being completely dominated: 'Far from being passive subordinates, some women developed strategies to modify or resist patriarchal authority, including marshalling support through friends, neighbours and kin to circumvent their putative subordination to their husbands.'[36]

Patriarchy and a Woman's Place

Deep-seated institutional misogyny persisted through the 1600s. Though the Catholic Church held no sway in England, its ideas had bitten deep into the male psyche, and suspicion of women was endemic in masculine thinking. The Church of Rome, systemically anti-female in its doctrines, saw women's secondary role as part of God's plan. The Church of England was more of the mind that men and women should respect one another, that husbands and wives should work in harmony, but was clear that ultimately the man was in charge. Women, as Eve's descendants, were thought more inclined to sin. Men too were sinners but a neat argument mitigated that 'though an husband in regard of evil qualities may carry the image of the devil, yet in regard to his place and office, he beareth the image of God'.[37]

No one statement or view can be universally true of the complexities of male–female relationships, but in general a woman's place was subordinate to the males within her family and social sphere. There were, of course, a number of strong-minded women who would not be dominated within their family or in any situation. Women did have some status: a mother had authority over her children (in the father's absence); a housewife had authority over her servants (in the master's absence); the wife of a guild master, a titled lady or a shop owner's wife was superior to anyone of an inferior station (male or female), but within her own rank was secondary to any adult male, even to a son of age if he had inherited from a dead father and was head of the family. Respect for her as a woman, as mother and as dowager (widow of a titled/ propertied man) would partially mitigate his authority. Women gained status through marriage, assuming the rank of their husband. Irrepressible women rose above all situations. It is clear in *King Lear* that the king's daughters are very much his property. As father and king he disposes of them as he sees fit. But once free of him, with his power diminished to a level where only affection might work in his favour, the two older daughters display a barbaric cruelty transgressing custom and civilized behaviour. In *The Tempest* Prospero's power, as father, ex-duke and magus, is great. His right to choose

Miranda's husband is not tested for she is happy to marry Ferdinand. Had she opposed her father, his love of her would have come into extreme tension with his political plan. Would his evident love for her have overborne his own wishes?

Women's subordination was part of an unfair hierarchical system within a social structure that designated a place for everyone and in which everyone (the monarch excluded) was subordinate to someone. Powerlessness increased as you descended the power pyramid. It was unjust but most of the social and legal structure was unfairly organized in favour of the rich over the poor and men over women.

In 1558, the year of Elizabeth I's succession, the most strident statement of female inferiority was made by the Scottish radical Protestant John Knox from his exile in Geneva:

> To promote a woman to bear rule, superiority, dominion or empire above any realm, nation or city is repugnant to nature, contumely to God, a thing most contrarious to his revealed will and approved ordinance, and finally it is the subversion of good order, of all equity and justice.[38]

Knox's views resonate with the fear that transgressing social, familial or gender order would herald anarchy and collapse. Even Montaigne, usually liberal and fair, expresses this orthodox view of females:

> Women should have no mastery over men save only the natural one of motherhood [...] It is dangerous to leave the superintendence of our succession to the judgement of our wives and to their choice between our sons, which over and over again is iniquitous and fantastic. For those unruly tastes and physical cravings which they experience during pregnancy are ever-present in their souls.[39]

This ignores the fact that people in restricted situations generally find ways of subverting the limitations put upon them and that some women have always tended to 1. oppose by a variety of means all attempts by males to repress them, and 2. achieve some independence for themselves by negotiation, by clandestine action or by default. Every relationship is different from every other. Some women failed to win any area of domination. Some ruled every area of family life, some a limited area. Some said 'Yes, dear', 'No, dear' and then secretly did what they wished. Some men could not be bothered about household matters or child rearing, so the wife/mother ruled by default. Some women gained rule of estates or businesses through their husband's decease, but largely Heaven's hierarchy persisted on Earth and religion backed it. Thus 'By marriage, the husband and wife became one person in law – and that person was the husband.'[40]

Just where women were placed in the day-to-day reality is problematic. The bulk of ordinary people were voiceless. Women provide even less evidence of their existence than men. Documents profiling actual relationships are scarce and differ between court and country and between the aristo-gentry and other ranks. The lower down the social scale the less material is available. The few remaining personal diaries or letters by women are held in archive, though probably more await discovery. It was a period in which few people committed personal feelings to paper. Cost of materials was one factor, but the culture was only slowly coming to accept that an individual's thoughts and feelings were of value. The various intersecting seventeenth-century controversies encouraged more people to put pen to paper. The 80 per cent male literacy rate in London effectively boosted this. Urban trading families needed literate heirs and dissenting groups began establishing their own small local schools. From the mid-seventeenth century Dissenting Academies provided excellent broad education, more liberal, practical and extensive than the limited classical studies of high-end families. There were many grammar schools and these often had endowments, bursaries and scholarships that enabled boys from poor families to gain formal education. Little formal schooling was given to girls, even from high-status families (apart from the royal family and a few cultured aristocratic households). Literacy and numeracy, taught at home, was often the only scope for girls. Individual tutors in individual households did provide more liberal studies and there were some institutions for girls set up by Puritans, but these were the exception, not the rule.

It was common (among Dissenters particularly) for Christians to make personal daily examination of their lives. In time this came to be written down in a spiritual journal and subsequently more material is available. The 1600s saw an increasing number of pamphlets (many by women) offering opinions on everything from politics to horticulture to horoscopes. By the Restoration (1660) there was a slightly higher proportion of female-to-male professional writers, reflecting some easing of male repressiveness, but as a demographic percentage figures for female writing are small. There are more questions than evidence to answer them. Did women write but not publish? Did women just not write much? Were they unable to access reading material that triggered their own writing? Was female literacy just too low to make a showing? Much female-authored fictional work circulated in manuscript among social networks like the court, London-based writers and literate and literary families and their friends. Prohibited from acting, women seem not to have written for the public stage until Aphra Behn.[41] Any assessment of women in the period 1600–1620 can largely only be reconstructed from male perspectives. The general picture seems to be that private individuals (male and female) were increasingly writing about their lives, opinions and personal struggles. This accelerated in the Civil War and afterwards. But much manuscript material remains locked away in scattered archives, public and private, awaiting analysis and publication.

The later Stuart period provides many spiritual autobiographies, but an interesting early example, giving insight into provincial life, comes from Lady Margaret Hoby's diary of 1599–1605.[42] A Yorkshire heiress, educated in a Puritan school for gentlewomen, run by the Countess of Huntingdon, she married three times, making alliances with high-profile court dynasties (the Devereux, Sidneys and Hobys). Her life was spent in Hackness near Scarborough, with a few visits to London. Her diary, the earliest known written by an English woman, records her local charity work, her running of the household and estate, and her domestic activities – managing servants, paying them, mundane activities like gardening, arranging the washing and ironing, preparing medicines, and her contacts with neighbours and estate tenants. It recounts her spiritual life – organizing household prayers and her personal devotions and reading – but does not delve into her inner feelings.

At every stage of life a woman was expected to be deferential, submissive and constantly aware of her different and separate expectations. Her infant education (if she received one) would be at home and limited to letters and figures, while her brothers attended school (or were home tutored) and then, once literate and numerate, moved on to Greek, Latin, mathematics, history and geography, followed by university. In the lower ranks a schooled boy might be apprenticed or simply join his father in the family business. A girl stayed at home and learned housecraft and needlework skills. Farmers' daughters joined the women in planting, tending animals, spinning, cooking and nursing younger siblings, while brothers ploughed, reaped, herded animals, made and used tools, went to market and met the world. Once of marriageable age, whatever her rank, she might be contracted to a man of her father's choosing if it was profitable to the family, or she might remain at home unmarried as general help (i.e., an unpaid servant). If lucky she might be sent away into service. While exposing her to innumerable risks, this could open up better prospects, allowing her to climb the ladder of service from housemaid to housekeeper. A prime fantasy was attracting her master's eldest son and marrying him. In practice parents reacted in horror at sons wishing to unite themselves to a maid and gentry sons tended to see female servants as sexual provender not marriage material. Girls from the governing ranks and bourgeoisie had fewer opportunities, so simply waited to be courted. Numbers from all ranks simply never married.

The tediousness of such limited horizons is well detailed in the eighteenth and nineteenth centuries, but the bored girls of Renaissance England are relatively silent. Like their brothers, they had virtues to cultivate: piety, chastity, discretion, modesty, gentleness, decorum, prudence, diligence and industry. If from a comfortably-off family, she was expected to join her mother in charity visits to the poor and other almsgiving. Lower down the social ladder things were better as regards active occupation, for you were expected to work and contribute to the family income. Middle- and upper-rank girls had to do much sewing, embroidery, cutting out and assembling of clothes for younger siblings or for charity children. Thousands upon thousands must have let their fathers marry them off to the first man who offered, simply to escape to another life and a home of their own to run. There were differences between how the court treated women and how they were expected to behave elsewhere. Court women were perceived (often correctly) to be promiscuous, flattering and fawning (therefore manipulative and devious hypocrites), overly interested in clothes and show, given to gossip and rumour mongering, and generally flirtatious and frivolous.

There were differences in how men regarded and treated women and what was expected of them according to their rank. Common girls were regarded as skivvies and sexual prey, middling ones as sexual prey and sources of fortune. A girl from a titled family could not easily be predated sexually if she had kinsmen to take revenge, but she could be courted for her money, married and left at home to nurture the offspring. Many girls in the two upper tiers did receive a good education, depending as always on parental attitudes (the father particularly) and there was a swing towards humanist ideals that saw female education as essential for the next generation of wives and mothers.

Renaissance Improvements

Richard Mulcaster, first headmaster of Merchant Taylors' School, then high master of St Paul's School, strongly favoured female education. His book, *Positions* (1581), declares that as 'our' closest 'companions', women should be 'well furnished in mind' and 'well strengthened in body'. Fathers have a 'duty' to educate their daughters. God 'require[s] an account for natural talents of both the parties, us for directing them; them for performance of our direction'. This alludes to the parable of the talents (Matthew 25:13–40; Luke 19:12–27) concerning one's God-given abilities. Mulcaster believed women's education should be selectively targeted towards strengthening virtue. He emphasized four essential skills: 'reading well, writing faire, singing sweet, playing fine', plus languages and drawing. Maths, science and divinity were less useful, but not excluded. Women, he felt, were weak by nature, but education could strengthen intellect and soul. Men should be educated 'without restraint for either matter or manner'. Countering the stereotypical view that women's education was neglected he asks:

> Do we not see in our country some of that sex so excellently well trained and so rarely qualified in regard both to the tongues themselves and to the subject matter contained in them, that they may be placed along with, or even above, the most vaunted paragons of Greece or Rome?[43]

How broadly spread was female education in the upper and middling ranks is unquantifiable. While masses of boys went to grammar school then university, and scholarships, bursaries and endowments enabled poor scholars to receive an education otherwise beyond their reach, such institutional learning was generally unavailable to girls, and such home tutoring as was provided has left few examples of its existence except among high-status ladies of evident learning.

Henry VIII's daughters, Mary and Elizabeth, were very well taught. Elizabeth, with Latin, Greek, Hebrew, Italian and French, was one of the most learned rulers in Europe. Her speeches use rhetorical devices that display her classical learning, but she insisted that a prince's education should be useful to ruling the nation. The princesses were tutored by leading scholars, including Juan Vives, the Spanish humanist. Vives – conservative, wary of a classical education because some political-historical material was unsuitable and the poetry of Ovid and Catullus immoral – based their curriculum on his own *Instruction of a Christian Woman* (1524), broadened to include Erasmus's *Paraphrases* (1517–24) and More's *Utopia* (1516). He believed 'most of the vices of women [...] are the products of ignorance, whence they never read nor heard those excellent sayings and monitions of the Holy Fathers about chastity, about obedience, about silence, women's adornments and treasures'. Women had to be obedient to their duties, needed their morals shaped and their virtues developed – as did men. Only 'a little learning is required of women' while 'men must do many things in the world and must be broadly educated'.[44] Women should confine their reading to works on chastity. This betrays the orthodox anxiety about female sexuality. Men felt that independent female sexuality would lead to increased illegitimacy thus obscuring fatherhood and confusing matters of inheritance, the central concern of patriarchally controlled marriage. Erasmus (*The Institution of Marriage*, 1526), friend of Sir Thomas More and key figure in the development of Renaissance ideas, suggests education is more effective than needlework in banishing idleness, preserving virginity and enhancing women's chances in the marriage market.

It should not be assumed that humanist ideas greatly influenced James's court or spread very far outside. Young women attending court would already be past the education stage. Their personalities and tastes already formed, they usually had more worldly matters in mind. Away from court there was a huge variety of attitudes among the country aristocracy and gentry as regards rearing and educating daughters. Learned education (Greek and Latin) was briefly fashionable for aristocratic girls from 1520–1560.[45] Thereafter it waned. Other positive influences did emerge, though again it is impossible to chart their influence. One was Castiglione's *Il Cortegiano* (1528; *The Courtier*, trans. Thomas Hoby, 1561). This important handbook suggested a little knowledge of 'letters' (classics, modern languages, history and literature) was acceptable for women, but that the social graces (playing music, singing, dancing, drawing/painting and needlework) were more civilized and made a woman more marriageable. Castiglione's discussions are presided over by two ladies, but the outcome of the debates illustrates that the refined Urbino court, a model of cultured elegance, valued more than good manners in ladies. It prioritized the intellectual and spiritual input women made. Webster's heroines in two Italian courts, the Duchess of Malfi in the play of the same name and Vittoria Corrombona in *The White Devil*, are learned, strong-willed women and show something of the influence of Renaissance Italy in English drama. Hoby claimed the book was 'to Ladies and Gentlewomen, a mirrour to decke and trimme themselves with vertuous conditions, comeley behaviours and honest entertainment toward all men'.[46] This new courtly ideal promoted the self-effacing but agreeable woman – witty, cultured and chaste. Renaissance courts could be centres of high culture where the ladies were scholarly, but they were also death traps of intrigue, plotting, power struggles, assassinations, political coups, rape and seduction. Court history in England exemplified that double-sidedness of culture and killing; for all the poetry, madrigals and dancing, executions, torture, the rise and fall of favourites, hothouse animosities and sexual intrigues made the English court (from Henry VIII to Charles I) like the set of a bloody play.

As evidence of some shift in attitudes to women, Thomas Campion (1567–1620), explores how women's restricted social opportunities encourage a vigorous inner life, while men are easily distracted by the world's superficialities:

Women are confined to silence,
Loosing wisht occasion.
Yet our tongues then theirs, men,

Are apter to be moving,
Women are more dumbe then they,
But in their thoughts more roving.[47]

Female-authored literature was beginning to emerge. Lady Mary Wroth (c. 1586–c. 1651) from the high-status, literary Sidney family, wrote a sonnet sequence and the first known prose romance by an English woman. Both texts contribute to the ongoing gender discourse. Elizabeth Carey (1585–1639), the first woman to write a history (of Edward II), also wrote the first female-authored tragedy. *The Tragedy of Mariam* (written 1602–04, published 1613), intended as a 'closet drama' to be read in domestic surroundings, contributes to the gender debate in contrasting the honest, principled Queen Mariam with the devious, promiscuous Princess Salome and presenting the violent absolutist patriarch King Herod. Another contributor to the man–woman question was Rachel Speght (c. 1597–?). A Calvinist minister's daughter, she entered the literary world with bravura, stepping straight into gender discourse controversy. Aged 19, with her name boldly attached, scorning anonymity, she published *A Mouzell for Melastomus* (*A Muzzle for Blackmouth*, 1617), an articulate, spirited, clearly and logically argued attack on the bigoted misogyny of Joseph Swetnam's *Araignment of Lewde, Idle, Froward, and Unconstant Women* (1615). Biblical and classical references reveal her religious background and education. Living at the centre of London commercial and clerical debate, she understood the current polemical climate and had seen many examples of husband–wife co-operation among merchant families. She claims respect is due to women as children of God and sees the possibilities for companionate relationships between men and women. Her lively style, often akin to the acerbic, insulting, combative language of male pamphlet polemics, makes her work readable, while her ideas make it convincingly sympathetic and reasonable. Marriage is a true union: 'as yoake-fellowes [married couples] are to sustayne part of each others cares, griefs, and calamities'. 'Marriage is a merri-age, and this worlds Paradise, where there is mutuall love [...] husbands should not account their wives as vassals, but as those that are heires together of the grace of life.' As 'head' of his wife, the husband must protect her and lead her to Christ. To 'exclaime against Woman' is ingratitude to God.[48] Swetnam focuses female vanity and lechery, Speght voices a new mood of companionship, shared piety and compromise between gender egotisms.

   The entrenched history and literature of Catholic misogyny, with its horror of the physical filthiness (i.e., menstruation and childbirth) and spiritual sinfulness of women, passed into male thinking and persisted after the Reformation. In religious thought the body (a temporary house for the soul) was considered corrupt and its sinful needs and dirty functions were to be minimized so the spirit could be kept pure and nourished. Subject to fleshly temptations and the vagaries of emotion, human beings were a comic treasure. One of Castiglione's disputants says, 'In each one of us there is some seed of folly which, once it is stirred, can grow indefinitely.' Another remarks, 'Our bodily senses are so untrustworthy that they often confuse our judgement as well.'[49] Folly, the senses, unreliable judgement – in these are the sources of comedy.

The virtue/sin, duty/desire conflict produced a body of 'sex war' literature focusing on the persistent hostility between men and women – men as bullying, rakish, lascivious brutes (or gullible weaklings), women as devious, unreliable, bullying (shrewish) in their own way (or innocent victims). Shakespeare addresses the virago–virgin polarity in *The Comedy of Errors* (Adriana and Luciana), *The Taming of the Shrew* (Katherine and Bianca) and *Much Ado About Nothing* (Beatrice and Hero). The trickiness of women is often a source of comedy, while their evil is fitting for tragedy. Contrast the polarities of the kite/tiger/wolf/monster sisters in *King Lear* with the gentle sensitivity of Cordelia. *Lear* has little to say of women directly, but many negative implications resonate round the words and actions of Goneril and Regan. Both sisters are white devils – a common metaphor for hypocrites who disguised their evil. The sisters are a study in the evil that females can perform. Shakespeare often explored the failings of women, but deep evil had only been explored through Queen Tamora (*Titus Andronicus*, c. 1588–93) and Queen Margaret, a 'she-wolf' with a 'tiger's heart wrapp'd in a woman's hide' (*Henry VI*, 1590–1591). His other great study of female evil is Lady Macbeth. The last plays, however, project much more positive images of women through Hermione, Paulina and Perdita (*The Winter's Tale*), Imogen (*Cymbeline*), Thaisa and Marina (*Pericles*) and Miranda.

Men had ambivalent, contradictory views of women. As the source of human sin they needed controlling to minimize their opportunities for tempting men. A multiplicity of pejorative terms – virago, termagant, shrew, Whore of Babylon, hussy, wagtail, punk and more – provide lexical markers of male suspicion. But men were ineluctably drawn to them, hormones being stronger than principles. In opposition to the Eve/Delilah/Jezebel image, medieval Courtly Love projected an idealized woman of beauty, intelligence, elegance and chastity, while Mariolatry raised the Virgin Mary to an archetype of gentle, sympathetic womanhood and loving, nurturing motherhood, partially redeeming women. Mary became a key human intercessor in approaching Christ, and an icon of the respect men should have for women. In loving a woman you re-expressed your love and respect for your mother, showing the love you first learned from her. Martin Luther asserted that Mary was 'the highest woman' and that 'we can never honour her enough [...]. The veneration of Mary is inscribed in the very depths of the human heart.'[50] While lauding Mary's model status, Luther made very derogatory remarks about women in general.[51] Castiglione leaves no doubt as to the fine qualities women could display, but despite some easing of extreme patriarchy and improvements in the status of women, negative views persisted and progress was slow.

Medieval hagiographies (lives of saints) celebrated the virtues of women martyrs, but Protestantism had banned statues, days, prayers and oaths associated with saints. This hampered the assimilation into church dogma of any ideology applauding women, though veneration of Mary persisted in people's private faith.[52] A small amount of literature iconized particularly virtuous women and applauded romantic, rational, affectionate relationships. From the medieval period there are Chaucer's *Legend of Good Women* and *The Book of the Duchesse*,[53] and later Thomas Elyot's *The Defence of Good Women* (1540) and Spenser's *The Faerie Queene* (1590 and 1596). Notable continental contributions include Boccaccio's *De Mulieribus Claris* (*Of Famous Women*, 1374) and Castiglione's *Il Cortegiano*, where, despite sharp misogynistic interruptions, Guiliano de Medici constructs the idealized court lady, ably acknowledges the female capacity for virtue and illustrates his case with classical and contemporary examples. There are the scattered references to courageous, faithful women in the Bible, but generally all churches were suspicious of women, sex and passion, encouraged men to control their own and female appetites and warned against women as provokers of lust. Men were supposedly more rational, while women were more emotional and vulnerable to fleshly temptations. Polemic writing tended to highlight female failings. Literature uses the constant interplay of tension between the positive aspects (affection and love) of the appetites and the dangers of following them excessively. Love was seen as a madness, an illness caught from women. For Castiglione, 'The emotions of love provide excuse for every kind of fault.'[54] In *A Midsummer Night's Dream*, Theseus describes love's insanity:

> Lovers and madmen have such seething brains,
> Such shaping fantasies, that apprehend
> More than cool reason ever comprehends. (V. i. 4–5)

Burton has much to say of the dangers of love, especially the blurred line between love and lust:

> If it rage, it is no more Love, but burning Lust, a Disease, Phrensy, Madness, Hell. 'Tis death, 'tis an immedicable calamity, 'tis a raging madness 'tis no virtuous habit this, but a vehement perturbation of the mind, a monster of nature, wit, and art.[55]

The Church of England's *Second Book of Homilies* (1571), which vicars used for sermons, includes 'On the State of Matrimony', defining the Church's views on women and how fathers and husbands, being in authority over them and being more rational beings, should approach them:

> The woman is a weak creature not endued with like strength and constancy of mind; therefore, they be the sooner disquieted, and they be the more prone to all weak affections and dispositions of mind, more than men be; and lighter they be, and more vain in their fantasies and opinions.

They were 'the weaker vessell, of a frail heart, inconstant, and with a word soon stirred to wrath'. A commentary in Matthew's Bible (1537) says that men, being intellectually stronger and in authority, had a duty to ensure their women conformed to the demand for chastity and modest behaviour. If she was 'not obedient and helpful to him, [he may] beat the fear of God into her head, and that thereby she may be compelled to learn her duty and do it'. Corporal punishment was common in the Renaissance. Whores and criminals were publicly whipped, children caned at home and school, wives and servants beaten.[56] The Bible exhorts wives to be in subjection to their husband, counterbalancing this by requiring that the husband should honour the wife and that they should have 'compassion one of another' (I Peter 3:8). Bishop Aylmer gave a sermon before Queen Elizabeth, outlining the best and worst aspects of women, in polarities evident in Shakespeare and most other dramatists:

> Women are of two sorts: some of them are wiser, better learned, discreeter, and more constant than a number of men; but another and worse sort of them are fond (simple), foolish, wanton, flibbergibs, tattlers, triflers, wavering, witless,, without council, feeble, careless, rash, proud, dainty (fussy), tale-bearers, eavesdroppers, rumour-raisers, evil-tongued, worse-minded, and in every way doltified with the dregs of the devil's dunghill.[57]

Legally women had few rights. Neither did most ordinary men, but they had the key ones. There were some shifts in behaviour, but how far they penetrated society as a whole is unclear. The sixteenth century saw an increase in stern patriarchy as regards marital and parental relations. In the seventeenth century there were countermovements against both. Imperceptibly slowly the stern, patriarchal, authoritarian father became more affectionate and considerate. Stone charts the gradual emergence of the more companionate marriage and more affective family relations: 'For a considerable period, two conflicting trends were at work at the same time, and the growing authority of the husband can only be seen in a relatively pure form during the first half of the sixteenth century.'[58]

Playwrights hint at the hope for harmonious, loving marriages at the end of comedies, but within them tend to use the dramatic possibilities of conflict between the sexes. Offering more opportunities for humour, tension and the exploration of violent emotions, it is better theatre. In George Wilkins's *The Miseries of Enforced Marriage* (1607), the character Ilford states the orthodox misogynistic view: 'Women are the purgatory of men's purses, the paradise of their bodies, and the hell of their minds: marry none of them. Women are in churches saints, abroad angels, at home devils.'[59] The play is partially based on the true story of William Calverley, who, provoked by his wife's denial that he was their children's father and the fear she was planning his death, severely wounded her and murdered two of his three children. It shows that women are supremely capable of verbal and psychological abuse. The tragedy *Arden of Faversham* (1592) shows them not incapable of commissioning murder.

Such lively possibilities are not explored between Miranda and Ferdinand. It is interesting to speculate how Prospero would react had Miranda either fallen for Ferdinand without his agreement or refused to marry him. In Marston's *The Dutch Courtesan* (1604), Malheureux says: 'The most odious spectacle the earth can present is an immodest, vulgar woman' (I. i. 154–5). Medea, Venus, the dockside doxies of Stephano's song, fall into that category. Miranda clearly does not. Marston, a member of Shakespeare's circle, worked in the same areas of problematic moral ambivalence central to *Measure for Measure* and touched on in *King Lear*. Freevill (his name conflating evil/freedom/free will), a libertine trying to terminate his relationship with the courtesan Franceschina so he can marry Beatrice, a respectable and wealthy heiress, passes on the whore to his friend Malheureux ('the unhappy or misfortunate one') who tries to repress his powerful sexual feelings. Freevill and Malheureux represent two significant forces in contemporary society – traditional male unfettered sexuality and the newer moral code of Puritanism attempting to control the sex impulse. Franceschina admits, 'Woman corrupted is the worst of devils' (*The Dutch Courtesan*, II. ii. 201). Her remark has relevance wider than London's sex trade and would have applied to some of the court ladies watching *The Tempest*. Shakespeare presents the counterargument when the hitherto chaste Angelo, feeling the prickings of lust, asks, 'The tempter, or the tempted, who sins most, ha?' (*Measure for Measure*, II. ii. 164). This acknowledges partial male responsibility for lust. King Lear makes sharps comments on lust and female lust in particular. His strictures sound as condemnatory as any Puritan preacher:

> Down from the waist they are Centaurs,
> Though women all above:
> But to the girdle do the Gods inherit,
> Beneath is all the fiends: there's hell, there's darkness,
> There is the sulphurous pit – burning, scalding,
> Stench, consumption; fie, fie fie! pah, pah! (IV. vi.)

In *The Tempest*, Prospero, fully aware of lust's power in young men, warns Ferdinand not to pre-empt the wedding with Miranda (IV. i. 13–23):

> Look thou be true; do not give dalliance
> Too much the rein: the strongest oaths are straw
> To th' fire in' th' blood,
> Or else, good night your vow. (IV. i. 51–4)

In different ways Marston, Jonson, Shakespeare and others explored the difficulties of trying to keep to virtue's path. While others mocked the pretensions and greed of contemporary London through their theatrical satires, Shakespeare dives deep into human depravity and cruelty in a universal setting, removed from readily identifiable topical references, but still with targets that prompt resemblances to his time and audience. By the time of *The Tempest* he has somewhat marginalized evil and focuses the more positive aspects of humanity.

Elizabethan-Jacobean dramatists show considerable sympathy for women in a male-dominated world, displaying their wit, virtue and sprightliness, but they are also alert to women's capacity for cunning and fierce brutality. It is disturbingly similar to men's.

Chapter 7

MAN IN HIS PLACE

First walk in thy vocation,
And do not seek thy lot to change.[1]

Maintaining order carried deep psychological resonances. Order meant social stability, but also was the outward sign of devotion to God's will. Disorder, any threat to the established hierarchies, stirred up the fear of Doomsday. By God's will you were born into a particular rank (your 'lot' in life). You were expected to know your place, keep it and work at whatever calling came within the scope of your family's position. Any family might rise, through hard work and God's grace. Small status improvements were not too disturbing for one's neighbours, but great success provoked envious suspicion of overreaching ambition. Doubts about the means by which you rose might arouse accusations of magic or devilish assistance, people being all too ready to take the Bible's point of view: 'He that maketh haste to be rich shall not be innocent' (Proverbs 28:20). The industrious, careful man, slowly improving his position, was safe from negative gossip: 'Wealth gotten by vanity shall be diminished: but he that gathereth by labour shall increase' (Proverbs 13:11). The rapid increase in bourgeois wealth created an interplay between envy, condemnation of luxury, suspicion of avarice and dishonesty, and fears of an upstart, ambitiously aspirational group rivalling the traditional ruling class.

The Jacobeans were highly suspicious of social movement. If God made the world, putting each man in his place, to alter your standing was to defy God's will. A poor man becoming poorer was thought punished for some unnamed sin, but some argued that God gave men abilities or talents, expected men to use them and rewarded hard work. If that meant you could climb out of your birth rank and better yourself then you could be said to be doing God's will and worshipping him by developing the talents he gave you. This approach appealed to Non-conformists for whom the work ethic was central.

They believed in industry, thrift and did not reject the idea of making money. A rise in fortunes, place and public status should not be accompanied by a complacent attitude to making money at any cost. It had to be ethical and the amounts within reason. Excessive gains should be redistributed through charities and the moneymaker and his family should avoid arrogance, ostentation and snobbery – in theory.[2] A hard-working shop assistant might marry the shopkeeper's daughter or his widow, he might rise to wealth and become master of his guild or a town councillor, but he was expected to give thanks by charitable donations and remain humble. Education could help a poor man's son to a government clerkship. Talented, active men could rise, particularly if they earned the patronage of someone of note and power. They could fall too if they followed a favourite who fell from favour. The court was a roller coaster of fortune where many rose by intrigues, plots, lies, favouritism and ruthless opportunism – and fell by the same. Antonio has risen by all of the above. 'King' Stephano contemplates rising by murder. His plot is ludicrous, unpromising and easily thwarted. 'Duke' Antonio, more clever and more devious, made haste to be rich by guilty means and it requires the superior power of magic to catch and expose him, though that could be seen as God's vengeance enacted through Prospero.

The astonishing rise to prominence of so many new men caused unease in conservative thinking about social mobility. Portrayed onstage, extreme reversals (*peripeteia* and *nemesis*) in rank or exceptional improvements (*hubris*) in status were seen as omens of impending disaster and social implosion that might engulf everyone.[3] Subversion of any sort was disturbing and threatening to the orderliness of society. *The Tempest*'s narrative is founded upon a primal order-threatening act: a younger brother supplanting an older. The Caliban plot (foster child against foster father) and Sebastian's planned supplanting of his brother treble the threat. Traditional family order is under attack, as is social hierarchy. In *Eastward Ho!* the goldsmith's daughter, Gertrude, obsessed with becoming a knight's wife, contemplates the pleasure of having gained superiority over her father: 'He must call me daughter no more now; but "Madam", and, "please you Madam", and, "please your worship, Madam", indeed' (III. ii. 63–5). Gertrude is suitably punished. She marries Sir Petronel Flash for title and property, but finds he resembles his name – all show, no substance, no castle, no money. He marries her for her money. Each has cheated the other and their pride is humbled. In addition to pride and ambition, Gertrude shows extreme disrespect to her father, striking at the very root of social order and breaking a Commandment. *King Lear* shows even worse subversion of family values and many City Comedies show disturbing threats to the fundamental basis of social life. *The Tempest* portrays sibling subversion, a planned coup and an assassination by commoners. Miranda is largely obedient and conforms to her role as daughter and female, but there are hints of a readiness to determine her own future. Without seeking paternal consent she pledges herself to Ferdinand.

As the seventeenth century progressed, increasing numbers of merchants, financiers, manufacturers and industrialists were making huge fortunes, becoming wealthier than some established aristo-gentry families. They copied elite cultural habits, seeking titles, estates and political power.[4] This aspiration frightened the ruling ranks. The bourgeois elite was well educated, with 2.5 per cent of males aged 14–20 even receiving university training. Reading, writing and accountancy skills were vital in trade and with male literacy improving (80 per cent in London) clearly life-enhancement possibilities were expanding. The middling sort was unstoppably on the move, though movement was not always upward. A third to a half of the seventeenth-century population existed at subsistence level and suffered acute unemployment. The majority of the lower sort suffered their hardship fairly stoically, but the urban underclass was always a worrying barrel of gunpowder. It took little to ignite it and regular outbreaks of riot occurred – in London particularly. Though the very poorest remained poor and their numbers increased due to enclosures, unemployment and inflation, those able to struggle upwards to literacy, and thereby to effective commercial activity, were also increasing. This widened the divide between those succeeding and the failing underclass with no means of reversing their downward spiral. The growth of capitalism created many different levels of sophistication and increased the need for minutely observed differentiations to distinguish between people. When a merchant's wife could afford to dress as well and in the same fashions as a lady at court, it was human nature to seek finer status identifiers to enable those with established rank to mark themselves apart from those newly arrived. For a society that valued order, such a broad sense of movement was psychologically destabilizing.

In the 1600s voices were beginning to speak up for the lower orders. The need to do so indicates growing tensions between the ranks. At the end of his progress south James I arrived at Theobalds, Robert Cecil's magnificent palace north of London. There he was handed the 'Poor Man's Petition'. Like others it demanded the new king promise religious uniformity and the purifying of public life, particularly attacking the legal profession: 'A pox take the proud covetous Attorney and merciless lawyer! […] Fye upon all close biting knaverie!'[5] Social divisions showed in other more public ways. Luxury clattered by on the streets in fine coaches. Successful men, their wives and families, displayed their newfound luxury in extravagant dress and lavishly decorated houses. Conspicuous consumption and ostentatious showing-off through carriages, horses, houses, furniture, clothes and expensive banquets were all forms of vanity. Expanding global trade and increasing plantation in the Americas provided many luxuries, the acquisition of which demonstrated your status. The many mocking stage representations of the purse-proud *nouveaux riches* had little effect. Sumptuary laws to control expenditure and regulate the types of clothing worn and the amounts/types of food consumed by the different ranks were ignored. Established in the Middle Ages, updated by Henry VIII and extended by Elizabeth, they officially claimed to restrain vain, wasteful habits and protect English trade, but were really an elite attempt to maintain the visual differences of rank. As everywhere else, there was hierarchy – in the fur trimming permitted for your level in society, the fabric you could wear, the headgear and the jewellery. To dress 'above your station' looked like pride. The laws were designed to discourage someone from one station imitating the manners and appearance of another, but were frankly a form of social control and means of identifying a person's rank and reinforcing the distinctions between the nobility and the up-and-coming entrepreneurial groups. Attempts to regulate extravagant expenditure on clothes by aspiring, fashion- and status-conscious bourgeois women were put in moral terms stressing restraint and humility. Elizabeth I's 1574 law declared the craze for fine show as

> the wasting and undoing of a great number of young gentlemen, otherwise serviceable, and others seeking by show of apparel to be esteemed as gentlemen, who, allured by the vain show of those things, do not only consume themselves, their goods, and lands which their parents left unto them, but also run into such debts and shifts as they cannot live out of danger of laws without attempting unlawful acts.

The words 'show', 'vain', 'consume' and 'debts' suggest disapproval based on medieval ideas of moderation, evoking the Deadly Sins and stereotypes linking suitability of behaviour to rank. Rank, income and gender were the criteria that decided what you could wear. Thus dress signifiers supposedly identified social rank and preserved 'degree'. Though there were harsh punishments for sumptuary infringements they were largely ignored and the laws were repealed in 1603–04 as simply unenforceable. To some this opened the floodgates that would swamp distinction between the orders and herald social collapse. In 1583 Philip Stubbes remarked on

> such a confused mingle mangle of apparel [...] that is verie hard to know who is noble, who is worshipful, who is a gentleman, who is not; for you shall have those [...] go daylie in silkes, velvets, satens, damasks, taffeties and suchlike, notwithstanding that they be both base by byrthe, meane by estate & servile by calling. This is a great confusion & a general disorder, God be mercifull unto us.[6]

High-end fashion became more lavish and impractical as a way of saying, 'I don't need to work, so my clothes are for show only.' Snobbery drove people to seek minute markers to show their superiority. Shakespeare's drama from 1600 onwards is much concerned with how clothing disguises what people really are. In *Measure for Measure*, *King Lear* and *The Tempest* he is much concerned with the discrepancy between appearance and reality relating to clothes and office, how fine robes suggest rank and rank implies virtue, while exposing how clothes hide sin, gold covers it, and office (or authority) does not mean the man occupying it is there by merit. Antonio is a prime example of this. Alonso too, for all his title and entourage, has a guilty secret. There are a few covert snipes at the sham gentlefolk in the audience whose money, clothes and flattery had gained them an entrée to court circles. Misleading appearance could apply higher up the power pyramid. Brachiano in *The White Devil* suggests that the Duke of Florence is all show:

> [...] all his reverend wit
> Lies in his wardrobe; he's a discreet fellow
> When he's made up in his robes of state. (II. i. 189–91)

This reminds us of Lear's remark on 'the great image of Authority': 'A dog's obey'd in office' (*Lear*, IV. vi.). People perceive and treat you according to your robes and accoutrements of office, regardless of the fool or knave you might actually be: 'Robes and furr'd gowns hide all' (*Lear*, IV. vi.). Judging by appearance, Alonso, Gonzalo and Antonio in his stolen clothes are men of probity and power. Yet all were party to deposing a legitimate ruler. Gonzalo, though provisioning the exiled Prospero, did not attempt to stop the coup. Ready as he is to offer advice he seems not to have spoken truth to power over Antonio's usurpation – an example of the cowed and complacent type of courtier, doing nothing to prevent the coup. Castiglione is clear about a courtier's duty in such a situation:

> Obey your lord in everything that redounds to his profit and honour, but not as regards things that bring him loss and shame. Therefore, if he were to order you to commit some treacherous deed not only are you not obliged to do it but you are obliged not to do it.[7]

Appearances are deceptive in many different ways throughout the play. Fine silks paraded in public simply emphasized the fact that some were rising fabulously while most were in the mire.

Each man, as guardian of his own soul, his own virtues, was responsible for his own sins. But he had other associations to whom he owed loyalty and responsibility – his family, village, trade or craft, county, nation, church humanity and the whole of creation. Family and community were the strongest bonds, though faith might take precedence and separate him from these commitments. Each man occupied a place in the detailed stratification of society, from king to pauper. The theory of the natural order was based on harmony. Each rank, high or low, had its part to play if concord and perfect working were to be achieved.

> This is the true ordering of the state of a well-fashioned commonwealth, that every part do obey one head, or governor, one law, as all parts of the body obey the head, agree among themselves, and one not to eat up the other through greediness, but that we see order, moderation, and reason, bridle the affections.[8]

This theory of order and orderliness was conceived by those who gave the orders and wished to preserve degree. It must be remembered always that the concept of world order was 'produced by power for its own interests' (church power and state power) and pre-dates the Jacobean reverence for hierarchy by centuries.[9]

Rulers were the brains and heart, the nobles the important organs. The others – the limbs – had little else to do but obey. But this often-voiced analogy is false. Society is not a body. If you cut off the head the body dies, but if you cut off the king's head or remove the aristocracy, society will make a new political settlement. The Civil War would show that. If the lavishly bedecked audience thought the play would be a light-hearted romance, with a little clowning to make them laugh, they were wrong. It carried in its texture warnings to the frivolous and the self-satisfied. It provokes questions about loyalty, rule, politics, education and parenting. Shakespeare never wrote a lightweight play; even his romances have dark undertones. In 1631 his colleague Ben Jonson wrote: 'All Repraesentations, [...] eyther have bene, or ought to be the mirrors of man's life, whose ends, [...] ought always to carry a mixture of profit, with them, no less then delight' (preface to *Love's Triumph*).[10] Jonson was not only referring to court masques. A classicist by education and inclination he was alluding to Horace's maxim 'He has gained every point who has mixed profit with pleasure, by delighting the reader at the same time as instructing him.'[11] How much profit and instruction would the court take from this representation? History suggests not much.

Chapter 8

IMAGES OF DISORDER:
THE RELIGIOUS CONTEXT

The sixteenth and seventeenth centuries were undeniably religious ages. Religion impacted all lives to varying degrees. The Church of England, present in everyone's life, was an arm of the established power that ruled England. The parish church, usually in or near the village, was visible from the fields as you worked. Its bells punctuated your day. The city parish church was likewise nearby. The priest would be visible haggling in the market like anyone else, perhaps occupying a corner of the local tavern. Sitting in judgement over your spiritual life, he was part of the civic power structure, reported your civil and moral misdemeanours, convened and presided over the church court, arranged poor relief and preached. One form of socio-moral re-enforcement was the homily the priest was obliged by his superiors to read out every Sunday. The *Book of Homilies* (the first published in 1547; the second in 1571) had 33 sermons, intended to bed in the ideas of the new reformed Church of England, to educate the masses and to assist conformity. They covered doctrinal and liturgical subjects but included moral sermons: 'Against Peril of Idolatry', 'Against Gluttony and Drunkenness', 'Against Excess of Apparel', 'Of Alms [Charity] Deeds', 'Of the State of Matrimony', 'Against Idleness', 'Against Disobedience and Wylful Rebellion'.

Religion meant much to the Jacobeans, but not all those who attended church did so in a spirit of devotion. Many went simply to avoid the various punishments meted out for non-attendance, but 'there was no escaping the rhythms of the Prayer Book or the barrage of catechisms and sermons'.[1] Though it was a largely churchgoing society, there were those who claimed (and believed) they needed no church or priest to intercede between them and God. Increasingly Dissenters asserted they could worship in the field, in the workshop, in their home. Enforced church attendance was increasingly resisted.

One sailor expressed the view in 1581 that 'it was never merry England since we were impressed to come to church'.[2] It was a criminal offence to not attend on Sunday, though the pursuit and prosecution of non-attenders depended on the zeal of the vicar. In London, large and anonymous, it was more difficult for parish officers to keep checks on local inhabitants, especially the constantly changing lodgers in the crowded tenements. Sunday worship was theoretically a time of communal affirmation of shared beliefs and values. That excludes those parishioners with rather different thoughts in their heads while the parson exhorted them to virtue and led their mumbled responses. There would always be some doctrinally opposed to Anglicanism. Though everyone was nominally Church of England, some in the congregation would be Catholics conforming to the law, others Puritans passively conforming while having more radical and aggressive beliefs about which they were mostly, but not always, quiet. Increasingly there were hostile interactions in the church that created simmering grievances in the outside community. Some vicars were too zealously reformist, some too lazily traditionalist. Some Dissenters separated from the church and formed their own unofficial congregations. These were illegal and the congregants subject to dispersal or arrest.[3] There were those who, indifferent to religion, called themselves Christian but did not allow faith to interfere with life more than they could help. Atheists tended to keep their views to themselves (or share them only with likeminded others); denial of God was punishable by arrest, interrogation, torture and imprisonment.[4] There were always those more concerned with the pint of ale in the inn after the boredom of the sermon was over. Some chatted, snoozed, made mocking comments on the priest and his sermon, laughed aloud or transacted business. Others would be more preoccupied with the members of the opposite sex seated across the aisle. The parish church was a place where the community's social differences were re-enforced as much as their shared faith. Finally, there were those who had genuine faith in the Anglican Church and lived in as holy and virtuous a way as possible. It is impossible to say what proportion of the population at any one time fell into these categories. The service was intended as a celebration of solidarity and a reminder of the demands and sacrifices faith and virtue required. The overarching zeitgeist was religious, though like a rainbow it was of many colours. Despite the various forms of internal, external, silent and vocal opposition to imposed worship, most English men and women were regular churchgoers and those who were not, those who moved away from their village community to the anonymity of the city, would nevertheless have the vestiges of religious upbringing and the remnants of biblical teachings still in their memories.

Another aspect of this structure, that all faiths agreed on, was that the orderliness of the cosmos and the natural world was fantastically varied and complex, with each part of the system working and doing its allotted job, and that all this was God's doing: 'The heavens declare the Glory of God and the firmament showeth his handiwork' (Psalm 19:1).

Unsettling Questions

Many fundamental beliefs were being questioned. Was God concerned with humanity or aloofly uninterested? Did he exist? Did the Devil exist? Did Heaven or Hell exist? Astronomers were gradually dismantling trust in the Ptolemaic system, but plays too could unsettle. Audiences watching the Admiral's Men perform Marlowe's *Tamburlaine the Great* (1587) at the Rose would have heard Alleyne declaim:

> Our souls, whose faculties can comprehend
> The wondrous architecture of the world
> And measure every wand'ring planet's course,
> Still climbing after knowledge infinite
> And always moving as the restless spheres,
> Wills us to wear ourselves and never rest
> Until we reach the ripest fruit of all,
> That perfect bliss and sole felicity,
> The sweet fruition of an earthly crown. (Part 1. II. vii. 21–9)

This combines traditional views – man's distinguishing faculties of understanding that separate him from the animals, the glory of God's creation (the 'always moving […] restless spheres') – with progressive, dangerously blasphemous views on man's restless search for knowledge that trespassed into the secrets of the divine. The final idea is unusual, for instead of seeing 'perfect bliss and sole felicity' as spiritual, a heavenly crown, Tamburlaine's goal is the 'earthly crown' of supreme material power – a very Renaissance ambition. This is the work of a restless, enquiring, turbulent young university man writing for an audience that would include some fairly sophisticated members, along with the posers and exhibitionists more interested in displaying themselves than watching the play.[5] But more than three-quarters of England's population was rural – landless farmworkers and small subsistence farmers with beliefs still primitive, basic and medieval. Many large-scale landholders, farmers and nobles were similar. Centuries of Catholicism could not be erased overnight. Changes of thinking take several generations when few are literate, have no access to academic research, and in any case have closed minds. Nationwide instant communication just did not happen and the church always stood in the way of the free sharing of intellectual ideas, especially if they were unorthodox. There was no organized dissemination of news; regular newspapers did not appear until the Civil War. There was also the normal monumental public resistance to change. The majority of the population was exceptionally conservative. Ignorance, fear and intellectual inertia played their parts as always. The Reformation changed the official outer world, but the private inner world of daily life and its cluster of beliefs lagged far behind. The Reformation had many fervent supporters, but was grafted onto a residue of long-ingrained beliefs and practices. Individuals, devoted to their faith, might conform to the new rites and liturgy of Anglicanism while still performing little acts of superstition.

The lines between magic and acceptable doctrine remained as blurred as they ever had been, but, given the growing print culture, and the spreading knowledge of what the Bible said, huge numbers of controversial debates sprang up as to what was orthodox and what was heresy, iconoclasm, superstition, idolatry, papist mumbo-jumbo or diabolic magic. Services in English made doctrine more accessible and as Anglicanism settled, Bible translations became more readily available and individuals could read for themselves the words that were the basis of a priest's hitherto unique and privileged interaction with his congregation. This newfound capacity for personal interpretation allowed many doctrinally divergent views to spring up and worry the Anglican hierarchy. In response bishops became more repressive, demanding greater conformity from vicars and parishioners. This encouraged stronger opposition though Puritanism's rise was slow. The Puritan drive to change religious thinking was regarded with irritation and new ideas in medicine, politics and science always provoked opposition. Puritans are almost always figures of fun and derided as hypocrites in plays. The mass of people just wanted to continue living as they had always done. But, regardless of this conservatism, seismic shifts were rumbling in many aspects of life. John Donne, in 'An Anatomy of the World' (1611), declares:

> […] new Philosophy calls all in doubt,
> The Element of fire is quite put out;
> The Sun is lost, and th'earth, and no man's wit
> Can well direct him where to look for it.
> And freely men confess that this world's spent,
> When in the Planets, and the Firmament
> They seek so many new; then see that this
> Is crumbled out again to his Atomies.
> 'Tis all in pieces, all coherence gone;
> All just supply, and all Relation:
> Prince, Subject, Father, Son, are things forgot.

Representing God's order, divine harmony, the Ptolemaic system gave reassuring coherence to life. To hear it questioned, to hear of old beliefs discarded by new science, was destabilizing, forcing doubts into people's heads in an age already full of changes, with a new religion, a new king and new worlds being discovered, new economic practices, new towns growing (and creating new problems), and old feudal relationships breaking down. The court coup of *The Tempest* in which the rightful duke is ousted echoed the crumbling times; to see family heads threatened by their brothers was disturbing. Family was the commonest, closest bond for everyone. Family history, family honour and family loyalty were central to the audience's thinking and feeling. It would be painful seeing taken-for-granted relationships called into question, especially if the answers suggest family love is a thin veneer of pretence.

Familial and societal disassembly is averted in *The Tempest*, though past fractures are not entirely mended. Hopes of a return to normality and order reside in Prospero's restoration and Miranda's marriage. Unbroken continuity of rule was essential. Those who knew Holinshed's *Chronicles* knew that breaks in the smooth running of royal power led to difficult times surrounding handovers to or takeovers by new dynasties. Shakespeare's history plays amply displayed the natural desire for order and peace. Political vacuums were dangerous, as was illegitimate rule – and both usually led to bloody struggles, generating uneasiness and repression, putting into perspective the desperate anxieties surrounding a queen's pregnancy and the nervous wait for a hoped-for male heir. Some audience members had experienced the traumas of the Tudor continuities and discontinuities. All remembered the recent shift into the Stuart line. Change was disturbing. From God to Earth's dust, everything had its place; man, man's communities and his states were part of that orderliness. The fast-changing, apparently disintegrating, world disorientated the Jacobeans. Courts were commonly sources of order-threatening discontent, but the mob too threatens in *The Tempest*. A warning perhaps, even as early as 1611.

The court audience collides with the difference between theory and reality, the discrepancy between what we would like to think and what we know is the truth. 'The great and the good' is how assemblies of various leaders are described. Yet we know that most of those so called were neither great nor good because they were morally compromised – flattering, lying, cheating, sleeping or buying their way to the top. They were just as susceptible to vice's temptations as the lowest in society and, in Jacobean times, were only where they were because of birth and rank. Peck states:

> Appointments to office and promotion were made through patronage and connections; officeholders were paid by those requiring their

services […]. An informal market grew up for the buying and selling of offices and their reversions, with the profits going to the officeholders, not the Crown.[6]

The disorderliness of courtiers was a common cause for concern, as was the unprofessional conduct of judges and justices of the peace. On 11 July 1604 Sir Philip Gawdy, MP described the Commons Speaker addressing the problem of

> Justices of Peace of wch ther wer two kyndes he founde great fault withal, the one wer such as go downe into the country, and presently fall to hawking, and other sportes, and yf any man comme about Justice, they sende him to their next neybur Justice; the others be suche as put downe one alehouse, and set vp two for it, set up one constable, and put down an other, and yf any matter be stirring whatsoeuer he must haue an ore in it.[7]

The double standard of the supposedly virtuous public man whose apparent probity masks private corruption recurs in drama, in the court and in real life. Part of the dramatic development in *The Tempest* involves stripping back appearances and exposing the realities hidden beneath. Sham virtue is visibly exposed in Antonio and Sebastian's conversations. Overt sin resonates in Stephano and Trinculo's behaviour. Middleton's City Comedy *A Mad World My Masters* (1605) has the mother of the courtesan Frank Gullman declare in a neat epigram:

> Who gets th'opinion for a virtuous name,
> May sin at pleasure and ne'er think of shame. (I. i. 164–5)

As regards the veneer of etiquette and politeness masking ambition and corruption, the stage court was no different from the court watching the play.

Part II

THE JACOBEAN CONTEXT

Chapter 9

THE CONTEXT OF EDUCATION: NATURE VERSUS NURTURE

Happy Families: Parenting Problems

George Herbert's view that infants are 'moulded more by the example of parents than by the stars at their nativities' indicates the uneasy co-existence of old superstitions and new ideas.[1] Though people still paid to have horoscopes cast to learn their luck and destiny and still believed zodiac birth signs predestined their personality and fortune, they also recognized that rank, lifestyle, education and above all parental intervention greatly influenced personality formation. Character was destiny, and character was formed by early experiences. Sir Thomas Elyot was adamant infants be reared in a virtuous atmosphere; mothers, nurses and maids responsible for or coming into contact with children should be of moderate behaviour and moral language. Similar qualities are required of tutors responsible for formal academic education. This sense of the importance of example in the formative early years was allied to recognition of the effects of parental influence and peer behaviour on later development and youthful conduct.

The ever-vexed question of education was much debated throughout the period, focused largely, though not exclusively, on the upbringing of elite males. It was not confined to narrow discourses on which classical texts should be studied and which were unsuitable. Early years training, the inculcation of virtue and faith, exercise regimes, and the dangers of the vices to which young men are drawn, as well as actual curricula, were all part of the problem and were argued over as much as whether Cicero was more valuable than Quintilian or Ovid more appropriate than Virgil. Erasmus's *The Education of a Christian Prince* (1516) had great influence throughout Europe. In England concern over training men for public office and social leadership had a history going back at least to King Alfred's translation of Pope Gregory the Great's

Pastoral Care, which comments on the duties and responsibilities of those in governing roles. More contemporary with Shakespeare are Sir Thomas Elyot's *The Boke Named the Governour*, the successive editions of *The Mirrour for Magistrates* (1574, 1578, 1587, 1610) and James I's *Basilikon Doron*. Relevant too as a handbook for the development of refined accomplishments and manners in courtiers is Baldassare Castiglione's *Il Cortegiano*. These, and the many sermons and pamphlets on the subject, indicate ongoing anxiety about what was suitable educational material, what was a workable stepped programme, and above all how to properly train the minds and conduct of young men of rank. The education debate was not just about assimilating facts or developing skills, but founded on the basic belief that upbringing should be moral and the aim should be to produce a virtuous Christian prince. Each young man of rank was potentially a future 'Christian Prince' ruling his little kingdom – himself, his family, his estate and his dependents. Essential to the argument about what and how children should learn is the belief that nurture will not work if nature is against it, that some types of personality resist learning how to behave according to the Renaissance idea of the cultured, civilized gentleman. Of Caliban Prospero says:

> A devil, a born devil, on whose nature
> Nurture can never stick; on whom my pains,
> Humanely taken, all, all lost, quite lost;
> And as with age his body uglier grows,
> So his mind cankers. (IV. i. 188–92)

This expresses the orthodox core belief that all men are born sinners, that evil is in us, and that some refuse the chance to redeem and reform themselves, resist learning, reject conformity to classroom behaviour, and fail to view schooling of any type as relevant to them. The City Comedies are full of ill-behaved, ill-intentioned young men whose privileged backgrounds should have inculcated virtue. Given the understanding that the early years were crucially formative, Caliban is the archetypal example of someone who, due to early deprivation, is unconformable. Miranda is a prime example of a child responsive to the process of careful home schooling by a parent, in isolation from the snares of a corrupt world. Prospero came upon Caliban too late; he is incorrigible and now resentful. If Ariel was in the pine tree prison for twelve years before release, Caliban was at least 12 years old before Prospero attempted to nurture him. The malign influences first of Sycorax and then, after her death, of a lack of parenting have formed his mind. Prospero tried but failed to educate Caliban. He succeeded with Miranda, but was able to influence her from birth. The difference could hardly be greater. Caliban represents incorrigible commonness, vulgarity and savagery such as teemed in the streets of London. The audience would incline to believe Miranda was born innately virtuous because she was born of high degree, though knowing also that people of rank could turn bad. Miranda also attempted the schooling of her foster brother, spending time and effort teaching him speech:

> When thou didst not, savage,
> Know thine own meaning, but wouldst gabble like
> A thing most brutish, I endowed thy purposes
> With words that made them known. (I. ii. 357–60)

Is the word 'gabble' simply a colonizer's description of a language not understood or did Caliban simply not have speech because he had no one to teach him and no one to copy? Either way, she made an effort to help him express himself, constantly taught him 'one thing or other', passing on what she had learned herself. This is the classic situation of one child teaching another, but reversed, with the younger teaching the older. Ultimately his 'vile race' predominated and displayed 'that in 't which good natures/Could not abide' (I. i. 361–2). This may euphemistically refer to his attempted rape or to a broader sense of his incapacity for becoming civilized. Miranda puts it thus:

> Abhorr'd slave,
> Which any print of goodness wilt not take,
> Being capable of all ill! (I. i. 353–5)

Given a second chance at family life and education Caliban has shown wild, untrainable predatoriness and non-responsiveness to civilizing nurture. Miranda's reaction to a child once treated like a member of the family is like the response of many white settlers to the Native Americans. First contact was friendly and co-operative until some act of innate savagery showed them unresponsive to conversion to Christian and European ways. The problem was partly that the Europeans, believing their culture superior, their religion the only true one, attempted to eradicate Native American culture and convert the tribes.[2] Tension led to rejection and violence, despite the early hopes of some that 'by a gentle and faire entreaty we may win them to be willing to heare and learne of us and our preachers'.[3]

The education context in *The Tempest* offers a range of groupings: Prospero's nuclear family (Miranda), his extended family (Antonio), his 'fostered' family (Caliban, Ariel and Ferdinand), Alonso and his son and daughter, and the 'family' of Alonso's court. There are the invisible family members too: two sets of parents that made two such different brothers in Prospero/Antonio and Alonso/Sebastian; the dead, barely mentioned mother of Miranda; Caliban's witch-mother; and Ferdinand's mother.

Antonio's nature seems irretrievably evil, his brother's essentially good – flawed but virtuous. Sebastian and Alonso are similarly positioned. There is no evidence indicating whether the pairs of brothers were given the same education, so we cannot determine whether nature predominates over nurture, or whether Antonio and Sebastian have simply made a conscious, free-will choice to be evil. It was perfectly possible for two children with identical backgrounds, identical education and parental encouragement to grow up with completely dissimilar personalities. An accumulation of minutely different influences – jealousies, cultural stimuli, brain wiring – would create different personalities, even between children close in age and of the same parents. Where today we would see that no two children can have absolutely identical growing experiences, the seventeenth century would see God's will at work: one child predestined to be bookish, inclined to be withdrawn, but affable and a leader inspiring love; the other capable of state business, but harbouring devious ambition. Such sibling polarities (with varied qualities) are displayed many times in Shakespeare.

With Prospero's 'children' we can be more definite at least about how they have been treated. With each he is consistent in utilizing a range of manners. He is harsh when they appear resistant to him, strict throughout, but with shows of benevolence. Ultimately he is benign in intention, though often imposing his power over them. In this he is a standard paternal figure, being what God and orthodoxy demanded. He has naturally favoured Miranda, his proper child, while the others are 'subjects' and servants. Underlying this seems to be the belief that some people are simply born virtuous and some evil; all are born sinners with a capacity to sin, but education can enhance natural virtue and encourage the readiness to prioritize virtue over sin – if it is the right sort of education. Miranda and Ferdinand fit this definition. Even vicious habits, learned from others, cannot completely annihilate virtuous qualities, which can resurface in crises. Conversely, the wicked soul can only be redeemed through suffering, punishment and repentance. Some remain irredeemable.

Prospero and Miranda

Miranda is regarded as completely accepting of patriarchy and being subordinate to her father. This is inevitable – without maternal input in her formation she owes everything to Prospero, has been under his sole influence for 12 years and is not yet of an age to be independent. Paternal authority, the orthodox default setting of this society, was part of the universal pattern of hierarchy. Heaven was hierarchical, governments were hierarchical and every citizen was automatically part of the hierarchy. A child was necessarily subject to the father's rule. It is pointless deprecating the 'internalization' of patriarchy by Miranda and seeing her as yet another victim of male exploitation in the play. This ignores her individual situation and the contemporary social context. She is necessarily influenced by her father; she will have absorbed his attitudes. Or internalized his patriarchy. There is too the automatic expectation of obedience by those hierarchically inferior. As a child she is subordinate, though it appears she is beginning to rebel. Children naturally internalize parental values, though as youths they may reject them. Children are dependent (materially and intellectually), emotionally unreliable and necessarily controlled by their parents. Transgressing deference evoked feelings of guilt for the transgressor and provoked horror in others. Infringing the rules of hierarchy evoked fear of punishment (divine or human). Submission valorized the system, though the people of England were learning to doubt, scout and flout their self-appointed betters.

Miranda is 14 and Ferdinand is only 'the third man that e'er I saw; the first/That e'er I sighed for' (I. ii. 448–9). She needs protection and yet there are signs in her interaction with Ferdinand that she is beginning to break free of paternal dominance. The awakening sexual awareness of a pubescent girl is another example of nature asserting itself. She is conscious of behaving contrary to paternal wishes: revealing her name against father's 'hests' and prattling 'too wildly' – slight faults. The plot demands she be compliant with Prospero's wishes (which, without her knowing, correspond with her own). These will deliver her into another situation of male control, an orthodox male-dominated marriage, but which seems likely to be loving, companionate and passionate. It bodes well, for Ferdinand seems open, honest and humane. Before Prospero's dynastic plans are revealed Miranda has already pledged herself to Ferdinand ('I am your wife if you will marry me' [II. i. 83]) and he to her ('with a heart as willing/As bondage e'er of freedom' [III. i. 98–9]). At this point their pledge is transgressive. They will presumably achieve a companionate union, negotiate for themselves the nature of their personal relationship while others make the political arrangements. As eventual King and Queen of Naples, both will again have to subsume part of their personal independence in adopting their new socio-political roles.

The father–daughter relationship is the closest familial bond displayed, the parent–child relationship we see most of and the closest to 'natural' or 'normal', but it is not complete nor completely natural. There is no mother involved and Miranda's nurturing has taken place in unusual circumstances, but we see enough to see the sincere love between father and daughter.

The relationship is on the verge of metamorphosis as the young woman, still really a girl, is about to fall in love. We are given information about her during the 'sea-change' from Milan to the island and there is the personality Miranda presents during the play. This is sufficient to project her as another innocent, gentle, pure, lively but somewhat naive female, as first shown in Luciana (*The Comedy of Errors*), repeated in Juliet, Cordelia, Marina (*Pericles*) and Perdita (*The Winter's Tale*). The affection is evident in their little terms of endearment ('my dearest father' and 'my girl'). She is formal with her father too, often addressing him as 'Sir'. This is orthodox for the time and does not indicate coldness. He is after all her mentor/schoolmaster as well as father and in this period address to authority figures was formal. Miranda's love shows too in her concern over her father's suffering as ousted duke.

The dangers and vagaries of their journey into exile (repeated in the marine adventure with which the play commences, with Alonso and Antonio made to undergo a hazard similar to Prospero's) prompt an interesting revelation. The description of the hardships of the sea journey involves a series of reversals. Prospero is ousted from his rightful place in the Milanese hierarchy, and during the voyage the child is smiling and 'infused with a fortitude from heaven' while her father weeps and 'under my burthen groan'd'. The child's insouciant placidity in adversity helps the father find 'an undergoing stomach, to bear up'. In other words the child taught the adult how to find the courage to face the ordeal. She was 'a cherubin', while he was weak and human. Far from being a burden to him she saved him: 'Thou wast that that did preserve me' (I. ii. 153). In greater detail than in referencing his wife he describes how Miranda was like an angel that 'infused' with her smiles 'a fortitude from heaven' (I. i. 154). The lexical choices here – 'drops full salt', 'under my burthen groan'd', 'undergoing stomach', 'bear up' – suggest also that Prospero is giving birth to a new self. Indeed, reborn and reshaped, the director of the fortunes of all the other characters is a more decisive, active man than the duke, who foolishly let his power be stolen. There is the suggestion that Miranda has some sort of divine influence in her – God's grace. As a learned man Prospero would know that the Cherubim were the second most high-ranking angels. Only Seraphim were more prestigious. He hints that the heavenly grace of the child 'saved' the parent and made him anew. This is a reversal of normality. Her name (meaning 'admired one') is suitable for she is to be admired both for her behaviour as an infant and as a loving, sensitive, intelligent young woman. Another reversal is Prospero being father-mother to his child: in the absence of a mother Prospero has had to be both. In bringing Juno into his masque, with her associations with childbirth and motherhood, Prospero is attempting to introduce some female influence as a necessary blessing and counterbalance or female corrective for his male-reared child. The link with Ceres as the deity of nature's fertility, albeit a controlled and cultivated agricultural nature, creates a traditional link that has been celebrated for centuries, joining pagan fertility rites with the hopes expressed in Christian marriage ceremonies. A bride is a reborn creature (metamorphosing from girl to woman) and represents the potential for a new generation of human life, like the new season's crops in the endless parallel of human procreation and nature's fertility cycle.

Further rebirths take place. While Miranda is transformed from submissive girlhood to lively, loving womanhood and prospective bridehood, the survivors have been cleansed by the threatening but merciful sea re-baptizing them. Their clothes are, as Gonzalo observes, 'as fresh as when we put them on first in Afric' (II. i. 66–7). It is a 'miracle' (II. i. 6) like the happy tempest that gave the Bermuda survivors a second chance. Alert audience members would see the final scene as an image of rebirth with religious overtones – a second chance for characters to confess sins, rethink values, rethink their past, repent and acknowledge God's loving Providence.

Through bereavement and despair Alonso is reborn as a rejoicing father and prospective father-in-law. His sins – betrayal and despair – are cleansed and atoned by suffering and repentance. Ferdinand is reborn too – saved from drowning and transformed into hopeful lover and prospective husband. It is for him a happy shipwreck, delivering him safely to an island where he meets, astonishingly, a lovely girl, as beautiful as she is lively and virtuous. For Ariel, release from enslavement and imprisonment by Sycorax shifted seamlessly into enslavement as Prospero's familiar, then rebirth in finally achieving freedom. Caliban too may become new if he actively seeks grace as he declares he will (V. i. 295). Finally, Prospero himself is reborn yet again by embracing forgiveness, relinquishing his magic powers, resuming his dukedom and shifting into the new role of future father-in-law, achieving a revenge of sorts through the marriage. He exposes his brother, annexes Alonso and inserts his family into extended power through the royal union with Naples.

There is evident affection shown by Miranda for her father and indisputable affection, though formal and sometimes strict, from father to daughter. He nurtured her and she has grown into a likeable girl full of the enthusiasm of someone on the edge of adulthood. Not quite three when she was exiled, twelve years on the island makes her nearly 15. Royal marriages were often contracted at that age. Brought up in a one-parent family (unusually, for the time, that parent is the father), she is naive through lack of contact with the wider world, but has the sort of intelligence that learns quickly, adjusts and is instinctively acute. All three familial relationships (Sycorax/Caliban, Alonso/Ferdinand and Prospero/Miranda) are sketchy and incomplete, with one parent absent. Shakespeare has a number of children brought up by lone fathers.

Antipholus of Syracuse (*The Comedy of Errors*) has a mother but is only reunited with her at the end of the play, having been reared by his father Egeus. The twin Antipholuses are of a similar character, though Antipholus of Ephesus is devious and short tempered due to a jealous and shrewish wife. Katherina and Bianca in *The Taming of the Shrew* have no mother though we do not know how recently she died. The sisters are very different, one decidedly resentful that her younger sibling was favoured over her. Hermia in *A Midsummer Night's Dream* is motherless and in conflict with a domineering father over her choice of mate. The cousins Hero and Beatrice in *Much Ado About Nothing* are both motherless though Hero has a father still. They are lively girls, though Hero is considerably more submissive and self-effacing than the irrepressible, independent, intimidating Beatrice. The three sisters in *King Lear* are without a female role model. The two oldest are strong-minded, transgressive, selfish and deceitful. The youngest is naive, virtuous, loving and father's favourite. The cousins Rosalind and Celia in *As You Like It* are without maternal influence but are well balanced and lively, though Celia is more inclined to orthodox submissiveness and follows Rosalind's lead.

The absence of the important female nurturing principle renders the psychological profile incomplete and the absence of information about the mother makes it impossible to ever complete it. Shakespeare presents many partially or completely orphaned heroes and heroines (some are only temporarily separated from parents), which usefully obviates conflict with a parent or parents over the choice of love object, shifting the tension and humour into the line of mad, bad and sad choices made without parental input and through personal misrule and misunderstanding of self, the world and the other. Many Shakespearean families are incomplete and dysfunctional, though to different degrees of gravity. Prospero, parenting alone, seems to have done a good job. He claims (and there is no reason to doubt him):

> I have done nothing but in care of thee,
> Of thee, my dear one [...]. (I. ii. 16–17)

His depth of love and care resonates in his declaration that Miranda is 'that for which I live' (IV. i. 4). This intensely strong father–daughter bond repeats that shown between Lear and Cordelia at the end of *King Lear*, but here tragedy is diverted. Fundamental is Montaigne's belief: 'A true and well-regulated affection should be born, and then increase, as children enable us to get to know them.'[4] Children should be cherished 'with a truly fatherly love' but also judged if they are unworthy. This reflects Prospero. Montaigne recommends consistency; the generous toy giver should not 'resent the slightest expenditure' or become 'miserly and close-fisted' once the child comes of age.[5] He recommends a father share power, influence and money with his children. This is not a concern in *The Tempest* as Miranda will soon be moving to wealth and power in Naples.

Overprotectiveness and overbearing control seem inevitable, natural reactions bearing in mind Prospero's past. Overcompensating for his disengaged parenting and rule in Milan, he has seen her grow at claustrophobically close quarters for the last 12 years. Miranda is judicious, alert, highly articulate, readily affectionate and compassionate. The love shown her during the island years is returned, though she is entering an age traditionally difficult for both sexes and begins (like Caliban and Ariel) to exhibit symptoms of opposition to his authoritarianism and of assertion of selfhood. His strictness was the cultural norm. Patriarchy, hierarchy and authority combine to trap him in orthodox parenting. Phrases like 'Obey, and be attentive', 'Thou attend'st not?' and 'Dost thou hear?' make him sound like a teacher (he calls himself 'thy schoolmaster' [I. ii. 172]). It is a parent's job to educate and discipline: he has had to be her tutor and moral/life mentor. He is proud to have

> [...] made thee more profit
> Than other princess' can, that have more time
> For vainer hours, and tutors not so careful. (I. ii. 172–4)

She replies, 'Heavens thank you for't!' (I. ii. 175) rather perfunctorily and hurries on to ask him to explain why he raised the tempest. This does not denote ingratitude. Rather it betokens the impatience of a young girl. For all his absorption in the 'liberal arts' Prospero is stereotypically paternalist with all four of his children. This authority is symbolically tied to his magic arts. He relinquishes that power by removing his 'magic garment' (I. ii. 24), by breaking his staff and drowning his book – as a king might discard his robes, orb and sceptre – to take on the appearance of ordinary humanity as a father.

Prospero and Caliban

Presented to us after we have met and assessed Miranda and Ariel, the Caliban–Prospero relationship is a stark contrast. Love and protection have not nurtured an affectionate or moral being. Nor has education dispelled Old Adam's sinfulness. Caliban, a sort of foster child, is the polar opposite to Miranda. Abandoned on the island after his mother died, he foraged for himself and was thus able to show Prospero all the places where wild food was available: the crab apples, pig nuts, filberts, and 'young scamels from the rock' (II. Ii. 167–72) he later promises to Stephano in a transfer of allegiance. While Miranda has been closely parented (perhaps too closely), Caliban, nature untamed, has grown up wild and unguided. How much rearing he received from his mother and what sort we do not know, but he must have been a partly formed, unloving personality when Prospero began to nurture him. There had been affection between them until Caliban's attempted rape. Even the gentle Miranda calls him 'abhorred slave' and 'savage' (I. ii. 353, 357). Her overprotective father calls him 'lying slave', 'hag-seed' and 'malice' (I. ii. 346, 367, 369), though his views are coloured by the attempted violation. Prospero claims he has treated Caliban 'with human care' (I. ii. 348) but he seems incorrigibly evil, a 'thing of darkness' (V. i. 275). Education has not worked at the moral level, despite the sort of view advanced by Robert Gray in relation to the Indians: 'It is not the nature of men but the education of men, which make them barbarous and uncivill, and therefore chaunge the education of men and you shall see that their nature will be greatly rectified and corrected.'[6]

To enhance interpretation of the play as a critique of imperial expansion and English involvement in the abduction of Africans for transportation to the growing colonies, critics have taken the word 'darkness' to mean Caliban is dark-skinned. Leo Africanus's *Geographical Histories of Africa* (trans. 1600), which Shakespeare consulted when writing *Othello*, added to the growing demonization of 'the other'. Hakluyt's *Voyages and Discoveries* described Africans as 'fiends more fierce than those in hell'. This was reported after a voyage to Guinea and added Moors and other African tribes to the growing literature that already demonized Jews and Moslems. Drama (for example, *Titus Andronicus*, *The Jew of Malta*, *The Merchant of Venice*, Peele's *Battle of Alcazar* and *Othello*) readily endorsed the stereotypes of its audience's xenophobia. Initially Prospero had made attempts to educate the young savage, teaching him about the sun and moon, 'made much' of him and offered the basic cuddling and physical contact ('strok'st me' I. i. 335) that animal behaviourists and child psychologists agree as being essential to developing emotional balance and affection in the young. Interestingly the nourishment exchange offered by the ex-duke was 'water with berries in 't' (I. ii. 336). This represents a small step from Caliban's wild food towards sophistication. Presumably Milanese cuisine made some contribution to elaborate their diet. Caliban's extempore freedom song declares that he will no more make dams for fish or fetch fire wood (II. ii. 180–81), indicating the use of primitive technology and cooking, presumably Prospero's innovations.[7] Then came the crisis moment when Caliban's implacable naturalness came out in the most natural form: lust. Sex drive is natural but in tutored psyches is repressed and controlled in the name of morality, virtue and decent concern for others. The sexual practice of the natives that Westerners met in America, the Caribbean, Brazil, Peru and Patagonia marked a collision of cultures.

Horror at promiscuity and polygamy ignores European sexual decadence, a common topic for moralistic writers.

Caliban is now a slave/servant kept strictly in his place with inducements, threats and punishments. It is tough love – repressive, harsh but not overly punitive. It is a paradigm of government. Prospero's 'Republic' is not ideal, but the realisms of life dictate the need for an externally applied system of punishments for those who will not conform to biblical or social demands for self-control of antisocial appetites. There is something of hierarchical and ethnic prejudice here. Those of high degree (ignoring the appalling conduct of many of their own rank) tended to look upon commoners as almost subhuman, irredeemable and naturally vicious both morally and physically. Christians tended to hold the same attitudes towards natives in the East and the Americas, seeing them as dangerous savages whom it was their God-driven, God-authorized duty to subjugate, convert and civilize. They applied the example of how Roman occupation civilized savage ancient Britain. Often the process of contact went through an early amicable stage, with natives welcoming the strangers (sometimes regarding them as gods) and the traders or adventurer/explorers regarding the natives as innocent and childlike. As the motives of the incomers became suspect unease and mistrust grew, erupting into conflict and killings. The final phase was large-scale massacre of natives as the visiting strangers became colonial masters, slavers and commercial exploiters.

Caliban and Prospero have been through this same development: 'When thou cam'st first,/Thou strok'st me, and made much of me' (I. ii. 333–4). In return Caliban acquainted Prospero with all the 'qualities o' th' isle'. The turning point came with the attempted rape of Miranda, a brutal abuse of the fatherly treatment Prospero had shown, tellingly exemplifying the natural sexual predatory impulse in man. It replicates the Fall, free will choosing to transgress the boundaries of decent conduct. Promiscuity, a common accusation levelled at the natives encountered in the New Worlds, was an inability to control themselves, particularly under the influence of alcohol. This assumption of moral superiority on the part of early colonists belies the immorality and drunkenness rife both at court and in society in general. Handy excuse or legitimate reason, this was perhaps the point at which Prospero appropriated ownership of the island by enslaving the sole inhabitant/owner. It seems that this was not his intention at the beginning when he 'lodg'd' Caliban 'in mine own cell' (I. ii. 349), made him one of the family, until the savage betrayed the trust invested in him and showed his inescapable nature. Central to this toxic bond is the fact that paying respect, being a servant or slave, or simply lower in rank to someone, creates a negative tension. No one likes to feel inferior. Caliban is likely to always dislike Prospero for being cultivated, educated and having power. His master has not helped. Punishment, necessary as it is, has activated unavoidable resentment. Though custom and law permitted Prospero to beat his servant, humanist theory warned against this. A man with servants 'ought speciallye to thinke that they are men, and not brute beastes, and that he should not rage with crueltye against them, […] for by scourging their hartes are made obdurate and hardened, neyther do they any thing but with evill wyl'.[8] The inevitable downside of rule is that the ruled resent. Prospero, negatively inclined after the attempted rape, has created Caliban anew, imbued with seething resentment. Like the urban mob, like the masses of poor, he is a factor that needs constant vigilant surveillance. He is danger waiting to erupt.

Prospero and Ariel

Ariel's appearance and his accounts of his exploits during the storm introduce a new dimension – magic realized in a moving, speaking spirit – and gives the play a special feel. After the relative normality of Prospero with Miranda this shifts the play further into a fantasy realm. We have been partially prepared for this by Prospero's reference to his 'Art', revealing he had called up the tempest and then laid down his 'mantle'. But Ariel is a whole new degree of drama. There is no reason why the simple direction 'Enter Ariel' should not have been by a flying wire. Admittedly the stage directions are detailed about the spectacle elements and one would expect the instruction here would specify 'flying' if that were required, but it was not such an unusual effect. The 'heavens' partially sheltering the stage in the open-air amphitheatres had a hut which housed the machinery for effecting flights down onto or across the stage. Such effects were common among the Boys Companies in the private hall theatres like Blackfriars, the King's Men's winter venue. Shakespeare used a descending god for the first time in *Cymbeline* in April 1611, but the performance location is not known. Ever more inventive staging arrangements for masques in the Banqueting Hall made wired flight possible. Whether or not Ariel flies in his description of how he split himself and flamed about the ship is itself enough to highlight the strangeness of this strange, unknown play.

This relationship is both parent–child and master–servant. Theoretically a master was seen as a parent to his servants with a duty of care for their safety, well-being and morals. Ariel owes his freedom to the 'master' or 'grave sir' who released him from the cloven pine imprisonment imposed by Sycorax. For a spirit this incarceration would not have been life-threatening, but was exceptionally painful, as Prospero reminds his 'moody' servant. Release required gratitude and, in the manner of Renaissance romances, Ariel puts himself at the service of his rescuer, thus going from one subordination to another. Caliban too, for all his complaints about Prospero's treatment, shifts his allegiance and freedom to Stephano without any thought. For all Prospero's occasional autocratic threats and severity and Ariel's occasional 'moody' complaints, the two are working as a team. There is affection and respect on both sides. Prospero, mixing praise with encouragement, several times expresses gratitude for Ariel's efficient hard work that enables the castaways to be manipulated and Prospero's overall plan to work out. There are moments of discord and discontent on Ariel's part, natural to servitude, but there is a warmer working bond than with Prospero and Caliban. Prospero calls him 'servant', 'my Ariel', 'my spirit', 'my industrious Ariel', 'my delicate Ariel' and 'chick'. The magician, firm in expectation of orders being carried out, praises work well done, and honourably keeps his promise to free his 'spirit' when the mission is complete. In keeping with the values of the time, Prospero claims ownership of his servant. Though there is never any doubt as to who is superior, much of the important action is triggered by Ariel. He is the hard-working stage manager to Prospero's aloof director. Similarly, government in England was really carried out by Robert Cecil, Earl of Salisbury, while James had the ultimate power of yea and nay, the name of king and the expected verbal deference. Prospero is far more determined, clear-minded and proactive than James ever was, but much of the action and humour is incited by Ariel. Their bond is crucial to the working of the narrative.

Prospero and Ferdinand

Ferdinand first enters in a trance, drawn to Prospero's cell by Ariel's music and singing, the first of many musical enchantments and songs. (There are seven musical events and five songs.) For most of the play Prospero assumes the role of substitute father for the bereaved prince. As such, through Ariel, Ferdinand is lured into meeting Miranda, falls for her and agrees to marriage. Prospero is so pleased with Ariel for managing this he shows instantly that important princely quality of acknowledging merit and rewarding accordingly: 'Spirit, fine spirit! I'll free thee/Within two days for this' (I. i.423–4). From the beginning Prospero adopts a stern authoritarian approach. Ferdinand is shown no commiseration for the loss he thinks he has sustained and is immediately treated as a spy and would-be usurper, enslaved and put to the same tasks as Caliban. This is all make-believe to test his qualities. Threatened with enslavement he naturally attempts escape and tries to draw his sword. This shows gentlemanly courage, indicates his nobility and blood. Prospero's magic renders him immobile in the act of drawing, displaying Prospero's power and symbolically thwarting Ferdinand's phallic threat.

Prospero is concerned that Ferdinand will behave like so many young men of rank, regarding all females as sex objects available for satisfying the natural appetites of young men. Having tested the physical mettle of this stranger he has to test his virtue too. He stresses the necessity of pure courtship, indeed goes too far in doing so. This seems to be another example of his overprotective nature, but then Miranda is his only child, is young, inexperienced and is the means by which he will publically reinvent himself and be restored to power. It is evident from the start that Prospero intends Ferdinand to be his son-in-law – if he passes the test. He tells Miranda to look at Ferdinand and comments, 'It goes on, I see' (I. ii. 421). Either this is love at first sight, natural sexual attraction or magic, though nothing indicates a spell has been cast. Either way Prospero has to be persistently vigilant. Miranda is entranced (love's magic) and thinks Ferdinand 'a thing divine'. Ferdinand too misperceives, thinking her a goddess, adding to the misunderstandings accumulating throughout the play from the mistaken tempest onwards. Both express in naive hyperbole the feelings of young love. Prospero maintains the master–slave relationship to test the young man, following the Baconian adage 'Prosperity doth best discover vice, but adversity doth best discover virtue.'[9] Prospero's lack of trust in Ferdinand stems from a deep suspicion of his sexual desires. Having seen how Caliban's sexual predatoriness overrode all sense of gratitude, Prospero is determined not to let any occasion arise for prenuptial sex. He knows what young people are like, how strong and amoral the sex drive. This is another pose, for he plans the union of the young couple, but feels the need to ascertain what Ferdinand's character is, so he may preserve his daughter's virginity and approach the marriage in the formal way orthodox morality demands. Prospero's strictures on masculine lust are highly relevant to a court audience made up of many young people. The early 1600s witnessed a powerful moral crusade against all forms of sexual excess and transgression, including the tradition of premarital sex following a betrothal.

Sycorax and Caliban

Caliban's case is one of classic maternal neglect and paternal absence, followed by separation by death. The child has innate incorrigible evil 'which any print of goodness will not take' (I. ii. 354). He has not been correctly nurtured. He starts from an unpromising base as an 'at risk' child – mother a witch, father 'the devil himself' (I. ii. 321). The seventeenth century believed that human women could and did have sex with demons and that on witches' sabbaths they had union with Satan. This, significantly, makes Caliban illegitimate and therefore ineligible to inherit the island, despite his claim that 'this island's mine, by Sycorax my mother' (I. ii. 333). English law barred bastards from inheriting (or even being part of the church) unless legitimized by the monarch.[10] This has not stopped many critics making much of the claim that the arrogance of Prospero, as evil colonizer annexing rule of the island, deprives the rightful heir. The audience would probably see the situation from the perspective of English law. To them Caliban has no claim to the property. Prospero, who could not hold what was his by right, has now stolen (or taken over) that which was not his from he who had no right to it. If legally Caliban was barred from inheritance, technically Prospero is not a usurper who has 'banished' the heir, but has appropriated rule by virtue of being an adult with experience and power. Caliban's attempted rape of Miranda indicates his unfitness to rule. The 'salvage', already morally corrupt and lacking grace, is further corrupted by resentment and then by alcohol. Hierarchies need people at the bottom of society to legitimize control by those at the top and Caliban's recalcitrance endorses Prospero's authoritarianism just as mob outbreaks justified repression (as a Jacobean audience would see it).

In yet another banishment and usurpation, Sycorax was exiled 'with child' (I. ii. 269) and took the island from Ariel, the spirit of the place. Presumably, whatever rearing Sycorax gave would have reflected her evil. Forced into servitude, Ariel was punished for refusing to obey 'her earthy and abhorr'd commands' (I. ii. 273) and imprisoned in 'a cloven pine' for 'a dozen years' (I. ii. 277, 279), during which time Sycorax died. Prospero's arrival led to the release of Ariel and his 'parenting' of Caliban. A wild child scavenging a savage living for himself up to that point, he might still have been redeemable. If Ariel was imprisoned in the pine for twelve years before Prospero arrived and Prospero has been there for another twelve, then Caliban is now 24 or 25 plus. His 'malice' persists, worsened now by being treated as a slave. To Prospero he is 'filth' and treated as such he behaves like it.

The process of initial nurture leading to an act of savagery leading to enslavement parallels the development of colonization in America and incorporates the themes of rule and service. Kermode suggests Shakespeare might have heard of 'certayne wild men [...] without any certaine language' and of Native Americans converted to Christianity, educated in a monastery 'with fatherly charity', who subsequently betrayed their benefactors.[11] Annexing the island Prospero disregards its two prior inhabitants. As a mature man with some experience of power and control the ex-duke naturally appropriates rule, 'stealing' or appropriating it from a child. All government (and paternalism) is necessary theft, taking freedom from those governed, whether subjects of a land or children within a family. Even government of self involves the restriction, repression or suppression of those features of appetite and passion that threaten balanced, rational, virtuous living.

But self-imposed repression of immoral, antisocial, antireligious impulses to achieve self-control is at least a choice the individual makes for himself. Government and colonization are imposed by superior force. Prospero, to protect his daughter and preserve order, is obliged to take control of Caliban, moving from surrogate father to stern ruler. Caliban's betrayal of trust and ingratitude for past kindnesses deserves punishment and his fitness to rule the island is in doubt despite his claim of legitimate inheritance. That legitimacy is doubtful because under English law bastardy barred him from inheriting and that is the view the audience would probably have taken. It was believed that some children were born with an innate tendency to nobility and honour, others with innate evil. Largely it was thought that all those of aristocratic rank were born virtuous (though clearly history showed many were not). It was also believed that individuals from the other ranks too *might* have such 'gentillesse' or 'noblesse', but were more likely to be irredeemably evil. It was after all an age that devoutly believed that evil existed. Caliban represents that element in humankind that is always going to break rules, despoil and destroy the order that civilization attempts to impose over the anarchic chaos of humanity unsupervised. By art, artifice, invention, domestication of animals and the manipulation and ordering of nature, man has cultivated the wild, turning it from wasted profusion into productive fertility. Some land was uncultivable. So were some people – Native American or English.

Alonso, Ferdinand and the Queen of Naples

Alonso and Ferdinand's grief at the assumed loss of the other indicates a warm bond, but the apparently strong father–son relationship is not fully represented because for most of the play they are apart. The absent (likely dead) Queen of Naples presumably had some influence on her son to have produced a personality so apparently noble, sensitive, honourable and lacking the deviousness his father showed in assisting the usurpation of Milan. What Ferdinand's relationship was with his parents is never revealed, but certainly father and son show genuine grief. Ferdinand describes himself 'sitting on a bank,/Weeping the King my father's wrack' (I. ii. 392–3). Alonso, rendered almost distracted with grief, inconsolable, is incapable of motivating himself for survival. This suffering is the means by which he atones and his soul is cleansed of the sin he committed in the joint coup to remove Prospero. Ferdinand is a counterbalance of continence to Caliban's lust. He seems to be one of those figures in drama who are naturally benevolent and noble and, like Cordelia in *King Lear*, redeem others by their grace. Like Miranda, Ferdinand represents the theological concept of man in a state of primal, prelapsarian innocence. Neither is tainted by the corruption around them.

Details of the upbringing of Prospero and Antonio might have explained how a good womb might bear such different sons. Was Antonio born bad and then drawn into temptation once Prospero delegated power to him? With the Neapolitan royals we have a flawed king who has spawned a good prince. In an age when some believed that individuals were born either predestined to be saved (the so-called elect) or to be damned, it was accepted that some are born naturally virtuous and others innately evil.[12] Sibling polarity is a theme that recurs in a number of Shakespeare's dramas. In *The Tempest* it is doubled by the presence of Alonso and Sebastian – one fallen but redeemable, the other potentially fratricidal, remorseless and easily led. It is a fruitful theatrical device, suitable to allegories or fables/fairy tales and opens up intricate matters of morality (Is goodness learned or innate?), conduct (What makes one brother evil and the other good?) and educational causes and effects (Can example-based schooling create a good, virtuous man or is the evil born in someone ineradicable?).

The Absent Female Principle

The Tempest has only one active female character. There are the goddesses in the masque, but their part in the drama is minimal. This is unusual. Other late plays have a normal range of female figures. *The Winter's Tale* has Perdita, Hermione, waiting gentlewomen Paulina and Emilia, and two shepherdesses Mopsa and Dorcas. *Cymbeline* has Princess Imogen, her mother the queen and Helen, the princess's gentlewoman. *Pericles* has Marina, her mother Thaisa, Marina's nurse and other minor roles: Antiochus's daughter, Dionyza, Diana and a bawd. Consequently, the contrasting female types that help open up the gender relationship discourse in the comedies from *The Comedy of Errors* to *The Winter's Tale* are absent from *The Tempest* in any active sense, and the piece loses the dramatic and comic possibilities created by the interplay between binary opposites (Adriana/Luciana, Katherina/Bianca, Hero/Beatrice, Viola/Olivia and Rosalind/Celia). Female wit and wisdom targeting men and the sex war are absent. Ferdinand and Miranda fall in love at first sight; there are no fallings out, no jealous mistakes, and the whole relationship is a rather tame, naive, juvenile romance. There is some playful banter between them, but it is slight. Miranda's readiness to oppose her father should he not allow the relationship is not developed since he controls everything and wishes them to marry. It is a curiously bloodless affair with minimal breathlessly gushing poetic effusion. They are stereotypes of young love – laughably silly, touching and naive – but represent the familiar hopefulness of the first flush of love at any age. The lack of obstacles on the course of their love, its very smoothness, diminishes theatrical interest.

Like the question 'How many children had Lady Macbeth?' it is futile to ask why Shakespeare gives so little detail about Miranda's mother when a few lines would have been so informative as to their home life, the nature of the parental relationship and Miranda's infant years. What characters do not say is sometimes as resonant as what they do say. Why does Prospero say so little of his wife? He has an obvious chance when asking Miranda what she can remember of her infancy. Why has he never, in the 12 years on the island, talked of his wife? He has often begun 'to tell me what I am, but stopp'd' and put an end to the subject: 'Stay: not yet' (I. ii. 33–6). What makes him stop? Distress at the harrowing memory of loss? A scruple inhibiting discussion of something he is unhappy to address? Or is there a deeper, darker reason? At most we can only say that Miranda's mother's influence must have been negligible, since her daughter has no memory of her. The simple statement 'She was a piece of virtue' suggests a holy, devout woman, dedicated to a godly life, perhaps more concerned about her soul and devotions than nursing her child.[13] The phrase may be spat out scornfully, suggesting she was far from virtuous. Like her husband she may have been more absent than present from Miranda's nursery years. The failure to say more suggests the marriage may have been a cold, formal, arranged union, with respect but without warmth or affection.

The shadows of other women are intermittently present, not as role models, moral guides or educators (that has all been achieved by Prospero), but as subliminal examples to the audience of other sorts of women. They are like a Renaissance tableau of allegorical figures, creating a range of female types stretching from evil through innocently virtuous to divine – from Sycorax to Juno. The shadow females are, in ascending order of virtue: Sycorax, Medea, Dido, Venus, Mall, Meg, Marian, Margery and Kate (the dockside whores of Stephano's song [II. Ii. 47–55]), the 'four or five gentlewomen that once tended' Miranda (I. ii. 47), the many imperfect ladies Ferdinand has been attracted to, Claribel, Miranda's mother, the nymphs in the masque, Iris, Ceres and Juno. Each represents different facets of womanhood, different features of female personality or behaviour, though none has had any effect upon the character of Miranda. She is Prospero's 'creation'.

1. Sycorax, witch mother of Caliban and previous ruler of the island, is referred to in more detail than any of the others. She is part of the evil principle in the play and represents the worst side of women (lustful, transgressive, malign and non-maternal). Her arts were dark and diabolic, she mated with a devil, bore a bastard, was banished to the island, and enslaved and imprisoned Ariel. There are multiple banishments in the play, though none more important than Prospero's. Sycorax is not needed. Dead before Prospero's arrival her influence is still there in the malice of Caliban.

Her presence would only complicate the plot, the whole weight of which is upon Prospero and his pursuit of revenge.

2. Medea, another witch (from classical myth), is present through the echoes and verbatim allusions to her buried in the language. Prospero's farewell to magic incorporates lines spoken by Medea, taken from Golding's 1567 translation of Ovid's *Metamorphoses*. This book was Shakespeare's favourite classical text, pillaged and cannibalized regularly throughout his career. Book VII tells the story of Jason at the Colchian court, where Medea, the king's daughter, fell in love with him. It is a love story with dark undertones and brutal overtones. Medea's magic is black, her love a distorted obsession. She represents the evil of which women are capable (particularly when fixated in love) and the twisted mazes into which love leads people. Medea was a niece of Circe the sorceress who held Odysseus spellbound and turned his companions into swine. The recognizable Ovidian echoes contrast Medea's summoning of evil forces with Prospero's renunciation of the dangers to which unrestrained magic could lead.

3. Intertextually Dido, Queen of Carthage, is there to symbolize the high drama and tragedy developing from uncontrolled passions – the dangerous power of love. In Virgil's *Aeneid* Venus makes her fall in love with Aeneas on his visit to her city and commit suicide when abandoned by the Trojan prince. It is a story interwoven with jealousy and trickery by gods and humans and offers a sharp contrast to the simple and innocent love of Ferdinand and Miranda. An alternative tradition has Dido as a virtuous woman, applauded for founding Carthage, for venerating the memory of her murdered husband and defending her chastity against the intended predation of Aeneas. This long tradition, supported by clerical writers, persisted into the Jacobean period, and was regarded as more historically correct. Contemporary authors saw Virgil's version as an attempt to blacken the origins of Rome's great rival imperial power.[14] The virtuous Dido might require moving to a position in the allegorical line-up next to Miranda's mother. Her precise position is less important than the idea that Miranda is virtuous despite the minimal female input into her formation. She has the innate goodness of high-born heroines in romances whatever their formative experiences. In this she reflects beliefs about the positive qualities the better sort were supposedly born with.

4. Venus, representing erotic love – selfish, lustful and animalistic – has no place in the pastoral bridal-blessing mood of the betrothal play-within-a-play and is banished from the masque.

5. The earthy side of life is further represented by Stephano's song referring to Mall and her companions. They are presumably prostitutes frequented by sailors. This fleeting allusion to London's sexual decadence (already of concern to preachers and pamphleteers) represents the commercial aspect

of sex, again contrasting with the relationship and attitudes of the young lovers. It is also a tiny reminder to those of the court whose morals were little different from dockside whores and their clients.

6. The waiting gentlewomen Miranda remembers from before she was hurried away from Milan are among her earliest memories, presumably for their kindness to the 2-year-old. She 'wast not/Out three years' (I. ii. 40–41) and recalls nothing else 'in the dark backward and abysm of time' (I. ii. 50). Her early years then were spent often without her father (withdrawn into his books) and seemingly without any remembrance of her mother, however virtuous she may have been. It was common that children of titled families, especially if mother and father were courtiers, were left mostly in the care of maids and waiting gentlewomen.

7. Ferdinand's admission to having 'lik'd several women' (III. i. 43) leads inevitably to his declaration of Miranda's superiority: 'so perfect and so peerless' and 'created/Of every creature's best!' (III. i. 47, 48). Each of his earlier loves had 'several virtues' and had that courtly accomplishment of speaking well:

> Th' harmony of their tongues hath into bondage
> Brought my too diligent ear […]. (III. i. 41–2)

But each had 'some defect in her'. Miranda is the *domna soisebuda*, the 'composite lady', of Courtly Love, combining all the necessary virtues demanded by morality, the physical requirements of love's aesthetics and what Ferdinand finds personally attractive. Following Caliban's craven and drunken submission to a new master, comes Ferdinand's willing submission to his 'mistress'. It is the traditional courtly lover's declaration of service, the willing enslavement to the will of the lady he loves. It is reciprocated by Miranda's refreshingly open declaration of her love. There is no game playing, no female wiles, no pretended coyness or wanton flirting. She is, however, aware that she is in some senses betraying her father.

8. King Alonso's daughter Claribel is a victim of politics and patriarchy, obediently but unwillingly married – 'Weigh'd between loathness and obedience' (II. i. 126) – probably as a hoped-for guarantee of peace between Naples and Tunis. Sebastian upbraids Alonso, in xenophobic and racist terms, for his readiness to 'loose her to an African' (II. i. 121). This example of patriarchy – forced marriage for dynastic or political reasons – starkly contrasts Prospero's proceedings. Force is unnecessary. Miranda's attraction to the man he wishes her to marry is unspoken consent. Political marriages were common at royal level and often loveless. At the time of the performance King James was already considering a union between the Spanish *infanta*

and the 17-year-old Prince of Wales as a means of bringing peace between enemies. It was a marriage James was adamant about despite intense anti-Spanish opposition from Parliament, court and commoners.

9. It is very strange that Prospero says so little about Miranda's mother. Her 'virtue' (which is all we learn of her) and his bookishness suggest a cold and formal union of separateness, not a warm and affectionate family situation.

10. It is a feature of Shakespeare and other contemporary writers that though they work within a Christian matrix morally, they refer regularly to the classical deities. This partially reflects their classical schooling, but also avoids prosecution for what might be construed as irreverent references to God on stage.[15] The nymphs and goddesses of the masque bring a mood of hopefulness. Iris, goddess of the rainbow, another stage manager, sets the scene and terms of this blessing for the infant love of Miranda and Ferdinand, automatically evoking thought of the rainbow God sent to symbolize hope after Noah's flood and as a token of Divine Providence. Iris here is part of the hope the 'god' Prospero stakes in his daughter's future, hoping, presumably, for a happier relationship than he seems to have experienced. As a goddess of the sea and messenger of the gods Iris brings together sea and sky (Ariel mentions Neptune and Jove in I. ii. 201, 204), and links humanity and the classical divinities. She is a sister of the Harpies (a form Ariel takes on) and like Ariel posts with speed over land and ocean (I. ii. 252–5) and into the underworld. She bears similarity to Prospero's spirit familiar. The classical images of pastoral plenty invoke a fruitfulness that acts as a correlative to the hope for happiness and fertility in the marriage. Ceres was a mother bereft of her daughter but who presided over the well-being of the land, nature and farming. Juno, though often involved in jealous revenge stories, is here in her benign form as a matriarch and goddess connected with childbirth and motherhood. So the three goddesses represent positive female forces brought to bless the planned marriage.

Finally there is Miranda, physically present and important to the play, there for the audience to measure against the range of other subliminal females and as a humorous romantic figure. She is Prospero's finest achievement. Some critics have seen her as completely bland, subjugated by her father, a victim of patriarchy, subservient to paternal rule, her self completely subsumed or colonized by Prospero's dominance and having internalized patriarchy and become subordinate to it.[16] This fails to take into account that she is only 14, has had no examples of womanhood to form her, knows nothing other than paternal rule and is naturally subordinate to a father she clearly adores. It is also evident that natural female teenage rebelliousness begins to emerge in response to the presence of a young man. This rebelliousness emerges before she even meets Ferdinand. Prospero's repeated exhortations for her to listen, to mark, to attend, suggest a restless expectancy common in puberty. She is waiting for something without knowing what. Her duty, in his eyes, is to remain obedient and chaste. This fails to take account of Miranda's projected subversion of father's power in favour of her new found love. It is a typical young girl's reaction to her first love, supplanting the father. She transfers her interest and energy to absorption with Ferdinand so readily it is as if she has been waiting for this to happen.

The shadow women mentioned in the play are doubly subordinated – by allusion rather than presence and by male report. Most of what is said about Sycorax is related by Prospero in repetition of Ariel's probably biased account. Medea is mediated through Ovid. According to Orgel, Prospero's suspicion of women makes him an unreliable informant. He suggests that the ex-duke is sceptical of female virtue in general, seeing ambiguity in Prospero's one remark about his wife and a hint of her infidelity.[17] The past is always biased by the relation it bears to the teller. Prospero reports his history to his daughter, but what degree of adjustment, what 'spin', he puts on it we do not know. He never addresses the audience directly through soliloquy so there is no opportunity to assess his real, unmediated nature.

Prospero and Antonio

The concern with sibling relationships, occurring in a number of other Shakespeare plays, is a family dynamic of some topical relevance. It focuses on the problem surrounding the nature of man and whether he is predisposed to evil, the discourse about civilization and the constantly debated difficulties connected with primogeniture. Inheritance by the eldest son raised numerous problems. Not least the jealousy of sidelined younger sons. Associated is the question of heirs who are unsuitable on the grounds of immoral lifestyle, mental incapacity (insanity or simple lack of ability, like Henry VI or James I respectively) or disinclination to duty, power and responsibility. Reason and common sense suggest rule should go to the most able rather than the firstborn if he is somehow unsuitable. Montaigne considered that while bonds can be strong between brothers or sisters, inheritance can cause friction. There should be no automatic expectation that siblings will remain friends:

> The name of brother is truly a fair one and full of love [...]. But sharing out property or dividing it up, with the wealth of one becoming the poverty of the other, can wondrously melt and weaken the solder binding brothers together. [...] Moreover, why should there be found

between them that congruity and affinity which engender true and perfect friendship? Father and son can be of totally different complexions [personalities]: so can brothers. […] And to the extent that they are loving relationships commanded by the law and the bonds of nature , there is less of our own choice, less 'willing freedom'. Our 'willing freedom' produces nothing more properly its own than affection and loving-friendship.[18]

In another essay, 'On the Affection of Fathers for Their Children', Montaigne addresses primogeniture. Cuckoo Antonio saw an opportunity to replace his less-than-effective brother who deserved to be ousted, though the act of usurpation was a sin (betrayal). Prospero neglected his duties for the pursuit of his own pleasures. King James did the same regularly, leaving the irksome drudgery of administrative business to his Privy Council while he went on hunting trips to Royston. His obsession with the chase, established early in his reign, did not diminish however complex national problems became. The Milanese duke's devotion to bookish study is somewhat different, but the result is the same – dereliction of duty – and this alone triggers connections with the king sitting on his dais watching the play. A more circumspect Prospero would have shouldered crucial aspects of his role, delegating clearly defined responsibilities to his brother, while reserving an overview of the state to himself. His withdrawal, his monomaniac devotion to books, is excessive – and excess, in Christian thinking, is a sin always liable to punishment.

Associated too is the question of why two privileged young men from the same family should have turned out so differently. As already suggested, the underlying possibility is that, like Caliban, Antonio was predisposed to choose evil. Regardless of their education (and we have no guidance on what that was and whether it was the same for both brothers), Antonio may be presumed to have been encouraged to be virtuous. That he chose of his own free will to do what he cannot but have known to be wrong is a reminder of the original sinfulness of man. Born with the curse Adam bequeathed to all humans, Antonio fails to use his free will to choose good and reveals himself as incorrigibly evil – in the backstory, in the planned betrayal of his erstwhile co-conspirator the King of Naples and in his failure to display or express any remorse at the end of the play. His blockish, obstinate silence, refusing to explain, is reminiscent of the immovably evil opposition to God shown by Satan. Antonio has less excuse than Caliban. Had there been extenuating circumstances in his upbringing to explain his greed for complete power they would surely have been mentioned. There is nothing to excuse his coup other than the corrupting attraction of power to a sinful mind or a deep desire to do his brother wrong. Relevant to rich families where the sons are not expected to work is the conundrum of what to do with the idle children of the idle rich once educated and of age. Thomas More had already signalled this problem:

> A great many noblemen [...] live idly like drones, off the labors of others, their tenants whom they bleed white by constantly raising their rents. (This is the only instance of their tight-fistedness, because they are prodigal in everything else, ready to spend their way to the poorhouse.) These noblemen drag around with them a great train of idle servants, who have never learned any trade by which they could earn a living.[19]

Resonant here is Montaigne's comment that neglected children 'are driven by despair to find some way, however unjust, of providing for their needs'.[20] This relates to Caliban too, prompting the question whether Prospero is right to persist in his mistrust, having perhaps created Caliban's persistent resentment by his failure to forgive.

Montaigne is clear about maintaining 'gentle relations with my children and so encourage in them an active love and unfeigned affection for me', and feels that 'it is also unjust, and mad, to deprive our grown up children of easy relations with their fathers by striving to maintain an austere and contemptuous frown, hoping by that to keep them in fear and obedience'.[21] He recommends a father be open and express his views and feelings frankly, wishing for no misunderstandings, either in his favour or against. Prospero's austere treatment of Miranda must have been counterbalanced by many instances of affection for towards the end of the play she sprinkles her dialogue with epithets and expressions of love.

Prospero's conduct raises doubt about uncontrolled patriarchy. Underlying the parent–children groupings in the play is the question of just how much real love existed between parents and offspring in a time when marriages were often arranged, and when many parents (fathers particularly) among the political elite were often not only physically and emotionally distant from each other but detached from the nursery, took little interest in their growing children, and were emotionally cold when they were together. Patriarchal strictness, if not ameliorated by love and softer moments, did not encourage close, loving bonds. Duty, the Commandment to honour thy father and thy mother, did not necessarily encourage love. Authoritarian males could be distant and family interactions often coldly formal. Parents were often figures of awe and an angry father, disobeyed or thwarted, could be like the wrath of God. Montaigne deprecates aloofness:

> I am against the custom of forbidding children to say 'Father', and requiring them to use some other, more respectful title, as though

Nature had not sufficiently provided for our authority. We address
God Almighty as Father and scorn to have our own children call us
by that name.[22]

After some initial distance, Prospero has been far from an absent father –
perhaps too present, but what option was there? He has been and still is
loving, sometimes cool, but ultimately affectionate.

> I have done nothing but in care of thee,
> Of thee, my dear one [...]. (I. ii. 16–17)

In keeping with the orthodoxy of patriarchal rule Prospero maintains his
power and control while mixing it with love and care. His circumspection
(or clairvoyance) fails him twice. Does he foresee Miranda pre-empting
the official announcement of her father's wish for her to marry Ferdinand
by pledging herself to him unilaterally? He forgets, during the masque, that
Caliban is leading the base plotters to his cell in order to assassinate him.
Alonso unquestionably loves Ferdinand, Prospero loves Miranda and Ariel,
and feels some responsibility for Caliban. What Sycorax felt for her 'freckled
whelp' (I. ii. 283) is unknown. We assume it was neither loving nor nurturing
or he would have a stronger moral sense. But then many courtiers present
behaved no better for all their privileged upbringing.

Chapter 10

THE CONTEMPORARY POLITICAL CONTEXT

The Word on the Street

Problems were mounting in England, a slow accumulation of anxieties – perceived moral decay, social tensions and economic difficulties. Dissatisfaction with the king persisted. There was increasing debate (not just in Parliament) about the nature of kingship, the limits thereof and the style of rule. Topics of special concern were not confined to the mechanics of government at the royal/ministerial/parliamentary level, but were moving into the arena of civil rights and individual status under the law. Arbitrary imprisonment at the whim of the king, royal intimidation of judges and judicial power biased in favour of the ruling ranks were subject to vehement vocal questioning. These concerns worsened. The Leveller Richard Overton indicated the degree to which they had risen by 1646 when, from his cell in Newgate (he was illegally incarcerated by the House of Lords) he wrote a pamphlet entitled *An Arrow against All Tyrants* that states:

> To every Individuall in nature, is given an individual property by nature, not to be invaded or usurped by any: for every one as he is himself, so he hath a self propriety, else he could not be himself, and on this no second may presume to deprive any of, without manifest violation and affront to the very principles of nature, and of the Rules of equity and justice between man and man; mine and thine cannot be, except this be: No man hath power over my rights and liberties, and I over no mans.[1]

Such views were being voiced thirty years before.[2] Overton asserts that self and property are protected by the law and are not to be predated by the will of any (i.e., monarch, lords or gentry). The full title makes explicit the intensity of the situation: *An Arrow against All Tyrants shot from the Prison of New-gate into the Prerogative Bowels of the Arbitrary House of Lords and All Other Usurpers and Tyrants Whatsoever*. This citizen selfhood was restated more succinctly in John Locke's key post–Civil War text *Two Treatises of Government* (1690): 'Every Man has a *Property* in his own *Person*. This no Body has any Right to but himself.'[3] This view has relevance to the matter of slavery – not only in the burgeoning colonies, but in the shires of England. More broadly it relates to the relationship between servants and masters, to land workers and tied cottages, to the lack of protection in law for anyone without high status, influential connections or money. In the early 1600s in country taverns, on city streets, ordinary men were beginning to raise questions and voices. Such views, expressed at the commencement of the century, grew louder up to, through and after the Civil War. The matter of personal right is pertinent to Prospero's rule, his appropriation of Caliban as slave and Ariel as servant, and his domination and punishment of them.

At the level of daily chatter in 1610 and 1611, people gossiped about the king's increasing indebtedness, his clashes with Parliament, the behaviour of his favourites and their depredations upon the nation's finances, various court scandals, the misfortunes of the Virginia colonists, some horrific domestic murders, the execution of two Catholic priests, the plague and a major robbery.[4] And as always, there was the uneasy sense that society might at any time collapse, that the ever-restless mob might rise, that law, order, control were fragile and precarious. This is reflected in the threat posed by Caliban, Stephano and Trinculo. The king's debts seemed a perennial, irresolvable problem. Since his succession James had racked up greater and greater expenses. His personal extravagance and that of his court were a persistent aggravation. The Great Contract (1610), put forward by the Lord Treasurer, Robert Cecil, required that Parliament vote a sum to clear the king's debts and agree to James receiving an annual sum of £200,000. In return he would give up his prerogative rights over wardships and purveyance[5] and cease to impose new import taxes. Entangled arguments over this, with both sides altering their aims, led to the plan being dropped, but the matter indicates the differences inherent in opposed perceptions of monarchical role, rule and the relationship with the Commons. In discussion between James and thirty members of the Commons, Sir Henry Neville had declared, 'Where your Majesty's expense groweth by the Commonwealth, we are bound to maintain it; otherwise not.'[6] This means costs related to public and national needs should be met by subsidies voted by Parliament, but personal expenses should not. Sir Henry went on to say:

> The King had received four subsidies and seven-fifteenths which is more than ever was given by any Parliament at any time; […] yet

withal they had no relief of their grievances. It is commonly said that the Parliament could be content to replenish the royal cistern of the King's Treasury were they assured that the King's largess to the Scots' prodigality would not cause a continual and remediless leak therein. Also, that one in the Lower House lately promised to produce a bill of £100,000 of debts owing to the Crown by Scotsmen who bear their creditors in hand that they shall all be paid when the new taxes come into the Exchequer.[7]

The Tempest, like *King Lear* and *Measure for Measure*, is a play based on a problem caused by imperfect governorship. Extravagance was not Prospero's flaw (that would invite dangerous identification with James) but rather a detachment from the rigours of administration, though it seems unlikely Antonio was an honest administrator. James was fond of lecturing Parliament and his court and had a tendency from his early years to put quill to paper to deliver his mind in print. In his late teens he wrote poetry (including an epic). Subsequently he turned to polemic and politics with *Daemonologie* (1597), *The True Law of Free Monarchies* (1598), *Basilikon Doron* (1599), *A Counterblaste to Tobacco* (1604), *An Apologie for the Oath of Allegiance* (1608) and *A Premonition to All Most Mightie Monarchs* (1609). Prospero shares some specific traits with James: a snappy temper, a disinclination to bureaucratic minutiae, a love of the liberal arts, and a childlike determination to control and have things his own way. These are serious enough, but, as with *King Lear* and *Measure for Measure*, Shakespeare distances his character sufficiently to be safe from arrest. The play addresses the question of what kind of man should rule and whether the philosopher-king was a workable model for effective political engagement. It shows the current duke as a man who, on his way to power, bought support (as James did), sold offices (as James did), sacked those who did not go along with him (as James did) and liked to keep control (as James did). These are common faults among governors. In other respects Antonio and Prospero are sufficiently far removed not to be treasonably identifiable with the king. One is deviously Machiavellian, the other a magician controlling the elements.

All this takes place on a Mediterranean island in an atmosphere of fantasy, with spirits, illusions, a wild man, a drunken butler, a drunken jester and a cluster of courtiers. Echoes of Whitehall are constant but tiny and distant. The whole play is of course, like all plays, pretence, illusion, ephemera and playacting – an unreal mirror of the reality beneath the surface. Arrogance, vanity, ambition, betrayal, lust and hypocrisy are all there under the magical playfulness. The tempest is simulated and harmless and Prospero's simulated anger is part of the edifice of pretences. The assumed deaths of Ferdinand

and Alonso, the pretended loyalty of Sebastian, the simulated friendliness
of Stephano to Caliban, the illusions created by Ariel, and the 'baseless
fabric' (IV. i. 151) of the masque, all cast doubt on what might be real. The
'cloud-capp'd towers, the gorgeous palaces' (IV. i. 152) of the masque fade
like an 'insubstantial pageant' (IV. i. 155). The description of what Ferdinand
saw during the masque may be either what he is imagined as imagining or a
description of a painted backcloth against which Ceres, Juno and Iris acted.
But they were all illusions, like the performance itself – dreams like life as if
life is a play, an illusion that will pass. Unrealism is so prominent in the play
that it has been interpreted as a piece of meta-theatre about the artificial
nature of drama, a play about being a play. Prospero's 'Art', his magic, is like
a dramatist weaving the magic of words to manipulate audiences' emotions,
making them laugh or cry at what is a make-believe 'insubstantial pageant'.
Prospero is the director/lead actor, organizing and focusing everything. Ariel
is his serving man of many parts – fire, light, harpy, sea nymph, Ceres and
invisible music maker – playing different roles as Prospero directs. All the
rest are his troupe of players, moving to his command. It sometimes feels as
if, with his need to remain omnipotent in order to control and execute his
plan, the whole action is going on inside Prospero's head, as if it is all the
wish-fulfilment daydream of a man imagining getting his own back on those
who have wronged him. It is the nature of things to go wrong and we have
all dreamed of gaining complete control and punishing those who have hurt
or thwarted us. But even Prospero cannot make Antonio say sorry or ensure
happiness for his son-in-law and daughter.

The Neapolitan Context

The King of Naples plays an important but muted role. His grief at the assumed
loss of his son provides a strong consistent element to the plot. For all his
power as ruler of an extensive realm in the south of Italy (including Sicily),
overlord of the Milanese dukedom, he is subject to that most levelling sorrow –
the loss of a child – and is immune to consolation. He is in many scenes,
but is depressed and uncommunicative. His reaction to his loss works both
as an indication of his true character and as a punishment for his past wrong
in materially assisting the removal of a rightful ruler.[8] In purely theatrical
terms his situation is a hook for the audience's emotions. In the Renaissance,
his kingdom was not only a sizeable area but an important collision point
in European politics claimed by both the French and Spanish crowns. A
recent ruler, Alfonso II, was married to Ippolita Maria Sforza. Her family
had been rulers of Milan and her father was the famous Ludovico Sforza,
nicknamed Il Moro (the Moor). Alfonso had been forced out of power by a

French takeover. His son, Ferdinand II, governed for only a year before dying and being succeeded briefly by Frederick, ruling from 1496–1501 before being ousted by another French attempt to gain a foothold on the peninsula and increase its strength against the stranglehold of Spanish domination in Italy and the Continent in general. The French Angevin usurper Louis XII was in his turn vanquished at the Battle of Garigliano in 1503 by Ferdinand III of Aragon (ruled 1504–16), in power at the time of *The Tempest*. Throughout the rest of this period Naples was part of the Spanish hegemony of Europe as Holy Roman Emperors and occupiers of the Netherlands. Both Naples and Milan were conflict areas that displayed in concentrated form many English prejudices about Italy and Italian politics. A 1561 reprint of William Thomas's *History of Italy* might have provided Shakespeare names and information on recent power struggles that underlie the political concerns of his play. *The Tempest* is not a docudrama about Italian dynastic conflicts, but uses some of the details to set up the Prospero–Antonio–Alonso backstory and their political entanglement. The Milan connection is there, Alonso is the Italian variant of the Spanish name Alfonso, several Ferdinands crop up, and there are usurpations, coups and grabbing of domains. At approximately two hundred and fifty thousand people, Naples was the largest European city and a thriving cultural and commercial centre. Rich, decadent, riven by political jealousies, too much in the thrall of the church, rife with syphilis, subject to regular outbreaks of the plague, overcrowded, resonant with sharp differences between rich titled families and the mass of poverty-stricken commoners, violent and restless, it was not dissimilar to London. Its recent violent history adds to the allusions that echo English court politics.

Chapter 11

ENCHANTMENT: THE CONTEXT OF MAGIC

The Ambiguous Status of Magic

John Bainbridge, a London physician, was also an enthusiastic astronomer and mathematician. In the predawn dark of 28 November 1618 he peered through his telescope, charted the path of a comet, recorded its appearance, calculating its speed and altitude, then wrote up his findings and conclusions in a book. Oddly, among the scientific data, algebraic equations, verse and flattering dedication to the king, Bainbridge claimed the trajectory between New Guinea and the Arctic, crossing Britain, was a sign that God would reveal to his chosen English race the long-sought location of the Northwest Passage to the Indies. This bizarre mix of scientific method and belief in revelation highlights the uneasy co-existence at the time of the growing body of natural philosophy (the name then for the sciences) and the vestiges of magic and superstition. It also indicates the indeterminate terrains a doctor inhabited as part magician, part scientist in a godly society. The blurred boundaries between magic and science are evident too in Isaac Newton's dabbling in alchemy while also authoring the severely rational and methodical *Philosophiae Naturalis Principia Mathematica* (*The Mathematical Principles of Natural Philosophy*). In 1687, when Newton published his work, magic's status was still unclear. The church disapproved of it strongly, yet, surviving from pagan times into post-Reformation England, magic was a continuing part of general life. Superstition is an innate constituent of the human psyche. Religion was beginning to be questioned, sometimes seen as institutionalized superstition. The church was undecided doctrinally whether witches and ghosts could be authenticated and officially believed in or not. Both were thought of as evil emanations linked to diabolism.

Most ordinary people believed in religion *and* magic. So too did the higher ranks, visiting high-end, high-profile, high-price 'wizards' like John Dee,

Simon Forman and William Lilly. The village wise woman or cunning man persisted into the nineteenth century.[1] These figures exercised white magic, much of it herbal and medicinal, based on centuries-old country lore, some efficacious, much superstitious nonsense, but satisfying people's beliefs in the predictability of the future and the effectiveness of charms, amulets and talismans for preserving good health (yours, your livestock's, etc.), finding lost items, discovering who would marry you or making someone fall in love with you. Along with spells and predictions about personal luck were charms to outdo or harm rivals in business or love, activities dangerously close to black magic, witchcraft or wizardry. Defining white or black magic often depended on whether the intentions were good or harmful and whether the local climate was vehemently anti-magic. That in turn depended on the zeal of the vicar and the attitudes of neighbours. Strongly Puritan localities were more likely to be obsessively alert to signs of magic activity. The Salem witch trials, though taking place in Massachusetts, are a prime example of how witchcraft accusations could be symptomatic of grievances in isolated communities about landholding, personal relationships, inheritance, boundary demarcation, and any of the many niggling squabbles that break out between neighbours.[2]

Among the various words for men with power over the forces of the world – magician, conjuror, charmer, wizard, necromancer or sorcerer – the last two carry occult implications. A necromancer learned of future events by communing with or calling up the spirits of the dead. The name 'sorcerer' derives from Old French *sorcier* and implies the use of black arts and therefore devilish activities. Whatever title you used you could be subject to accusations of witchcraft depending on the climate of the time. Epidemics of accusations rose if the local vicar or the diocesan authorities were active and if the register of communal fear was high, with anxieties about outbreaks of disease (among humans or animals), extreme weather or the activities of Catholics. Prejudice in the locality was often stoked by the vicar if he was personally vehement against witchcraft, but individual laypeople might also be activated against a specific old man or woman who practised the cunning arts and was thought responsible for illness among animals or bad luck in the family. People are always quick to point the finger of blame at others and not too fussy about evidence. There were intermittent outbreaks of zeal against such shadowy characters as the cunning man and the wise woman and they might be unlucky enough to be taken up as dealing in black arts, tried and burned. Unusual birth deformities could provoke charges the unfortunate mother had had dealings with the Devil.

The presence in a locality of a 'witch finder' like Matthew Hopkins tended to produce a spike in accusations. These would dwindle once he left the area. This seems to be due to: 1. the general suggestibility of people (if you tell them there is witchcraft in the village they will soon find a culprit), and 2. specific factors in the region (tensions in religion, commerce, farming, landholding or personal rivalries). Particular regions seemed to be more prone to 'discovering' witchcraft than others. Scotland had more trials and burnings than England. The Holy Roman Empire (largely Catholic) was subject to periodic witch hysteria and mass trials, while England was largely free of such extreme outbursts.[3] Extreme Protestant demonologists made no distinction between white and black magic, associating all magical practices with diabolism. Despite the official stance on any form of magic, ranging from suspicion and disapproval to extreme punishment, plays seemed a permitted medium for its portrayal, sometimes for didactic condemnation (as in *Faustus*), sometimes as a vehicle of satirical comment on the corruption and follies of society (as in *The Devil is an Ass*, 1616, and *The Witch of Edmonton*, 1621) or more commonly for its comic potential (producing mayhem and mistakes) and its visual sensationalism (as in *Friar Bacon and Friar Bungay*, c. 1598).

Like *A Midsummer Night's Dream* (1594–96), where magic is riotously humorous in its effects, *The Tempest* inhabits a strange no man's land between the fleshly world of men and the airy world of spirits. It is suffused with an atmosphere of magic, enchantment, tricks, illusions, disembodied music and spectacle (ingredients skirting the edge of diabolism), yet is embedded in Christian values. The mad, inexplicable enchantment of love at first sight is there in the Miranda–Ferdinand storyline (manipulated and partially manufactured by Prospero). There is the hypnotic effect on Prospero of his studies to the extent that he neglects his civic duties. Was that devil-inspired madness or personal aberration? There is the spellbinding effect of theatre, illusion masquerading as reality and – sometimes comically, sometimes chillingly and potentially tragically – reflecting the actions and outcomes of reality. There is, above all, the overarching magic of Prospero's 'Art' that creates and drives the storyline.

The title itself may echo an alchemical term for distilling the contents of a retort to remove impurities as part of the process for transmuting base metals into gold.[4] The 'tempest' was the boiling of the fluids prior to condensation. The process of the play metaphorically parallels the violent boiling (the storm) and the subsequent purification (the reconciliation and planned marriage). What magic does Prospero display? He divines that the nearby fleet contains his intended victims, raises an apparently life-threatening storm, brings the passengers safely to shore and the crew and vessel safely into a sheltered bay. At will he puts Miranda into a hypnotic sleep, freezes Ferdinand as he attempts to draw his sword, and threatens Caliban with pinches and cramps, punishments he has received before. These are impressive skills and useful for theatrical effect and amusement. Most of the other conjuring is performed by Ariel. It is Prospero who commands Ariel but it is the spirit who executes them. At his own will he displays extra visual and sound effects aboard the ship and has free rein to play with the various castaways. The fire and light on the vessel (a well-known phenomenon called St Elmo's fire)[5] are Ariel's own spectacular additions to the storm. Prospero also has his spirit servant supervise surveillance of the court and servant groups and play various tricks (invisibly teasing Stephano and Trinculo, leading them through mire and briars). Ariel organizes other spirits to bring in a banquet and act as hunting hounds. He may play Ceres (IV. i. 167) in the masque, which requires three spirits as deities and others as nymphs and reapers. He creates the disembodied music, hypnotizes the court characters into sleepwalking, and forces the low-born plotters through muddy discomforts. These tricks are left to the inventive spirit to improvise, much as Oberon in A *Midsummer Night's Dream* outlines his broad strategy but leaves the details to Puck. The more spectacular magic happens offstage and is only reported. Prospero claims magical necromantic acts predating the play's timeframe:

> I have bedimm'd
> The noontide sun, call'd forth the mutinous winds,
> And 'twixt the green sea and the azur'd vault
> Set roaring war; to the dread rattling thunder
> Have I given fire, and rifted Jove's stout oak
> With his own bolt; the strong-bas'd promontory
> Have I made shake, and by the spurs pluck'd up
> The pine and cedar: graves at my command
> Have wak'd their sleepers, op'd, and let them forth
> By my so potent Art. (V. i. 41–50)

These claims all relate to command of elemental forces. He called up Ariel at midnight to fly to the Bermudas to collect dew and has him 'tread the ooze' at the ocean's bottom and dig in 'the veins o' th' earth' (I. ii. 252–5). Critics have seen this as indicating Ariel's connection with all four elements (air, water, earth, fire) and as a possible reference to the hopes of mining gold and silver in Virginia. What was the point of these activities? Creating an eclipse, calling up storms, making an earthquake, splitting oaks and ripping up other trees shows command of Earth's forces, though why he should have done any of this is unclear. It seems pointless and has led to no good for mankind, though, if confined to the island, then they have done no ill either. Was Prospero just practising his skills, testing his progress? Loosing dead bodies from graves is the most disturbing. Why do it? Where did he do it? The island is uninhabited apart from himself, Miranda and Caliban, unless there had been an earlier population. Perhaps he does it at long distance in another location. This is the most morally questionable magic, close to necromancy – divining the future by contact with the dead – and is a form of spiritualism. Raising the dead, even if they did not then return to normal living, is blasphemously near to imitating Christ – but to no apparent good or ill. This was not like calling Lazarus back to life. If Prospero could open graves and let out rotting corpses and skeletons could he not at any time have brought Antonio and Alonso to the island or transported himself to Milan to take revenge? Perhaps his powers have only recently progressed to such a pitch. Perhaps he possessed this power but chose not to use it, his sense of the theatrical and his liking for control perhaps dictating he bring an audience to his realm to see his power and witness the humbling of his enemies. That could have been achieved sensationally and with the same outcome in Milan. He talks of his 'Art' as being 'so potent', yet much of his power seems dependent upon luck and a fortunate combination of the stars:

> By accident most strange, bountiful Fortune
> (Now my dear lady) hath mine enemies
> Brought to this shore; and by my prescience
> I find my zenith doth depend upon
> A most auspicious star, whose influence
> If now I court not, but omit, my fortunes
> Will ever after droop. (I. i. 178–84)

Is his 'so potent Art' another illusion? We rely upon Prospero for much of the backstory. Retelling his past he may adjust it, understating his own role and blame, overstating his brother's responsibility, being curiously evasive about his wife and inflating his powers. Should we believe all his claims to magical events? Should we take the magic seriously? Or should it be regarded simply as a device to manipulate the plot of what is essentially an unbelievable story in which we suspend our disbelief for the sake of entertainment, amusement and the lessons it embodies? Prospero's status as magician is inconsistently realized.

The inconsistencies between his claimed power (and what it might have done) and the actualities of what he does do, suggest Shakespeare was not concerned to create a credible magician, but perhaps to display the absurdity of the mayhem leading ultimately to one remorseful king, two recalcitrant villains, an unconvincingly stoic slave and a forthcoming marriage. Immense power achieving petty ends is an ironic reflection on monarchy. Whatever his power Prospero cannot make Antonio confess and reform or socio-psychologically engineer Caliban's mindset any more than

Christ could change the impenitent thief crucified with him. In the words of Feste, 'What's to come is still unsure' (*Twelfth Night*). Attempting to logically analyse motive and opportunity are out of place. We are supposed to accept what he has done, what he can do and what he does, without looking too closely into it. Many of the court audience would anyway have accepted that such magic was possible and would be too lost in the illusions of the play to analyse the story and identify inconsistencies. They would also have been fascinated to know the outcome. This is inherent in the telling of any story: it is more impelling to ask 'What is going to happen next?' and 'Where will it lead?' than to logically dissect every minute detail.

Magic and religion are central to the atmosphere of the piece. Magic is essential to most of the developing action and religion is central to its ethical framework. Abjuring his 'rough magic', divesting himself of the traditional mage's cloak, burying his staff and drowning his book are acts of renunciation heralding a return to normal human life. Unlike Faustus, Prospero is able to draw back from the lure of power (magic's power at least). He comes close to sorcery, but retreats from it. Within the play's scope he does nothing evil, casts no malefic spells, and his powers diminish once he removes his 'magic garment'. He is not guilty of the sort of devilish sorcery that Friar Bacon performs in Robert Greene's *Friar Bacon and Friar Bungay* (c. 1590–91), where two characters are transported through space. This is achieved by simple theatrical means (they exit one scene and reappear in another location). The first event involves Bacon (in Oxford) striking dumb Bungay (in Suffolk) so that he cannot marry Margaret and Lacy; the stage directions then state: '*Enter a* Devil, *and carry off* Bungay *on his back*' (II. iii). The direction does not have the devil appear through the trap door as was normal practice, but as he carries Bungay on his back perhaps it was easier for a simple stage-level entrance and a piggyback exit through one of the doors at the back; spectacular effects would not be needed. The second act of transportation occurs when a German magician who challenges Bacon to a contest of skill calls up the spirit of Hercules and is then, at Bacon's command, carried away to Hapsburg by the spirit. Just prior to that, Bungay, safely delivered to Oxford, conjures the tree of the Hesperides, '*with the Dragon shooting fire*'. These props might be kept in the inner room and the curtain drawn back to reveal them. The spirit of Hercules could use the trapdoor to rise from the Underworld. All this indicates the attractiveness to audiences of spectacle, theatrical trickery and illusion.

Bacon is persuaded to renounce his art by what may be seen as a warning from God. He has made a huge bronze head that will speak. Giving life to an inanimate object is an act of blasphemy; in appropriating the prerogative of the divine, Bacon transgresses unacceptably. The head speaks three times gnomically: 'Time is', 'Time was', 'Time is past'. Then '*a lightning flasheth forth, and a hand appears that breaketh down the* Head *with a hammer*' (IV. i.). This is dramatic and could be frightening if realized effectively. The hammer represents retribution, God's vengeance. *The Tempest* presents a rather muted spectacle by comparison. Bacon predicts bad luck is coming. Two scholars ask him to show them their fathers back home. In his 'prospective glass' (i.e., a crystal ball) they see the two men fight and kill each other. The sons then argue about who was to blame and stab each other too. This convinces Bacon his skills are dangerous and he breaks the glass. He fears damnation for 'using devils to countervail his God' (IV. iii. 98); he regrets:

> The hours I have spent in pyromantic spells
> The fearful tossing in the latest night
> Of papers full of necromantic charms,
> Conjuring and adjuring devils and fiends,
> [...]
> The wresting of the holy name of God. (IV. iii. 88–93)

But he seeks forgiveness:

> Sins have their salves, repentance can do much:
> Think Mercy sits where Justice holds her seat,
> And from those wounds those bloody Jews did pierce,
> Which by thy magic of did bleed afresh,
> From thence for thee the dew of mercy drops,
> To wash the wrath of high Jehovah's ire,
> And make thee as a new-born babe from sin. (IV. iii 157)

Prospero has never meddled with devils. The supernatural creatures in *The Tempest* are called 'spirits of shapes', never devils, but Friar Bacon admits:

> I have dived into hell,
> And sought the darkest palaces of fiends;
> That with my magic spells great Belcephon
> Hath left his lodge and kneeled at my cell;
> The rafters of the earth rent from the poles,
> And three-formed Luna hid her silver looks,
> Trembling upon her concave continent,
> When Bacon read upon his magic book. (IV. i. 8–13)

Prospero, though he has a cell, a book and spells, and reportedly has 'rifted' oaks and made the Earth quake, he has no truck with devils and has no compact with Hell. His magic is solely focused upon regaining his dukedom. Ariel is not a demon familiar. Refusing to obey Sycorax's 'abhorr'd commands', he indicates a moral dimension and emerges as a servant who will not do that which is wrong. More mischievous than malign, Ariel is a spirit or fairy. Is Prospero suspect simply by being a magician? Leading Puritan William Perkins, for whom all magic was diabolic, would have condemned him. Is magic itself suspect? The church certainly saw all human attempts to harness more than human powers as dangerous, possibly diabolic, probably heretical and definitely to be discouraged. Divination (using supernatural means to ascertain the future), necromancy, selling magic talismans, casting love spells, writing spells on paper notes worn in a pouch hung about the neck, making love potions and astrological predictions, all came under the heading magic, but were less seriously opposed by the church than the summoning of devils, selling your soul to Satan, demonic possession, putting pins into wax effigies or causing disease and death. These were Satanic works. The church was unhappy with both white and black magic. This explains the uneasy and sometimes punitive reaction to scientific advance; it often looked magical, diabolic or as if it were trespassing into God's domain. The church was desperately trying to consolidate its hold on England's faith. It was besieged – by Catholics who never gave up their religion and by the inertia of those who did not much conform to any religion devoutly but tended to cling on to semi-superstitious vestiges of old pagan lore. Even sincere Protestant believers were generally reluctant to give up belief in magic. In 1584 it was claimed, 'Three parts at least of the people [remained] wedded to their old superstition still.'[6] Black and white magic were delicate matters in this time. All occult or diabolic dealings were punishable by death. Astrological predictions and all those forms of 'magic' relating to medical, amatory or monetary needs and a host of other personal matters were open to suspicion, however benign they might be.

For the purposes of theatre the make-believe display of magic was acceptable, but the whole subject was controversial. The representation of spirits, elves and fairies was part of many comedies. The Devil, goblins and demons were brought onstage, but it had to be made clear that they were condemned doctrinally and represented evil. The supernatural in general conflicted with church doctrine and with the growing knowledge of science. Magic was in decline, but eradicating the superstition attached to it was very slow. The Church of England had officially banished all papistical superstitions – in the miraculous powers of saints' statues or the thousands of relics held in churches and cathedrals all over the country. Holy shrines like those at Canterbury and Walsingham were destroyed. Holy wells and other sacred places like springs and grottoes were prohibited (though secretly still visited). Non-Christian superstitions were regarded as dangerous pagan beliefs deviating from prescribed orthodoxy. As recently as 1600 the Italian intellectual Giordano Bruno, who had met with Dee's circle during a stay in England, was burnt for various heresies, including interest in the occult, questioning church doctrine about the Trinity, Christ and the Incarnation, whether Jesus was Christ, whether Mary was a virgin, and whether bread and wine turned to Christ's flesh and blood during communion. Satanic allegiance was a handy label to put on anyone who raised awkward questions about doctrinal inconsistencies.

The English Church was just as intolerant of intellectual freedom of thought. The good (i.e., white) magician was, like the good prince, expected to be an example, expected to aim at the bettering of people. He should cleanse himself of appetites and passions: those 'disturbances experienced by [...] intemperate souls [...] afflicted [...] by the stupor of ignorance, and [...] by the turmoil caused by their blind and perverse desires'.[7] He should pursue learning in order to make himself a better man. But the pursuit of knowledge was fraught. A truly learned king would have a broader range of judgement to apply in his duties. But he had to cultivate those branches of knowledge that assisted him in ruling wisely, virtuously, like a follower of Christ. Knowing where to draw boundaries was essential. Prospero, lured into areas of study that became addictive, lost contact with his role, his court and his state. Adam fell by crossing the boundary into prohibited knowledge. Prospero too. But by the end of the play he has patiently, at the cost of humiliation and suffering, learned humility, wisdom and how to make positive benefits out of forgiveness.

Prospero's 'secret studies' are a danger he pulls back from in time. Faustus fatally could not. Renouncing his powers Prospero reassumes and reasserts his virtues, evident before but overshadowed by his aura and power as a magician. There would be sceptics who saw the minor magic and the reported greater acts as merely part of the fiction and spectacle of theatre. They had seen actors as devils (and other supernatural effects) before. In *Macbeth* they had 'seen' witches, the goddess Hecate, ghosts and speaking oracles. It was all part of the fiction, illusion and fun of plays. Sometimes witchcraft was shown as evil and leading to the damnation of a soul, but often it was playful hokum. In books of merry tales the Devil was often portrayed as a foolish, gullible figure. The evil evident in *The Tempest* comes from humans (and the subhuman Caliban). Ariel, apparently invisible to Stephano and Trinculo while standing beside them and teasingly impersonating Trinculo's voice, is a fiction in which actors and audience are complicit and suspend disbelief (and reason) for the sake of the humour and the play. The disappearing banquet is a common enough conjuring trick using the trapdoor or a reversible table top. Though produced to look like magic these were the sort of comic episodes found traditionally in *commedia dell'arte* scenes (see Chapter 13) and other populist drama. Accumulatively the onstage illusion of illusions remind us of the essential fictional nature of all stage representation. It is mimetic – not reality but an imitation of it. The magic also serves to remind us that sometimes it takes luck or magic, leaps of faith or acts of forgiving and forgetting to solve the otherwise irresolvable. In some respects too, the magician is like God or a king; he can make things happen that otherwise would not. In *A Midsummer Night's Dream* the maze of love needs Puck's mischievous magic to make all come right. In *The Tempest*, after the major magic feat of the storm (which harms no one), the other trivial acts of magic are only to comically punish those who deserve it. *The* achievement of the play, the *real* magic, is the change wrought in Prospero (by himself) repressing his natural passions and turning not to revenge but to forgiveness. That is perhaps the greatest magic of all. Orgel claims that 'by relinquishing his special powers, he becomes at last fully human'.[8] To go further, we can say that by forgiving those who so completely changed his life Prospero becomes an imitation of Christ, an extension of the merely human.

What 'magic' effects did the audience actually witness? The tempest that is simulated by the actors' actions and words, by stage effects too possibly, is fictionally fabricated by Prospero and Ariel. Thus it is an illusion in so far as it is not naturally occurring and though it seems real it is not dangerous; it is a controlled illusion, an illusion of an illusion, for it is represented on a stage in actions and words. Other theatrical illusions are Ariel's reappearance as a water nymph, his songs as an invisible voice, Ferdinand frozen immobile as he tries to draw his sword (a piece of acting trickery used in *Friar Bacon*), Ariel playing solemn music-inducing sleep, then singing in Gonzalo's ear to wake him and thwart Sebastian and Antonio's murder of Alonso, and Ariel (invisible once more) playing tricks on Caliban, Trinculo and Stephano. In Act III Scene iii 'several strange shapes' set out a banquet for the king's party; then, with thunder and lightning, 'Ariel, like a Harpy; claps his wings upon the table; and, with a quaint device, the banquet vanishes'. Apart from the visual effect of Ariel as a harpy, the 'quaint device' would have been a surprising effect. Various means might effect this. Possibly wires or ropes attached to a pulley system in the above-stage area to lift the foodstuffs up and out of sight, a drop through the trapdoor, or a mechanism in the table top that allowed the food to 'disappear' into a space under the table which would not be visible if the table were covered with a cloth.[9] During the masque 'Juno descends' either in a 'car' or on a wire. This is achieved by the conventional *deus ex machina* set-up that was part of the public open-air theatres. The masque ends with 'a strange, hollow, and confused noise' as the characters exit. There is 'a noise of hunters [...], divers Spirits, in the shape of dogs and hounds' (something to make the king laugh). All these are the usual paraphernalia of masques, but there are so many it is like an overload of illusions to leave the audience gasping and wondering what next. Finally the court characters are drawn 'charm'd' into a ring as Prospero, ringmaster/God/conjuror, reveals who he is. Ariel completes the circle by 'driving' in the bewildered, oddly dressed Stephano, and Trinculo and Caliban.

The stage directions are more numerous and detailed than anywhere else in Shakespeare. Many are achievable either with straightforward conjuring tricks, theatrical pretence or the sort of machinery that was becoming more frequent in the many masques that were a particular feature of James's court. The collaboration of Inigo Jones and Ben Jonson in producing masques had brought about the development of intricate movable scenery, traps and 'flying' devices. Jones is credited with designing the proscenium arch and this would have helped hide from sight many of the gadgets by which tricks were achieved. Prospero's control by magic is not omniscient for, absorbed by the masque and its underlying meanings, he forgets Caliban's plot. Such a very human lapse is absurd in a man Ariel calls 'great master'. His magic has limitations, but his inability to affect Antonio's free will (he chooses not to repent his sins) is less important than the fact of his relinquishing revenge. Forgiveness is always as much (if not more) about the forgiver than the forgiven, and in performance we may forget Antonio's morose silence as the hopeful lovers usurp attention. Uncertainty about Antonio and Sebastian is in keeping with a play where nothing is fully resolved and the new beginnings are full of unanswered possibilities.

James was unsympathetic to the discussions of how the wonders of science were colonizing much that had once been considered supernatural. Telescopes and microscopes opened up a world beyond sight, but the dark psychic corners opened up by belief in black magic remind us that most men were still primitive in their thinking. James's *Daemonologie* (1597) combatively opens its preface thus:

The fearefull aboundinge at this time in this countrie, of these detestable slaves of the Devill, the Witches or enchanters, hath moved me (beloved reader) to dispatch in post, this following treatise of mine, not in any way (as I protest) to serve for a shew of my learning and ingine, but onely (mooved of conscience) to preasse thereby, so farre as I can, to resolve the doubting harts of many; both that such assaultes of Sathan are most certainly practized, and that the instrumentes thereof, merits most severely to be punished: against the damnable opinions of two principally in our age, whereof the one called SCOT an Englishman, is not ashamed in publike print to deny, that ther can be such a thing as Witch-craft: and so mainteines the old error of the Sadducees, in denying of spirits. The other called WIERUS, a German Phisition, sets out a publick apologie for all these crafts-folks, wherby, procuring for their impunitie, he plainely bewrayes himselfe to have bene one of that profession.

James wrote to counter Reginald Scot's *The Discovery of Witchcraft* (1584), which attempted to persuade readers that witchcraft was a hoax, that most instances of so-called witchcraft were illusion, conjuring, mistaken perception, criminal trickery or ignorant prejudice. Prospero's illusions are clearly distinct from the diabolic evil of Sycorax. While black magic was prohibited and punished severely when discovered, many apparently 'magical' results of spells and potions were shown to be the outcome of scientifically explicable processes. Though intellectuals and scientists were beginning to develop rational, chemical, biological and physiological explanations of supposed magic they still faced a highly critical conservative opposition backed by the immense power of the Roman and English Churches.

Prospero and John Dee

Jonson's play *The Alchemist* (performed October 1610) focuses its satire on the greed and gullibility of men, but also targets the long-held fantasy of alchemy that base metals could be turned into gold by means of the *lapis philosophorum* (philosopher's stone). ''Tis said that Jonson had his hint of the Alchemist from Dr John Dee.'[10] If Shakespeare needed a model on which to loosely base his main character, John Dee was a high-profile possibility. An internationally renowned scholar, and astrological and navigational consultant to Elizabeth I, Dee was charged with necromancy under James, after living most of his adult life under the shadow of rumours of wizardry. His death in 1608 or 1609 is close enough to the writing of *The Tempest* to make it not implausible that he was a partial inspiration for Prospero, though folk tales are full of stories of wizards and princesses. The fantasy of a man with extra-natural power, able to control the elements, able to marshal spirits and manipulate people, is potent.[11] It would have been intensely attractive to Jacobeans considering the sea and land storms, floods, bad harvests and eclipses that littered the weather calendar of the early 1600s. This was a time when the 'New World' offered immense potential as a new start for the corrupt European cultures, a second Eden of fruitful fertility – if the Caliban cannibal natives could be controlled, subjugated and Christianized. A wizard whose powers stretch across the wide seas, deploying legions of spirits and administering a new paradise island is a powerful folk fantasy taking on a contemporary resonance. All sorts of subliminal angsts and hopes reverberate in Prospero.

John Dee (1527–1608/1609) was a highly skilled mathematician and astronomer who knew Tycho Brahe[12] and was conversant with Copernican theories (though not a heliocentrist). Such was his knowledge of these fields he became a mentor/trainer of numerous navigators and a committed supporter of England's colonial expansion. His studies, his obsession with gaining knowledge and discovering the intricate truths of the universe, would eventually, like Faustus, take him across the dangerous border between science and magic into astrology and occultism. He often faced charges of divination. Though acquitting himself successfully these constant accusations show how fine was the line between science and prejudice and indicate the precariousness and unpredictability of such borderline studies. Like Newton he was drawn to alchemical experiments and dabbled in divination. Divining the future, especially by means of scrying (looking into a glass), was very close to occult magic. Aged 15 he entered St John's College, Cambridge. Graduating in 1544 he lectured in Greek studies and was made a fellow of the newly founded Trinity College in 1546. He created the stage effects for a performance of Aristophanes's comedy *Peace*, the most spectacular of which was a beetle-shaped machine or chariot that flew up to the heavens carrying a man with a basket of victuals on his back. At this time stage machinery was rare and simple. Though the *deus ex machina* device lowering a god from 'the heavens' to Earth had been used in classical theatre and, along with the trapdoor, would become a standard feature in public theatres from the 1570s, in the mid-sixteenth century they were unusual and would look like the results of magic. Prospero, a similar scholar/conjuror, stage manages numerous illusions, but by 1611 audiences were relatively blasé about spectacle, especially the court audience.

Dee's stage effects gained him a reputation for extra-natural powers that would stay with him for the rest of his life. His arrest for casting horoscopes for the princesses Mary and Elizabeth in 1555 led to a treason charge investigated in the Star Chamber. Acquitted, he began building a career and reputation as a scholar and adviser to the Crown, especially on astronomical matters related to voyages of discovery. In *General and Rare Memorials Pertayning to the Perfect Arte of Navigation* (1577) Dee formulated a justification for colonial claims in the New World that became the guiding light of imperial expansion. Then, like Faustus, becoming discontented with his status and the limits of earthly knowledge, he turned to wilder supernatural ventures, including alchemy, reading the future and seeking to talk to angels through a crystal-gazing scryer called Kelly. He also began to invent fantastic assertions about England's claim to America predating that of Spain.[13] Like most people of the time, though more notoriously, Dee lived in two worlds – the day-to-day world of Christian faith and that of the semi-magical/semi-scientific. Along with his practical skills in navigation and mathematics he pursued alchemy, astrology and the Hermetic philosophy[14] that had got Ficino and Bruno into trouble in Italy. For Dee, mathematics, navigation, astronomy, astrology, alchemy and speaking to angels were all part of an exploration to discover the 'pure verities' of the universe, the unifying spirit, the divine harmony, with which God suffused creation and made everything part of everything else. At a time when much magical belief was metamorphosing into science his explorations often brought him into conflict with the authorities and with ordinary folk afraid of the rumours of his occultism and of the sometimes magic appearance of scientific phenomena. In 1604 he petitioned King James for protection and planned to exile himself in Germany, but died before he could effect this. His scholasticism had drawn him into the political elite, mixing with Cecil, Walsingham, the Earl of Leicester, Sir Philip Sidney and Sir Christopher Hatton.

Prospero and Sycorax

From the beginning a clear distinction is made between Prospero's non-malign, white magic and the evil practices of Sycorax. This is only one of a series of binary oppositions. Prospero is a rational non-occultist. He does not call up the Devil, does not use demons, wishes ill to no one – not even his brother. Only 15 lines after Gonzalo calls 'the wills above' to save him for 'a dry death', Prospero declares, 'There's no harm done' (I. ii. 15). The audience is not kept long in suspense about the outcome of the storm and apparent wreck. By contrast the magic of Sycorax is unquestionably connected to evil, with her sexual union with the Devil and her 'earthy and abhorr'd commands' I. ii. 273). She committed 'sorceries terrible' (I. ii. 264). She is first mentioned as Prospero, berating Ariel, reminds him how Sycorax had imprisoned him in a cloven pine. This first reference to the 'foul witch' (I. ii. 258) deformed by 'age and envy' into 'a hoop' shape, implies that not only had age bent her back, but her sinful envy had distorted her from uprightness. Renaissance people believed inner qualities showed on the outside. Virtue and grace would be reflected in a sweet and serene face, evil would be visible in the eyes, in the expression and ugly appearance. Shakespeare reflects that in Miranda's appearance and comportment contrasted with Caliban's ('disproportion'd in his manners/As in his shape' [V. i. 290–91]), but he also demonstrates how it was slowly being realized that looks and behaviour are not true guides to the malevolence a person harbours (witness the courtly appearance of Antonio and Sebastian). Every mention of Sycorax is accompanied by a damning epithet – 'damn'd witch' (I. ii.263), 'hag' (I. ii. 269) – and evil connotations ('mischiefs manifold', 'sorceries terrible', 'earthy and abhorr'd commands'). Her name incorporates the Latin for raven (*corax*), a bird associated with witchcraft. It may be that she is a parallel to the sorceress Circe, infamous in *The Odyssey* for attempting to enchant and hold Odysseus on her island. She was born in Colchis, a town long-established as a centre of witchcraft (situated in the tribal land of the Coraxi) and home of that other famous sorceress, Medea. Circe was banished to a Mediterranean island as Sycorax is banished from Algiers. Algiers was in the public mind in 1610 on account of news that Marseilles merchants were sending three galleons to hunt down the pirates that were based there and in Tunis. The Algerian connection allies her to the suspect, demonized Muslim world of 'the other' – Moors, Saracens and the notorious Barbary pirates. Thus black magic is associated with the Arab world in contrast to Prospero's benign powers representing the Christian West. Along with Jews, Mohammedans were figures of devious evil to the audiences and playwrights of the time. Sycorax is dehumanized as well in the figurative description of her as a bitch dog whose 'litter' (i.e., Caliban) is 'a freckled whelp hag-born – not honour'd with/A human shape' (I. ii. 283–4). Bent double and referenced as a hag (Caliban is 'hag-seed' and 'hag-born'), she conforms to the traditional crone image of a witch – deformed, old and ugly.

There are several layers of significance amalgamated here. The island has been rescued from devilish influence by a Christian, hinting at the bringing of light to the benighted heathens of the West Indies and Americas. The power of Prospero is benign, administered in order to prosecute his planned revenge. His summoning of the tempest is an act of near black magic close to the commonly held belief that witches created storms in order to wreck ships, drown sailors and use their body parts.[15] Prospero is saved from the accusation of using occult powers by harming no one and only using the storm to bring his victims to the island. Christians regarded hurricanes, floods, earthquakes, eclipses and storms as signs of God's anger and as part of his secret plans. In that respect Prospero is similar to God. Astrologers predicting weather events by reading the stars and planet positions were regarded as little different from astronomers who predicted eclipses, comets and astral events. Both inhabited a suspect terrain between God and the Devil. The church denounced the impiety of predictive divination as distracting people from seeing Divine Providence at work in all things. Foretelling the future by reading the alignment of stars and planets (called judicial astrology) was regarded as occult and heretical.

Natural astrology dealing with medical problems (zodiac alignments affecting the efficacy of herbal and physiological remedies) and meteorological astrology predicting the weather were just about tolerated. Both were suspect but accepted as part of the natural sciences, using the forces and cross-connections existing in nature. From the village cunning woman to the king's physician, much medical knowledge and practice rested on herbal and other natural remedies handed down the ages and semi-mystic correspondences like believing the stomach was the organ influencing courage, the liver ruling love, and that certain foodstuffs affected certain organs.

Where the unacceptable boundary was crossed was when the Devil, malign intentions, anti-Christian ritual and the pursuit of power became involved. Though he has appropriated the land from the original inhabitant, Prospero represents a better form of human activity – cultivated, humane and civilized. He educates the native ex-owner but finds his benevolence disregarded in Caliban's attempted rape. This may be seen as a figurative way of referencing the outbursts of violence by Native Americans against settlers with whom they had previously co-existed peacefully. It is also a way of saying that some human types need strict control because they are uneducable and irredeemably evil. William Strachey reflects Prospero's experience with Caliban in a letter about the wreck of the *Sea Venture* (on its way to re-provision the Virginia colonists): 'How little a faire and noble intreatie workes upon a barbarous disposition.'[16] This is an example of Prospero's fair dealing being taken advantage of (as Antonio did). In all this Prospero takes on the presence and power of God, sometimes affectionate and caring, often severe and punitive. He displays this double aspect with Ariel, with Miranda and certainly with Caliban.

Sycorax worshipped the pagan god Setebos, and is asserted to have had sex with 'the devil himself' (I. ii. 321) and to have spawned the 'hag-seed' (I. ii. 367) Caliban. Setebos was the deity worshipped by a Patagonian tribe described in Richard Eden's 1577 account of Magellan's voyages, *History of Travel*. This allusion indicates the diversity of texts Shakespeare drew on to provide him with the references, allusions and lexis to create the mood he wanted. In building the image of Caliban's absent mother with her diabolic arts and her 'unmitigable rage' (I. ii. 276), we see the contrast with Prospero's rational 'Art' and his stern but loving patriarchalism. Sycorax, for all her diabolic power was unable to make Ariel act diabolically. The spirit of air and fire (divine qualities) refused to carry out certain acts and was imprisoned.

Prospero too is unable to control Caliban or Antonio. He can punish them physically but not manipulate their minds. Prospero has formed a bond of sorts with Ariel. It is a relationship based on gratitude and respect, unless Ariel addressing Prospero as 'great master' (I. ii. 189) and 'commander'

(IV. i. 166) is merely flattering. Prospero needs to remind his servant that he released him from his prison. Like king and subject, Prospero has the upper hand, but needs Ariel's service. It is also a relationship based on fear of punishment that works while both sides do their allotted tasks. Nurturing Caliban until the attempted rape, successful in rearing Miranda to be sensitive and compassionate yet sharply demanding of obedience from both, Prospero appears like the Old Testament God and like the occasionally needed sternness of human authority. A Jacobean audience would recognize both personae; many would endorse them.

Prospero also represents the emergence of a science that looks like magic, while Sycorax represents dark, pagan cults largely banned but not entirely banished in Europe, and still dominant in the unenlightened 'New World'. His takeover of the island symbolizes the bringing of rational, Christian (i.e., merciful and positive) belief to the benighted. It is the Old World's new beliefs cleansing and saving the New World's ancient brutalism. Except it is not quite so neat as that. Antonio and Sebastian, Trinculo and Stephano – a usurper, a would-be fratricide, two drunken fools and hubristic would-be murderers – are hardly ideal representatives of Western culture. At the same time Caliban is hardly a suitable example of the noble savage Montaigne and others applauded. He is given both some of the nastiest comments in the play and some of the most hauntingly beautiful. Prospero's rational goodness enables him to use Ariel's powers where Sycorax can only trap him in a tree. Sycorax's magic is frequently described as destructive and terrible, where Prospero's is only temporarily frightening and ultimately aimed at good. Prospero seeks to set things right in his world through magic, and once that is done, he renounces it, setting Ariel free. At no point does his magic contain *maleficium* (evil with destructive intention).

Some intellectuals, like Bruno and Agrippa, were beginning to explore magic, superstitious and supernatural beliefs in a rational and scientific way.[17] It was a precarious line of study with the church on guard to identify heresy and punish. Like the image of the mad scientist, Dee was drawn to push his studies further and further. For all his claims of serious scholarly research into unusual phenomena and the scientific bases for the workings of the world and nature, he often ran up against the church authorities for crossing boundaries into the occult and frankly cranky.[18] Prospero too was drawn deeper and deeper into his studies, from the 'liberal Arts' to more arcane (and dangerous) matters, until, after 12 years on the island he has mastery of natural forces. It is ironic that he accuses his brother of being lured by 'ambition growing' (I. ii. 105), while falling victim to the same sin himself. Small, everyday aspirations were acceptable, but overblown, overweening, overreaching ambition, what Macbeth calls 'vaulting ambition', was a grave fault.

It was the Devil's sin – pride, a desire to rival or equal God. Delving into the knowledge of God's designs and the workings of his creation was trespassing into prohibited territory. That said, Prospero's magic, as displayed, is pretty limited. Apart from the large spectacle of the storm, sending Miranda into hypnotic trances, rendering Ferdinand immobile and making the banquet disappear are low-level conjuring tricks. The calling of Ariel and his 'quality' (companions) is more disturbing, but never goes further than mischievous tricks played upon characters who deserve to be lured through 'tooth'd briers, sharp furzes, pricking gorse, and thorns' and into a 'filthy-mantled pool' (IV. i. 180, 182). These Puckish antics are similar to what happens to the lovers in *A Midsummer Night's Dream*. It is a staple of comedy that human pretension and dignity should be degraded and mocked physically as well as verbally and ideologically.

Chapter 12

THE CONTEXT OF COLONIALISM AND CANNIBALISM: THEFT OR DUTY?

The principall effect which we can desier or expect of this action is the conversion and reduction of the people in those parts unto the true worship of God and Christian religion.[1]

Radix malorum est cupiditas.[2]

All the law is fulfilled in one word […]. Thou shalt love thy neighbour as thyself. But if ye bite and devour one another, take heed that ye be not consumed one of another.[3]

From early in the Elizabethan period England had been increasingly excited by gossip, rumour and tales reflecting the achievements of various English sailors. Some of these achievements were military and patriotic, but many were piratical, greedy and unethical. Famous names like Hawkins, Drake, Raleigh, Frobisher and Grenville are tarnished by the unedifying scrabble for treasure. Ships of various European nations were seized and their cargoes stolen. The queen was not above claiming Crown rights to some portion of the loot. The contents of victim ships predated were not always commodities like spices, silks, cotton, gold and silver. In the 1560s Sir John Hawkins made voyages to the coast of Africa to buy or steal natives for exchange as slaves in the Spanish West Indies in return for saleable goods. Sometimes he simply captured Portuguese slave ships and took their human cargo, sailed to Hispaniola,[4] Puerto Rico or the islands off Venezuela (Curacoa or Margarita). Hakluyt describes how Hawkins 'made vent of the whole number of his *Negroes*' and calmly calls this 'peaceable traffic' (trouble-free trade) for which he got in exchange 'hides, ginger, sugar, and some quantity of pearls'.[5] Hawkins is just one of many entrepreneurs who made fortunes from Atlantic trade ventures, feeding the greed of those who invested in them and the vanity of those who desired the goods they brought back. In a fine example of the hypocrisy surrounding the slave trade, the Spanish ambassador, whose nation pillaged people and commodities all over the Indies and the Americas, complained to Queen Elizabeth of 'the greed of these people'.[6] England was late entering the rapacious colonization of America and late too in joining the human trafficking, but once the Spanish began utilizing black slaves to provide the labour-intensive needs of mining and agriculture, the English colonies on the east coast of North America rapidly realized the value of such a cheap workforce. In 1607 an English ship, specifically there for the purpose, carried slaves from the Guinea coast to Ghana and the highly lucrative slave trade had officially begun. Isolated private slave trading quickly developed into a thriving transatlantic business that made the fortunes of many Bristol and Liverpool merchants and London investors. By 1619 tobacco planters in Virginia were buying slaves from the Dutch.[7] Though the records are scanty for this early period, it may be assumed that English vessels were also by this time regularly transporting slaves to the rapidly spreading English colonies of Carolina, Massachusetts, New England and Virginia. Voices raised against plantation tended to be more concerned with the greedy excesses it released than with human rights.

The Tempest coincides with the expansion of the Virginia colony, so that the taking of the island from Caliban and the enslavement of the 'salvage' may be seen as *a very distant* signification of this imperial venture. It does not make the play a discourse on colonialism. Though many of the men central to the activities of the Virginia Company were acquaintances of Shakespeare, there is very little in the text to link it specifically to the Virginian situation. The subtext is more broadly and abstractly concerned with displaying all rule as theft. There is a pattern of role stealing and usurpation that relates as much to European politics as to empire building. It is worth pointing out that Ariel was the indigenous inhabitant supplanted and subjugated by Sycorax. Her malign magic and cruelty *may* be seen as a criticism of the tortures and terrors the papist Spanish exercised in the West Indies, while Prospero's more benevolent rule may represent how the English wished their conversion/ civilizing/commercial intentions to be perceived.

Numerous pamphlets and sermons at the time were conducting a lively discourse on the pros and cons of colonial occupation.[8] Some in the audience would have been involved as Virginia Company investors or directors, but if not connected with the inner workings of the company many would miss the very subtle allusions. To annexe the play as part of the colonial discourse requires it to contain sustained and unquestionable reference to the Virginian situation. It does not. It has a few verbal echoes of Strachey's *True Declaration* and peripherally touches upon who has the right to rule the island, but is hardly a full engagement with the moral questions clustered round the plantation of America.

Contemporary Britain is acutely embarrassed by its rampantly imperial past. Critics, reflecting Europe's post-colonial guilt, have been very eager to claim the play as a contribution to the discourse on the ethics of empire. They have built a substantial edifice of arguments and articles about colonialism, based on Caliban losing the island and being called a slave and Ariel a 'servant'.[9] Post-war, post-empire guilts and racial collisions are highlighted in the anthropological-ethnic explorations of Franz Fanon's *Black Skin, White Masks* (1948) and are central to Octave Mannoni's *Prospero and Caliban: The Psychology of Colonization* (written 1948). The demystification of colonization is continued in Edward Said's *Orientalism* (1978) and *Culture and Imperialism* (1993). These texts have fed the cultural conflict aspects of recent criticism. *The Tempest* is now viewed in terms of post-colonial theory and black struggles for civil rights. For Mannoni both Ariel and Caliban are victims of white paternalist exploitation – the one subsumed into conforming to white culture, the other creating an identity by contempt for it, opposition to it and attempted subversion of it. Mannoni is determined to demonize Prospero as colonizer, appropriator, usurper and oppressor. In relation to his 'paternal omnipotence', telling his daughter to 'obey and be attentive', Mannoni claims Prospero 'tries to treat Miranda as an equal; but he fails', punctuating his 'recital [...] with other orders [...] all absurd and quite unwarranted'.[10] This fails to understand a father's position. Miranda is not an equal. Prospero is entitled, indeed would be expected, to order her silence and attention. She is still partially a child. Prospero is snappy and touchy, but he is also affectionate.

In relation to Ariel, Mannoni asserts Prospero has 'promised him his liberty, but fails to give it to him. He constantly reminds Ariel that he freed him from the knotty entrails of a cloven pine.'[11] The 'absolute authority of the father' would have been entirely expected and acceptable in 1611. In their argument about Ariel's freedom (I. ii.) Prospero mentions that once a month he has to remind the complaining spirit of the painful imprisonment his master freed him from. This seems reasonable and hardly deserves the word 'constantly'. Prospero reminds Ariel he is bound for a set period (out of gratitude) and will not be delivered from his servant role 'before the time be out' (I. ii. 246). In two days' time, says Prospero, 'I will discharge thee' (I. ii. 299). Ariel is a spirit of air and fire and understandably longs to be free. But he owes gratitude and is a servant working out a term of employment. Like all employees, he moans, but during the rest of the play is happy to serve, enjoys the responsibility he is given for tormenting and teasing the various men of sin on the island, is warmly praised and then, in the last line, freed.

Caliban is 'ruthlessly exploited'.[12] Again Mannoni misses the contemporary context. Rape was a capital offence. Attempted rape would have been given a more severe punishment than becoming a hewer of wood and drawer of water. Caliban gets off lightly; he is kept within the family, not banished to fend for himself. Mannoni sees Prospero's actions as extreme, as a mask for his own hidden incestuous desires for Miranda: 'He wants to rid himself of guilt by putting the blame for his bad thoughts on someone else.'[13] This displacement implies that the attempted violation is a fabrication, yet Caliban acknowledges, 'Thou didst prevent me' (I. ii. 352). Prospero is right to punish, right to be wary. Caliban's easy exchange of master is seen as 'the dependence complex in its pure state'.[14] If, as Mannoni suggests, Caliban is betrayed by Prospero withdrawing his co-operation, he is also betrayed by Stephano in a worse way: the butler plans to exhibit him as a 'monster' or rarity, making him a slave and a moneymaking commodity. Prospero does at least eventually reach a state where he is ready to give Caliban a second chance by acknowledging him as his own and perhaps leaving him to resume habitation of the island. This may suggest acceptance that Caliban is the way he is because of how Prospero has treated him. Mannoni concludes, 'What the colonial in common with Prospero lacks, is awareness of the world of Others, a world in which Others have to be respected.'[15] Prospero has acted in the punitive way that conforms to contemporary orthodoxy. Caliban's human rights would not have been considered, nor would his psychology of deprivation. His sin has to be punished. Rehabilitation might come later – after sin Hell, after Hell Purgatory, after Purgatory Paradise. There is a vicious circle of punishment and resentment. Prospero punishes Caliban for the attempted violation, Caliban resents being punished, Prospero continues to punish him because of his persistent refusal to repent, Caliban seeks to murder Prospero out of resentment for being punished. Only forgiveness (by Prospero) and repentance (by Caliban) will break the circle. Caliban has certainly lacked respect for others and it is noticeable that while Mannoni is critical of Prospero he seems unaffected by the seriousness of what Caliban tried to do.

Interpreting the text as an exploration of the effect of the colonizer (Prospero) on the colonized (Ariel and Caliban) and Ariel as not so much exploited by the colonizer as subtly exploiting his master's needs, misses the contemporary 1611 point, and distorts the narrative to satisfy the agendas of critics with more modern concerns in mind. If we attempt to return the play to its time, the anti-colonial elements are minimized in favour of seeing it as a palimpsest of various discourses: on parenting and education within the patriarchal structure, a series of vignettes on the nature of rule, and a series of usurpations and repeated metamorphoses. Viewed thus we can compare Ariel and Caliban as children of Prospero (servants were considered as under the fatherly wing of their master). Thus Ariel, often relegated as less interesting than the enigmatic and threatening Caliban, apart from being a tool of power is reinstated as the good servant, in comparison with the conniving Caliban as the untrustworthy servant. This is a view to which Shakespeare's audience would have responded. The theme was common in Shakespeare and precipitates questions about the tensions between the ranks in a hierarchical society where a large proportion of Englishmen were subordinate to a master of some sort and often treated like slaves. The paternalist parenting patterns are extended when we add Prospero as 'father' to Ferdinand and Alonso as father to Ferdinand and Claribel.

The dynamic of the servant–master nexus (where service, honesty and exploitation were active factors) is far closer to Renaissance thought than that of colonial master–colonized slave. The colonial interpretation ignores the ideological climate of the time. Renaissance thinking in general simply did not consider the claims to self-determination of native peoples. The view that English subjects had rights was only slowly gathering credence. The elites of Europe largely thought the common sort had a duty to obey out of respect for God's established hierarchy. Neither on the grounds of political nor theological theory would many have supported the rights of heathen savages over the duty of European Christians to civilize Native Americans and Africans and bring them to God. The races of the New Worlds were regarded as less than human and certainly inferior to white Europeans. In both the western and eastern hemispheres, Portuguese and Spanish discoverers established trading posts as a first stage in the process of trade turning to land theft. The European intruders would not have seen it as stealing. For them it was a superior race rightly appropriating underutilized land, maximizing its agricultural fertility, extracting mineral resources, bringing nature under effective control and bringing light to the benighted. Even Eden needed taming by Adam and Eve's gardening. Strachey asserts, 'God sels us al things for our labours, when Adam himself might not live in Paradice without dressing the garden.'[16] Annexing the land involved annexing the minds of the native populations; colonization and conversion came as an indivisible package. Both Catholic and Protestant Churches accepted slavery; it was the curse Noah put upon his son Ham, a curse they would lift by bringing the light of Christ to the dark places of the world.[17] Prospero's appropriation of the island cannot be claimed as engaging with the ethical complexities of colonialism. It is at the very most Shakespeare tenuously, distantly, peripherally embellishing the texture of his play with references to topics of common gossip, using a few of the details in the available voyage accounts to provide mood and factual authentication to a setting that was unusual. The theft of the island can be seen as a practical political move in the repression of a dangerous savage unsuitable to rule it, and parallels Prospero previously being removed from power on the grounds of his own unsuitability. The pattern of sovereignty threatened by theft is repeated in the attitude of Sebastian and Antonio to the Boatswain and in the plots to kill Alonso and Prospero.

What would have happened if Caliban had not tried to rape Miranda? Would Prospero have educated him for governorship and allowed him to rule while preparing himself to reassume power in Milan? His magical powers would enable him to reinstate himself at some time and in some way. His choosing to remain as ruler of the island is hardly credible, given other options. The savage's misbehaviour, both before the play starts and during its action, is justification for Prospero's 'usurpation'. The main thrust of the plot is the working out of Prospero's revenge through the exposure of Sebastian and Antonio, the atonement of Alonso, the marriage of Ferdinand and Miranda and the rehabilitation and restoration of himself. Caliban's situation is relatively minor, an auxiliary issue. His fate at the end of the play is not even mentioned. Is he left behind on the island as sole proprietor, left to return to his savage ways, leaving nature to run wild, happy to do nothing to improve it, like the inhabitants of the 'Utopia' Gonzalo had envisaged? Will Prospero, in acknowledging 'this thing of darkness', take him to Milan? In what role? As a grotesque to be displayed at court – part jester, part family member with 'learning difficulties'? It was common for courts to keep dwarves and naturals[18] as curiosities allowed the freedom of the palace. Will he be commodified as a monster, a sixpenny public exhibit? Trinculo displays the mercenary baseness of the common sort when he meditates making the 'monster' into a street show:

> Were I in England now [...] and had but this fish painted, not a holiday
> fool there but would give a piece of silver: there would the monster
> make the man; any strange beast there makes a man: when they will
> not give a doit [a small coin] to relieve a lame beggar, they will lay out
> ten to see a dead Indian. (II. ii. 28–34)[19]

This satirical barb targets the selfish priorities of the mob putting their silly pleasures before their Christian charitable duties. It is a point made often about the ruling elite too and implies all ranks can be trivial and callous.[20] Stephano, adored by his unexpected subject, is ready to exploit him as 'a present for any emperor' or sell him. Immediately on finding Caliban both men consider him as a commodity from which to profit. This is the world of Hobbes where men predate each other in different variations of metaphorical cannibalism. Caliban serves a function at the other extreme of the polarity associated with Miranda and Ferdinand that addresses the question of education (the nature/nurture discourse). He also engages with the socio-political strands of the play allied to Stephano and Trinculo, reflecting the nature of the base mob as inconsistent, easily led, slave-ish, ignorant and superstitious. Peripherally he precipitates questions related to colonization and slavery and is a graphic counter to the idea of the noble savage. In the political context he represents the lowest form of common man, the freeborn Englishman whose rights had been stolen and whose conduct was unreliable.

In Shakespeare's day the world was still being discovered by European seafarers, and stories abounded of distant islands, with true accounts and inflated myths about the cannibals of the Caribbean, metaphors of paradise, new Edens and tropical Utopias. Caliban has been made the focus of recent studies. His name, a not-quite-perfect anagram of cannibal, his enslavement, the process leading to that, his angry resentment, his attempted retaliation and restoration and Gonzalo's imagined ideal society, have all been taken as proof of the play being engaged with the unethical grabbing of foreign lands, oppressing the native peoples and exploiting the natural resources. Caliban is also similar to 'Cariban' (from the Carib, an Amerindian tribe believed to originate round the Orinoco River in South America and migrating to the Antilles and Domenica). Critics asserting that *The Tempest* explores the morality of the infant Jacobean imperialism see Caliban speaking up for his natural rights when he sturdily declares to Prospero:

> This island's mine, by Sycorax my mother,
> Which thou tak'st from me. (I. ii. 333–4)

His account of their early relationship seems metaphorically to portray the progress of colonization:

> When thou cam'st first,
> Thou strok'st me, and made much of me; wouldst give me
> Water with berries in't; and teach me how
> To name the bigger light, and how the less: and then I lov'd thee,
> And showed thee all the qualities of the isle (I. ii. 334–8)

This time of peaceful exchange of knowledge and co-operation ended with Caliban's attempted rape. Previously he had been housed in Prospero's cell, father and daughter trying to educate him as one of the family. This story seems an allegory of conquest: compromise and sharing developing out of initial contact, a period of co-operation, then the growth of tensions, disagreements and outbreaks of violence. The experiences of Columbus, Ponce de Léon and the Roanoke settlers all followed this pattern. These associations do not however constitute a fully articulated argument about colonialism. Critics tend to reflect the prejudices, values and fascinations of their age and they often have their own political agendas. Imperialist appropriation is only a tiny element of the play. Gender politics and Marxism/socialism have also skewed interpretations. In rediscovering how Jacobeans might react to the main elements of the play we need to acknowledge that while exotic stories of American settlement were of current interest, particularly in the circles in which Shakespeare moved, the New World pamphlets and conditions on the Bermudas are little more than background information adding to the overall ambience of the play, and the bulk of any audience would know little about the documents so lightly alluded to.

Inevitably, Ireland too has been seen as the possible correlative to the presumed anti-plantation stance of the play. It was regularly a focus of trouble. At the end of Elizabeth's reign, Essex's mission there had foundered and shown him as a flawed governor. Raleigh and many other titled Englishmen had extensive estates there. Most recently James had quietly sown the seeds of future simmering resentment. When the Earls of Tyrone and Tyrconnel had fled Ulster, the king ceded their lands to Scots and English landlords – a colonial appropriation.

Gonzalo's fantasy of the island (and worse still, its imaginary population) in a natural state is introduced to highlight the impossibility of all such dreams given the unavoidably malicious, selfish, sinful nature of men. Given European man's natural tendency to proactively engage with his environment, it is unthinkable that the population would not want to change and improve it. The idle state Gonzalo imagines is excessively slothful. The many would happily do nothing, but the restless, organizing streak in some men would not allow nature to remain uncultivated. In *Leviathan* (1651) Thomas Hobbes referred to man's life as 'solitary, poor, nasty, brutish, and short' if not protected by a society or political community based on co-operation.[21] Without community (family, village, tribe, etc.) men would prey on each other like animals in a savage, primitive, might-is-right world. That would be the likely outcome of Gonzalo's society. Hobbes asserted that nature can be counterbalanced by men co-operating to protect themselves from brute-force robbers. Montaigne said, 'There seems to be nothing for which Nature has better prepared us than for fellowship.'[22] Co-operation is a signifier of civilization and incorporates Christian beliefs that validate the exercise of sympathy, help, decency and respect for the individual. But fellowship is chosen, not imposed. Native Americans and English did sometimes get on, but often did not. The settler mix too was troublesome and less than harmonious. Many colonists were artisans without farming experience and young gentleman with no intention of working. After Raleigh's imprisonment the right to administer the planting was handed over to the greedy Justice Popham. From 1606 the brave new world was 'stockt and planted out of all the gaoles of England'.[23]

Without this socialization, Hobbes says, there would be no industry and commerce, 'no arts; no letters; no society; and worst of all, continual fear, and danger of violent death'.[24] This is highlighted by Caliban on the one hand (as an ignoble savage) and Sebastian and Antonio on the other (as supposedly civilized men); all are corrupt, savage and untrustworthy. Caliban may represent the cultural collision of sophisticated European values (and corruption) with the different, but equally savage, cultures of the Americas. He is man in a natural state, primitive, without Adamic godlike beauty, a 'salvage' deformed in body and mind. He has a poetic sensitivity to nature but an uncivilized attitude to sex; his appetites are uncontrolled. He is a sycophantic superstitious subhuman, ready to exchange one master for another for the price of a swig of wine. Resentful of Prospero, his readiness to kiss the foot of a new master reflects the readiness of the mob to worship and follow whoever captures their imagination – and promises to satisfy their immediate base needs. Rousseau in the eighteenth century championed the idea of the noble savage, but this savage is no better than the base Stephano and Trinculo. Alluding to Montaigne, as Gonzalo's ideal commonwealth speech does, does not automatically signify Shakespeare's agreement with his vision. If he is less than supportive of Caliban he also portrays Antonio and Sebastian as examples of sophisticated man perverted.

The savage is the unregenerate rump of the mob – resisting education, resisting religion and resisting morality. Caliban is that lazy part of society that lives from hand to mouth, scrounging, scavenging and thieving. He will eat wild fruit and raw meat but will not cultivate or farm them. He is that part of society always ready to riot and wreck, less for political principle than for the loot that can be stolen or simply for the enjoyment of destruction. He represents what some political theorists were increasingly emphasizing – the people's right to choose their government. But he chooses foolishly, making a 'god' of a 'drunkard' (V. i. 296). King James himself was a heavy drinker yet always expected deference despite his frequent less-than-dignified behaviour. But as Shakespeare has King Lear remark: 'A dog's obey'd in office.' For Caliban to pick Stephano because he has wine to give him and because he was the first means presenting itself to eliminate the 'tyrant' Prospero is a poor choice made on unsafe grounds and an unworthy waste of loyalty. Repentance for his sins and a determination to reform would be a better plan. 'Cacaliban' has 'a new master' and celebrates drunkenly his newfound 'freedom! freedom! high-day, freedom!' This is not freedom, but an exchange of bondage, the short-sighted elevation of a man of limited qualities (and those not good) by an unthinking savage led by the desire to satisfy short-term appetites (wine and revenge). It is the mistake of rebels throughout history to throw off one tyranny only to be drawn or swindled into another. It is also the nature of all government to exploit subjects as Trinculo and Stephano envisage exploiting Caliban. Apart from his drunkenness, lust and greedy disloyalty, Stephano's reaction to Caliban's 'the isle is full of noises' speech (III. ii. 133ff.) indicates his mercenary baseness and unsuitability for governorship. To one of the most poetic and rhapsodic declarations (indicative of some imaginative soul in the savage) Stephano merely responds, 'This will prove a brave kingdom to me, where I shall have my music for nothing' (III. ii. 142–3). Civilization is a very thin veneer.

For free alcohol – the age-old price/bribe of the fool/slave's support – Cacaliban gives away his freedom and what he had claimed as his birthright, for Stephano announces 'we will inherit here'. His celebratory song includes signs of inebriation in mispronouncing his name, but may also unwittingly undermine his 'rebellion'. Shakespeare may be delivering a covert message by hinting the need to ''Ban, 'Ban' such unreliable, volatile forces in society. His muddled version of his name may also carry the implication that such people are excrement, for 'caca' is Spanish slang for shit.[25] His behaviour (attempted rape, surliness, morose conversation, lack of respect for a 'better', drunkenness and planned murder) would mark him as vulgar and uncivilized. A court audience would laugh at him and see him as authenticating their prejudices about the 'common sort'. Whether we view Caliban as correlating by implication to the native Virginians, or simply as a traditional wild man of the woods of Western folklore, he represents that irredeemable streak in society of people who will not conform to any form of authority. He is uneducable, immune to conscience, illogical, vengeful and destructive. Jacobean society had many such men. A similarly cynical view of the common sort was presented in *Measure for Measure* (1604) and *Coriolanus* (1607–09), though the ruling classes were shown as no better. Romantic critics saw Caliban rather idealistically because they cherished revolutionary hopes of overthrowing the old European order and saw in him a fantasy image of the noble savage, innocent, dignified, without the artificialities of *ancien régime* elite European culture. The Whitehall audience of 1611 would have seen him as a filthy, fish-stinking, craven, deformed savage and untrustworthy heathen, much as they regarded the poor. Shakespeare seems to regard most men as savages whatever their background.

Chapter 13

LITERARY CONTEXT

Genre

The Tempest is difficult to define generically. It is a little bit of everything – a hybrid amalgam with elements of potential tragedy, actual comedy, romance, melodrama and masque. It is not a thoroughgoing comedy, but has some physically amusing 'clown' moments, some verbal wittiness and some topical satire. It is not a tragedy but has some plotlines that have the potential for disaster. The fall of a man of power (a key aspect of Renaissance tragedy) has happened before the play begins. The first scene ends with the apparently imminent drowning of a group of characters. There are two (unfulfilled) plots to commit murder. Revenge (a popular and common motif in tragedy) is the driving impulse of the narrative, but is diverted. These uncompleted tragic possibilities, combined with the comic elements, make the play a tragi-comedy with some features of the romance-pastoral derived from tales of chivalry and masques. The drama may be seen as an anti-pastoral, debunking the nostalgic sentimentalism of 'Golden Age' idylls. There was a literary fad for setting tales in unbelievably peaceful rural settings. This island's potential idyll was broken by Caliban and is now infested with corrupt outsiders.

At times the action is almost like a pantomime derived from the Italian *commedia dell'arte* and English Mumming Play traditions. The story has whimsicality, occasional knockabout humour and a haunting melancholy. It appears fairly light-hearted but has dark undertones. It is fast moving, short and is almost unique among the late plays in its adherence to the classical unities (time, place and plot) that hark back to the Terentian–Plautine structure pattern of Shakespeare's early work. We must not be misled. It is a play packed with serious implications, including centrally the competing demands of vengeance and forgiveness, justice and mercy. It is about reconciliation and regeneration, education and parenting, political legitimacy and usurpation – particularly by brothers – and questions the right to rule and the desirable limits of control over subjects. It raises questions about sexual imperialism, male predatoriness and the dangers of sexuality, but also glances at the ethical complexities of political imperialism in its allusion to colonial ventures in North America. It also carries a naive love story ending with a betrothal and anticipated marriage, but presents humorous moments associated with classical comedy stereotypes – an over-strict father, villains, a subhuman clown, drunken clowns, and young lovers with unrealistic emotional declarations of attraction excessive enough to provoke amusement.

Commedia dell'arte

This early form of comedy, coming from Italy in the sixteenth century, presented short improvised sketches or scenes with masked actors playing stock characters like the angry father, foolish old man, devious servants, lovers, the braggart soldier, quack doctor and drunken clowns. Though there were a number of common basic storylines involving adultery, love and jealousy, with sex, cheating and trickery as staple features of the plots, the custom of introducing improvisation allowed the set stories to be adapted and updated with topical, satirical, political or personal references. Song and dance were integral components and though most of the *scenari* were comic some incorporated more serious plot strands.

The *I Gelosi* troupe, formed in Milan in 1569 by Flamineo Scala, toured Europe and helped spread the form to England. In 1611 Scala published fifty scenarios and roles in Italian. This is too late for Elizabethan-Jacobean writers to have pillaged them for stories and ideas, which strongly suggests that a troupe visited England at some time during the period, and that the various types of playing companies copied their subjects and style.[1] There are records of sixteenth-century tours, but no evidence for performances in the 1600s. However, so many elements appear in English plays and then in court masques that some direct viewing of an Italian company's performances must have taken place or else returning tourists had recounted pieces they had seen.

Some of Scala's scenes incorporate mischievous spirit servants, magic books, a character imprisoned in a rock by a necromancer, wild men, illusionary banquets removed by spirits, drunken sailors, a magically raised tempest and other small items. No one *commedia* provides all the multiple elements in *The Tempest*; it looks as if Shakespeare made a pastiche of relevant elements he saw or recalled from accounts by others. The pantomime content – goodies, baddies, fairies, magic, bawdy clowns and a happy ending for a pair of lovers – is very much in the *commedia dell'arte* style. A magus and his daughter with spirit attendants are motifs found in the form. Clown types (rustic buffoons, not circus clowns) are common and may be originals for Stephano and Trinculo. A key character is the devious and nasty Pulchinello, a lecher with a long nose and hunch back. His physical deformities and malevolent personality (expressing his moral state) may have suggested Caliban, 'salvage and deformed'. His lust, which Prospero refers to and Caliban jokingly acknowledges, is an important factor in the characterization of Shakespeare's savage as ignoble. *Commedia* clowns are obsessed with sex. The three baser 'men of sin' (Caliban, Stephano, Trinculo) have origins in English medieval folk plays (mumming or guisings), where buffoonery provides comic relief to the serious main theme. Common themes were duality (e.g., virtue and sin, life and death, a Christian knight and the Devil) and resurrection after a struggle between paired characters representing good and bad. All these allegorical and magic elements occur in *The Tempest*. The mummers (or guisers) usually came in disguise, with make-up to hide their features or with actual masks on. Here then is an English origin for the Elizabethan-Jacobean court masques.

Masque

Other than the actual betrothal masque in Act IV, the frequency of music, song and dance in *The Tempest* make the whole play like a masque. Such entertainments were played at court from the 1600s, but increasingly masque elements intruded in the plays performed at the Blackfriars Hall theatre and the Globe public open-air arena.

The masque proper, as a courtly entertainment, combines dialogue between allegorical or classical figures, song and dance and the wearing of masks. While appearing trivial, lavish, extravagant and ephemeral, often designed to celebrate special occasions (particularly nuptials), they carry coded meanings usually of a political-ethical nature. The subjects are allegorical treatments of moral themes of some direct import to the aristocratic leaders forming the audience. They endorse those courtly values that are morally and religiously acceptable, deprecate ignoble behaviour, and point the way to improvement, reform and virtuous living. The linguistic style was high-flown poetry studded with classical allusions. The masque was a sign of the increasingly inward-looking court detached from the rest of the state. It is doubtful whether the lofty sentiments were as interesting to the audience as the expensive and elaborate costumes, the music, the grace and intricacy of the dancing and the cleverness of the stage machinery and scenery. No doubt the lofty sentiments and moral guidance had little effect on what was already in 1611 a politically, financially and morally bankrupt collection of narcissists.

Masques became a favourite court event under King James largely through the efforts of his queen, who often pushed for their production and took part in them. It was a Tudor tradition to have plays specially presented at court. During Elizabeth's reign masques also became a part of court festivities, but under James and then Charles it was a regular enough feature added to the performances of the King's Men and other companies to eventually become the dominant theatrical form. Jonson alone composed over thirty masques and, from James's accession to the performance of *The Tempest*, had already written eight specifically for the court. The King's Men, royal household employees, would attend any court festivity that involved plays and masques and their expertise (and possible participation) was regularly called upon. Jonson was an associate of the King's Men, and professional interest alone would have encouraged Shakespeare to watch his friend and colleague's productions. He would have seen that, like his own pieces, Jonson's were not sugar-coated flattery simply celebrating majesty and aristocratic life. Using praise to disarm and flattery to draw in the audience, his masques sought by instruction and admonitory satire to encourage the court to rediscover the ideals that underlay the chivalric romances of earlier times. By opposing polar allegorical abstracts – virtue/vice, pleasure/virtue, *Love Freed from Ignorance and Folly*,[2] ugliness/beauty, wicked sorcery/royal virtue, etc. – Jonson aimed to reconcile and resolve the moral conflicts on display.[3] He appealed to the Renaissance's love of allegorical high-art representations and symbolic iconography.

The Tempest too offers such binaries, but does not see their resolution in such simple terms. Juno descends like a classical goddess at the end of a play, but does not resolve the drama's central problem; that remains a human conflict partly unresolved. Prospero's masque is intentionally not completed. It is interrupted by real life as he remembers the plotters and the urgency of thwarting them. In the Act IV masque, real-life values assert themselves too. Venus makes no appearance, is given no voice and is banished before Ceres and Juno come to bless the betrothing couple. Thus lust is excluded because it has already been argued down by Prospero's strictures to Ferdinand and defeated by Ferdinand's respect for Miranda. Erotic love needs no place in the masque because it has already spoken through the naive declarations of the lovers and is controlled by their essential virtue. The masque, offering idealized hopes, may be seen as yet another piece of directorial control and spectacle produced by the arch-showman Prospero. It is also a gesture towards the hope that accompanies all engagements and marriages. It calls for the magic and luck needed for all such undertakings to succeed in a vile old world that 'has such people in't' as Caliban, Sebastian, Antonio, Stephano and Trinculo. It does so within the orthodox framework of marriage, with its expressions of hope for natural fertility within the orderly impositions of moral human intervention – Ceres representing controlled agriculture and Juno representing controlled sex (i.e., within a loving marriage). But there are uncertainties. How will Miranda react to sudden transportation into court life? Will she retain her honesty and virtue? Will Ferdinand remain faithful, unchanged by power and the enchanting corruptions of a court?

The public as well as the court was attuned to allegorical figures, for civic pageantry commonly used them. The London celebrations of James's accession were full of deities representing images of justice, mercy, concord, wisdom and hope. Prospero's masque displays two goddesses who offer fertility to the land and fertility to a couple who will hopefully rule lovingly and within the prescribed regulation of the passions permitted by marriage. This ideal is counterbalanced by the rest of the play, which acts as an anti-masque. Binary opposites of the ideals of Prospero's masque are the sexuality of Caliban and Stephano, the malign past and future intentions of Antonio and Sebastian, the querulous nature of Prospero, Ariel and Caliban, and the array of other sins displayed. Gonzalo's vision of an ideal state is not only rejected by the sneering interjections of Sebastian and Antonio but by the behaviour and attitudes of Caliban. The anti-masque represents those anarchic and vicious elements in society that threaten peace, order and all positive projects. Much of the hopefulness of both play and masque is threatened by the evil possibilities of the anti-masque characters. The contrast between Ferdinand/Miranda and Caliban/Stephano/Trinculo reminds the court that the privilege of indulging in such refined, prettified art relies on the maintenance of hierarchy and that harmony of distinct social ranks depends on the top tier doing its duty and taking the sting of resentment out of social tensions by aiding the disadvantaged. The device of an anti-masque developed from 1609 on, particularly in Jonson's work. His acerbic, combative, critical nature (sharply evident in his later satirical comedies *Volpone*, *The Alchemist* and *Bartholomew Fair*) could not be muffled and in the anti-masque he diverts his thorny wit through this adaptation of the gentler masque form. The threat posed by the grotesque figures of the anti-masque is prevented by the main masquers, who close the piece with promises of harmony. Shakespeare shows that real life is never so neat as fiction. Prospero's masque, with its courtly registers and refined lexis, is interrupted when he remembers the plot of the anti-masquers. It is a warning that the protected court life with its artificial rituals should not ignore the discontent building outside the Whitehall enclave.

Though the masque was a courtly entertainment, it had lowly origins; the folk 'guisings' (disguisings) of Tudor times and earlier involved dressing in costume and masks and visiting local people's houses – often the lord of the manor's or a local gentleman's – especially (but not exclusively) at Christmas. The lord's birthday or a family marriage were other typical occasions for local amateur mummers to bring gifts and show respect or allegiance by performing a primitive play, starting possibly with a dumbshow[4] and including crudely rhymed dialogue. The programme would finish with music, song and a dance or tableau, before the actors unmasked and completed the evening with food and carousing. It was a community entertainment and the 'drama' was often a traditional piece (like the St George play or a Robin Hood tale) from folklore and legend. The communal dancing, drinking and feasting at the end were a form of social bonding allowing the different classes to mix. A well-known example is the *Pyramus and Thisbe* offering made by the mechanicals at the end of *A Midsummer Night's Dream* to celebrate the three marriages.

Guisings developed more refinement at the Burgundian court in the fifteenth century, when more elaborate displays were put on to entertain the ducal household or to celebrate marriage or birth. They acted too as a show of conspicuous wealth for visiting ambassadors or foreign royalty, moving the subject matter into tales or allegories in classical pastoral settings with gods, goddesses and nymphs, where characters like Riches, Poverty, Justice, Fortitude, Mercy and Might debated moral conflicts. Early on it became customary for the masque to carry a message or teach a lesson on a relevant political, social or religious theme, though the imagery tended to be classical rather than biblical, perhaps to obviate straying into blasphemy.

In the early Tudor court the masque developed out of a simpler form where a masked allegorical figure addressed the guests. By Elizabeth's time the whole device was more complex, with interacting characters and themes relating to national unity and social concord. It was almost obligatory that the masque would include a eulogy on the queen. Under James the masque, the dominant courtly entertainment, was hugely more lavish in costumes, astronomical in costs, more ingenious in its staging and effects, and involved much more music and dancing. A space was left between the king's dais and the stage so that at the end the court might join in a dance. For many the dance was the most interesting element, offering opportunities for intimacy and flirtation. The whole subgenre celebrated the privileges of one rank rather than a bonding of the wider community.

Stage design became more architectural, introducing the proscenium arch and wings to create perspective. The machinery used to create effects became ever more ingenious at evoking surprise and admiration. Costumes became more fantastic. The event became a means of displaying wealth and power and could sometimes be fawningly flattering to the patron footing the bill. Professional actors and musicians were hired for the speaking and singing parts. The King's Men were always on call, but increasingly courtiers too participated. From her accession until 1611, Queen Anne frequently danced with her ladies. The king did not participate but Henry, Prince of Wales did and after his death in 1612 his brother Charles also took part.

As national political fractures opened the splits were reflected in the matters debated in the masques shown at court, but, as with Shakespeare, controversial topics had to be dressed up in serious language and surrounded by comments flattering to both court and king. Plots retelling well-known classical stories could be given a topical political slant.[5] The masques presented at James's court were 'located […] ever more precisely in the political world' and reflected the manifold political issues of the time.[6] Jonson, more than any other contemporary dramatist, was involved in developing the Jacobean masque. His sometimes testy relationship with the architect and stage set designer, Inigo Jones, took the form to a whole new level of sophistication as regards both staging and writing. In his masques Jonson was more successful in criticizing policy and covertly advising the king than he ever was in his satirical dramas. The masque was 'an arena […] in which discreet criticism could be advanced, or in which analogy and oblique allusion could be employed to insinuate a commentary on contemporary events'.[7] It is thought that Jonson's masques influenced Shakespeare in the writing of the betrothal masque in *The Tempest*. He had occasionally used brief masque-like elements (in *Love's Labours Lost*, *Romeo and Juliet*, and to comic purpose in *Much Ado About Nothing*). These tended to be for comic effect and as an extension of the metaphor of appearance and reality, blurring the boundary between truth and trickery. Prospero's masque is the most extended form Shakespeare produced. What then is its significance? It works as a formal blessing for the betrothing pair, it states the usual hopes for future happiness, but is interrupted to symbolize how the vision it presents is unreal or precarious. It was a lesson the audience, including the current and future monarchs, did not learn. Reality would interrupt their fantasy world too.

Romance

The late plays are different from the densely written, ethically combative, complex and cynical works Shakespeare wrote in the period 1600–1609. They are generally accepted to be romances. This does not just mean that the plots are love stories. Originating in medieval chivalric tales of Arthur and his knights, the romance persisted into the Renaissance. It was a long prose or verse story recounting the improbable, sometimes fantastic, testing adventures of an idealized hero travelling to strange and remote lands (often arriving through a shipwreck), facing a variety of obstacles, some human, some monstrous and supernatural. Virtue's fortitude in the face of adversity and temptation was the common theme, and though the hero has strength, courage and martial skills, the emphasis was on his personal chivalric qualities. Readily helping all sorts and conditions of people, he is decent, chaste and charitable, a Christian warrior fighting evil in whatever form encountered. Romances typically featured motifs of sin, repentance and redemption that comprise loss and retrieval, exile and restoration. There is a love element and the hero's adventures may be in quest of rescuing a lady in distress or he may meet her during his journeys. The amatory aspect is set within the Courtly Love tradition. The most famous example is Ariosto's *Orlando Furioso* (first part 1516; complete publication 1532; English translation, Sir John Harington, 1591). Spenser's *The Faerie Queene* and Sidney's *Arcadia* are influential English romances. *Pericles*, *Cymbeline*, *The Winter's Tale* and *The Tempest* all incorporate standard romance. One recurrent feature in these last plays is that the heroes/heroines are all from royal, aristocratic or better sort rank and of unquestionable, unswerving, natural virtue. They are chaste, have quick intelligence, and are readily sympathetic and courteous in all social interactions.

Another romance feature, figuring in *The Winter's Tale* and *The Tempest*, is the pastoral. This involves a country setting (in this case an uninhabited, uncultivated island) and a hero/heroine of noble rank falling in love with a heroine/hero of humbler origin (the peasant character is, like Miranda, often a noble person in disguise). Pastoral usually stresses the contrast between nature and art, the simple, honest, unpretentious community spirit of rural life and the artificial, affected, malicious atmosphere of the court or city. While stressing the calming, meditative value of returning to rural life, pastoral is essentially unreal. Court life might be artificial and full of insincerities, but pastoral, a literary device, rarely addresses the realities of country life. The swains and nymphs are Golden Age fantasies set in a mythical Arcadia. Their loves are sincere, their lives sanitized. *As You Like It* has effective anti-pastoral, with down-to-earth rustic types who acknowledge the stink, muck and hard work, but the attraction of the etherealized, literary form of this subgenre persisted as European courts became more detached from the hardships of the people.[8] Pastoral was an elaborate game as unreal as Prospero's masque, with erotic love banished and winter removed from the year's agricultural cycle. *The Tempest* as a whole has minimal hints of lust, and no bloodshed, death or violence. An isolated, simple, non-court upbringing has given Miranda pastoral heroine characteristics in her naturalness, openness and chastity, derived perhaps from Book VI of *The Faerie Queene*. Kermode sees the play as a 'romance of the *Mucedorus* type'.[9] This early romance play (c. 1590) was immensely popular, being acted before Elizabeth and James, and reprinted more than any other drama of the time. With its plethora of incidents and coincidences, its juxtaposition of humour and danger, it has some stock elements (including pastoral) that may have influenced Shakespeare. Shakespeare offers a corrupt pastoral where the courtly folk come to nature and we find that some of them are as evil by nature as the beastly natural Caliban. *The Tempest* being listed as a comedy in the 1623 Folio and later reclassified as a romance indicates its indeterminate identity generically.

The recurrence of romances at court, together with the proliferation of masques, marks a move away from satirical realism into a fantasy world. Such idealized entertainments, remote from the realities of life, indicate a court becoming more detached from its political responsibilities and escaping into its own world of lavish productions, extravagant costumes and unrealistic stories. Prospero's masque has many traditional pastoral elements. John Gillies sees it as a celebration of the climate and fertility of Virginia, but pastoral traditionally presents a 'Golden Age' setting in such terms.[10] There is abundance of wild food on the island, but Prospero seems not to have suffered the privations of 'the starving time' experienced by the Virginian settlers in the winter of 1609–10 and there is little specific detail to link the island with the unhealthy Jamestown plantation. Pastoral is meant to be an enactment of ideals, how the world would be if all worked out perfectly, an age of innocence, of leisure and pleasure (with pastoral work a peripheral, undemanding add-on). From its beginnings it ignored the realities of toil, the vagaries of weather and the subsistence nature of most farming.

Prospero's masque is a consciously artificial artistic fabrication, intended as advice to re-enforce Prospero's insistence on chastity and a blessing of good luck to the soon-to-be married couple. It is, as engagement parties, wedding ceremonies and wedding receptions are, a declaration of hope, while the cruel realities niggle at the mind's edge reminding us all that relationships fall short of expectation, are hard to maintain, and romance does not often last long in the face of the realities of the everyday struggle to feed, clothe and house oneself. This couple will not face those hardships but will have the insidious temptations of court life to contend with. The masque acts as a proxy handfasting of the lovers, publicly declaring before witnesses their intention to marry. The *sponsalia de praesenti* (betrothal in front of witnesses) was a well-established ceremony whereby a couple announced their intention to marry. It had legal weight and was in essence a marriage to which the church ceremony put the official sanctifying seal. As they were regarded as 'married', many ordinary couples took the *sponsalia* as justifying their subsequently having sex. For a royal couple like Ferdinand and Miranda, however, continued chastity would be demanded until the display of power and pomp and the traditional rituals of the formal wedding ceremony were complete. But the masque's public intentions have already been subverted, pre-empted by Miranda and Ferdinand's private mutual promises to marry (III. i.). They have contracted a clandestine marriage in so far as parental permission was not sought or given. This fault, indeed a sin and a crime, is overtaken and annulled by Prospero's tacit agreement to the union. Their personal contracting is overseen by Prospero ('at a distance, unseen' [III. i.]). Only the audience is privy to his secret agreement. Through the masque, a public, theatrical enactment of betrothal, Prospero reinforces his orthodox views of continence before marriage. Betrothal was no guarantee of subsequent marriage. A breach of promise incident in Stratford (c. 1604) may have come to Shakespeare's mind as he wrote Prospero's warnings to Ferdinand. The town bailiff, Daniel Baker, a prominent Puritan, was excommunicated by the church court for failing to attend a hearing to answer the charge of getting a woman pregnant then breaching his promise to marry her.[11] Not that there was any shortage of other examples. Virginity at marriage was important as a mark of moral restraint but also for ensuring the legitimacy of any issue born nine months afterwards the ceremony. Chastity was a long-established Christian virtue. Elizabeth had made it a regal attribute (for reasons of state) and had been severe against her unmarried waiting gentlewomen for sexual misconduct. James's court was considerably more lax.

Tragi-comedy

Another generic label assignable to The Tempest is the form amalgamating elements of tragedy and comedy. It mixes lighter moments with more ominous and potentially dangerous incidents, but averts disaster and ends happily. The Tempest develops tragic complications, looks as if it is leading to confrontations, death and sorrow, but these are ultimately avoided in the last scene's partial resolution. Tragi-comic endings are often wish-fulfilling, romantic and improbable. Tragi-comedies are largely about noble characters, but have lowborn clown types to provide comic relief. They occasionally display love relationships between a nobleman and a young woman of lower degree. Thwarted love is often the central inciting factor, offering contrasts between the purity and fidelity of the heroes and lustful villains threatening the heroines. This type may simply present a complex mix of both comic and dramatic situations without ever approaching the truly tragic. It originated in the work of Guarini in sixteenth-century Italy, particularly in Il Pastor Fido (The Faithful Shepherd, 1583). Guarini introduced both high- and lowborn characters. A popular contemporary English example is Beaumont and Fletcher's Philaster, or Love Lies a-Bleeding (c. 1610).[12] Fletcher defines the subgenre as follows: 'A tragi-comedy is not so called in respect to mirth and killing, but in respect it wants deaths, which is enough to make it no tragedy, yet brings some near it, which is enough to make it no comedy' (Preface, *The Faithful Shepherdess*).[13] Many of the elements of tragi-comedy are similar to the materials found in romances. *The Tempest* comprises numerous potentially tragic incidents: the assumed drowning of the crew and passengers, the malice of Caliban and his death plot, Antonio and Sebastian's plot, the overarching revenge theme that could lead to a clash between Prospero and Antonio and a possible trial and execution. None of these tense or conflictual situations ends badly. Ferdinand and Miranda are the rather too-perfect romance hero and heroine. Their love is not questioned, but it is not deeply explored either.

The Text Alone

To take the text alone, without considering the contribution of any context to its meaning, highlights the story's extreme simplicity. A duke is deposed by his brother and the King of Naples, set adrift in a boat with his infant daughter, cast ashore on an island, uninhabited except for a deformed savage, an imprisoned spirit and a variety of other spirits. The ex-duke releases the spirit, takes under his wing the savage and rears both the girl and the growing young man. The savage's nurturing ends when he attempts to rape the girl. The ex-duke then treats the savage as his slave. The duke's studies in natural science lead him to attain magic powers. When his brother and his co-conspirator are sailing within the scope of the ex-duke's powers he conjures up a tempest. The courtly characters jump into the sea and are washed ashore. The ex-duke then subjects them to tricks and mishaps until he draws them all together, reveals himself, forgoes his revenge, forgiving his wrongdoers and arranging for his daughter to marry the King of Naples' son. Such a basic recital makes the play sound like a fairy story for children – and a lightweight one at that. The plot is made slightly more complex by the survivors being in three separate groups kept separate until the final scene. They involve: 1. the king's entourage (where his brother is encouraged to think of killing him to usurp his power), 2. the king's son, and 3. two servants who meet the savage and concoct a plot to murder the magician and take over the island. All three strands are part of the overall plan of the magician and his spirit servant, are under constant surveillance and are brought together in a 'name, blame and shame' final scene. Prospero and Ariel are in nearly all scenes except Act I Scene i and Act II Scene ii. Like a stage manager and his assistant they control and direct everything, and their presence incites, links and monitors most of the action.

This compact narrative is relatively brief – only 2,020 lines. *Hamlet* is over 4,000, *King Lear* 3,275. The average Elizabethan play at the end of the sixteenth century had 2,500.[14] The first act is concentrated in its dramatic effects with only two scenes – one only 67 lines, the other the longest in the play with 504. Beginning on board a ship in a storm is audacious and has impact visually, audibly, verbally and thematically. There is scope for sound and visual effects as well as in the words, creating the feel of stress and danger.

The narrative is so simple that moving into contextual dimensions is unavoidable and necessary. Storms and shipwrecks, as already discussed, have a long tradition as literary devices and symbols, initiating action in epics and long Renaissance verse romances, bringing out characters' qualities in adversity and bringing them to new lands, adventures and dangers. This storm presents some social tension between the boatswain and the court characters, reflecting the growing fractures in English society. The boatswain's questioning of how effective people of privilege, power and control are in this situation raises questions on the limits of authority that reverberate throughout. His attitude to Antonio and Sebastian is a reaction to their arrogance and is a *proleptic* contrast to Ferdinand's humble readiness (activated by love) to endure his mean task (III. i.).[15]

Disorder in the elements foreshadows the transgressions of morality in the play and parallels the growing disharmonies between the courtly ranks gathered to watch and the mass of people in the kingdom. It also introduces the personalities of Sebastian and Antonio as less than noble, and Gonzalo as well intentioned but rather pompously sententious. Symbolically storms represent the vicissitudes of life's journey (often likened to a voyage seeking safe haven in Christ). A shipwreck thus becomes emblematic of how vulnerable man's security is, how helpless he is in the face of Fortune, and how, as a victim of events he cannot control, he needs Providence. This was an area of considerable debate between those who, like Webster's character Bosola, see men at the mercy of astrology and the randomness of Fortune ('We are merely the stars' tennis-balls, struck and bandied/Which way please them')[16] and those who, like Bishop Cooper, saw everything as part of God's plan even if we cannot see how: 'That which we call Fortune is nothing but the hand of God, working by causes and for causes that we know not [and nature] nothing but the finger of God working in his creatures.'[17] For Bishop Cooper plague was not a natural, preventable medical problem: 'Whensoever misery or plague happeneth to man, it cometh not by chance or fortune, but by the assured providence of God.'[18]

Act I Scene ii is a protracted *protasis*. This device, found often in classical literature, introduces characters and explains the backstory. We learn immediately the tempest was fabricated specially, has not been fatal, and that the conjuror, the ousted Duke of Milan, is now in a position of power over the two conspirators who deposed him. We begin to see the relationship of Prospero and his daughter and, with Ferdinand's introduction, we see romantic possibilities. The magic element is extended considerably with the entry of Ariel, a non-human, supernatural creature, and the story of his past and his present services. In contrast to the bond of affection between Prospero and Miranda and Prospero and Ariel, Caliban represents bonds broken. Once again the backstory is sketched in and future trouble anticipated in the resentment of the savage. Another polar opposition is evident in the gentle cultured manners of Miranda compared with the vulgarity of her foster brother. A final plot strand for development is the figure of Ferdinand. Drawn by music, magic and curiosity to Prospero's cell, he is almost immediately recognizable as a romantic lead, a youth with 'gentillesse' – natural gentleness and decency. He and Miranda are instantly attracted. The audience sees this is part of Prospero's plan, as is the character test Ferdinand undergoes during his enslavement. The bases of the fairy story are thus displayed and the forward developments initiated: Prospero's revenge, Caliban's resentful longing for retaliation and the love theme. The rest of the play is relatively straightforward. There are some minor complications that beguile us on the way (Sebastian's plan to take power – weakly motivated and lacking drive; Caliban's recruitment of Stephano to exact retribution on his enslaver – clumsy and drunkenly confused), but there is little strong drama and nothing deflects the key impulse that will bring Prospero face to face with his brother and Alonso. The dramatic arc from beginning through middle to end is mechanical and lacking any great tension. What gives the piece weight and interest are the political, topical, ethical and satirical contextual components buried in the text. All would be assessed by biblical values. There is also some curiosity whether the love and revenge stories will work out suitably.

The Tempest's Place in Shakespeare's Oeuvre

Coming at the end of the writer's career the play inevitably echoes many themes, subjects and ideas already established.[19] Its fairy-tale narrative, its mood of healing and reconciliation, and its barely credible events ally it to the romances that preceded it. It clearly has more in common with *Pericles*, *Cymbeline* and *The Winter's Tale* than with the social, moral, satirical and political entanglements of the Problem Plays, the Great Tragedies and Mature Comedies of 1599–1606. It shows little affinity with the cynicism of *Antony and Cleopatra*, *Timon of Athens* or *Coriolanus*. Its tight structure and story shaping are reminiscent of the neoclassical early comedies (keeping to the classical unities of plot, time and location). There is one main plot; though split into the three strands already identified, they all relate to and reunite with each other in leading to Prospero's intended outcome. But in its use of spectacle, detailed stage directions and frequent musical accompaniment to the action *The Tempest* is experimental and groundbreaking. These features suggest a closer kinship to the prevailing mode of the court masque than to his other works. Economical structure and focused action should not betray us into thinking it a simple play, for throughout the texture carries sets of reflective symmetries that give different perspectives on integral themes. This patterning is common to Shakespeare's work. There is the working hierarchical team of the ship's crew, the unbonded hierarchy of the dispersed Neapolitan court, the partially fractured hierarchy of Prospero's polity, and the dysfunctional hierarchy of the Milanese court under Prospero.

There are two active sets of parent–child relationships (with the shadows of others in the background) and two pairs of brothers where one is unsuspecting of the evil aims of the other. There are two conspiracies within the play (echoing the original plot that removed Prospero from power). Sycorax's banishment from Argier and her arrival on the island is duplicated by Prospero's banishment and arrival. The latest set of arrivals form into two false trinities from the top and bottom of society. The repeating mirror images are continued in Ariel as unacceptable servant to an evil mistress but as effective servant to a virtuous master. Good servant/bad servant binaries are recurrent in Shakespeare. Ariel is a reworking of Puck in A Midsummer Night's Dream and Prospero a reconstituted version of Oberon, King of the Fairies, in the same play. In some senses they are updated stock Plautine characters, the master and his mischievous servant, such as are found in The Comedy of Errors and The Taming of the Shrew. There is love at first sight, a device occurring in The Comedy of Errors, The Taming of the Shrew, As You Like It, The Winter's Tale, Much Ado About Nothing and magically enforced in A Midsummer Night's Dream. Appearance/reality images (found throughout Shakespeare) are repeated in many of the play's situations. The claustrophobic effect of all the plot strands being part of the one central and driving action, with a controlling manager figure directing everything to a personal and particular end, recalls the tense plotting of both Oberon and Duke Vincentio (Measure for Measure). Critics who see the play as meta-theatre have also seen Shakespeare as shaping everything to his own ends, choosing the words and images to repeat patterns and similarities, choosing the developments and complications, rejecting one possibility and accepting another. Just as Prospero does not have complete control (he forgets the Caliban plot, cannot make Antonio express repentance, etc.) so Shakespeare cannot ultimately control just what gestures the actor makes, how he paces a line or emphasizes words, or how the audience will react.

The Literature of the Time

It has already been suggested that the contemporary literary forms The Tempest most resembles are romance, tragi-comedy and the masque. The latter, tending towards the simplicity of allegory, avoided complex psychological exploration of characters' motives and personalities. As such it reflects the inward-looking narcissism of a small privileged elite. Orazio Busino (chaplain to the Venetian Embassy), generalizing about London playgoers, describes them thus:

> People devoted to pleasure, who, for the most part, dress grandly and colourfully, so that they appear, if possible, more than princes, or rather *they appear actors* [emphasis added]. Similarly in the King's court after Christmas day begins a series of sumptuous banquets, well performed plays, and very graceful masques of knights and ladies.[20]

Theatregoing became a distinct feature of the cultural profile of London, though the percentage of the population regularly watching drama in any of the varied venues was relatively small and its social range diminished as private theatres increased. At the time Busino was writing (1618) admission costs had risen. Private theatres charged sixpence entrance, a shilling for a gallery seat and half a crown for a lord's box.[21] The open-air amphitheatres had very short seasons and were often closed for months when plague deaths rose above 50 a week for three consecutive weeks. The cost of entrance to the pit was one pence in the early days. Seats in the galleries ranged from two to six pence and a 'lord's box' (at the side overlooking the stage) was one shilling. All doubled by 1611. The theatre was slowly becoming a niche cultural marker for the privileged and financially secure that precluded most Londoners. Sixpence entry to Blackfriars represented a twelfth of a workman's average weekly wage of six shillings. By the Restoration (1660) drama had not only become an elite interest but tended to be about that narrow section of society. At the beginning of the century, the two popular forms of play were the bloody Revenge Tragedy and the satirical City Comedy. Both had highly political elements and were critical of the ruling class. Both subtypes continued though the satirical bourgeois-mocking City Comedy began to fade, to be reborn as Restoration Comedy when the theatres reopened in 1660. They had been closed in 1642 at the beginning of the Civil War, considered inappropriate in such difficult times. In 1657 William Davenant opened a small venue at Rutland House and with Charles II's restoration matters returned to normal but with a difference. Theatre had become much more the preserve of the comfortably-off, and the drama offered sophisticated, witty court-focused and city-focused comedies of manners about and appealing to the top two tiers of society, marking the clear detachment of the rich from the rest. The violent Revenge Tragedy survived in its previous form, but from 1610–1640 the masque and tragi-comedies began to emerge and eventually dominate. This reflects the economics of entrance becoming too expensive for the many and the withdrawal of the ruling class into their own cosseted world.

Sources

Like *Love's Labours Lost* (1588–94) and *A Midsummer Night's Dream* (1594–96), *The Tempest* lacks a dominant narrative source. This last solo-authored work is a story of Shakespeare's own imagining. The student of *Antony and Cleopatra* has North's translation of Plutarch's *Lives* to provide material for the play. The student of *King Lear* has Holinshed's history and an earlier drama version of the story, *King Leir*, to enable comparisons of what is left in, what is omitted and what is adapted. There is no such source for *The Tempest*. A source needs to contribute storyline, character or language in such substantial amounts as to show the degree to which a writer has cannibalized parts of the original narrative, discarded others or crucially changed it. With *The Tempest* all we have are echoes of *The Aeneid*, Ovid's *Metamorphoses*, and some passing allusions to contemporary writings about the colonization of America. None of these contribute greatly to the story and are only subliminal presences in the dialogue or the ideological contexts. Yet from scattered, sparse allusions to and verbal echoes of the travel writings relating to the Virginia Company, critics have raised a whole edifice from the few straws available; the terms of its charter, its Jamestown colony, clashes with the native Indians, provoked discussion about the nature of imperial acquisition and the trigger it gave to greed, but these are not engaged in *The Tempest*.

The Aeneid

Virgil's epic would have been well known by the audience, particularly the men, who would have read, translated and analysed parts of it at school and university. Some of its incidents and characters were common models of good and bad conduct. Some of its lines and descriptions were well known and well loved. Largely its contribution is that of distant echoes of situations and some tenuous verbal similarities. Orgel notes that some see 'the meaning of the play as controlled by Shakespeare's response to *The Aeneid*'.[22] Wiltenburg sees it not as the source of the plot 'but the work to which Shakespeare is responding, the story he is retelling'.[23] The fact that the fleet is sailing from Tunis (near the site of Carthage) to Naples, retracing Aeneas's voyage to Italy, is sufficient for some to see Virgil's work as a framing source. On his way Aeneas descends into Hades. This would make the survivors' island 'visit' a reworking of the Trojan hero's underworld episode, a strange encounter with a happy outcome – near death and resurrection – and Aeneas's lustful relationship with Dido as a contrast to the chaste Ferdinand and Miranda. Lindley sees Francisco's brief description of Ferdinand struggling bravely to reach the shore as reworking the opening storm in *The Aeneid*.[24] Prospero pulling aside the curtain covering his cave to reveal Ferdinand and Miranda innocently playing chess is supposedly reminiscent of the curtain closing off 'the counsel-keeping cave' that offers Dido and Aeneas refuge from a storm and an opportunity for lust. Here the curtain reveals them both reborn – Ferdinand back from death by drowning, Miranda to prospective bridehood – playfully teasing each other, thus furthering the chaste relationship contrast. It is all fairly tenuous and looks like the critics were struggling to find connections.

Ariel as a harpy removing the banquet echoes Book III (225) of *The Aeneid*, referencing the story of Phineus's food despoiled by harpies, or perhaps it is a parallel of the Eucharist being withdrawn from the unworthy. Ferdinand's apostrophe on first seeing Miranda ('Most sure, the goddess/On whom these airs attend!' [I. ii. 424–5]) echoes Aeneas's response to meeting Venus: 'O dea certe' (O goddess surely).[25] This at least is a verbatim translation of a tiny moment. When Ceres describes Iris in Prospero's masque she says

> Hail many-colour'd messenger, that ne'er
> Dost disobey the wife of Jupiter;
> Who, with thy saffron wings , upon my flowers
> Diffusest honey-drops, refreshing flowers. (IV. i. 76–9)

According to Orgel, Shakespeare 'appropriates a Virgilian description of the goddess' from Book IV. 700ff. which reads:

> So Iris, on her saffron wings through heaven,
> Glides dewy down, trailing a thousand tints,
> That shift against the sun […].[26]

In Ovid Iris is described as 'clad in rainbow hue', 'trailing her robe of a thousand colours' and 'gliding to earth down the gaily-coloured rainbow'.[27] Iris was the goddess of the rainbow, but the saffron wings seem to only occur in Virgil. This limited borrowing hardly justifies Orgel's term 'appropriates'. Slightly more substantial are the references to 'widow Dido' in the exchange between Antonio and Sebastian (II. i.). The brief discussion possibly resituates *The Aeneid* in the play as an allusive archetype of the quest tale. The epic begins with a storm and shipwreck caused by an angry deity and has a dramatic tragic love story. Shakespeare's shipwreck will turn out to have a more potentially positive outcome to its love interest, but that hardly justifies claiming *The Aeneid* is 'the work to which Shakespeare is responding, the story he is retelling'. Some writings (the Bible, for instance) have such an influence they become embedded in the culture and memory, individual phrasing, words and moods infiltrating other works without the writer being aware. A borrowing that is suitable to what a writer wants to say does not elevate the original piece into a source. The Virgilian echoes are so distant and faint as to probably be no more than Shakespeare remembering (perhaps not knowing he was) or using a phrase because it says what he wants to say. It is how poets work.

Ovid

The Metamorphoses, a collection of love stories from Greek and Roman myths involving incidents of physical transformation as metaphors of what love does to the psyche, was a 'source' Shakespeare regularly resorted to, a text he studied at school and seems to have lived with him throughout his career. Prospero's renunciation speech (V. i. 33–57) incorporates much of Medea's speech (Book VII) where she calls upon the Queen of Night, the witch-goddess Hecate, to help her transform her lover's aged father into a young man.[28] This transgressive act trespasses into the sphere of the gods' powers and perverts nature. It distinguishes her from Prospero, who seems content only to use magic to bring his enemies within his grasp.

Arthur Golding's translation appeared in 1567 and Shakespeare certainly knew it. Prospero's address to the spirits – 'Ye elves of hills, brooks, standing lakes and groves' (V. i. 33) – is virtually the same as Golding's 'Ye Ayres and windes: ye Elves of Hilles, of Brookes, of Woodes alone,/Of standing Lakes'.[29] Shakespeare adds spirits sporting with the tide, making fairy rings in the fields and making mushrooms grow overnight. These folkloric beliefs are perhaps remembered from local tales heard during his Stratford boyhood. He uses some of the later elements in the speech – magic forces making the seas rough and the Earth shake, the winds ripping up trees – but makes slight alterations. Where Golding has Medea claim, 'I call up dead men from their graves', Shakespeare is more graphic: '[…] graves at my command/Have wak'd their sleepers, op'd, and let 'em forth' (V. i. 48–9). This allusion to Ovid's sorceress acts as an anti-correlative, establishing Prospero as having power over the elements, but without her evil intents. Turning round three times, sprinkling river water on her head, giving a wailing cry and calling on the dark goddess Hecate, Medea is allied distinctly to the dark arts. Prospero may have come close to that but turned away from black magic. The Ovidian reference serves to differentiate Prospero from the evils Medea committed. Again this is a borrowing not a source.

The New World pamphlets

The borrowed verbal echoes from texts related to Virginia loom larger in recent critical approaches than they do in the play itself. An allusion needs to be recognizable by a reader/spectator or it has no effect upon meaning. A few of the first audience would have seen the relevant documents, but most would probably not. As Virginia was a topic of gossip, the storm and shipwreck might well have triggered connections with news of a vessel grounding in the Bermudas and the subsequent hardships and tensions of the survivors. It is unlikely the masses (or anyone) would see the play as engaging with the discourse on the legitimacy or otherwise of acquisition of foreign territory other than in the loosest way.

England's first steps into the imperial race to grab the Americas were a source of persistent excited interest and rumour in the taverns, the city and the court. The 1583 attempt to set up a colony in Newfoundland failed when Sir Humphrey Gilbert drowned, but the following year his half-brother, Sir Walter Raleigh, took over his charter and in 1585 sent a fleet to North Carolina to found the Roanoke settlement. This had failed by 1587 and already clashes with Native Americans tainted the imperial venture. Conflict was inevitable as the appearance of simple trading interests turned to the reality of colonization. Raleigh, with some elaborate fantasizing (largely to persuade the king to support the venture), elevated his 1595 expedition to Guiana into a mesmerizing discovery of limitless gold. It failed to produce anything other than marcasite ore. The first surviving North American colony, Jamestown, Virginia, nearly collapsed in the winter of 1609–10. Established by the newly chartered Virginia Company (1607), it too became a focus for greedy dreams of gold which were soon exposed as baseless, but the hazardous transatlantic voyage to re-provision the struggling settlement and bring in new colonists, and the sometimes difficult interchanges between natives and intruders, began very quickly to generate a thriving literature of written accounts retold in the taverns (and growing in the retelling).

Whatever the morality of sailing round the world and stealing land for the queen or king, the imperial adventure was exciting, opened up exotic new worlds, led to contact with strange new peoples and produced a new literary genre: the travel book. From the beginning the blatant avarice of the commercial aspect of creating an English empire was justified by moral imperatives (Christianizing, civilizing and educating the heathen) and embellished with morally resonant stories of happy shipwrecks and the uplifting effects of adversity, co-operation and comradeship.[30] The network of people variously involved with the Virginia Company included Shakespeare. He knew company directors, was privy to inside stories, and may have read some of the accounts or heard their details. The key documents are Sylvester Jourdain's *Discovery of the Barmudas* (1610), the Council of Virginia's *True Declaration of the state of the Colonie in Virginia, with a confutation of such scandalous reports as have tended to the disgrace of so worthy an enterprise* (1610), and William Strachey's *A True Reportory of the Wracke and Redemption of Sir Thomas Gates, Knight.* This last was initially a letter dated 15 July 1610 and published first in *Purchas His Pilgrimes* (1625).[31] Shakespeare probably knew the contents of Strachey's letter through conversations with one or other of the members of the 'Board' of the Virginia Company. He may have even read its account of the storm dispersing a fleet going to Virginia and how the *Sea Venture*, separated from the rest, ran ashore on the Bermudas.[32]

Among the network of Shakespeare's acquaintances connected with the plantation, the Earls of Southampton and Pembroke, Sir Robert Sidney, Sir Henry Nevile and Lord De La Warr had money invested in the venture. All had been members the Earl of Essex's political group. In May 1609 a fleet set sail under Sir George Summers and Sir Thomas Gates to bolster the struggling plantation. Aboard the *Sea Venture* was William Strachey, a possible protégé and certainly an acquaintance of Sir Dudley Digges. Strachey is considered to be one of Shakespeare's primary sources. The problem is to explain how Shakespeare might have learnt the details of the wreck. The event would have been a subject of tavern discussion, especially as the Jamestown settlement was of considerable topical interest. The founding and subsequent difficulties of the settlement would have been a hot talking point as it comprised two potent features: danger and invested money.[33] Some details Strachey gave and Shakespeare used suggest the playwright had seen the manuscript sometime during that year. Bate has identified a probable stimulus to writing about a shipwreck, namely Shakespeare's contact with Sir Dudley Digges, a member of the Council of the Virginia Company. Bate suggests Digges or the Earl of Pembroke (another acquaintance of Shakespeare), both associated with the company, had 'passed him one or more of the "Bermuda pamphlets" describing the shipwreck of Sir Thomas Gates in the Caribbean'.[34] If Digges had passed material to the playwright, he might also have let him see Strachey's letter. These are all connections by which information could have filtered through to the playwright.

Jourdain, another *Sea Venture* survivor, wrote a pamphlet (dated 13 October 1610) which is another possible source and was publicly available. The Virginia Council of London's *A True Declaration* (published 8 November 1610), provides another possible trigger for writing about appropriating foreign land regardless of the native inhabitants. The *Declaration's* full title suggests controversy was building about the motives and behaviour of both company and colonists. The new colony raised moral questions of profit versus principle. Exploration, hazardous journeys and colonization greatly occupied people's minds. This marks a step-change in English political history. Shakespeare's shipwreck takes up only 67 lines. The nautical details and description of the storm are unimportant. They are replicated in *The Aeneid*, in many other texts and could be acquired from tavern conversation. The unfolding story of Prospero's plan to be restored to Milan, the bulk of the play, is Shakespeare's own. The key features of the opening scene are the introduction of the court characters surrounding the King of Naples and the theme of authority, deference and hierarchy in crisis.

Sea ventures, narrow escapes and shipwrecks formed part of Western literature from its earliest beginnings. Two great classical epics, *The Odyssey* and *The Aeneid* tell of voyages incorporating storms and dangers at sea. Shakespeare uses the handy device of a storm that separates characters in *The Comedy of Errors*, *Twelfth Night* and *The Winter's Tale*. Strachey's *True Reportory* describes vividly the storm that assailed the ship for 24 hours, the prayers and cries of the passengers, the roaring of the wind and sea, and

> an apparition of a little round light, like a faint Starre, trembling, and streaming along with a sparkeling blaze, half the height upon the Maine Mast, and shooting sometimes from Shroud to Shroud [...] running sometimes along the Maine-yard to the very end, and then returning.[35]

This is very similar to Ariel's description of how

> I boarded the king's ship; now on the beak,
> Now in the waist, the deck, in every cabin,
> I flam'd amazement: sometimes I'd divide,
> And burn in many places; on the topmast,
> The yards and boresprit, would I flame distinctly,
> Then meet and join. (I. ii. 196–201)

Strachey describes how Summers 'both by his speech and authoritie' heartened everyone, and how (to lighten the ship) they threw overboard 'many a Butt of Beere, Hogsheads of Oyle, Syder, Wine, and Vinegar'. He says that the Bermudas 'be called commonly, the Devils Ilands [...] given over to Devils and wicked Spirits', but that in fact they were 'as habitable and commodious as most Countries of the same climate and situation'. On the subjects of culture, cultivation and civilization he reports the idleness of some mutinous colonists in eating raw fish rather than making the effort to gather wood and cook. This indicates a weakness of drive and spirit among so-called civilized men. His conclusion that even Adam had to tidy up Eden raises the question of nurture improving nature. Some breakdown of discipline in Jamestown also showed the need for strong leadership. Prospero nurtured Caliban in weaning him from the raw, wild food he gathered for himself to giving him 'water with berries in 't'.[36] Caliban may be seen as a simple hunter-gatherer or scavenger. Clearly Prospero brought the civilized knowledge of how raw food materials could be prepared, cooked and mixed in interesting, tasty ways, since one of Caliban's tasks (allotted also to Ferdinand) was to bring in logs. The development of livestock and crop farming was a civilizing step-change from nomadic hunter-gathering and cooking was a marker of primitive societies developing.

One feature all the accounts of the Bermudas incident share is the moralizing of it as a salutary experience, proving God's merciful Providence and how good can come of what appears evil. Kermode puts this into context:

> The central figure of Jacobean travel-literature, Samuel Purchas, perceived the need for presenting the new facts about foreign lands with full reference to classical voyages, and to the theological and moral implications of voyaging and colonizing.[37]

Verbal and situational echoes strongly suggest Shakespeare had seen the Strachey document, but this does not make it a source. It provided a few ideas and some verbal borrowings. It is an influence, not a source, and does not promote the play as participant in the colonial discourse. Many Renaissance texts (including sermons) promulgated exploration as a duty to spread the word of God. Some questioned the sanctity of conquest. It is stretching credibility (and the textual evidence) to claim *The Tempest* for either argument.

Marine material: An Erasmus connection?

It is claimed that a dialogue in Erasmus's *Colloquies* (*Conversations*) provided technical information on how the sailors attempt to save the ship. Some features of the marine tactics used have been alleged to follow closely the colloquy 'Naufragium' (Shipwreck).[38] Published first in 1518, *Colloquies* was translated into English in 1606 and 'exercised a pervasive influence on many later Renaissance writers'.[39] This collection of short dialogues attracted English readers with its sustained ironic mockery of the superstitions and failings of the Catholic Church. 'Naufragium' was added to the growing list of colloquy topics in 1523. According to Stritmatter and Kositsky, Shakespeare appropriated the rhetorical style, language and themes from Erasmus and 'several features […] *unambiguously confirm* its unmediated influence on *The Tempest*'.[40] The work might have been available to the playwright to read in someone's library, but the mechanics of trimming a ship in a storm are limited and are what any sailor in a tavern could have supplied.

Another suggested source for the idea of a shipwreck as the initial phase, bringing the characters to the island, was discovered in the eighteenth century as editors began trying to tidy and rationalize Shakespeare's texts. Richard Eden's translation (1555) of Peter Martyr's 1530 collection *De Orbo Novo* (*Of the New World*) came well before Shakespeare began writing. There is no need to speculate that he may have read the translation; Martyr's accounts provide fairly standard details of shipwrecks that anyone could have imagined. However, Eden's *History of Travaile* (1577) refers to Setebos the Patagonian god, whom Caliban claims as his mother's deity. However he encountered the unusual name, it stuck in Shakespeare's memory and was exotic enough to be usable, but it does not prove Shakespeare read Eden or that Prospero's island is in the Patagonian archipelago.

Other storm 'sources' suggested are Ariosto's *Orlando Furioso* and Henry May's account of being wrecked on the Bermudas in 1593. Any of these texts (or none) may have contributed flimsy details, tiny elements that formed thought sources or imaginative stimuli. None provides a storyline. The many pamphlets and books published attest to the marketability of accounts of voyages to the 'New World' and the Far East. These records inevitably foreground not only the hardships, dangers and excitements of long sea voyages, but also the interface between the European adventurers/explorers/ merchants and very different cultures. They also provoke moral questions on how to react to foreign cultures, how to interact with the natives, how legitimate it was for Europeans to assume the superiority of their civilization and whether they should impose their Christian beliefs. The missionary impulse was very strong, justified by the sense of duty to bring the heathens to Christ, but these themes are only very distantly hinted in *The Tempest*. The storm, briefly, and the island more lengthily, provide a test for the castaways, but the core of the play is Prospero's renewal.

Other origins for the story and characters have been suggested. Part III of Diego de Calahora's *Espejo de Principes y Cavalleros* (1578; translated as *The Mirror of Knighthood*)[41] has the hero land on an island that had been ruled by a witch whose son was fathered by the devil. It includes the story of Palisteo, second son of the King of Phrygia. Rejecting the art of governorship he studies magic, escapes to a magic island, falls in love with a picture of Lindaraza, daughter of Emperor Trebacio, and magically transports the emperor to the island. In William Thomas's *History of Italy* (1549, reprinted 1561) Shakespeare might have found the name Prosper. Deposed as Duke of

Genoa, returned to power as deputy for the Duke of Milan, he became a friend of Ferdinand, King of Naples. There was an Alfonso, King of Naples, who resigned in favour of his son Ferdinand to devote himself to 'study, solitariness and religion'. Jonson's early satire *Every Man in His Humour* (1598) has characters called Prospero and Stephano. Shakespeare acted in the play and possibly witnessed its revival at court in 1605. Vaughan and Vaughan suggest that as marriage negotiations with the Palatinate were ongoing at the time of the composition, the problems of the Milanese dukedom might reflect the 1608 usurpation of the Austrian, Hungarian and Moravian states by the brother of Rudolph II, Holy Roman Emperor.[42] In 1611 he also lost the crown of Bohemia. In the 1580s he had become interested in occult studies and Dr John Dee (a possible model for Prospero) had sought his support. Rudolph retreated into his library when political troubles became too much. It is further suggested that Alonso's grief at having lost his son in the wreck and his daughter to a foreign prince might be seen as a mirror of the situation in the English court, except that the Prince of Wales died in 1612 – after the first performance of the play.

The clearest source for *The Tempest* is Shakespeare's own work and its persistent revisiting of the themes of usurpation (often by brothers), vengeance, reconciliatory healing and the complex magical mystery of love. The audience would have no precise idea how matters might develop after the storm, but experience of the writer's work would suggest possibilities. There are hints of potential tragedy in the revenge of Prospero as it emerges that this is why he has drawn the characters to the island and we learn of the power he has through his magic. Is it to be retribution or reconciliation? The outcome is uncertain until the end. The theme of protagonist and antagonists being thrown or drawn together in an isolated or unusual location that forces them out of their comfort zone is recurrent in Shakespeare. Kermode points to wandering/enchantment/disenchantment motifs in Jonson's *Masque of Beauty* (performed January 1608),[43] but there are also the lovers lost enchanted in the forest in *A Midsummer Night's Dream*, wandering, separated, eventually reunited, with intermixed scenes of broad comedy with Bottom and the mechanicals, just as Trinculo and his companions provide light humour between more serious scenes and raise serious themes mixed with their clowning. Whatever the influence(s) for the shipwreck, the major factor is that it was a handy device to bring castaways to a strange shore. Isolating characters was a device used often by Shakespeare. In *As You Like It* the banished Duke and his followers refuge in the Forest of Arden while various young couples tread the comic mazes of the moves and countermoves of love. The storms, wrecks and separations in *The Comedy of Errors*, *Twelfth Night* and *The Winter's Tale* serve to force protagonists out of their comfort zones, testing their virtues, their self-rule, their fortitude and their judgements. The storms activate new beginnings or second chances. Muir sensibly concludes that although there 'is little doubt that Shakespeare had read […] William Strachey's *True Reportory*' and other accounts,

> the extent of the verbal echoes of [the Bermuda] pamphlets has, I think, been exaggerated. There is hardly a shipwreck in history or fiction which does not mention splitting, in which the ship is not lightened of its cargo, in which the passengers do not give themselves up for lost, in which north winds are not sharp, and in which no one gets to shore by clinging to wreckage.[44]

Nautical disasters naturally proliferated as the 'Age of Discovery' took adventurers to farther and farther shores of the opening world. Tales of such events would have been excitedly picked over in conversation.

The Montaigne influence

One undeniable, important influence is Montaigne's essay *Of the Cannibales*. This provides the ideas and words for Gonzalo's speech on the sort of idealized community he would institute given the chance. This favourite topic for political theorists is presented as a distracting daydream to divert Alonso's thoughts from the presumed loss of his son, and is undermined and interrupted by Sebastian and Antonio's mocking comments. It is an unrealistic fantasy and Shakespeare undercuts it in order to draw the viewer/listener's attention to its unworkability and inconsistency. Theoretical Utopian societies do not take account of the malice, greed and brutality of those in any society who subvert good intentions and peaceful co-existence. Sebastian, Antonio, Trinculo, Stephano and Caliban represent those sinful, criminal elements. Gonzalo subverts his own ideal commonwealth by making himself 'King on 't' despite asserting there would be 'no sovereignty'. Implicitly Shakespeare is suggesting that although all government is theft, leadership is essential or society would simply drift, would never improve and would probably sink into brutal anarchy.

It is well proven that Shakespeare knew of John Florio's 1603 translation of Montaigne's *Essais*. Verbal affinities indicate he had read at least certain individual discussions. More important than the use of Montaigne's ideas and Florio's words is how they contribute to the thematic texture of the play. In eulogizing the natives of the Caribbean, Montaigne says:

> It is a nation […] that hath no kinde of traffike, no knowledge of Letters, no intelligence of numbers, no name of magistrate, nor of politike

superioritie; no use of service, of riches, or of poverty; no contracts, no successions, no dividences, no occupation but idle; no respect of kinred, but common, no apparrell but naturall, no manuring of lands, no use of wine, corne, or mettle. The very words that import lying, falsehood, treason, dissimulation, covetousnes, envie, detraction, and pardon, were never heard of amongst them.[45]

Gonzalo repeats almost verbatim Florio's words, but although some writers viewed Native American society thus, most Renaissance political theorists regarded it as anarchic, savage and immoral. Gonzalo's speech (II. i. 143ff.) adds another dimension to the complexity of the discourse on how to rule, what makes a good ruler, and how to arrange an effective state. Prospero and his island are a microcosm of these larger issues. Gonzalo envisages a return to ground zero with no trade, no need for magistrates (for there would be no crime), no liberal arts, no disparity between the very rich and the very poor (for property would be 'in common'), no servitude, no property to inherit, no legal contracts, no land boundaries indicating who owned what, no agriculture, no production of metal and no need to work. The flaw in his dream is that it is predicated upon the impossible belief that all men and women are 'innocent and pure'. Living off the fecundity of nature, Gonzalo's 'innocent people' would be free of 'sweat or endeavour'. His 'Golden Age' society would be free of all the things that were wrong in England – 'treason, felony,/Sword, pike, knife, gun or [...] engine', corrupt magistrates, the growing gap between those at the top and bottom of society, etc. – but it would be a very primitive and unstimulating society. It is patently impossible and undesirable but works as the means to introduce a satirical reminder of English shortcomings. These English infrastructural features would be fine if it were not for the greed and dishonesty of those who find loopholes, who cheat and bribe, twist the laws and corrupt commercial practices. Alert, strong government would identify and crush such criminal self-interest and jobbery. Characteristic of James's reign was his ineffectiveness and lack of interest in curtailing the growing perversion of national political and mercantile institutions. Gonzalo's vision is also set up to be critiqued by a more realistic assessment of human nature than that held by those who eulogized the 'noble savage' of the New Worlds. Ironically Gonzalo's Utopia is mocked by two men who represent exactly why such an ideal is impossible. This idealism can be countered by Machiavelli's cynical realism:

One can make this generalisation about men: they are ungrateful, fickle, liars, and deceivers, they shun danger and are greedy for profit; while you treat them well, they are yours. They would shed their blood

for you, risk their property, their lives, their children, so long [...] as
danger is remote; but when you are in danger they turn against you.[46]

The devious self-interest of Antonio and Sebastian endorses the need for the
firm governorship Prospero now seems capable of wielding. The new Duke of
Milan has learned something from Machiavelli.

Chapter 14

TENDER PATRIARCH OR TYRANT? THE LIMITS OF AUTHORITY

Boatswain: What cares these roarers for the name of king? (I. i. 16–17)

The island is Prospero's Platonic 'Republic', an attempted (and failed) Utopian polity based upon justice – the justice of an authoritarian paternalist patriarch, kindly but strict when necessary. Given its smallness and the fact that Prospero had control of the subjects – Miranda subordinate as respectful daughter under paternal rule, Ariel subordinate as grateful servant, Caliban subordinate as an presumed grateful 'adopted' child and then subordinate as a punished criminal – it should have succeeded. But order was threatened by an attempted sexual assault, a rebellion against hierarchy and civilized conduct and harmony. Harmony is broken by the continuing enslavement and resentment of Caliban. A household was a state, a political entity, reflecting the structure of the larger state. Prospero's polity is a microcosm of the realities of politics with its tensions and fractures more or less held in control, needing strong leadership and repression of antisocial elements, but threatening to disassemble. It is a reminder that even the simplest ideal state is impossible to maintain, always foundering on human sinfulness. Prospero rules, Miranda is presumably being educated to take over, Ariel is the high-level serving body like the nobility or government ministers and Caliban the vulgar mob always threatening to break into destructive disorder. They reflect (along with the Neapolitan court) the socio-political problems facing contemporary England.

A long tradition of political philosophy sought to establish the ideal way to run a state and prepare ideal rulers. Prospero's current 'state' originated in usurpation the moment he decided to appropriate governorship, however justified. Taking independence from the people inhabiting it renders a king's state illegitimate. If he inherited the crown, but becomes a tyrant or a careless governor, his legitimacy remains but his rule is deviant. From its backstory of deposition to its putative afterlife with the marriage of Ferdinand and Miranda, the play's narrative shows Prospero's journey from neglectful ruler to engaged autocrat to tender patriarch. At each stage his conduct and manner of rule can be measured against innumerable writings about how rulers should govern, not least according to the principles laid down by the very king watching the piece. As already seen, *Basilikon Doron* says much about the duties and commitments required of rulers. Prospero's faults might well be seen as reflecting the inconsistencies of the royal author. James warned his son:

> As for the study of the other liberal arts and sciences, I would have you reasonablie versed in them, but not preassing to be a passe-master in any of them: for that cannot but distract you from the point of your calling.[1]

Distraction from his calling is precisely what Prospero allowed. He is punished for it and is displayed during the play's time frame as a prince humbled and overcoming his own flaws and passions. Theoretically James accepted that kingship was a serious role, not a hobby, not part-time employment, not irresponsible access to power and wealth, but a commitment requiring full engagement. James was intermittently engaged, sometimes deeply embroiled, in the arguments and conflicts that inevitably flared up in an increasingly complex society, but at other times he was indifferent, disengaged and distracted by pleasures. Writers agreed that rule was a skill to be learned, a calling of immense importance on which thousands of lives relied.[2] Others warned that the magnitude of the role should not blind anointed monarchs to the fact that they were still human. It was a warning to which James seemed deaf despite innumerable reminders. In 1603 Sir William Alexander's closet drama *Darius* carried this admonition:

> Let greatnesse of her glascie scepters vaunt;
> Not scepters, no, but reeds, soone brus'd, soone broken:
> And let this worldlie pomp our wits inchant,
> All fades, and scarcelie leaues behind a token.
> Those golden pallaces, those gorgeous halles,
> With fourniture superfluouslie faire:
> Those statelie courts, those sky-encountring walles
> Evanish all like vapours in the aire.[3]

In 1610 John Davies put it more succinctly:

> Wee all (that's Kings and all) but Players are
> Upon this earthly Stage.[4]

The Tempest shows the human limits of power or power limited by human frailty. Prospero's legitimate rule is marred by his lack of role engagement, Antonio's is marred by its being usurped – the shadow that lay over innumerable rulers real or fictional; Alonso's is tainted by complicity in the theft of Milan. For every charismatic Caesar or godlike Alexander (and they too were flawed) there were thousands of ordinary, weak princes. Prospero's newfound power resides partly in his magic, partly in his newfound confidence. The magic metaphorically emblematizes the quasi-divine presence, the aura of authority, attributed automatically to any ruler. Innate or learned it cannot be applied without strength of character. It is a role that, once assumed, has to be kept up. Born to power, but not expressing it, Prospero has learned about power during his exile and now is able to dominate and direct. The audience would endorse the need for rule and hierarchy. Such a structure gave them their position. A wider demographic would also agree with the need for a ruler and for hierarchy, but was increasingly questioning how such a system should be administered and how the rights of subjects related to monarchical assumptions of supremacy.

The storm scene is not just a dramatic story opening, but a vehicle for introducing some of the concerns about authority that underpin and overlay the whole text. Hierarchy and deference are reversed; the courtly characters threaten order, insurrection and insubordination. The ordered hierarchy, and therefore proper working of the ship, is assailed by Antonio and Sebastian in another (albeit slight) attempt at usurpation. They try to impose land values in a marine environment, assuming court superiority in a workplace in which they have no knowledge, use or influence. They are quite rightly put in their place. Their irrelevance and powerlessness are neatly expressed by the boatswain, who tells them that the roaring waves are indifferent to rank and offers a sarcastic invitation to Gonzalo: 'If you can command these elements […] use your authority' (I. i. 21–3). It serves as a reminder that no man should neglect his place and function, that the world's elemental power is ultimately in God's hands and not man's, that princely power is weak and limited in the face of nature. Prospero's deposition is restaged through his deposition of Caliban, the Antonio/Sebastian plot and the intended coup of the counter-court commoner trio. Prospero makes a grudging, limited admission of responsibility for passively tempting Antonio's treasonable behaviour. A soliloquy delivered by Prospero might give insight into his relationship with Antonio, how they discussed his brother's deputizing for him, and why Prospero was so drawn to study. Inserting some expression of his current feelings about Antonio would not have been impossible. Soliloquies allow the audience to enter the mindset, motives, fears and hopes of the speaker. Prospero remains distanced. Everything we learn about his past he reports to Miranda, Ariel and Caliban. It runs the risk of being mediated by distorted 12-year-old memories, by grievances, by a concern to maintain his position with each listener. Ferdinand comments that Prospero is the 'famous Duke of Milan/Of whom so often I have heard renown' (V. i. 192–3), but does not say for what the duke was renowned. The ex-duke remains aloof, largely keeping his own counsel, like a brooding God developing his plans. This would accord with the general view of the need for authority, the need for it to be firm and its necessary loneliness:

> Government is the prop and pillar of all States and Kingdoms, the cement and soule of humane affaires, the life of society and order, the very vitall spirit whereby so many millions of men doe breathe the life of comfort and peace; and the whole nature of things subsist.[5]

All contemporary political theorists agreed that dereliction of careful governorship was the origin of widespread national consequences. In Milan it led to illegitimate rule. Questions of royal legitimacy bedevilled the age. Henry VII was a usurper, Henry VIII's will barred inheritance of the crown to all but those born in England, and declared his daughter Elizabeth illegitimate after her mother was executed for adultery and incest. Lady Jane Grey sought to prove her right to rule. Mary Queen of Scots (James's mother) was Scots born, so her claim to the English throne was false, though that did not stop her. Her husband, Darnley, was English born, his mother moving south to legitimize his claim as a direct descendant of Henry VII. James's anxiety about his own status stemmed from rumours that he was the product of an illicit liaison between Mary and her alleged lover, Rizzio.[6] This did not inhibit him assuming in *Basilikon Doron* that he would eventually succeed Elizabeth. Elizabeth had been declared illegitimate by her own father when he had had her mother executed. The Pope too had declared her a heretic and a bastard. Evil mothers, stolen inheritance, legitimate inheritance, unsuitable sons and fraternal friction are recurrent features in Shakespeare's history plays and in *Hamlet*. They are embedded in *The Tempest* and create resonances relevant to the king and court, but indirectly enough to evade reprisal.

Prospero rules the play from start to finish. He may have been negligent as Duke of Milan, but on the island he is fully engaged with power, committed to control and direction. His 'Republic' is far from ideal for he has only three subjects, but he does try, like Plato's philosopher-king, to be just. His sternness perhaps repels us, but was acceptable in its time. Our attitude to power is different. His authority and style instil fear and demand obedience. He believes in a hierarchy founded on God's authority devolved through him. He manufactures the tempest with which the action starts and from then on dominates it like God. Like Plato's, Prospero's state is devoted to justice. It is justice, as conceived by Prospero, to expose his brother's perfidy and retake his dukedom, justice to repress Caliban's unrepentant lust. Hierarchy underpins much of the action as one might expect in an age when social stratification was the explicit and implicit structural feature of all relationships. Antonio subverted justice and hierarchy by supplanting his older brother in the post he inherited according to the tradition of primogeniture. Though Prospero governs the play as God was believed to govern the universe, he is not immutable or immaculate. He changes as the piece progresses towards its expected revenge. He morphs from an Old Testament, severe, punitive, retributive deity to a New Testament power intent on forgiving, reconciling and regenerating.

The long *protatic* second scene reveals the first form his governorship took in his account of the coup that ousted him. This 'confession' presents him as neglectful, self-centred, avoiding the rigours of daily government in favour of the pursuit of his studies, and enabling an ambitious, false brother to supplant him. Now, as a magician of allegedly stupendous (but largely pointless) powers, he is ready to take revenge. It is a revenge he would not need to take had he done his duty in the first place. His studies have led him to perfect an art (controlling natural forces) he would not have needed had he ruled Milan properly. In actuality Ariel conducts the large-scale actions, but always on behalf of Prospero. In some scenes Prospero stands over the set like the Almighty, controlling and invisibly surveying his handiwork. In Act III Scene i, he enters 'at a distance, unseen'. In Act III Scene iii, as 'several strange shapes' bring in a banquet for Alonso, the stage direction describes 'Prospero on the top (invisible)'. In Act IV Scene i, 'Prospero and Ariel remain, invisible'. In Act V Scene i, once Prospero has drawn his puppets into a circle, they 'stand charm'd', he reveals himself and then he speaks. Like God he manipulates the destinies of those he has brought to his new realm, but is often invisible. The play is his creation and its actions the progress of his plan. It is a working out of his fantasies of retaliation.

The Banqueting House at the Palace of Whitehall had a stage, possibly a proscenium and a set of machinery used in masques. A balcony (as in the Globe) could enable Prospero to observe above like God in majesty. In *King Lear* a storm heralding mental and social dissolution comes roughly in the middle of the play. *The Tempest* begins with the event that gives the piece its name and metaphorically parallels stormy disruption in the social arrangement. The ship is a little 'kingdom', with its hierarchy reflecting the larger social structure. There is the master, then the boatswain, then the mariners. They echo the three basic ranks of society – the ruler, the nobility and the labourers. Each has his place and function and they need to work in harmony. The master is like a king, the boatswain represents the nobility passing on the king's commands, and the mariners are the commoners whose muscle power does the necessary physical work. But there is from the very beginning the threat of strife as hierarchies collide; the sailors, desperately trying to make the vessel secure, are distracted and abused by their high-status passengers. As the boatswain implies, rank – the higher degree of king and courtiers – means nothing here. Crashing waves, thunder and lightning do not recognize the 'authority' of these land lords. There is an implication linking 'these roarers' to the gods, i.e. to the forces of fortune and destiny. Neptune, Roman god of the sea, was thought to roar like a bull in his anger at men and was capable of sending destructive storms, tsunamis and earthquakes to punish human sin or *hubris*. Jove, king of the gods, could punish sinners with his bolts of lightning. Both are mentioned in Act I Scene ii when Ariel describes his antics during the storm intended to frighten the sailors and the passengers. The sailor sharply orders the courtly passengers, 'Out of our way', after mocking their useless assumed superiority: 'If you can command these elements to silence, and work the peace of the present, we will not hand a rope more – use your authority.' Shakespeare satirically hints at the limitations of power as he did in *King Lear*. Kings may liken themselves to God (James often did), but they were only human. Their power was apparently absolute, but relied on the ready service of courtiers and other minions. They could not command the elements or even at times their own population. Act I Scene ii displays further types of authority and hierarchy. First the simple patriarchal authority Prospero has over his still-young daughter. This is mitigated by his love for her, his doing everything 'in care of thee'. This raises a question related to Prospero's treatment of Ariel and Caliban as well. Is he a tyrant or a tender patriarch? Perhaps the question is not so simple, for he demonstrates different behaviour at different times with each of his four 'family' members – varying in tone, always authoritarian, threatening sometimes, but not violent or vicious. Prospero's backstory reveals the hierarchy of primogenitive inheritance overturned by ambition in the usurpation of Milan. Under primogeniture younger brothers and sisters got nothing other than by special arrangement made by their father (e.g., a lump sum or a property). Antonio, a beloved brother ('he whom next thyself/Of all the world I lov'd' [I. ii. 68–9]), has been given access to power. The audience would be horrified at Antonio's theft – an order-threatening transgression of custom – though the younger sons might quietly applaud it. Biblical stories – Cain and Abel, Jacob and Esau, Joseph and his brothers, etc. – were all warnings resonating within Prospero's revelation of fraternal treachery.

The desire for security and peace was deeply ingrained in the English psyche. The instabilities of the Wars of the Roses and the upheavals of the Tudors had made people long for reliable rule. They had seen enough dynastic in-fighting in the nation's history represented and repeated in the innumerable chronicle dramas so popular throughout the period. The personal and political rivalries between siblings and relatives, recurrent in the history plays, appear too in the comedies and the tragedies. James too was a neglectful king, irregularly involved in administration (unless he wished to browbeat the Privy Council or the Commons into accepting a policy of his own devising or voting him more money). He too was intermittently bookish, intervening in controversy, writing books, seeing himself as supremely intellectual and more learned than his bishops or leading scholars. His belief in Divine Right had seeped so far into his thinking he believed his thoughts divinely inspired, his every idea inevitably right. His regular withdrawal from personal control, putting deputies in his place (be they politicians like Robert Cecil, Sir Francis Bacon or favourites like Carr and Villiers), and his frequent hunting trips were a dereliction of duty and an irritant. The personal power and family interest of favourites was to become an increasingly conflictual aspect of governing England. Prospero encourages Antonio's sin by similar withdrawal from his duties. The plan to correct this subversion of primogeniture impels the plot. Though the stage duke is not to be identified with the king in the audience there are issues in the fictional world of the island that evoke echoes of the court and its king and provoke judgement of both.

Other reflective, parallel subversions emphasize the importance of hierarchy and order. The stratification of roles and authority on the ship as the sailors work to save it, governed by the master, mediated by the boatswain and executed by the crew, is a co-operative effort, but the master's orders are not questioned. Effectiveness is threatened by the interference of the courtly characters, especially by the aggressive snobbery of Sebastian, less so by the pompous philosophizing of Gonzalo. The image of a body needing all its parts to work in unity was common. Here it makes plain the need for the relevant, qualified part (the limbs) to do their job without interference or distraction from the other 'organs'. As Sir Thomas Elyot asserts, the hierarchies of Heaven are reflected on Earth; the elements have their 'spheris' and men do not all have the same gifts from God. Potters cannot administer justice. Similarly, a courtier cannot handle a ship.

Another aspect of the concern for order is the appropriation of the island by an incomer (i.e., Prospero taking over from the apparent heir). As already discussed, Caliban's claim to the island is defective. His mother appropriated it from Ariel and her son's bastardy makes him ineligible to inherit what was anyway not his by right. The dénouement of the play, with Prospero about to return to his rightful domain, does not resolve either Caliban's future or the next ownership of the property. The newly enfranchised Ariel might be considered the rightful claimant. Prospero's withdrawal sets right what might be perceived as his high-handed theft but leaves unanswered the question of how this move relates to the imperial penetration of the 'New World'. Interpretations that see the play as engaging with the colonial debate must logically see Prospero's return to Milan as advocating withdrawal by the colonizing power, something none of the interested English investors contemplated and would not thank Shakespeare for suggesting. The attempt to overturn order inherent in Sebastian's desire to usurp his brother's governorship is similarly unresolved, like Antonio's situation, in so far as it is not revealed to Alonso, but is retained by Prospero as a secret lever holding Sebastian to good behaviour under threat of exposure.

Hierarchy is shown in the relationship between Ariel and Prospero. Released from the prison of the pine tree where the spirit had been incarcerated 'a dozen years' (I. ii. 279), Ariel became Prospero's servant/ slave. Though hard worked and occasionally resentful, Ariel is grateful for his release from imprisonment and willingly works with Prospero. But they have a verbal contract; Ariel is promised release from his indentured service and receives it. Miranda is subordinate according to nature and custom. All children are naturally dependent, under the command of their parents during their minority and training for adulthood. Custom makes her subordinate as a son would be. In all, Prospero, though a tyrant to the ignorant, irrational, resentful Caliban, is a tender patriarch to everyone else.

The English longed for peace, for the 'Golden Age' blessing of Prospero's masque, with foreign foes kept at bay and the arts of agriculture, trade and commerce prospering at home. They had peace under James from 1603–25, but paid the price – corrupt monarchy, corrupt government, increasingly restless parliaments, increasingly restless people and humiliating foreign entanglements. There was only peace in international affairs. The declining state of farming (rising rents, high corn prices caused by a series of bad harvests, increasing unemployment caused by the general decline and the expansion of enclosure) created an undercurrent of discontent among the mass of common people who made up approximately 80 per cent of the population. Other matters related to right of rule are raised as the Caliban story emerges. Prospero educated Caliban, but has taken over the island. It is one power subjugating a weaker, culpable one – for the protection of a victim 'subject' (Miranda). Castiglione asserted, 'If one is too forgiving with a transgressor, one injures the innocent'[7] and Shakespeare had similarly warned:

Mercy is not itself, that oft looks so;
Pardon is still the nurse of second woe. (*Measure for Measure*, II. i. 280–81)

This age believed forgiveness should only come after instructive punishment. Caliban proves himself an unfit companionate family member, likely to be a tyrannical, brutal, sexual predator as ruler. Should Prospero have forgiven Caliban and given him a second chance? Might that not have merely provoked a second attempt at rape? Shakespeare seems to be saying that rule is necessary for a state to function in an orderly way; if that ruler is improper he or she must be supplanted and another put in their place, but rule there must be in order to repress the disorderly impulses of mankind. This is exactly what happened in Milan and on the island. The resentment felt by the person removed gives Prospero and Caliban something in common. But Prospero has metamorphosed into a better man. Whether Caliban truly accepts his mistakes and genuinely intends to improve is unclear. His final words hint at possible reform:

> I'll be wise hereafter,
> And seek for grace. What a thrice-double ass
> Was I, to take this drunkard for a god,
> And worship this dull fool! (V. i. 294–7)

This process reflects the imagined ideal state where flawed monarchs become aware of their imperfections and adjust and rebellious subjects are punished, put in their place and determine to improve. The dénouement, like the rest of the play, abounds in uncertainties and ambiguities, but achieves an apparently happy ending. In the real English state the flawed monarch remained flawed, withdrew into lavish seclusion with his court and the resentments of his restless subjects escalated, becoming increasingly adversarial until civil war became inevitable.

Chapter 15

THE MORAL CONTEXT:
SINS, VIRTUES AND TRANSGRESSIONS

From the beginning, with the boatswain advising Gonzalo to 'keep below' and 'make yourself ready [...] for the mischance of the hour', the play is underpinned by Christian values and beliefs. Making ready, a sailing term, is here applied to preparing for the last voyage body and soul undergo. Due and proper preparation for death was something Christians were supposed to do every day, by prayers for forgiveness (as in the Lord's Prayer), by repentance and above all by living a virtuous life. Readiness for death was key in preparing for the afterlife and death could come at any time, especially for those braving the dangers of the sea. Hooker's *Of the Laws of Ecclesiastical Polity* (1594, 1597) reminds readers of the state in which all humans existed theologically:

> A general perswasion that thou art a sinner, will neyther soe humble, or bridle thy soule: as if the catalogue of thy sinnes examined severally, bee continually kept in minde [...] wee must force it, wee must constraine it thereunto.

Pertinent to the process we observe in *The Tempest* are Hooker's comments on penitence and restitution:

> Let noe man decyve himself; from such offences wee are not discharged [...] till recompense and restitution to man accompanie the penitent confession wee have made to Almightie God.[1]

Whatever moral questions are articulated, it is the religious context, in which every member of the audience was brought up and by which they would mediate any play viewed, that underlies each stage in the development of the story. It is not overly dominant or overtly verbalized, but it is the default position and the text is littered with both positive and negative words that had moral, Christian connotations informing the atmosphere of the piece. The misleading, apparent reality of wreck and death in the storm is dissipated by Miranda's opening lines. Like God, Prospero summoned the 'wild waters' and their 'roar' and he can 'allay' them, but her sympathy for the wretches apparently drowning is instinctive and sincere, seemingly in contrast with her father's apparent cruelty in raising the tempest. Throughout the play Miranda's emotions, conduct and empathy exemplify right thinking and right feeling in keeping with the Seven Cardinal Virtues, particularly the Christian quality of compassion (see I. ii. 27). They reflect the grace she showed during their voyage from Milan.

Other positive qualities displayed or implied by their absence are obedience, good parenting, pity, bearing up (stoic fortitude), nobleness, gentleness, mercy, penitence and forgiveness. Among the sins displayed are various forms of foul behaviour, perfidy, falseness, neglect of duty, ambition, ignobleness, desperation, envy, lying, attempted violation, lust and malice. Some Commandments are implied ('Thou shalt not kill', 'Thou shalt not steal', 'Thou shalt not covet), but all the Seven Deadly Sins are evident. The play's moral matrix references the Cardinal Virtues of temperance, justice, fortitude, faith, hope and charity, and two of the Spiritual Works of Mercy: 'to bear wrongs patiently' and 'to forgive injuries'. The Corporal Works of Mercy are displayed in Prospero's nurturing of Caliban: feeding the hungry, giving drink to the thirsty, clothing the naked and harbouring a stranger. In its broad development the plot's driving force, Prospero's planned revenge, turns at the end to the central idea of the New Testament: forgiveness. The Prospero of Acts I–IV represents the stern Old Testament God – harsh, vengeful and punitive. With the presence, teachings and example of Christ, the New Testament takes a different approach. At the beginning of Act V Prospero provides a clear indication of how the play will end, confiding to Ariel:

> Yet with my nobler reason 'gainst my fury
> Do I take part: the rarer action is
> In virtue than in vengeance. (V. i. 26–8)

During his banishment Prospero bore his injuries with controlled fury. They have built up to an angry desire for revenge. Resentment speaks strongly in his comments and the epithets used to describe his usurping brother to Miranda. He expresses astonishment

> [...] that a brother should
> Be so perfidious! – he whom next thyself
> Of all the world I lov'd. (I. ii. 67–9)

If this is the truth it indicates, on Prospero's part at least, there had once been a close bond between the two. Something happened to change that. Perhaps it was simply the corrupting lure of power when Prospero trusted Antonio enough to leave him to act as his deputy. He deprecates 'thy false uncle' (I. ii. 77) and the 'evil nature' of 'my false brother' (I. ii. 92–3). He outlines the Machiavellian process by which Antonio 'new created/The creatures that were mine' (I. ii. 81–2), granted suits, promoted new men, got rid of those not supportive of him and slowly won 'all hearts i' th' state' (I. ii. 84). It was an insidious process, devilishly tempting others to sin. It led to a rebirth or replacement, like ivy slowly enveloping a tree, shrouding it and draining its life. Though openly admitting his preference for retired study ('my library/ Was dukedom enough' [I. ii. 109–10]) he acknowledges responsibility, but offers no assessment whether he was suited for governorship, self-pityingly calling himself 'poor man' (I. ii. 109). Prospero is guilty of putting temptation in his brother's way by being so naively trusting. Miranda puts into words what the audience may be thinking: 'Good wombs have borne bad sons' (I. ii. 119).[2] It is a tale as old as the Old Testament – sibling rivalry, with one brother evilly ambitious, the other naively unsuspecting.

Antonio's first words on deck in the storm are to ask for the master of the ship. A tempest is raging, the boatswain and mariners are desperately trying to save the vessel, and Antonio demands to talk to the man in charge – the classic pride of a man full of an overweening sense of his own power and importance. He abuses the boatswain for telling Sebastian to stop interfering, with comments inappropriate for a gentleman and counter to the requirement of moderation in a governor ('cur', 'whoreson, insolent noisemaker' [I. i. 43]). James I was equally prone to slip into invective and foul language when lecturing his Privy Council or the Commons. Sebastian and Antonio's abuse, the impatient arrogance of men used to being obeyed instantly, is a negative aspect of hierarchy. Sir Thomas Elyot required any sort of prince to display comeliness in language and gesture, dignity in deportment and behaviour, an honourable and sober demeanour, affability, mercifulness, placability, humanity, benevolence and liberality, and 'the faire vertu pacience'.

When Antonio appears on the island and we realize who he is, we soon see that his deviousness is still active as he begins to tempt Sebastian into treason and fratricide. He seems a figure of unregenerate evil, for there seems little apparent motive in his plot. Is it just doing evil for the instinctive impulse to do evil? Does he hope to regain full independence for Milan as a reward for helping Sebastian to power? When forgiven by Prospero he says nothing. While Alonso, as Hooker demanded, immediately asks pardon and relinquishes his overlordship of Milan in penitent reparation, Antonio maintains an impenetrable silence. Like Iago, once his sin is exposed, he closes out the world, expresses no remorse and seeks no reconciliation. Is it the silence of deep shame that cannot express itself or does the evil remain, unexorcised, unadmitted and impervious to guilt? Antonio seems, like Satan, to have 'a mind not be changed by Place or Time'.[3] The three men of sin, plus Gonzalo, Adrian and Francisco initially stand 'spell-stopp'd' (V. i. 61) as Prospero addresses them. Whether they can hear or not is not clear, but he makes the charges against them. To Antonio he says:

> Flesh and blood,
> You, brother mine, that entertain'd ambition,
> Expell'd remorse and nature
> [...]
> I do forgive thee,
> Unnatural though thou art. (V. i. 74–8)

As 'their understanding/Begins to swell' and they resurface from their trance, Prospero addresses each individually, leaving Antonio until last:

> For you, most wicked sir, whom to call brother
> Would infect my mouth, I do forgive
> Thy rankest fault, – all of them; and require
> My dukedom of thee, which perforce, I know,
> Thou must restore. (V. i. 130–34)

It is a simple charge and a simple forgiveness, but to pardon someone, especially in front of others, albeit relatively few, raises awkward psychological difficulties. Though it may be good for Prospero's soul to do the Christ-like thing, Antonio will feel humiliated, angry and unready to acknowledge guilt and show repentance. He clearly is not ready to say sorry. Perhaps he never will be. Presumably Prospero notes this and will be aware Antonio is a continuing threat. He previously declared, 'They being penitent,/The sole drift of my purpose doth extend/not a frown further' (V. i. 28–30). What he will do in the face of Antonio's dumb impenitence we are not told, but perhaps he does not need to do anything, for the marriage of Miranda and Ferdinand blocks Antonio. Prospero restored will bequeath Milan to his daughter and it will, on his death, be subsumed to Naples through Ferdinand's assumption of his wife's property. It is a strategy Machiavelli would have applauded. Prospero's odd comment about his imminent death thus makes sense. It is a way of saying to his intractable brother that, penitent or not, he has been outmanoeuvred. A substantial body of religious writing exhorted the forgiving of trespasses against you. In 1609 John Hoskins published *A Sermon upon the Parable of the King that Taketh Accompt of His Servants*. He commented: 'To pardon and forgive, is the part of man, to revenge is the part of a beast.' Prospero has publicly forgiven his erring brother, but privately barred him from further advancement. Audience members, whatever their level of faith, would know the exhortation at the heart of the Lord's Prayer to 'forgive us our trespasses as we forgive those that trespass against us'. Forgiveness allies Prospero with Christ and implies Antonio belongs in the wild with the beasts.

None of the 'men of sin' is made to suffer severely. Little more is meted out to them than being in a state of confused distraction ('thy brains/[…] boil'd within thy skull' [V. i. 59–60]), 'unsettled fancy' (V. i. 59), frightened by spirits, driven through muddy bogs and torn by briars. Public exposure, in keeping with the practice of the time, is humiliating, but it is limited: 'At this time/I will tell no tales' (V. i. 128–9). Alonso suffers most through the emotional turmoil of grief for a son believed drowned. Much audience sympathy is drained from this situation by knowing from Act I Scene ii that Ferdinand lives. Everyone already knew Antonio was a usurper/betrayer deserving greater punishment, yet he suffers nothing more than the public humiliation of being required to restore what he stole. Even the conspiracy to kill Alonso is kept quiet, though there is the suggestion in Prospero's words that he will guard the secret on condition of good behaviour by the two sinners. Perhaps for Prospero Alonso was the appropriate target of suffering for encouraging a tributary to commit evil. Alonso is a victim more easily punished: he is a parent and therefore vulnerable.

The Prospero of the early scenes is strict, demanding, loving to Miranda but severe and intent upon getting his own way. We see him playing a power role with her, as well as with Ariel, Caliban and Ferdinand (to whom he is a surrogate father figure). A harsh but loving God-like patriarch, he is an authority figure the audience would recognize and endorse. He is like their father, their king, their God. He is naturally protective of Miranda and has alone moulded her character during all the formative years of her life. She has no memory of her mother and only dimly remembers the women who served her in infancy. He has had the unaccustomed luxury of nurturing her without corrupting incursions by outside influences. She is therefore his creation. Her trusting lovingness is presumably reflective of a deeper, caring private character in him as opposed to the public projection of himself, though she had innate virtue as displayed in her behaviour during the voyage to the island. Miranda's first words, sympathetic, merciful, empathetic with the suffering souls on the ship, betoken a readiness to comfort those in sorrow. Running in parallel are other virtues overtly represented or implied by their absence. Each virtue implies its correlative sin, each sin evokes its opposite virtue.

As emphasized throughout, this was a culture infused through and through with ethical markers related to the Bible and the teachings of the old and new churches. The drama too reflects, debates and questions personal, social and political morality within the same context. For all its apparent narrative simplicity and brevity, *The Tempest* addresses both implicitly and explicitly the discourses that exercised contemporary anxieties. The transgression that brought Prospero to the island is the only one where resolution is completed. Other sins are contemplated, put in motion, but remain incomplete. Planned but unacted sins were still regarded as sins committed. The contemplation alone was sufficient to taint you. The resolutions too are incomplete. The forgiving of Antonio and his refusal to repent leaves unanswered the question of what will happen to him subsequently. Similarly Sebastian's guilt is known by Prospero, but not revealed or dealt with. Caliban's fate is unresolved. Like the interrupted masque, Alonso's joy at Ferdinand's survival and his betrothal to Miranda is also cut short. And as always with the marriage plans that end so many plays, 'what's to come is still unsure' (*Twelfth Night*, II. iii. 51). It is the nature of tragi-comedy to display the weakness and sinfulness of humankind but to artificially 'fix' the endings. In a tragedy it is the vices and sins of man that predominate in the language and actions portrayed. In *The Tempest* sins and sinful intentions are deflected, virtue is persistently evident and positive actions prevail – but only through the intervention of magic. That the luck works is Providence, the will of God.

Of the Ten Commandments, the fifth ('Honour thy father and thy mother') is clearly demonstrated in the respectful and loving attitudes and behaviour of Miranda and Ferdinand. The exhortations prohibiting murder, theft, bearing false witness and coveting are all broken. Antonio has borne false witness in breaking his oath of loyalty to his liege lord. This is made worse by it being fraternal betrayal. Dante put betrayers against family, guests, lord or country into Nether Hell. Antonio has sinned against kindred, state and governor. His betrayal also involves theft, though his illegitimate and blasphemous stealing of power does not seem to have bothered his conscience as it does some characters in other plays (e.g., Richard III before the Battle of Bosworth, Claudius in *Hamlet*, Macbeth and Henry IV). Any forced deposition, usurpation or murder to gain a crown would be regarded as blasphemy – a heinous disregard of God's will, bearing in mind the divine status accorded kings and other rulers, re-enforced by the religious trappings of coronation and other formal state ceremonies. Alonso's guilty betrayal of a fellow ruler provides a precedent for his own potential removal. Ariel includes Sebastian as part of the sinful trio 'that did supplant good Prospero' (III. iii. 70) and he is guilty as an accomplice in a planned repetition of the supplanting. Contemplating a sin, mentally enacting it, is seen much like committing the sin.

Sebastian's planned murder of his brother, then, even though it comes to nothing, marks him as guilty and implicates him further in the case against the defendants in Ariel's indictment. Ariel speaks as the counsel for the prosecution, arraigning them and outlining their offences. Before Prospero can make his summing up as God the Judge, he must clear himself of personal animosity. He announces his intention of mercifully forgiving the culprits, forgoing revenge and completing his final metamorphosis, his return to humanity, by renouncing his 'so potent Art' (V. i. 50). He draws the court characters into a circle in his court. Judgement Day has arrived.

Historically, deposition of a ruler included his death and the massacre of his family. This was a reality of politics. Machiavelli comments, 'The family of the old prince must be destroyed' if a new ruler is to maintain possession.[4] No new leader of state wanted to live with the fear of family revenge being taken against him.[5] Antonio failed to do this. Prospero claims this was due to 'the love my people bore me' (I. ii. 141) and a fear of marking the act with blood. Casting them adrift in 'a rotten carcass of a butt' (I. ii. 146) was, however, tantamount to murder, had it not been for 'providence divine'. After 12 years Antonio must assume his brother lost at sea. For all his kindness in provisioning the boat, Gonzalo is party to this crime, an accomplice before and after the fact, an example of moral failing among the courtiers of Naples to parallel the moral cowardice in the Milanese court and a failure to live up to Castiglione's requirement of a courtier's aim in life. Stephano, Trinculo and Caliban, equally guilty in their plotting to wrest rule and life from Prospero, at least have the strength of Machiavelli's conviction in intention, but are hopelessly inept in execution.

All the Deadly Sins are present. Prospero's arrogance in setting aside his God-ordained role and retreating into his library, thinking himself entitled to neglect his duties, is pride and sloth. This *hubris* invites punishment. Retribution comes, but, unlike the expectation of tragedy, his fall is followed by an eventual second chance to resume power, to be resurrected. Prospero's pride also involves sloth – his reluctance to take on all the tedium of day-to-day bureaucratic government drudgeries. His vanity in his newfound magical power is displayed by the magisterial manner of his ordering Ariel's managing the various elements of the plan to bring the 'men of sin' to judgement. He is reminded of his human weakness when he nearly forgets to forestall the clowns' attempt on his life. Antonio's vanity is in thinking himself entitled to supplant his brother. His *hubris* is punished by the sudden reappearance of that brother, being brought to book in public and losing what he stole. Antonio is unaware his providential survival of the storm will lead to a surprise reunion with his sibling. Stephano's fantasies of rule display a degree of pride. Contemporary thought would see comic *hubris* and hierarchical subversion in a mere butler contemplating assuming the aura of majesty. Mixed with this are murder and lust in his plot to take power by killing the ruler of the island and forcing his daughter into marriage.

Wrath is a dominant sin, present in Prospero, Caliban, Antonio, Sebastian, Stephano and Trinculo. Even Miranda displays anger in berating Caliban's ingratitude. Prospero's varying degrees of anger are present until Act V. There is his bitterness about his once-beloved brother which drives the revenge motive of the play. Revenge was a 'kind of wild justice'. In 'taking revenge a man is but even with his enemy, but in passing it over he is superior, for it is a prince's part to pardon'.[6] Bacon identifies the anger element in wanting revenge and warns that 'a man that studieth revenge keeps his own wounds green, which otherwise would heal'.[7] Prospero kept his 'wounds' open for 12 years, but ultimately plays the prince. Moments of irritation with Miranda's inattention, snappy anger and threats responding to Ariel's complaints and reminders of his promise to free the spirit, indicate a natural irascibility perhaps provoked by his vengeful mood and nervy anxiety whether his plan will work. His anger against Ferdinand is partly simulated, part of his fiction to enslave him in order to test him and bring he and Miranda together. Even when the union with Miranda is openly accepted Prospero persists with a fabricated belief that the prince will seek sex before marriage. But is it a simulated anxiety? This fiction has an underlying reality. Young men were unreliably lascivious and lustful feelings were a danger to even the most intentionally chaste. Male vulnerability to lust, forcibly acknowledged by Castiglione (Book III), was explored in the figures of Claudio and Angelo in *Measure for Measure* and revisited in the satire of *King Lear*. Prospero speaks as a wary, rightly cautious father and as mouthpiece for a perennial concern in society. Unwanted pregnancies were rising. General laxity in society and the unfettered sexuality of young men in particular were blamed.

Perhaps the strongest anger is Prospero's and Caliban's against each other. There is also the minor irritation of Antonio and Sebastian against Gonzalo for his endless Polonius-like chattering; he has an opinion on everything. Mixed with this is the unadmitted awareness that essentially, though he may be a prattling annoyance, Gonzalo is good; his loyalty and virtue persistently contrast with their deviousness, sinfulness and disloyalty. Again, all these outbursts of anger and plans for retaliation come to nothing. Most importantly Prospero's genuine cause for revenge is diverted. Some of the audience might remember Proverbs 19:11: 'The discretion of a man deferreth his anger; and it is his glory to pass over a transgression.' It is a sign of Prospero's fitness now to rule that he has learnt princely moderation and wise conduct. James, on the other hand, regularly exploded in angry outbursts. Orazio Busino records an incident when some dancers became tired during a performance of Jonson's masque *Pleasure Reconciled to Virtue* (performed 6 January 1618 in the Banqueting Hall, Whitehall):

> The king, who is by nature choleric, grew impatient and shouted loudly, 'Why don't they dance? What did you make me come here for? Devil take all of you, dance!'[8]

This transgresses a number of qualities thought essential to regal and gentlemanly decorum.

Lust was the commonest sin. Caliban's lust is set up in opposition to Ferdinand's moderation, control and abstinence. The occasion of lust, like the cause of revenge, took place before the play began. Its distasteful enactment and effects have no place in the atmosphere of reconciliation suffusing the play. It was a sin Shakespeare had discussed often elsewhere, most recently in *Measure for Measure*, where it is at the centre of complex moral discourses in a plot wrestling with the suitability of the death sentence for a gentleman who has got his wife-to-be pregnant. In contemporary England adultery, fornication, rape and all sexual uncleanliness were severely punished. Caliban's sin is bad enough but exacerbated by his joking lack of remorse. Not repenting made a sin worse. There is some spark of lust in the drunken Stephano's ready response to Caliban's description of Miranda's beauty. He has seen no other female except his mother, but senses that Miranda 'as far surpasseth Sycorax/As great does least' (III. ii. 100–101). Hearing of 'so brave a lass', Stephano immediately imagines 'his daughter and I will be king and queen' (III. ii. 105). No thought of seeing her first, becoming attracted, attracting her, courting and winning her consent. It is an imagined animal relationship like that implied in his song about Mall, Meg and company. Miranda not only has beauty, but grace and modesty. Stephano does not, and, if his song is a sign of his inclinations and attitudes, it signifies another form of imperialism – the forced appropriation of the female body. His unrealized fantasy of marriage is balanced by the more suitable and more hopeful union of Miranda and Ferdinand which at least has the important element of mutual love, however new, untried and youthful.

Envy is exhibited in Antonio's reaction to his brother retaining the title and aura of duke while he (Antonio) was doing the work. Having assumed the public appearance of being the duke he wanted to become it for real. But the robes of authority do not automatically endow you with majesty any more than Stephano and Trinculo by adorning themselves with 'trumpery' and 'glistering apparel' become men of quality. Their motley appearance is merely an imitative, mocking re-enactment of Antonio stealing the ducal robes. How many people in the audience bore more quality on their outside than in their character? Clothing as symbols of disguised reality is a common theme in Shakespeare. Envy reappears in Sebastian's ambitions to replace his brother.

Gluttony is only physically represented in the drunkenness of Stephano, Trinculo and Caliban, but avarice broods in the greediness for power evident in various plot strands. There is spiritual, intellectual and cultural sloth in Caliban's undeveloped state and his rejection of Prospero's nurturing. Without inclination to cultivate or improve himself, his laziness is evident in his reluctance to do the work he is forced to do, though that is exacerbated by his being a slave with no choice. This is the consequence of his own behaviour. He is not over-harshly treated for Prospero is too humane, but he has offended the expectations of decent conduct and is now a bond slave controlled by the will of his master. He calls Prospero a tyrant, but this is the exaggeration of the wrongdoer who refuses to admit his sin. It is the morose recrimination of the child who has been justly punished. Prospero is strict with him, but not oppressive. He exhibits none of the usual marks of tyranny:

> Tyrants are incorrigible – because of their pride, because they love adulation, because they are unwilling to return the booty they have plundered. They give bad officials free rein; they yield to flattery; they disregard the needs of the very poor; they do not criticise the rich; they expect farmers and the labouring poor to work for them; they allow their officials to expect the same; they fix elections; and increasingly try the people's patience.[9]

Caliban, like the unthinking mob, dislikes any form of authority controlling him, but society needed protecting from those who refused to see the need for repressing antisocial natural drives. Ferdinand's forced labour would be 'as heavy […] as odious' (II. i. 5) but for the delight he feels in serving Miranda. For him, love makes service a delight, bondage a freedom. He uses the language of Courtly Love (as does she) in vowing to devote himself to her service. It is subversive of male dominance, but is the traditional language of a young man's overwhelmed sense of finding a soul mate. Miranda subverts obedience to her parent, breaks his 'hest' and subverts patriarchy in giving her heart to a man without seeking her father's approval. This too is an illusory trick, for the audience knows Prospero observes them and blesses their love ('Heavens rain grace' on these 'two most rare affections!' [III. i. 75]). In choosing to remain unimproved Caliban condemns himself to never being anything other than a drudging slave. He exemplifies what Aristotle said: 'Some things are so divided right from birth, some to rule, some to be ruled.'[10] The early colonists believed the natives of both North and South America naturally indolent.

Caliban appears to prove this, but the inciting action of the plot is Prospero's own slothful disinclination to take on the burden of his inherited duties. Strachey acknowledged that the settlers marooned on the Bermudas showed signs of inertia instead of being fired by providential survival. Spiritual sloth (*accidia*) is evident in Alonso's downcast, spiritless melancholy that refuses to believe Providence might have saved Ferdinand.

In keeping with the overall mood of the play, and becoming more dominant as it progresses, the virtues have a greater presence than in *Timon of Athens*, *King Lear* or *Measure for Measure*. Even the sins are muted compared with their strength in the tragedies and Problem Plays. All seven of the Cardinal Virtues make significant contributions to *The Tempest*'s moral context. Temperance, prudence and charity are shown by the newborn Prospero. His apparently intended revenge was delayed for 12 years until Fortune offers an opportunity, but he has been patient – he is mostly moderate in his behaviour, not over-punitive and shows foresight, circumspection, mercy and wise conduct. He waits until the Miranda–Ferdinand situation is well in hand and under control, tests the young man's mettle and ensures his daughter is attracted to a worthy object. He plays Antonio and Alonso with skill but displays justice and fairness in bringing them to judgement. He is not over-severe in the manner of some who seek justice but simply intend brutal 'eye for an eye' retaliation. He is magnanimous in victory. He has shown fortitude throughout the 12 years, rearing and educating his daughter, sheltering Caliban and attempting to educate him. Faith is shown in attributing his survival to Providence and of course there is the underlying Christian theme of vengeful ferocity mitigated to forgiveness. There is little overt allusion to Christian beliefs, but they are implied throughout and made explicit in Miranda's compassion for those on the storm-tossed ship and in her sympathy for Ferdinand and Prospero's crucial shift at the beginning of Act V. Hope is there in the new beginning promised in the forthcoming marriage. The despair of Ferdinand's and Alonso's grief is cancelled like all the other negative impulses in the play, which are either blunted, thwarted or diverted into positive drives.

The (Spiritual and Corporal) Works of Mercy are strongly present. They are shown particularly in Prospero's treatment of Caliban. He has fed him, given him drink (parodied by Stephano's alcoholic contribution), clothed him too presumably, and has harboured the stranger (the survivors too). He has instructed the ignorant (with Miranda as a recipient who passed on her knowledge to Caliban), has born wrongs patiently and ultimately forgiven the injuries done him.

The major transgressions – betrayal and deposition of a prince, attempted rape, planned murders – are obvious, strong and useful plot elements. The virtues and some of the sins are integrated into the text rather than signalled openly, but this was an audience attuned to spotting such things. Whether they took much notice and applied it to their own lives is another question. In his dedicatory introduction to *Cynthia's Revels* (1600), Ben Jonson, with heavy irony, addressed the Elizabethan court, 'the special fountain of manners':

> Thou art a bountiful and brave spring, and waterest all the noble plants of this island. In thee the whole kingdom dresseth itself, and is ambitious to use thee as her glass. Beware then thou render men's figures truly, and teach them no less to hate their deformities, than to love their forms: for, to grace, there should come reverence, and no man can call that lovely, which is not also venerable. It is not powdering, perfuming, and every day smelling of the tailor, that converteth to a beautiful object; but a mind shining through any suit, which needs no false light, either of riches or honours, to help it.

This was a model for James's court too. It was ignored. The corruption witnessed among the court characters on stage in *The Tempest* would have been readily and embarrassingly comprehensible to the silk-clad sycophants and drunken Roaring Boy savages in the audience. The happy ending might have amused even cynical hearts, but the shadows were gathering in England. The new philosopher-king was proving as much of an illusion as Prospero. Death saved James from disaster, but his son and his court, their figure deformed, their spring polluted, would face a tempest of their own making. The play began with a storm and ends with calm broken by a squall of applause. England's tempest was still to come.

NOTES

Introduction

1 Tillyard, *The English Renaissance: Fact or Fiction?*, 28, 27.
2 *The Prince*, XV, 90–91.

Prologue: The Setting

1 Chambers, *William Shakespeare*, ii, 342.
2 Though there are no records of performances at the Globe or the Blackfriars Theatre (an indoor venue bought by the King's Players in 1608), this does not preclude earlier presentations at either place. Gurr (*Shakespeare Survey* 41) suggests the availability of the Blackfriars consort explains the frequency of music in the piece and the definite act breaks were typical of indoor performance, allowing candles to be trimmed. Both factors would equally apply to a Whitehall first night.
3 Squibs were rarely used for hall or court productions because of the reverberation, smoke and smell inside the auditorium.
4 *The Odyssey* is a Greek epic by Homer. *The Aeneid*, a later Latin epic, is by Virgil. Neptune is the Roman name for Poseidon (Greek), the god of the sea.
5 It includes lightning striking the ship, intense darkness and being driven aground in a creek.
6 In *Cymbeline* (1609) Jupiter descends on an eagle amid thunder and lightning and throws a thunderbolt. The term *deus ex machina* (god from the machine) has come to mean any external authority intervening to resolve a problem.
7 Preface to *The Masque of Blacknesse* (*Ben Jonson's Plays and Masques*, 315).
8 Introduction, Arden edition, lxxvi.
9 *The Westminster Magazine* criticized Sheridan's 1777 Drury Lane production as too like a pantomime and pandering to 'the childish taste of the times'.
10 Sir James Lancaster led the first, Sir Henry Middleton the second, after earlier abortive voyages. The company, officially formed and receiving its royal charter in 1600, imported spices, tea, opium, cottons, silks and saltpetre. The Caribbean and Central America were raided and robbed from the 1560s.
11 Hawkins made voyages in 1562–23 and 1564–65, but established no permanent plantation. Richard Hore (1536) and Sir Humphrey Gilbert (1583) also made aborted expeditions to the American east coast.

12 Harrison, *A Jacobean Journal*, 140, quoting Samuel Purchas, *Purchas His Pilgrimes* (1625). Purchas recounts exploration in the Americas and West Indies in vol. IV.

13 Jonson produced 36 masques, mostly for the court.

14 Orgel, *The Illusion of Power*, 38.

15 'Hallowed' meant holy or sanctified. 'Hallowmas' therefore means 'mass for the holy ones'.

16 Hutton, *The Stations of the Sun*, 371.

17 Hutton, *The Stations of the Sun*, 379.

18 The chosen plays for Christmas 1613 were a strange mix: 'One play called Filaster, One called the Knott of Fooles, One other Much Ado Abowte Nothing, The Mayeds Tragedy, The Merry Dyvell of Edmonton, The Tempest, A King and no Kinge, The Twins tragedie, The Winters Tale, Sir John Falstaffe, The Moore of Venice [*Othello*], The Nobleman, Caesars Tragedye, And one other called Love lyes a bleeding' (Chambers, 343). *Philaster* and *The Winter's Tale* are romances and *The Merry Dyvell* involved mischief and magic. *Much Ado* is a sex war comedy. *The Knot of Fools* sounds like a comedy but is untraceable. The rest are unusually gloomy for a marriage celebration.

Chapter 1. The Historical Context: An Overview

1 Weldon, *The Court and Character of King James I* (1650). Sir Anthony Weldon, a courtier and politician, was banished from Court for criticizing the Scots.

2 See Nichols, *The Progresses, Processions, and Magnificent Festivities of James the First*.

3 Troynovant was the ancient name for London, supposedly founded by Brutus leading a band of Trojan exiles. This pseudo history in Geoffrey of Monmouth filtered through Holinshed into a play, *Locrine*, performed c. 1595.

4 James's inaugural speech to Parliament declared, 'I am the husband, and the whole island is my lawful wife; I am the head and it is my body' (McIlwain, *The Political Works of James I*, 272). Revisionist historians have tried to rehabilitate James but the overwhelming evidence of contemporaries is highly critical of him.

5 Davies, *The Early Stuarts*, 7.

6 After Jean Calvin the radical French Protestant theologian.

7 In 1513 Machiavelli had referred to 'the great changes and variations, beyond human imagining, which we have experienced and experience every day' (*The Prince*, 130; written 1513, published 1532). In 1611 the European world was still morphing from its medieval past.

8 Historical Manuscripts Commission, *Calendar of the Manuscripts of the Most Honourable the Marquess of Salisbury*, vol. 12, 272.

9 Peck's work (*Northampton*) uncovers how privy councillors gathered advisors from court, scholarly and merchant communities. Much counsel was focused on self-interested profit making by the networks involved and the king ignored what would not increase his revenue or simply went his own way, exercising absolute, personal power.

Chapter 2. The Elizabethan World Order: From Divinity to Dust

1 Uranus was only discovered in 1781.

2 In *The Boke Named the Governour* (1531).

3 See Revelation 21.

4 A *Defence of Iudiciall Astrologie* (quoted in Thomas, *Religion and the Decline and Magic*, 414).

5 A court comprising privy councillors and judges, instituted to try cases of suspected treason by powerful lords whom the ordinary courts were unable to bring to book. Under the Stuarts it became a means of curbing the Crown's political opponents, most of whom belonged to the dissenting religions.

6 See Tillyard, *The Elizabethan World Picture*, for other aspects of the Elizabethan world picture.

7 A tribe with eyes in their shoulders and a mouth in their chest was reported by Raleigh after his 1595 trip to Guiana and recorded in Hakluyt's *Voyages* (viii). Richard Hakluyt, personal chaplain to Sir Robert Cecil was a leading petitioner to James for granting the Virginia Company charter.

8 *Psychomachia* is the struggle between good and evil for the mind/soul of man. Often portrayed onstage as a good and a bad angel – advising or tempting the protagonist (as in *Faustus*) – by the 1600s they had lost their allegorical state and were integrated into secularized characters, like a good friend and a false friend or a wise, disinterested adviser and a flattering self-seeker.

9 For revisionist analyses of the times see Bouwsma, *The Waning of the Renaissance*.

10 Literacy was accelerating and cheap books and pamphlets increasingly numerous. By 1600, 25 per cent of males and 10 per cent of women could read (Mortimer, 102). In London male literacy was 80 per cent.

11 Its reliance upon mind, reason and will marks the Renaissance's divergence from medievalism.

12 The church tried to keep track of unlicensed presses producing heretical or treasonable matter, but smuggled imports from Holland and the mobility of printers made it very difficult to police thought.

13 St Augustine, *City of God*, 548.

14 Milton (*Paradise Lost*, 1667) has Hell specially created by God from the materials of Chaos to receive the falling angels after their defeat and expulsion from Heaven.

15 The Catholic Church had imagined another level – Purgatory – an escape route for avoiding Hell. Venial sinners, after death, could purge their souls of sin and make themselves suitable for Heaven. Masses paid for by money left in wills were believed to assist in cleansing the soul of the departed. Protestantism saw Purgatory as a doctrinally suspect, corrupt, moneymaking scheme and dropped it from Anglican teachings.

16 Beier, *Masterless Men*, 125.

17 Formalized by St Thomas Aquinas, seminal Christian thinker of the medieval period. Some theologians placed the mother of Christ closer to her son. Hell's hierarchy is variously organized by different writers.

18 Incubi were male demons thought to have sex with sleeping women. Succubi were female demons coupling with men.

19 Theurgy is magic designed to call up and use good spirits. It was used to discover the secrets of the universe and to approach closer to God.

20 Aristotle, *Nichomachean Ethics*, X. 9. 199.

21 Increasingly, successful merchants like Cranfield, Ingram and Swinnerton were drawn into government advisory groups. Some inevitably took advantage of the opportunities for jobbery. See Peck, *Northampton*, ch. 7.

22 A royal proclamation announced a recall of monopolies, ordered lawyers to cease excessive charges, instructed royal household officials not to abuse their positions

when procuring goods for the court, and (a sop to the Puritans) banned bear baiting, music, plays and 'disordered exercises' on Sundays. These intended reforms were forgotten once James secured power.

23 Nichols, *The Progresses, Processions, and Magnificent Festivities of James the First*, 128–32. 'Placemen' held court or government posts, often through family influence.

24 *Basilikon Doron* (*A King's Gift*), a conduct book for his son Henry, Prince of Wales, justifies the principles of divine right.

25 Castiglione, *The Book of the Courtier*, 320.

26 In Elyot's Lucianic satire *Pasquil the Plain* (1532) Gnatho is the flatterer, Pasquil the plain speaker and Harpocrates (after the Greek god of silence) is the man who says nothing even when he sees wrongdoing.

27 '[...] the miserable and useless gang
Of those who please neither God nor his enemies' (*Inferno*, III. 62–3).

28 The overwhelming view of his contemporaries is of his escalating absolutism, inconsistency, extravagance and ineffectiveness.

29 Many gained military experience fighting the Spanish in the Netherlands.

30 Increasingly the better sort invested in speculative ventures (industrial, commercial and colonial).

31 See Peck, *Northampton: Patronage and Policy at the Court of James I* and *Court Patronage and Corruption in Early Stuart England*.

32 As plantations in Virginia and New England became settled and Newfoundland and Nova Scotia were exploited, importation of materials (timber, beaver fur, minerals, fish, tobacco, etc.) became valuable commercial investments.

33 Five 'young gentlemen' were imprisoned for 'ill beseeming' drunkenness for three weeks in November 1606. They were brought before the Star Chamber and fined as well 'for example's sake' (Harrison, *A Jacobean Journal*, 346).

34 Public theatre audiences too knew how often flashy, attention-seeking gallants crowded the stage and interrupted performances.

35 Many aristo-gentry families put younger sons into professions and trades so they should have an income, since land and fortune were bequeathed to the eldest male.

36 I. i. 114–16, 138. See under Jonson in the Bibliography.

37 Cited in Stone, *The Crisis of the Aristocracy*, 27.

38 Ashley, *England in the Seventeenth Century*, 18.

39 Ashley, *England in the Seventeenth Century*, 18.

40 Wilson, *State of England* (quoted in *Camden Miscellany*, vol. 16, 43).

41 Kishlansky (*A Monarchy Transformed*, 44) describing the huge network of family members given posts under the influence of royal favourite the Duke of Buckingham.

42 Edmund Bolton, antiquarian, refers to 'the vent of Virginia' as used by the government to resettle the idle multitude (Peck, *Northampton*, 119).

43 Recently discovered legal documents show Shakespeare being fined for hoarding food, presumably to sell at inflated prices (*Sunday Times*, 31 March 2013). His role as a moneylender puts a hypocritical slant on his comments about usurers and tarnishes his stance as someone concerned for the poor.

44 Burton's *The Anatomy of Melancholy* (1621) explores this multiplicity of psycho-emotional types.

45 Campbell (*Shakespeare's Tragic Heroes*) interprets heroic flaws from physiological diagnoses.

46 Cf. 'No animal fawns so much as a dog, and none is so faithful' (*Erasmus*, 134).

47 'Those who have deliberately preferred a life of irresponsible lawlessness and violence become wolves and hawks and kites' (Plato, *Phaedo*, 134). See also Leviticus 11:14, where kites are listed with many other birds that are 'an abomination'.

48 'A Most pleasant Comedie' with 'merry conceites [...] acted before the Kings Maistie at White-hall on Shroue-sunday night. By his Highnes Seruantes vsually playing at the Globe.' Printed in 1610 it is described as 'Very delectable, and full of conceited Mirth'.

49 Vaughan and Vaughan, *The Tempest*, 61–2.

50 Socrates calls bees, wasps and ants 'social and disciplined creatures' (*Phaedo*, 134).

51 In *The White Devil*, the corrupt Duke Brachiano is described as a yew tree. This negative connotation associates him with death as this tree traditionally grew in graveyards. Brachiano causes deaths and dies horribly himself.

52 Webster, *The White Devil* (1612), III. iii. 49–50.

53 Thomas, *Rivers of Gold*, xvii. Davy Ingrams claimed that, walking the Atlantic coast from Florida to Nova Scotia, he saw Indian buckets of solid silver and fist-sized gold nuggets (Milton, *Big Chief Elizabeth*, 22).

54 Milton, *Big Chief Elizabeth*, 126.

55 After his visit he built Guiana into a fabulous treasure resource to encourage James to support his colonization of the place. His *Discovery of Guiana* (1591) refers to 'the great and golden city of MANOA, which the Spaniards call EL DORADO' and laid out his plans to colonize 'for return or profit' but also for 'let or impeachment' to the Spanish (cited in Hill, *Intellectual Origins of the English Revolution*, 159). He fell foul of James's pro-Spanish policy.

56 'The Order for the Burial of the Dead' (*Book of Common Prayer*, 86).

57 Gawdy, *Letters*, 132. A sewer seated you at table and might also serve you.

58 'Over-topping' means overstepping their authority or overestimating their favour.

59 Quoted in De Lisle, *After Elizabeth*, 205. Scaramelli revealed to the Signory that English politicians, aristocrats and courtiers blamed the government for 'having sold England to the Scots'.

60 Gawdy, *Letters*, 131.

61 Quoted in De Lisle, *After Elizabeth*, 210, from *The Calendar of State Papers Relating to English Affairs, Existing in the Archives and Collections of Venice* (London, 1900), vol. 10. 1603–7.

62 Montaigne, 'On Anger', 810.

63 Bacon, 'Of Anger', 226. The translation is Bacon's.

64 By 1604 eight hundred and thirty-eight new £30 knights had been created.

65 Aristotle, *The Politics*, 67.

66 *Basilikon Doron*, 4. All quotes from the EEBO Editions reprint of the 1682 edition.

67 Nichols, *The Progresses, Processions, and Magnificent Festivities of James the First*, 327.

68 Daunton, *Progress and Poverty*, 137.

69 Historical Manuscripts Commission, *Calendar of the Manuscripts of the Most Honourable Salisbury*, vol. 12, 272.

70 Clapham, *Elizabeth of England*, 98.

71 Peck, *Northampton*, 156.

72 Strype, *Memorials of Thomas Cranmer* (1690), rec. 114.

73 Wootten, *Divine Right and Democracy*, 94–8.

74 Younger sons of aristocratic families were often forced into the church. It could be lucrative and access to clerical power was useful to the family.

75 For confrontations between congregants and clergy see Cressy, *Agnes Bowker's Cat*, ch. 9.
76 See Bunker, *Making Haste from Babylon*, 103. Some Mayflower separatists came from this area of Nottinghamshire, West Riding and Lincolnshire. John Cotton, Puritan minister of St Botolph's, Boston, also gathered followers.
77 Critics who see the play as a critique of colonial expansion have suggested the island is off the coast of America. Ariel is presumably capable of diverting the fleet from its Tunis–Naples route to the Caribbean, but the text tells us the ship was close to the island and the fleet had regrouped and sailed on for Naples. Transatlantic detours are unnecessary to the meanings of the piece.
78 *Basilikon Doron*, 18, 19, 18.
79 Brathwait, *The English Gentleman*, 115.
80 Brathwait, *The English Gentleman*, 115.
81 Webster, *The White Devil*, III. ii. 64–6.
82 Percy, *Advice to His Son*, 119.
83 One reason the Roanoke colony failed was that gentlemen settlers refused to do construction work (Milton, *Big Chief Elizabeth*, 126). Roanoke was on an island off the coast of North Carolina, USA.

Chapter 3. Sin, Death and the Prince of Darkness

1 Wycliffe, Prologue to the Apocalypse, 493.
2 After fornication (prohibited sex), nonattendance was the second most common offence.
3 For growing prosecution of prenuptial sex, adultery and bastard birth, see Dabhoiwala, *The Origins of Sex*, 41.
4 See Chaucer, *The Wife of Bath's Tale*, 1109–1130.
5 Castiglione, *The Book of the Courtier*, 55.
6 Lucifer was a prince of light before he fell. The testaments call the Devil a prince, and as darkness denotes sin joining the two terms is natural. Edgar's comment, 'The Prince of Darkness is a gentleman; Modo he's called, and Mahu' (*King Lear*, III. iv.) takes these names from an anti-papist pamphlet by Samuel Harsnett and links evil with the sham politeness of gentlemen that masks devious intent.
7 *Basilikon Doron*, 12–13. See *Two Elizabethan Puritan Diaries*, ed. M. M. Knappen.
8 See Dabhoiwala, *The Origins of Sex*, 41. Family dysfunctionality of different sorts was also worryingly increasing (see Beier, *Masterless Men*, 56), not only among the homeless, but in settled communities and in the governing classes. The Prospero–Antonio power struggle was repeated in the French court as well as among those gathered at Whitehall.
9 Nearly half of all babies never reached their first birthday. High mortality among teenagers affected not just the poor but ended many direct dynastic lines. James's eldest son, the promising and popular Prince Henry, would die aged 18 (probably of typhus). Shakespeare lost his only son aged 11. Jonson lost his first son aged 7.
10 The anonymous *Memorial* (addressed to James on his accession) demanded the reintroduction of the Edwardian reforms, more practising preaching ministers, strict observance of the Sabbath and the banishment of the ring exchange in marriage and other 'superstitious' remnants of popery. Cited in De Lisle, *After Elizabeth*, 192.
11 'To Philosophize Is to Learn How to Die', *The Complete Essays*, 96.
12 *Basilikon Doron*, 13.
13 Marlowe, *Tamburlaine*, pt 1, II. vii. 24.

14 Such a network of astrologers, mathematicians, atheists and navigators is discussed in Christopher Hill, *Intellectual Origins of the English Revolution*, ch. iv. There was an uncertain mix of genuine scientific discovery and superstition and magic among these groups. The 'Wizard Earl' of Northumberland, one of the Raleigh group, experimented in alchemy.

15 Archbishop Laud (elevated 1633) is particularly associated with the growth of increasingly Catholic ritual, but this corrupting of the original bases of the Church of England had begun much earlier.

16 Bacon, *The Advancement of Learning* (1605), 157.

17 See Botticelli's painting *The Abyss of Hell* (1480).

18 Sorcerers used occult, diabolic powers. Prospero is a conjuror or white magician, harnessing nature's forces and not intending harm.

19 *A Direction for the Government of the Tongue*, 1593. Cited in Cressy, *Agnes Bowker's Cat*, 141.

20 *Confessions*, VIII, 7.

21 Dabhoiwala, *The Origins of Sex*, 42.

22 'Of women's unnatural, insatiable lust, what Country, what Village doth not complain?' (*The Anatomy of Melancholy*, 656–7).

23 'If they cannot contain, let them marry: for it is better to marry than to burn' (I Corinthians 7:9).

24 'Prospero's Wife', *Representations* 8 (October 1984), 2.

25 'Superflux' is excess, superfluous money or food the rich were supposed to give to the poor.

26 *On the Good of Marriage*, ch. 21.

Chapter 4. The Seven Cardinal Virtues

1 *The Book of the Courtier*, 87–8.

Chapter 5. Kingship

1 Graham-Dixon, *Caravaggio*, 24.

2 Machiavelli had warned 'study and books are insufficient' to preserve states (cited in Viroli, 112).

3 One-fifth of all plays from 1588–1608 were histories (Harbage, *Shakespeare and the Rival Traditions*, 85, 260).

4 Hill, *Intellectual Origins of the English Revolution*, 175.

5 *Daemonologie*, 10.

6 City-state (Greek). In theology, morality and political theory a person was seen as a state, governed well or ill.

7 Plato's *Republic* is the starting point (much referenced in James's *Basilikon Doron*), but others took up the theme: Xenophon (*Cyropaedia*), Isocrates (*Oration to Nicocles*), Cicero (*De Officiis*), Seneca (*De Clementia*), John of Salisbury (*Policraticus*, 1159), St. Thomas Aquinas (*De Regimine Principum*, c. 1265), Erasmus (*Education of a Christian Prince*, 1516), Machiavelli (*Il Principe*, 1532).

8 All quotes from the 1970 Scolar Press unpaginated facsimile reprint.

9 *The Prince*, IX, 67.

10 *The Prince*, IX, 68. Cf. 'Men willingly change their ruler, expecting to fare better' (III, 34).

11 Cf. Castiglione, *The Book of the Courtier*, bks I–III.

12 It was not, at this time, usual for sons of the nobility to go to university. This had begun to change by the end of the sixteenth century, but for reasons of social prestige rather than concern for education (see Secor, 76).

13 Combining the medieval university courses, the *trivium* (grammar, rhetoric and logic) and *quadrivium* (arithmetic, geometry, music, astronomy) with Renaissance subjects: classical literature, philosophy, history, modern languages and natural sciences.

14 They might have received separate instruction, with Prospero, as the heir presumptive, prepared specifically for governorship. Henry VIII (as second son) was educated in a different establishment from his older brother, Arthur. Elizabeth and Mary (with a 17-year age difference) received similar academic education, but separately.

15 *The Tempest* (Oxford World's Classics edition), 36.

16 Stone, *The Crisis of the Aristocracy*, 617.

17 Speech to Parliament (1610). See Wootten, *Divine Right and Democracy*, 107.

18 Prospero claims his people loved him. Possibly they did. Perhaps they simply complied with automatic traditional loyalty to a distant prince or Prospero is putting a positive spin on his reputation.

19 Chute, *Ben Jonson of Westminster*, 130.

20 Quoted in Scott, *James I*, 263. This comment by Roger Aston, a messenger in James's service, provoked laughter at the Privy Council. It soon proved hollow.

21 *A History of England*, cited in *Basilikon Doron*, 62.

22 See *The Duchess of Malfi*, I. i. 11–15. The same speech mentions the French king clearing his court of 'flatt'ring sycophants, of dissolute,/And infamous persons'.

23 'Of all the responsibilities that fall to a prince, the most important is justice. And to maintain this, there should be appointed to hold office men of wisdom and probity, who must be good as well as judicious' (Castiglione, *The Book of the Courtier*, 307).

24 'On the Vanity of Words', 343.

25 Two of the three authors of *Eastward Ho!* were briefly jailed for mocking the Scots.

26 This note must have been added for the 1603 edition as the plot postdates the 1598 first edition.

27 According to Winwood's *Memorials* it was 'twice represented by the King's Players, with exceeding concourse of all sorts of people; but whether the matter or manner be not well handled, or that it be thought unfit that Princes should be played on the stage in their life-time, I hear that some great Councellors are much displeased with it, and so 'tis thought shall be forbidden' (Winwood, 470; cited in Harrison, *A Jacobean Journal*, 172).

28 Buchanan had been a tutor to James (who saw monarchy so very differently) and had taught Montaigne at the Collège de Guyenne in Bordeaux.

29 Republicanism or anti-monarchism were not yet discernible movements, but Buchanan's *Law of Kings* (1579) and Raleigh's *Prerogative of Parliaments* (1603) were beginning to question absolutism and suggest ways of controlling it.

30 Nichols, *The Progresses, Processions, and Magnificent Festivities of James the First*, 327. Ben Jonson wrote part of the address. He criticized the political state in *Sejanus* (1603), then became integrally involved with court masque production, using them to praise but also admonish and instruct.

Chapter 6. Patriarchy, Family Authority and Gender Relationships

1 A useful corollary to this chapter is Dusinberre, *Shakespeare and the Nature of Women*, ch. 2.

2 Ephesians 5:22–3. See also I Corinthians 11:3.

3 Genesis 3:16.

4 Hallelujah (1641).

5 *Basilikon Doron*, 54.

6 *Basilikon Doron*, 58.

7 *Basilikon Doron*, 60–61.

8 Education in the classics brought many males into contact with negative examples of female behaviour, particularly among Roman empresses.

9 *De Cultu Feminarum.* Cited in Ellerbe, *The Dark Side of Christian History*, 115.

10 Homily XV to the People of Antioch.

11 Cited in Starr, *The 'Natural Inferiority' of Women*, 45. Clement also advocated equality of the sexes and female admission to leading roles in the church.

12 *Malleus*, sect. 1.

13 *The Duchess of Malfi*, II. v. 6.

14 See Dusinberre, *Shakespeare and the Nature of Women*, 156–7.

15 Quoted in Milton, *Big Chief Elizabeth*, 201.

16 Similar orthodoxy is voiced by the unmarried Luciana in *The Comedy of Errors* (1588–93), II. i. 15–25.

17 A gull was a fool, someone gullible.

18 Cited in Stone, *The Crisis of the Aristocracy*, 615.

19 Stone, *The Crisis of the Aristocracy*, 614.

20 See Dusinberre, *Shakespeare and the Nature of Women*, 2–4.

21 Further detail in Berry and Foyster, *The Family in Early Modern England*; also see Stone, *The Family, Sex and Marriage in England, 1500–1800*.

22 Ann Thompson sees Miranda as having 'internalized' patriarchy so completely she does not question her father's behaviour ('Miranda, Where's Your Sister?', in *Feminist Criticism: Theory and Practice*, 1991).

23 See Schleiner for a discussion of the small coteries of women authors.

24 *Norton Anthology of English Literature*, vol. 1, 1553–5.

25 The letters between the gentry couple Sir John and Margaret Winthrop in the second decade of the seventeenth century testify to both a loving marriage and a highly articulate woman. Similarly, Lovell recounts the affection Bess of Hardwick achieved with her several husbands.

26 *Basilikon Doron*, 61–2.

27 Dusinberre, *Shakespeare and the Nature of Women*, 278.

28 See, for example, Elizabeth Hoby (Laoutaris, *Shakespeare and the Countess*) and Elizabeth Talbot (Lovell, *Bess of Hardwick*) – both formidable and not always pleasant women.

29 'Almost half of all babies died within twelve months of birth' (Lovell, *Empire Builder and First Lady of Chatsworth*, 1) and the teenage deaths of longed-for heirs litter the records. Elizabethan and Jacobean family monuments in churches display sad little sculpted groups of dead children.

30 Stone, *The Family, Sex and Marriage in England, 1500–1800*, 37.

31 See Dusinberre, *Shakespeare and the Nature of Women*.

32 Mothers often bequeathed money or property to a younger son to ensure he was not left destitute when his father died and the eldest inherited all.

33 The early 1600s saw increasingly punitive action by various authorities against fornication, adultery, incest, homosexuality and prostitution. See Dabhoiwala, *The Origins of Sex*, ch. 1.

34 Berry and Foyster, *The Family in Early Modern England*, 3.

35 Berry and Foyster, *The Family in Early Modern England*, 3.

36 Berry and Foyster, *The Family in Early Modern England*, 3.

37 William Gouge, *Of Domesticall Duties* (1622).
38 *The First Blast of the Trumpet against the Monstrous Regiment of Women* (1558).
39 'On the Affection of Fathers for Their Children', 448.
40 Stone, *The Family, Sex and Marriage in England*, 136.
41 Her first play was *The Forced Marriage* (1670). Private masques were female-authored before this and dramas for private reading.
42 See Hoby, *The Private Life of an Elizabethan Lady*.
43 *Norton Anthology*.
44 *Norton Anthology*.
45 Stone, *The Family, Sex and Marriage in England*, 143.
46 'The Epystle of the Translatour' from Hoby's translation (1561).
47 See Campion in *Norton Anthology*.
48 *Norton Anthology*, 1036–9. For the texts of Speght, Swetnam and others see Butler, *Female Replies to Swetnam the Woman-Hater*.
49 *The Book of the Courtier*, 47, 108.
50 Sermon, 1 September 1522.
51 'The word and works of God is quite clear, that women were made either to be wives or prostitutes' (*Works* XII, 94). 'God created Adam master and lord of living creatures, but Eve spoilt all, when she persuaded him to set himself above God's will. 'Tis you women, with your tricks and artifices, that lead men into error' (*Table Talk*).
52 See Rubin, *Mother of God*, Part VI.
53 There was a subgenre of books on famous and virtuous women. Christine of Pizan's *The Book of the City of Ladies* and Boccaccio's *De Mulieribus* were most influential.
54 *The Book of the Courtier*, 198.
55 *Anatomy*, pt 3, sect. 2, memb. 1, subs. 2, 650–51.
56 Resentful, beaten servants could not legally run away and leave the parish. That was to become a masterless man/woman and carried a prison sentence. This implication that the servant was the property of the master was yet another of the ancient practices that restricted the liberties of the English.
57 Stone, *The Family, Sex and Marriage in England*, 137.
58 Stone, *The Family, Sex and Marriage in England*, 136.
59 Stone, *The Family, Sex and Marriage in England*, 137.

Chapter 7. Man in His Place

1 Robert Crowley, *Voice of the Last Trumpet* (1550).
2 For attitudes to commercial enterprise Weber (*The Protestant Ethic and the Spirit of Capitalism*, 1904–05) and Tawney (*Religion and the Rise of Capitalism*, 1926) are still relevant. So too is L. C. Knights, *Drama and Society in the Age of Jonson* (1937), chs 1–4.
3 *Peripeteia* is Aristotle's term for the tragic process of reversal of a successful man's fortunes. *Nemesis* is the Greek Goddess of retribution. *Hubris* is the Aristotelian term for the overconfidence that is punished by a fall.
4 See Peck, *Northampton*, ch. 7.
5 Quoted in De Lisle, *After Elizabeth*, 195.
6 Stubbes, *Anatomie of Abuses*, sig. C. 11v.
7 Castiglione, The Book of the Courtier, 131.
8 From Bishop Burnet, 'King Edward's Remains: A Discourse about the Reformation of Many Abuses', in *History of the Reformation*.

9 Shuger, *Habits of Thought*, 1.
10 Jonson, *Works*, VII, 735.
11 *Ars Poetica* (*The Art of Poetry*), I, 351.

Chapter 8. Images of Disorder: The Religious Context

1 Cressy, *Agnes Bowker's Cat*, 139.
2 Keith Thomas, *Religion and the Decline of Magic*, 179.
3 1606–07 was the period when separatists exiled themselves to Leiden before sailing to America, fleeing increasing persecution. See Bunker, *Making Haste from Babylon*, pt 2.
4 Cressy, *Agnes Bowker's Cat*, ch. 10.
5 Marlowe associated with a group (including Raleigh and the Earl of Northumberland) interested in alchemy, astronomy, exploration and intellectual discussion that brought them close to deism and atheism.
6 Peck, *Northampton*, 146.
7 Gawdy, *Letters*, 148.

Chapter 9. The Context of Education: Nature versus Nurture

1 Cited Keith Thomas, *Religion and the Decline of Magic*, 384.
2 Before setting out in 1583 Sir Humphrey Gilbert sold huge areas of land in the America he had not yet reached (Milton, *Big Chief Elizabeth*, 24). He planned to impose English laws, punish crime as he saw fit and, anticipating clashes with the Native Americans, planned to take settlers who were 'thieves, murderers and wastrels' and 'such needie people [...] which now trouble the commonwelth' (Milton, *Big Chief Elizabeth*, 25). This determination to impose values is not a positive attitude and looks like a recipe for conflict.
3 Strachey, *The History of Travaile into Virginia Britannia* (1612), quoted in Oberg, *Dominion and Civility*, 53. Some early settlers were criminals, others were looking to exploit the newfound land and its peoples, and thus provocation could come from either side. Sir Humphrey Gilbert's aborted voyage (1578) was manned by 'a motley crew of pirates and criminals' (Milton, *Big Chief Elizabeth*, 16) and Hore's (1536) explorers resorted to cannibalism to survive. The early planters often lacked drive and needed strong leadership.
4 'On the Affection of Fathers for Their Children', 435.
5 'On the Affection of Fathers for Their Children', 435.
6 *Good Speed to Virginia* (1609), quoted in Oberg, *Dominion and Civility*, 54.
7 The 1585 Roanoke settlers used fish traps, foraged for berries and shellfish, but such technology as dams to catch fish had been used since Mesolithic times in Europe as well as in North America (Milton, *Big Chief Elizabeth*, 140, 150).
8 Francesco Patrizi, *A Moral Methode of Civile Policie* (1576).
9 Bacon, 'Of Adversity', 75.
10 Deuteronomy, 23:2.
11 Peter Martyr's *De Novo Orbo* (*Of the New World*). See *The Tempest*, Arden edition (1989), xxxiii.
12 In *A Preservative against Death* (1545, sigs. D1, D3) this doctrine is preached by the Devil; Elyot emphasizes how man can save himself by his own efforts (repentance, atonement, reform, faith and virtuous living) and by Christ's grace.

13 'Piece' can mean 'masterpiece', suggesting formidable virtue, or 'a component', suggesting she was a part of the essential quality of virtue. Either is unattractive, perhaps hinting at excessive piety.

14 For further detail see Orgel, *The Tempest*, 40–41.

15 A 1606 act 'To Restraine Abuses of Players' fined actors £10 for blaspheming God, Jesus, the Holy Ghost or the Trinity.

16 Thompson, 'Miranda, Where's Your Sister?' (45–55).

17 See Orgel, 'Prospero's Wife', *Representations*, 8 October 1984.

18 Montaigne, 'On Affectionate Relationships', in *The Complete Essays*, 208.

19 More, *Utopia*, I, 10.

20 Montaigne, 'On the Affection of Fathers for Their Children', in *The Complete Essays*, 435.

21 Montaigne, 'On the Affection of Fathers for Their Children', in *The Complete Essays*, 441.

22 Montaigne, 'On the Affection of Fathers for Their Children', in *The Complete Essays*, 441.

Chapter 10. The Contemporary Political Context

1 Aylmer, *The Levellers in the English Revolution*, 68.

2 By among others, Raleigh and Buchanan, as already cited.

3 Locke, *Two Treatises of Government*, bk II, para. xxvii, 287.

4 In August 1610 over 250 died of plague, 333 in September, 250 in October. Sixteen servants of Lord Clifton were arrested and imprisoned for stealing £1200 from a trunk on the London–Bedfordshire road.

5 Wardship gave the Crown the right to administer the estates and income of orphaned minors. Purveyance was the right to requisition services and goods for royal use (worth approximately £40,000 p.a.). Both were unpopular, long-established means of supplementing royal income and provided extensive opportunities for corrupt officials to bribe and intimidate.

6 Harrison, *A Second Jacobean Journal*, 232.

7 Harrison, *A Second Jacobean Journal*, 232.

8 An 'inveterate' enemy (I. ii. 121–2) to Prospero (with no reason given), he levied an army and, when Antonio had Milan's gates opened, the army occupied the city and had Prospero 'hurried thence' (I. ii. 131).

Chapter 11. Enchantment: The Context of Magic

1 'Cunning', a corruption of 'conning' (knowing), suggests knowledge beyond the normal.

2 See Frances Hill, *A Delusion of Satan*.

3 Oldridge, *The Devil in Tudor and Stuart England*, 162.

4 *The Tempest*, Arden edition (2011), 63.

5 Known of since ancient Greek times, reported by an early English explorer in Hakluyt's *Principle Navigations*.

6 Cited in Keith Thomas, *Religion and the Decline of Magic*, 84.

7 Castiglione, *The Book of the Courtier*, 300.

8 Orgel, *The Tempest*, 52.

9 C. Walter Hodges (*The Globe Restored*) sees this standard conjuring trick as achievable by a revolving table top.

10 Harrison, *A Second Jacobean Journal*, 227.

11 *Faustus* was based on a legendary character but Roger Bacon (*Friar Bacon and Friar Bungay*) and Peter Fabel (*The Merry Devil of Edmonton*) were real men reputed to be magicians.

12 Internationally renowned Danish astronomer and alchemist.

13 He claimed Madog Gwynedd discovered the continent and Robert Thorn and a Mr Eliot of Bristol had claimed America in 1494. To cement the English Crown's right to America he declared that Brutus (legendary founder of the English monarchy) and Arthur had conquered lands in America. See A. L. Rowse, *The Elizabethans and America*.

14 A form of mystic belief recently resurrected by Florentine intellectuals, combining the early philosophy of Plotinus and the even earlier mysticism of Hermes Trismegistus and the Jewish Kabbalah.

15 See *Macbeth*, I. iii.

16 Cited in Oberg, *Dominion and Civility*, 61.

17 Henricus Cornelius Agrippa. His *De Occulta Philosophia* (*On Occult Knowledge*, 1531) influenced Dee's thinking.

18 Though he defended his researches as non-occult and simply seeking to understand the divine, he did get into some unusual areas.

Chapter 12. The Context of Colonialism and Cannibalism: Theft or Duty?

1 Charter of the Virginia Company (1609), quoted in Andrews, Canney and Hair (eds), *The Westward Enterprise*, 251.

2 The root of evil is greed. See I Timothy 6:10: 'For the love of money is the root of all evil.'

3 Galatians 5:14–15.

4 Now the island split between Haiti and the Dominican Republic.

5 Payne and Beazley, *Voyages of Hawkins, Frobisher and Drake*, 7–8.

6 Thomas, *The Slave Trade*, 157.

7 Thomas, *The Slave Trade*, 175, 174.

8 See Sokol and Sokol, 'The Tempest and Legal Justification of Plantation in Virginia'. Also see Lindley, 'Courtly Play', in *The Stuart Courts*, 47ff.

9 See Orgel, *The Tempest* (Oxford World's Classics edition), 83–5.

10 Mannoni, *Prospero and Caliban*, 105.

11 Mannoni, *Prospero and Caliban*, 105.

12 Mannoni, *Prospero and Caliban*, 106.

13 Mannoni, *Prospero and Caliban*, 106.

14 Mannoni, *Prospero and Caliban*, 107.

15 Mannoni, *Prospero and Caliban*, 108.

16 *True Reportory*, in Purchas, *Purchas His Pilgrimes* (1625), 255.

17 See Thomas, *Slave Trade*, 23. Both Christianity and Islam believed the black races were turned black as part of this curse.

18 Naturals were born with mental deficiencies, employed at court or in a titled man's house as curiosities to amuse and entertain. Cosimo de Medici kept a famous dwarf fool called Braccio de Bartolo. Il Moro also had one in Milan. Is this the deformed salvage's destiny?

19 Kermode comments that such displays were common spin-offs of voyages to the Americas. Under James they were as much part of the investment plan as importing tobacco, cotton or sugar.

20 Richard Hore's voyage (1536) and Walter Raleigh's (1584) both had as an objective the taking back to England of a native for various forms of commercial and investment purposes. See Milton, *Big Chief Elizabeth*, 4 and 53.

21 Hobbes, *Leviathan*, 186.

22 Montaigne, 'On Affectionate Relationships', 207. 'Fellowship' here means company, society.

23 Milton, *Big Chief Elizabeth*, 293.

24 Hobbes, *Leviathan*, 186.

25 The word may have become known after Drake captured the Spanish treasure ship *Cacafuego* (Shitfire) off the Panamanian Pacific coast.

Chapter 13. Literary Context

1 Chambers, *William Shakespeare*, I, 494.

2 Performed 1611.

3 In Jonson's *Masque of Queens* (1609) diabolic female magic was defeated by the regal virtue of 12 queens led by Bel-Anna (a personation of Queen Anne).

4 Dumbshows precede each act. These are mimes in which the actors allegorically represent the imminent action and dialogue.

5 *The Triumph of Peace* (staged 1634), financed by money given to Charles I by Parliament, offended the Puritans. It showed how the divide was widening between an idle, wasteful court and the country.

6 Lindley, *The Stuart Courts*, 43.

7 Martin Butler, 'Reform or Reverence?', 121.

8 It is most vividly portrayed in eighteenth-century France in the beautiful unrealisms of Claude and Poussin's paintings and in Marie-Antoinette playing at being a shepherdess while her subjects starved in the real country.

9 Arden edition (1989), xvi.

10 Gillies, 'Shakespeare's Virginian Masque', *English Literary History*, vol. 53, 1986.

11 Bate, *Soul of the Age*, 179. Breach of promise was a key plot twist in *Measure for Measure*.

12 One of the 14 plays, along with *The Tempest*, performed at the wedding celebrations in 1613.

13 See Bowers's edition, vol. III.

14 Gurr, *The Shakespearean Stage, 1574–1642*, 178.

15 *Prolepsis* is a device by which an event or situation foreshadows a similar event/situation yet to come. *The Tempest* is full of such parallelisms. The usurpation of Prospero's power pre-dates the play's action, but is reflected in a number of other usurpations within the narrative enacted.

16 *The Duchess of Malfi*, V. iv. 53–4.

17 Cooper, *Certaine Sermons* (1580), cited in Keith Thomas, *Religion and the Decline of Magic*, 92.

18 Cooper, *Certaine Sermons* (1580), cited in Keith Thomas, *Religion and the Decline of Magic*, 91.

19 It is generally accepted that this was Shakespeare's last solo-authored piece. *Henry VIII* (performed 1613, printed in the 1623 Folio) was probably in collaboration with John Fletcher.

20 Orgel and Strong, *Inigo Jones: The Theatre of the Stuart Court*, I, 282.
21 The prices need multiplying by several hundreds to give modern equivalents.
22 *The Tempest*, Oxford World's Classics, 39.
23 Wiltenburg, 'The Aeneid in *The Tempest*', *Shakespeare Survey* 39 (1987).
24 *The Tempest* (New Cambridge edition, ed. Lindley), 26.
25 *The Aeneid*, I, 328.
26 *The Aeneid*, IV, 698–700.
27 *Metamorphoses*, 36, 261, 333.
28 The witches in *Macbeth* summon Hecate, their witch queen.
29 Cited in Kermode's Arden edition (1989), 148.
30 Early accounts remarked how idle and unmotivated the settlers were. Often they were disaffected criminals, unemployed men or thriftless gentlemen escaping debtors. Later planters, there by choice, made the necessary efforts to establish proper communities and thriving agriculture.
31 Samuel Purchas, rector of St Martin's, Ludgate, London, chaplain to the Archbishop of Canterbury, collected and anthologized various travellers' tales.
32 Atlantic islands, 640 miles off the American coast. A small Virginia Company settlement, set up in 1609, was a useful staging post for the incoming voyage to the new colony or the outgoing return to England. The company ran it until 1614.
33 Bate, *Soul of the Age*, 64–5.
34 Bate, *Soul of the Age*, 155.
35 Quoted in Kermode, Appendix A, *The Tempest*, Arden edition (1989).
36 Jourdain, talking of the plentiful natural foodstuffs, mentions cedar berries.
37 Kermode, Introduction to *The Tempest*, Arden edition (1989), xxx.
38 Other influences claimed, apart from Strachey, are storm descriptions in Ovid, a brief piece in *The Aeneid* and St Paul's shipwreck in the Acts of the Apostles.
39 Stritmatter and Kositsky, 'Pale as Death', 145.
40 Stritmatter and Kositsky, 'Pale as Death', 146.
41 Part III appeared c. 1586.
42 The Palatinate was one of a loose conglomerate of states in what is now Germany. See Introduction to *The Tempest*, Arden edition (2011), 38.
43 Kermode, Introduction to *The Tempest*, Arden edition (1989), lxxii.
44 Muir, *The Sources of Shakespeare's Plays*, 280.
45 Quoted in Kermode, Appendix C, *The Tempest*, Arden edition (1989), 146.
46 Machiavelli, *The Prince*, 96.

Chapter 14. Tender Patriarch or Tyrant? The Limits of Authority

1 *Basilikon Doron*, 70.
2 Castiglione asserts, 'Although the potentiality for these virtues is rooted within our souls, it often fails to develop unless helped by education' (*The Book of the Courtier*, 291).
3 *Darius* was a classical style drama. Prospero's speech (IV. viii.) 148–58, about theatre's ephemeral nature, is similar to Alexander's comments on the insubstantiality of power.
4 *The Scourge of Folly*, cited in Gurr, *The Shakespearean Stage, 1574–1642*, 80.
5 Robert Bolton, *Two Sermons Preached at Northampton* (1635), quoted in Sommerville, *Politics and Ideology in England 1603–1640*, 17.

6 Rumours of this were recurrent in England in the 1580s. While Elizabeth was iconized as a virgin goddess, Mary Queen of Scots was demonized as a lustful sorceress.

7 Castiglione, *The Book of the Courtier*, 65.

Chapter 15. The Moral Context: Sins, Virtues and Transgressions

1 Hooker, *Of the Laws of Ecclesiastical Polity*, III, 20, III, 61.

2 In *King Lear* (less succinctly) Kent (referring to Lear's daughters) says: 'It is the stars,/ […] govern our conditions;/Else one self mate and make could not beget/Such different issues' (IV. iii.).

3 Milton, *Paradise Lost*, I, 253.

4 *The Prince*, III, 36.

5 'Any injury a prince does a man should be of such a kind that there is no fear of revenge' (*The Prince*, III, 38). 'When he seizes a state the new ruler ought to determine all the injuries that he will need to inflict. He should inflict them once for all, and not have to renew them every day' (*The Prince*, VIII, 66).

6 Bacon, 'On Revenge', 72.

7 Bacon, 'On Revenge', 73.

8 Orgel and Strong, *Inigo Jones: The Theatre of the Stuart Court*, I, 284.

9 From a sermon by Savonarola against Lorenzo de Medici, 6 April 1491 (cited by Maurizio Viroli, *Niccolo's Smile: A Biography of Machiavelli*, 17).

10 *The Politics*, 67. See also Castiglione, *The Book of the Courtier*, 298.

BIBLIOGRAPHY

Andrews, K. R., N. P. Canny and P. E. H. Hair (eds). *The Westward Enterprise*. Liverpool: Liverpool University Press, 1978.

Aristotle. *The Nichomachean Ethics*, trans. David Ross. Oxford: Oxford World's Classics, 2009.

_____. *The Politics*, trans T. A. Sinclair. London: Penguin, 1981.

Ashley, Maurice. *England in the Seventeenth Century*. Harmondsworth: Penguin, 1960.

Augustine, Saint. *City of God*, trans. Henry Bettinson. London: Penguin Classics, 2003.

_____. *Confessions*, trans. R. S. Pine-Coffin. London: Penguin Classics, 1964.

_____. *On the Good of Marriage*, ed. P. G. Walsh. Oxford: Clarendon Press, 2001.

Aylmer, G. E. (ed.). *The Levellers in the English Revolution*. London: Thames & Hudson, 1975.

Bacon, Sir Francis. *The Advancement of Learning*, ed. Arthur Johnston. Oxford: Clarendon Press, 1980.

_____. *The Essays*. London: Penguin Classics, ed. John Pitcher, 1985.

Bate, Jonathan. *Soul of the Age*. London: Penguin Books, 2009.

Beier, A. L. *Masterless Men: The Vagrancy Problem in England, 1560–1640*. London: Methuen, 1985.

Berry, Helen, and Elizabeth Foyster. *The Family in Early Modern England*. Cambridge: Cambridge University Press, 2007.

Brathwait, Richard. *The English Gentleman*. London [1631].

Book of Common Prayer, ed. Brian Cummings. Oxford World's Classics. Oxford: Oxford University Press, 2011.

Bouwsma, William J. *The Waning of the Renaissance*. New Haven, CT: Yale University Press, 2000.

Bunker, Nick. *Making Haste from Babylon*. London: Pimlico, 2011.

Burnet, Bishop. *History of the Reformation*. London [1681].

Burton, Robert. *The Anatomy of Melancholy* [1621], ed. Dell and Jordan-Smith. New York: Tudor, 1927.

Butler, Charles. *Female Replies to Swetnam the Woman-Hater*. Bristol: Thoemmes Press, 1995.

Butler, Martin. 'Reform or Reverence? The Politics of the Caroline Masque'. In *Theatre and Government under the Early Stuarts*, ed. J. R. Mulryne and M. Shewring. Cambridge: Cambridge University Press, 1993.

Campbell, Lily B. *Shakespeare's Tragic Heroes*. London: Methuen, 1961.

Castiglione, Baldassare. *The Book of the Courtier*, trans. George Bull. Harmondsworth: Penguin Classics, 1981.

Chambers, E. K. *William Shakespeare: A Study of Facts and Problems*. Oxford: Clarendon Press, 1988.

Chute, Marchette. *Ben Jonson of Westminster*. London: Souvenir Press, 1978.

Clapham, John. *Elizabeth of England*, ed. E. Plummer Read and C. Read. London, 1951.

Cressy, David. *Agnes Bowker's Cat: Travesties and Transgressions in Tudor and Stuart England.* Oxford: Oxford University Press, 2000.

Crowley, Robert. *Voice of the Last Trumpet*. London [1550].

Dabhoiwala, Faramerz. *The Origins of Sex: A History of the First Sexual Revolution*. London: Penguin, 2013.

Dante. *l'Inferno* in *The Divine Comedy*, trans. David H. Higgins. Oxford World's Classics. Oxford: Oxford University Press, 2008.

Daunton, M. J. *Progress and Poverty*. Oxford: Oxford University Press, 1995.

Davies, Godfrey. *The Early Stuarts*. Oxford: Clarendon Press, 1976.

De Lisle, Leanda. *After Elizabeth*. London: Harper Collins, 2005.

Dusinberre, Juliet. *Shakespeare and the Nature of Women*. Basingstoke: Macmillan, 1996.

Ellerbe, Helen. *The Dark Side of Christian History*. Orlando, FL: Morningstar & Lark, 2001.

Elyot, Sir Thomas. *The Boke Named the Governour*. Menston: Scolar Press, 1970.

_____. *A Preservative against Death* [1545].

Erasmus, Desiderius. *Praise of Folly*, trans. Betty Radice. London: Penguin Classics, 1971.

Fletcher, John. *Dramatic Works of Francis Beaumont and John Fletcher*, vol. 3, ed. F. Bowers. Cambridge: Cambridge University Press, 2008.

Gawdy, Sir Philip. *The Letters of Sir Philip Gawdy*, ed. Isaac H. Geaves. London: J. Nichols, 1906.

Gillies, John. 'Shakespeare's Virginian Masque'. *English Literary History* 53 (1986).

Gouge, William. *Of Domesticall Duties* [1622].

Graham-Dixon, Andrew. *Caravaggio*. Harmondsworth: Penguin, 2011.

Gurr, Andrew. *The Shakespearean Stage, 1574–1642*. Cambridge: Cambridge University Press, 1991.

Hakluyt, Richard. *Voyages and Discoveries* [1589].

Harbage, Alfred. *Shakespeare and the Rival Traditions*. New York: Barnes & Noble, 1952.

Harrison, G. B. *A Jacobean Journal*. London: Routledge and Kegan Paul, 1946.

_____. *A Second Jacobean Journal*. London: Routledge and Kegan Paul, 1958.

Harsnett, Samuel. *A Declaration of Egregious Popish Impostures* [1603].

Hill, Christopher. *Intellectual Origins of the English Revolution*. London: Panther Books, 1972.

Hill, Frances. *A Delusion of Satan: The Full Story of the Salem Witch Trials*. London: Penguin, 1997.

Historical Manuscripts Commission. *Calendar of the Manuscripts of the Most Honourable the Marquess of Salisbury*. London [1883].

Hobbes, Thomas. *Leviathan*, ed. C. B. Macpherson. London: Penguin Classics, 1968.

Hoby, Lady Margaret. *The Private Life of an Elizabethan Lady: The Diary of Lady Margaret Hoby*, ed. Joanna Moody. Stroud: Sutton, 1998.

Hodges, C. Walter. *The Globe Restored*. Oxford: Oxford University Press, 1968.

Hooker, Richard. *Of the Laws of Ecclesiastical Polity*. Folger Library edition, ed. Georges Edelen. Cambridge, MA: Belknap Press of Harvard University Press, 1977.

Hutton, Ronald. *The Stations of the Sun: A History of the Ritual Year in Britain*. Oxford: Oxford University Press, 1996.

James I. *Basilikon Doron*. EEBO Editions reprint of the 1682 edition.

_____. *Daemonologie*. San Diego, CA: The Book Tree, 2002 (reprint of G. B. Harrison's edition, 1924).

Jonson, Ben. *Ben Jonson's Plays and Masques*, ed. R. Harp. New York: Norton, 2001.

_____. *Ben Jonson: Works*, ed. C. H. Herford and P. Simpson. Oxford: Clarendon Press, 1925–52.

Jonson, Ben, George Chapman and John Marston. *Eastward Ho!* New Mermaid edition. London: Ernest Benn, 1994.

Kermode, Frank. *The Tempest*, Arden edition. London: Routledge, 1989.

Kishlansky, Mark. *A Monarchy Transformed: Britain 1603–1714*. London: Penguin, 1996.

Knappen, M. M. (ed.). *Two Elizabethan Puritan Diaries*. London: SPCK, 1933.

Knights, L. C. *Drama and Society in the Age of Jonson* [1937]. Harmondsworth: Penguin, 1962.

Knox, John. *The First Blast of the Trumpet against the Monstrous Regiment of Women* [1558].

Laoutaris, Chris. *Shakespeare and the Countess*. London: Fig Tree, 2014.

Lindley, David. 'Courtly Play: The Politics of Chapman's *The Memorable Masque*'. In *The Stuart Courts*, ed. Eveline Cruickshanks. Stroud: The History Press, 2009.

_____, ed. *The Tempest*, New Cambridge Shakespeare. Cambridge: Cambridge University Press, 2002.

Locke, John. *Two Treatises of Government*, ed. Peter Laslett. Cambridge: Cambridge University Press, 2004.

Lovell, Mary S. *Empire Builder and First Lady of Chatsworth*. London: Little, Brown, 2005.

Machiavelli, Niccolo. *The Prince*, trans. George Bull. Harmondsworth: Penguin Classics, 1961.

Major, John M. *Sir Thomas Elyot and Renaissance Humanism*. Lincoln: University of Nebraska Press, 1964.

Malleus Maleficarum (*The Hammer of Witches*), trans. Christopher S. Mackay. Cambridge: Cambridge University Press, 2009.

Mannoni, Octave. *Prospero and Caliban: The Psychology of Colonization*. Ann Arbor: University of Michigan Press, 1990.

McIlwain, C. H., ed. *The Political Works of James I*. Cambridge, MA: Harvard University Press, 1918.

Milton, Giles. *Big Chief Elizabeth*. London: Sceptre, 2001.

Montaigne, Michel. *The Complete Essays*, ed. M. A. Screech. London: Penguin Classics, 2003.

More, Sir Thomas. *Utopia* [1516], Norton Critical edition, trans. Robert M. Adams. New York: Norton, 1992.

Mortimer, Ian. *The Time Traveller's Guide to Elizabethan England*. London: Vintage Books, 2013.

Muir, Kenneth. *The Sources of Shakespeare's Plays*. London: Methuen, 1977.

Nichols, John. *The Progresses, Processions, and Magnificent Festivities of James the First* [1828].

Norton Anthology of English Literature, vol. 1. New York: Norton, 1962.

Oberg, Michael. *Dominion and Civility: English Imperialism and Native America, 1585–1685*. New York: Cornell University, 2003.

Oldridge, Darren. *The Devil in Tudor and Stuart England*. Stroud: The History Press, 2010.

Orgel, Stephen. *The Illusion of Power*. Berkeley: University of California Press, 1975.

_____. *The Tempest*. Oxford World's Classics. Oxford: Oxford University Press, 2008.

Orgel, Stephen, and Roy Strong. *Inigo Jones: The Theatre of the Stuart Court*. Berkeley: University of California Press, 1973.

Ovid. *Metamorphoses*, trans. Mary M. Innes. London: Penguin Classics, 1955.

Overton, Richard. *An Arrow against all Tyrants*. In *The Levellers in the English Revolution*, ed. G. E. Aylmer. London: Thames & Hudson, 1975.

Patrizi, Francesco. *A Moral Methode of Civile Policie*, trans. Richard Robinson [1576].

Payne, E. J., and C. R. Beazley. *Voyages of Hawkins, Frobisher and Drake*. Oxford: Clarendon Press, 1907.

Peck, Linda Levy. *Court Patronage and Corruption in Early Stuart England*. London: Routledge, 1993.

_____. *Northampton: Patronage and Policy at the Court of James I*. London: Allen & Unwin, 1982.

Percy, Henry. *Advice to His Son*, ed. G. B. Harrison. London: Ernest Benn, 1930.

Plato. *Phaedo*. In *The Last Days of Socrates*, trans Hugh Tredennick. London: Penguin Classics, 1971.

Purchas, Samuel. *Purchas His Pilgrimes* [1625].

Rowse, A. L. *The Elizabethans and America*. London: Macmillan, 1959.

Rubin, Miri. *Mother of God: A History of the Virgin Mary*. London: Allen Lane, 2009.

Scott, O. J. *James I*. New York: Mason Charter, 1976.

Schleiner, Louise. *Tudor and Stuart Women Writers*. Bloomington: Indiana University Press, 1994.

Sellers, Susan (ed.). *Feminist Criticism: Theory and Practice*. London: Harvester Wheatsheaf, 1991.

Secor, Philip B. *Richard Hooker: Prophet of Angicanism*. Tunbridge Wells: Burns & Oates, 1999.

Seneca. 'On Mercy'. In *Dialogues and Essays*. Oxford World's Classics, trans. John Davie. Oxford: Oxford University Press, 2008.

Shuger, Debora. *Habits of Thought*. Berkeley: University of California Press, 1990.

Sokol, B. J., and M. Sokol. 'The Tempest and Legal Justification of Plantation in Virginia'. *Shakespeare Yearbook* 7 (1996).

Sommerville, J. P. *Politics and Ideology in England 1603–1640*. London: Longmans, 1986.

Starr, Tama. *The 'Natural Inferiority' of Women*. New York: Poseidon Press, 1991.

Stone, Lawrence. *The Crisis of the Aristocracy*. Oxford: Clarendon Press, 1966.

_____. *The Family, Sex and Marriage in England, 1500–1800*. London: Penguin, 1979.

Stritmatter and Kositsky. 'Pale as Death: The Fictionalizing Influence of Erasmus' "Naufragium" on the Renaissance Travel Narrative'. The Renaissance Society of America, 2006.

Strype, John. *Memorials of Thomas Cranmer*. London [1690].

Stubbes, Philip. *Anatomie of Abuses* [1583].

Tawney, R. H. *Religion and the Rise of Capitalism* [1926]. Harmondsworth: Penguin, 1990.

Thomas, Hugh. *Rivers of Gold*. Harmondsworth: Penguin, 2010.

_____. *The Slave Trade*. London: Macmillan Papermac, 1998.

Thomas, Keith. *Religion and the Decline of Magic*. London: Penguin, 1991.

Tillyard, E. M. W. *The Elizabethan World Picture*. Harmondsworth: Penguin, 1970.

Vaughan, V. M., and A. T. Vaughan. *The Tempest*, Arden edition. London: Bloomsbury, 2011.

Virgil. *The Aeneid*, trans. James Rhoades. Oxford: Oxford University Press, 1920.

Viroli, Maurizio. *Niccolo's Smile: A Biography of Machiavelli*, trans. Antony Shugaar. London: I. B. Tauris, 2000.

Weber, Max. *The Protestant Ethic and the Spirit of Capitalism (1904–5)*, trans. T. Parsons. London: Unwin University Books, 1968.

Webster, John. *The White Devil*. New Mermaid edition, ed. Christina Luckyj. London: A & C Black, 1996.

Weldon, Sir Anthony. *The Court and Character of James I*. London [1651].

Wilson, Thomas. *State of England* [1600], ed. F. J. Fisher. 1936.

Wiltenburg, Robert. 'The Aeneid in The Tempest'. *Shakespeare Survey* 39 (1987).

Winthrop, Sir John, and Lady Margaret. *Some Old Puritan Love-Letters*, ed. J. H. Twichell. London, 1893.

Winwood, Ralph. *Memorials of Affairs of State in the Reigns of Queen Elizabeth and King James I* [1725].

Wootten, David. *Divine Right and Democracy: An Anthology of Political Writings in Stuart England*. Harmondsworth: Penguin, 1986.

INDEX

Lightning Source UK Ltd.
Milton Keynes UK
UKHW012135180121
377089UK00012B/337